Best Wishes

To Pete,

Tom Melvin

Danny's Tavern

617 571 5473
MelvinTom73@gmail.com

Dr. Tom Melvin, P.E.
Facilities Manager
Professional Engineer

Melvin Consultants
92 Taxiera Road
Stoughton, MA 02072

www.DannysTavern.net
Author: Danny's Tavern; Memories Of A Working Class Neighborhood, Dorchester, MA 1935-1975

Danny's Tavern

A Collection of Neighborhood Stories 1935-1975

Dr. Tom Melvin, P.E.

AuthorHouse™
1663 Liberty Drive
Bloomington, IN 47403
www.authorhouse.com
Phone: 1-800-839-8640

Published by AuthorHouse 06/07/2012

ISBN: 978-1-4772-0331-6 (sc)
ISBN: 978-1-4772-0332-3 (e)

Library of Congress Control Number: 2012908120

This book is printed on acid-free paper.

Dedication

To My Wonderful Children: Jackie, Brian, Janet, and Timmy

To the Memories of Two Fine Ladies: My Wife, Helen (Flynn) Melvin,

And My Mother, Mary (Melvin) Walsh,

To the Memories of My Two Fathers, both Newfoundland Fishermen: David Melvin and John Walsh

ABOUT THE AUTHOR

Tom Melvin spent his first twenty-nine years growing up in Dorchester, Massachusetts. He attended St. Peter's elementary school followed by the long closed, High School of Commerce. He learned the meaning of a dollar by hustling a buck working at any job that would pay him; newsboy, tomato factory worker, cutting weeds around the oil tanks on Chelsea Creek, steam pressing clothes in the heat of the summer, and washing cars in the dead of winter. As he matured so did the danger in his job choices; roofer, Plate Boy in the Herald Traveler pressroom, deckhand on a tug boat and, finally, volunteering as a U.S. Paratrooper 1953.

After graduating from the school of "Hard Knocks" Tom's fate took a turn when he graduated from Boston University with a degree in Aeronautical Engineering. He continued with his education and received a MS in Engineering from Northeastern University. In the early 1990's he received a CAS from Harvard University's School of Education and went on to finish his Doctorate degree from Nova University in 1996.

Tom's career focused mostly on the construction industry. He was a long time Capital Project Manager at Harvard University completing over 100 projects during his years at Harvard. He also taught Facilities Management at Wentworth Institute of Technology.

He wrote *Practical Psychology in Construction Management* which was published by Van Nostrand Reinhold in 1979. Danny's Tavern is his first novel.

Tom lives in Stoughton, Massachusetts with his Black Lab, Jenny.

ACKNOWLEDGEMENTS

Time and space limit giving adequate recognition to the many individuals who generously contributed to the backgrounds material for this novel. To all, my thanks.

I would like to single out a few individuals and convey my gratitude. First to my family, my daughter Janet and her brother Jack, who generously gave their support over the years to every adventure that I contemplated. To my son Brian who took on the yeoman's task of being "Red the Roofer" and created all the sketches for the book. And thanks to my son, Timmy who resurrected the novel from a dusty shelf deep in the cellar where it was buried since 1972.

I thank the following: Betty McIntyre, who's calm demeanor and support helped smooth out the hills and valleys associated with writing the book; Jackie Bassett, whose marketing expertise proved invaluable to the completion of the novel; and finally Gaylene Do Canto and Jackie Gauthier for their patience and talent in deciphering the original manuscript and typing it into workable pages. To the staff of Author House and a special nod to Larry Grabb and Kathy Lorenzo who offered many solid recommendations.

And finally, thanks to my good friend and colleague for over 25 years, Phoebe Chamberlain who took my dream and pieced it together into this book. She took the scribbles, hieroglyphics and my notes which I gave her on a sow's ear and turned it into a silk purse. I could not have achieved this goal without her; in fact, I am not sure I would have even tried.

Of course to all of my Dorchester pals from Danny's Tavern, real or imaginary.

Thanks,
Muzzy

Editor's Preface

Dr. Tom Melvin, P.E., Editor

1977

Danny's Tavern was owned by a bookie, named Timothy Brennan, AKA "Booker T." and herein is a collection of stories preserved by the part-time bartender, Billy Flynn, concerning hundreds of characters over a forty-year period (1935-1975).

Through his filter, Bill observed all types of personalities in varied extremes and situations. Bill noted the truths and the lies, the hopes and the uncertainties, the joys and miseries, all of which occurred over five decades as the denizens migrated through the phases of life: birth, maturation, marriage, aging, and, finally death. With the detail of an historian, he witnessed the demise of a city neighborhood, as well as the cataclysmic changes in economics, religion, values, family life, and government in Dorchester as well as throughout the country.

I suppose you could call his collection a definitive history of a city block. Well, maybe, history is a misplaced choice of word. History implies a rational scheme of presentation. In actuality, what we have here is a potpourri chronicle of newspaper clippings, magazine articles, folklore, sketches, and Bill's reflections and conversations. This is not a story in the sense of a novel with characters and a defined plot. More accurately it is a collage of trivia, no more, no less. Nevertheless, it is highly subjective because I'm part of Danny's myself. Maybe that's why the word "history" strikes the right chord with me. I personally know many of the individuals and the events.

Danny's Tavern is named after Bill's brother, Danny, Booker's best friend who was killed in the first World War. The tavern was opened just after Prohibition, and before I was born in 1935. Knowing the owner, Timothy

Brennan, I would strongly suspect that it was open before prohibition ended.

But first, let me explain how I got involved in editing Bill's story. I'm a city kid, born and brought up on a corner in Dorchester—St. Peter's Parish. (G.V. Higgins wrote about Dorchester in "Friends of Eddie Coyle." And Jerry Murphy of the Boston Globe always writes about Dorchester guys as 6 pack Joes). Fact is that neither of them lived there. Which to some people is critical. It's a closed society, like South Boston, Mission Hill, or Charlestown—either you were born there or you're not in the clan, so to speak. Make no mistake about it, city kids are different from suburbanites; they are conditioned early to a "street savvy" which time and degrees can never quite erase.

However, I've always loved to read; in fact, I would have majored in English, but there are too many BA's in English working as security guards or dishwashers for $2.50 an hour. A few years ago I wrote a novel—The Great American Story—so I thought, "Two Winds to Vandalia" it was about two Cain and Abel Brothers and an accident at a nuclear plant. But 20 or so rejection slips convinced me otherwise. Now it happens that the bartender, Bill, loved words too. Many a Friday or Saturday evening we talked about this book or that author. Both of us were Thomas Wolfe buffs. Also Bill mentored me in 1953 when I was a senior in high school in writing an essay for college admission. Bill became not only a dear friend but also a surrogate father. It is uncanny that our backgrounds are similar; his parents were from Newfoundland; his father was a fisherman. And he attended St. Peter's Parochial School and Commerce High School.

"Bill" to the older guys, and the "Fossil" to the younger Turks, was the undisputed poet laureate of St. Peter's parish. I can still picture him sitting at the end of the bar early in the morning, or during a slow Friday night, jotting down some event or conversation, or clipping magazine or newspaper articles and photos.

A drunk would yell "C'mon, for chrissake, give us a couple of beers!" Or one of the young guys would bust his aggies, "Put me in a story Bill. I don't care if you got me honking a midget. Make me famous . . . will ya?"

Undaunted Bill wrote on. Eyes, soft grey—ruddy face, gave one the impression of a good guy. Seldom got angry. Rarely did he curse. To him profanity was the sign of an undeveloped mind. Certainly an unusual characteristic in a tavern when generally every other word that is heard is an expletive, such as the "F-bomb and various combinations with other swears. Bill was moody in a lot of ways. Maybe frustrated, I don't know. Other than Booker T., Tommy O'Hara, and very few others, Bill had no solid open friendships. But who does?

One thing I do know: for as long as I've associated with Danny's, Bill wrote. And according to one old timer, Scotty Burns, Bill always kept a record of happenings: notes, clippings of front pages from the Dorchester Monthly Tribune, souvenirs, sketches by Red Driscoll (the artist of Danny's), Jap swords, flags, mementos, model ships, all stored in several of cardboard beer cases in the backroom. He stayed in a changing neighborhood and kept the grand diary while I, like most of young guys (and whites now), moved out to the suburbs. Knock on wood, I'm out of the busing, the taxes, the crime, the burnt out houses. I still return, but less frequently. Things change too fast. Every time I return another house is boarded up or burnt down. Last year I drove down my old street, my house was a wreck—the parlor windows were knocked out. Some fat guy was yelling through the middle window, swearing in Spanish, I guess. Look, prejudiced or not, I could do without all this. And I'm sure anyone who's fled the neighborhood feels likewise.

About two summers ago, while passing through Dorchester, I dropped into Danny's for a beer on Saturday afternoon.

Booker T., by then he must be in his seventies still tan and fit, and slightly inebriated, said to me, "Hi Muzzy," my nickname, most city kids have a nickname, "I heard that you wrote a book?" He leans on the bar, drains the glass and stares through me as though he's sizing me up. "I remember Bill telling me that. You know, my buckaroo, me and Bill grew up together. In fact, his brother, Danny, joined the Army with me. Two great pals we were. But Danny got killed in France; named this place after him, I did. All I got now are the memories. And the older I get, the more it means. My best chum, I miss him, you know that? No, you wouldn't know." He nods his head. "And Bill's the only guy I'd trust with a million bucks or even my life. The only one. It's tough to find someone you can trust one hundred percent."

I mumble, "Ya, he was a nice guy. Everybody liked him."

He leans close to me. I can smell the alcohol and nicotine on his breath. "You know how he was always writing and all that. Never got published big time, except for the Dorchester Monthly Tribune. That bothered him." Lights a smoke, eyes squint in thought." I'll admit some of his stories he showed me were OK All the others sucked. Course I ain't much for books. My interests are with the tavern and a few ventures here and there."

"But listen Muzzy," arm on my shoulder, "You want to make a couple of bucks?" He jerks his thumb towards the back room. "I got most of Billy's stuff. Five or six boxes locked in a beer chest. Pretty safe, but it's just gathering dust. I owe it to my buddy to do the right thing. It meant a helluva lot to him."

"Ya, I'm sure," I answer.

"He collected a lot of stuff . . . and this is where you come in," He cuts me off. "I'll give you the papers and boxes and all and I want you to put it together. Make a story and get it published." He squeezes my shoulder. I'm amazed at the strength of his grip. "I want someone who knew him to do it. Someone who likes books and understands this neighborhood. Most of these clowns around here can't get past the sport's page. Now what'd you say?" His grip tightened.

Booker continues, "If it don't get published, then that's the way it goes, but you'll still make a few dollars." His final comment, "All I really want to do is the right thing. You know what I mean? Do Bill right. In fact, can you watch his dog Jenny for a while? A bar is not the place for a dog."

I took the boxes, six of them, and a black lab puppy named Jenny. To be perfectly honest, he forced the task on me. Booker, old as he is, still has a certain way of getting messages across. At home the dog finds a bed and the boxes lay in the cellar untouched for a couple of weeks. Then, one day I began to rummage through a jumble of bundled papers. Like a junk photo box under grandma's bed or in an attic, once you start, you can't stop. It's akin to the evil attraction of spying on someone, or reading a diary. I know how Max Perkins must have felt with Wolfe's giant jigsaws.

The dog, the story, and my family began the bonding process.

As I said, I can personally verify some of the events, especially the late fifties when I was in my twenties and a steady patron. A lot of mysteries and coincidences are explained. Who robbed what or who stole the bronze statue of Mayor Curley and cut it up for junk? How a couple of taverns got burnt down in Southie? Or who was screwing who? Who was paying off what pol or cop? Or how the booking system works? Or how to beat welfare, taxes, the phone company, credit cards, and the insurance companies, etc.,—Bill didn't really moralize. Sure, you know it's wrong. But this is the city and there are all types and mixes. He just reported as he saw it. Of course, answers to some of the more illegal mysteries I destroyed primarily because I value my gonads to the utmost.

Billy saw guys survive World War I only to be crippled in the Depression. Watched their sons and grandsons go into World War II, Korea, and Vietnam. Met a hundred and one immigrants from the four corners of the earth. Hob-knobbed with the best and the baddest—people at their finest and worst. And he wrote it all down, along with his victories and defeats. He believed that if you want to explore people, go to a tavern. You'll see what a birth, a death, joy and sorrow, and a win or loss really means. Witness someone leap and laugh with no holds barred. It's here where all the statistics and surveys (unemployment, casualty figures, birth and death rates, cost of living index, cancer and heart attack probabilities) get translated into human terms. If you want to understand what the Depression did to people, then read on. Or World War II, or drugs—some people shrugged and rode with it, others cried and croaked, or as Widow Magaletti would say, "The fire that melts the butter hardens the egg". Or to see the dream of an immigrant—a good life for his children so he works at some stinking, back breaking, and dangerous job. Sometimes physically and verbally abused and exploited so that his kids experience no hunger, no pain, nothing but opportunity—all for the children.

Now as far as editing goes, my biggest problem is what to include and what to delete. In a story such as this what is really important? How can you attempt to assemble a meaningful story from a pile of papers? You'd have to be an engineer—a logician—to piece together this puzzle. The track I took was to illuminate the changes that have occurred with respect to the neighborhood. We're all aware that change is part of life. And in forty years (1935-1975) there have been a lot of changes. Maybe people basically don't change but their environment certainly does, resulting in various responses, some positive and some negative.

As I said, reader beware, although Bill never swore, the language, as quoted, is rough, the humor is sometimes black, the characters at time empty and spiteful, the plot is definitely lacking. But for each minus, there is a plus, even more so. Without bordering on the philosophical, isn't life the same? I mean, what do I know? My job was to assemble the information. You be the judge.

After rummaging through the boxes, I decided that the best approach was to divide each section of the book into decades, in chronological fashion when possible, as follows: (Bill did date some of his stories in a haphazard way)

1) Newspapers/magazines clippings I used a local publication—the Dorchester Monthly Tribune for most of the historical data.
2) Conversations recorded by Bill. Note: I have not the slightest idea which are facts and which are fiction.
3) Diary notes. What I call a "diary" is little more than Bill's innermost thoughts. The diary notation is solely my doing. Eventually I discontinued the word diary. Bill had his private thoughts but I delete many of more privates ones. Little was written about his woman friends—he was a widower—in fact, his wife and only son died tragically from the flu. Bill buried his pain in a dungeon vault deep, deep in the earth below and deepen in the recesses of his mind.
4) Short stories written by Bill which were ppublished in the Dorchester Monthy Tribune. He was seldom published by a major publishing house. A large novel was written but never published nor included herein.

5) Jokes/graffiti as seen on any tavern toilet wall or heard in the bar were heavily edited to weed out those comments which bordered on savage or pornographic.
6) Sketches. Most were done by Red Driscoll, a roofer and the neighborhood artist.
7) The Odds and Ends are a random selections taken from Bill's "stuff"—Copious notes (short stories, observations, conversations, news and radio media.) Bill had exceptional hearing ability. It was said that he could hear a roach walking across the bar. Often he would write down what he heard for posterity. Hopefully as they related to Danny's Tavern, Dorchester, and/or the city of Boston, the reader finds interesting, informative, humorous, or some other redeeming value. If not, then lay the blame on the editor's ineptitude
8) Danny's Bulletin Board was the brainchild of Booker T., to provide an outlet for the customer's thoughts and new comments—often to his dismay.
9) Original characters. Billy listed 26 patrons in 1935, and many later proved central to the cast. As the years passed the list dwindled—of course, new patrons entered the scene, but were not added to original list. As a finale in 1977, I tracked down the whereabouts (or demise) of the more prominent patrons—no easy task, let me assure you.

Another specific deletion has to do with sports and politics to some extent. Bill wasn't particularly a sports nut, and neither am I. But in a tavern, sports are extremely important whether it be professional baseball, park league football, or the tavern bowling team. I've watered sports down. What I tried to do is select those stories or sketches, which best describe the people and the times. Hopefully, I am successful—this story is for real. The only comments I'll make will be in the form of a postscript.

Note: Some of the names and specific descriptions have been changed to fit the story.

WELCOME TO DANNY'S TAVERN!

The 1930's

Bill's Forward

October 1935

It's Halloween, 1935, and the place is Danny's Tavern, located under the Dorchester Citizen's Club, right down the street from St. Peter's Church. We opened exactly one year ago today. And I am finally logging the first entry of this tavern—of the people, the times, and the events. For a year I've played with this idea. But now it's a reality.

Let's say it'll be a diary (Sam Pepys?). I have little idea what will happen. Certainly I'm a frustrated writer because I want to create something. Where I developed a love for words I'll never know. Except for random grunts between fishing trips and smoking a pipe, I never really knew my father—how he lived and loved and how he felt and why. Neither of my folks passed beyond the fifth grade—immigrants from Newfoundland. Maybe my heritage originates in Ireland, where writing is instinctual in that race. Who knows? In any case, I may be a bartender (only for a while until jobs pick up), but I could hibernate in a library and escape into books. God, I love literature—and traveling.

Here's what I plan to do: track a group of guys—document the history of their lives—as honestly as I see it. Win, lose or draw, let's see what life deals to us all.

In one sense, we all have a bad poker hand in this neighborhood. Death remains a certainty and any talent or energy or potential dissipates to nil in scratching out a living. Sure, some of us delight in our wins, but right now its 1935, and most of the guys in this place hurt economically. They all live hand to mouth. Just one accident, a long illness, a strike, and a guy's family suffers.

How bad is it? Mickey Smith, the plumber, crushed his toe on a job—dropped a six inch gate valve on it. He could hardly walk, but if you don't show up, there goes your job. So he leaves for work at 5 a.m. and limps along to make sure he's on the job at 7:30. Said he actually cried it hurt so badly. Thank God, it was Friday. He rested in bed all weekend. Now that's what you call hurting. Or take Jack Walsh, the fisherman, last winter he fished ten days off George's Bank—caught in a blizzard—two fingers and a spot on his cheek got frostbitten. An all he earned was seven dollars—a real broker. Seven dollars for ten days.

So let's say this at the outset—this will be a tale of real people in a real neighborhood. I'll report what I see and hear. You ask why write about a tavern? Because in a city, the corner tavern is the people. A microcosm with ill defined rules, laws and customs, and loosely governed by a group somewhere between a laughing brotherhood (as the radio commercial would have you believe) and a mindless mob. I want to tell my story of these men of Danny's Tavern.

It has been said, "War and politics make for strange bedfellows." In fact, a tavern makes for stranger bedfellows. Where else can you rub elbows with the young and the old, the high rollers and the destitute, cops and robbers, and guys with damn near every conceivable trade, occupation or method of survival? At one time or another they all cross the portals of most taverns. In Danny's, we specialize in certain trades. You have one guy who gets on the MTA, driving a trolley. In turn, he cements his buddy, brother, or cousin, and so on. For example, we have our cliques; cops, fireman, MTA, Edison, telephone, city, state and federal workers—typical Irish jobs—secure and stable with a small but steady paycheck. We've also got roofers, carpenters, truckies, shoe workers, laborers, fisherman, and the high iron guys to form unique little groups. Then we have the strays, the one's and two's: a couple of machinists, Peter Z the printer, a steam-fitter, Mickey the plumber, two electricians, a clerk, a bookkeeper, a few guards, and a lot of unemployed. Of course, every tavern claims a bookie (Frank Vento) and a lawyer (Ira Gold, Law Student).

Where else can you find so many different occupations under one roof with very few formal rules? (St. Peter's doesn't apply. They've got more rules than you can count). When you consider all the varied personalities with a kaleidoscope of different traits, joined with a cacophony of heritages and changing environments, you realize how fantastically diverse a tavern can be. However, in Danny's, all men are created equal, as long as they possess the cash for beer or wine (no whiskey or hard stuff—the Monsignor influences the licensing board).

Banish the idea that Danny's is one in a kind; the albino of the breweries. It's unique, for sure, in its own distinct way. But there are a thousand identical taverns in a hundred cities—only the names changed. I want my stories to be their stories. By outward appearances the patrons are not famous, nor rich, nor great. But to know some of them is a rare privilege. Because within them lives a basic honesty, a solid generosity, and a tenacious bravery that one could rarely imagine. Possibly it's a bartender's viewpoint. Drunkenness reveals what soberness conceals, and a tavern can be a revealing place—places where guys sometimes meet and drink and live and grow old and die, to be replaced by others.

If I seem sentimental, bear with me. This neighborhood really touches my soul. I'm only thirty-five, but already too much of my life has whizzed by. Where are all my wild boyhood pals—the old corner, the girls, the games, the jokes, the freedom; the lofty dreams; the Foreign Legion, the Mount Everest climb? Now swapped for a grocery list, a new pair of baby shoes, the eternal paychecks—God, where did the time fly? You read the same questions in many eyes. But no one offers an acceptable answer.

Back to reality. A tavern reaches extremes, a warm friendly place one minute—a suspicious jungle the next. If you don't believe me, visit any unfamiliar neighborhood tavern. Dress or act differently. Say nothing. Just be different. I'll bet within a week a regular will knock your block off. So don't expect to read of man at his noblest, elegantly dressed, discoursing in the King's English. Be prepared to hear a roofer, tar from his backside to his elbow, call a guy an "expletive punk". As I said, you'll read it the way I see it and hear it—life inside of the tavern. I make a yeoman's effort to limit the swears and especially any outright pornography but in a tavern, especially the jokes, and graffiti, are at times offensive—sexually, racially, religiously. If I fail, my apology. If you can't stomach it, if it doesn't interest you, no one's twisting your arm. Stop. Close the book. Each dog to his own smell. There's no plot other than fate itself. I no more have any idea of what's up for tomorrow than the Wizard of Oz. I have no control what a person says or does, or writes on the latrine wall and/or the bulletin board. My approach is to describe twenty, say twenty-six guys—the ones I know the best, the regulars. Let's see what happens to them.

That's the plot. Life itself is a great mystery, probably the greatest. What's in the cards? For them? Danny's? Boston? The U.S.? Me? Changes we'll see for certain, but when and how. Will life throw in a cruel twist of fate?

November 1935

Original List of 26 Regulars

Above me, a five dollar bill hangs from the ceiling, stuck there by the owner. The first fiver ever earned in here by Booker T. Brennan. Serial No. 4821679. Each and every day Booker plays some combination of the numbers in the numbers pool. Across the bill are scribbled seven signatures—the first seven customers.

Therefore, a logical beginning for my list:

1) Booker T. Brennan, Owner
2) Frank Vento, Bookie
3) Jerry Collins, Telephone Lineman
4) Peter Vessy, Building Engineer
5) Mickey Smith, Plumber
6) Gunny Steel, Mailman, Ex-Marine
7) Jack Walsh, Fisherman

Let's see, down at the end of the bar, the young fellows, Peter Z. and Jackie Dwyer.

8) Peter Z. or the Polack, Printer
9) Jackie Dwyer, Pipefitter, Gas Company

Who else? Dinty—(the Dim)—not all there in his head. Booker lets him sweep the floor. Gives him a couple of bucks to live on. No, don't have him, I tell myself. Nothing happens to him. We need for interesting guys, variety in what way? Age? What else? Obviously jobs. Married? It's amazing how we stick people into slots. Describe a guy in a few words—name, age, job, marital status. We begin to know him, or form an opinion of him just by knowing these simple pieces of information. A name pinpoints his origin somewhat and usually implies quite a bit. And a nickname sometimes tell all (What image is flashed by the name: Rags Maloney or Old Tony, the shoemaker?)

Age—very important. In fact, this dictates how long he will be in the story?

So let's get variation with age—some young, some old. Who's the youngest around here? That Quinn kid? So help me God, he doesn't look twenty-one (actually I think he is 20). But he's got the identification. Anyway he works for a living. Good boxer, great athlete, the pride of Dorchester.

10) Richie Quinn, Meat Packer

Who's the oldest? Vassarian. He must be seventy five or eighty. Comes in here every afternoon for two glasses of wine, not one—not three. Nice old-timer. Quiet. Got the blackest eyes I've ever seen—shiny wet—almost black aggies. He is an interesting man from another era and a strange culture, but I discount him because he will probably die within a year or two. Not that many men is this neighborhood live to reach 80—maybe the women, especially Italian widows who don't drink, smoke, fool around, or swear.

11) Bill Morrissey, Fisherman, Age 32, Bill's the hand who brought in the huge lobster claw which is mounted on the wall behind the bar. The inscription reads: "The Flying Cloud, Georges Bank, Newfoundland, 1935, Bill Morrissey"

Can't forget Tommy O'Hara. A janitor at St, Peter's but a recognized Irish intellectual. Great guy.

12) Tommy O'Hara, Janitor, Age 41.

Let's see, fourteen names to go. This list gets a little complicated. Who's middle aged? Boss McDonough. 50. Big strapping construction boss.

13) Boss McDonough, Construction Superintendent

Origin. We need various origins for the list. Mostly Irish, English, Scottish, Italian around here. I've already had enough Irish; Danny's is crawling with harps. Let's pick other nationalities—Let's see . . . Scotty Burns—born in Scotland . . . Joe Scarletta—Italy . . . Blackie Hession—born in Germany . . . Karras the tailor—born in Syria.

14) Scotty Burns—Scottish
15) Joe Scarletta—Italian
16) Blackie Hession—German
17) Karras—Syrian

Married? If a guy's married, he'll put with a fair measure of abuse, especially in his job. And don't think companies aren't aware of this. Furthermore, if the guy has kids—he'll bear all the more abuse. One striking feature of these guys is their love for kids. For the family, they work under some terrible conditions. Like Boss McDonough, when asked how he could work in the freezing mud on a construction site, said, "For the kids, bye, for seven little ones." Some of the guys above are married, some single. Jerry Collins is separated—a great guy but with the disposition of a exuberant puppy when it comes down to family responsibility. As Booker says, "He's got the taste." And more than one night, he has slept with the weeds in the back yard instead of the bed in his rented room.

Jobs—critical. Reflects the man as sure as the mirror. We've already got all kinds of working stiffs. Let's see. I definitely want a cop. A school teacher too. A priest would be great—but none come in here. None that I know of. What about a politician? No regulars. A lawyer will have to do. Ira Gold is in Suffolk Law at night. That's enough.

Teacher—Bob McNamara. Nose as ripe as a raspberry. A real drinker. Guy told me that the school department would have ditched him long ago except that's he's permanent—tenured so to speak. Secure as a spike hammered into granite.

18) Bob McNamara, Teacher
19) Ira Gold, Law School Clerk

Police—the one and only Iron Mike Kelly. Doesn't really drink, but he's a regular, especially on cold nights.

20) Iron Mike Kelly

To complete our list, let us pick six more—just for uniqueness. Let me think:

21) Danny O'Neil, Trolley man—left Ireland in a hurry. He was involved with a shooting of an English soldier.
22) Chico—a merchant mariner—traveled throughout the world, Not quite a fanatic but when he sees an injustice he tries to correct it.
23) Red Driscoll, a roofer by trade, tells tall tales but is the undisputed artist of the tavern. Great sketches. As a young man, attended The Museum of Fine Arts School but the Depression dented his plans. Roofing is tough but it puts meat on the table.
24) Casey—a very dark personality. You can actually sense an aura of evil oozing from his being. He never looks at you—he stares through you. Any person who has "LOVE" and "HATE" tattooed on his fingers bears a little leeway.
25) Bill Flynn, me—35, part-time bartender and midnight shift boiler operator at Wenworth Institute, a post high school on Huntington Ave.
26) Tonto—last but certainly not least is Tonto, a Mic-Mac Indian from Canada. Being as sure footed as a cat he became a high iron worker. Over six-foot with a dark complexion and a solid body form, your first impression is to not invade his space—or tickle the dragon's tail. He is, in fact, very good natured. When he enters Danny's, the boys give him the high pitched war cry—tapping your hand over your mouth. OOOOwoowoo! He responds in a deep resonant voice—somewhat threatening, "Nice scalp, white man. It'll look good in my wigwam." The boys laugh.

There we have it. Twenty-six men. I'll follow them along until they leave or die. It's eerie and I know we're all going to die, but it gives me the willies to think of who'll go first. Who's going to succeed in life? Fail? To the reader these fellows are simply names. But, to me, they are people—blood and bone and sinew. They live and breathe and laugh and cry.

So far I've been too sketchy. Let me, for completeness, list each person and give age, occupation and marital status. If I have time, I'll follow some of up with a sketch. You know, as I review the list, these guys have more stories and legends than you can imagine. "Canterbury Tales" of the barroom. For example, you know of Black Jack Pershing. Well, Iron Mike Kelly rode with him on that expedition into Mexico. How an Irishman from Aran ended up in the calvary puzzles my imagination.

Or Jack Walsh—sailed around the world more times than I've been out of New England. He's put Jack London to shame. Actually sailed before the mast. In fact, almost froze to death in Labrador (1916) while hunting seals as a nineteen year old boy.

Jerry Collins—served in India with the British Army. And the way he swills down the beer, he's reliving Gunga Din. Great talker, a superb raconteur.

So you see each guy has his own tale, his moment of glory. Some more interesting than others. It may be "full of sound and fury, but signifying nothing," still it's for real. Diamonds in the rough. Always we hear of the generals—the leaders. Well, this is the story of the privates—the followers. Be they saint or sinner, we'll hear their stories. A weekly, monthly, even yearly log of the events—the songs, the jokes, the legends, the straw and the stuff that make up the scarecrow.

December 13, 1935

As a final note, after I chose the names, I feel guilty that I was somehow spying. Peeking through a keyhole. So I spoke with each guy—it took a month to touch all bases—and asked their permission. No one objects. I don't intend to bare their souls (or do I?) (Thomas Wolfe was an outcast in Ashville after his "Look Homeward, Angel" was published) Sensitive area. Let me leave it this way. If the stories are too sensitive, I'll be the one who gets his head torn off.

But fair's fair—so I'll include me and bare my soul.

DANNY'S TAVERN—Original List of Patrons, November 13, 1935

	Name	Age	Occupation	Family Status
1.	Booker T. Brennan	32	Owns Several Businesses	Married; 2 Daughters
2.	Frank Vento	34	Bookie	Single
3.	Jerry Collins	34	Telephone Company	Separated; 5 Children
4.	Peter Vessy	41	Building Engineer, City of Boston, Curley Appointment	Single
5.	Mickey Smith	24	Plumber	Married; 2 Boys
6.	Gunny Steel	62	Mailman, Ex-Marine	Married; 4 Children
7.	Jack Walsh	36	Fisherman	Single
8.	Peter Z.	27	Printer (part-time)	Married; 3 Children
9.	Jackie Dwyer	23	Street Gang-Gas Company	Single
10.	Richie Quinn	20	Meat Packer	Single
11.	Bill Morrissey	32	Fisherman	Widowed; 0 Children
12.	Tommy O'Hara	41	Janitor (St. Peter's)	Married; 4 Boys, 3 Girls
13.	Boss McDonough	43	Construction Superintendent	Married; 7 Children, 1 newborn
14.	Scotty Burns	33	Fireman	Married; 2 Boys
15.	Joe Scarletta	23	Truck Driver	Single
16.	Blackie Hessian	22	Tomato Factory Worker (part-time)	Single
17.	Tony Karras	53	Tailor	Married; 3 Boys, 1 Girl
18.	Bob McNamara	49	Teacher-Dorchester High	Married; 4 Children
19.	Ira Gold	29	Clerk—Law student	Single
20.	Iron Mike Kelly	52	Policeman	Married; 5 Children
21.	Danny O'Neil	35	Trolley Man (MTA)	Married; 6 Children
22.	Chico	33	Seaman (unemployed)	Unknown
23.	Red Driscoll	24	Roofer (part-time artist)	Single, No Children
24.	Casey	28	Unknown	Divorced; 2 Boys
25.	Bill Flynn (me)	35	Bartender (part-time) Wentworth Institute (Boiler Operator, Fireman 3rd Class)	Widowed
26.	Tonto	27	Iron Worker	Married; 3 Children

In addition, during the first week, Booker had customers sign the "Danny's Tavern Honor Roll." There were 73 names on the chart, which were framed at Peter Z's Print Shop and mounted on the wall.

HONOR ROLL

HONOR ROLL

In Honor of Daniel Flynn
Killed in WWI 1 November 1918
The Names Below are Entitled to Participate in a Celebration
on
Every 1st of November as Long as This
Tavern Stands

Booker

Dorchester Monthly Tribune

A community newsletter serving the Dorchester neighbourhood.

Special Edition
August 19, 1934

Peter Z's Print Shop
Bowdoin Street

Nearing the 5th Anniversary of the

WALL STREET CRASH

UNEMPLOYMENT IS 25%
WAGES FALL 42%
WORLD TRADE FALLS 65%

170,000 N.E. MILL TOILERS FIGHT STRIKE COLL SEPT. 1

LABOR CHIEF ATTACKS REDS IN BOMBINGS

HITLER SURE DF 33 MILLION VOTES TODAY

Curley Raps Hurley

Says 'Economy' Hits Little Men

01 Employment for Men

ATTENTION TAYLORING MEN!
Big money assured selling – All Wool Suits $18.95, you make $4.00 to $7.50 each sale plus bonuses. New fabrics, guaranteed fit. Union made. Outfit free. Write Dept. 55 Glem

02 Employment for Women

WOMEN! Local company is opening women of good appearance for permanent positions paying $15 to $20 according to past experience. Apply personally Monday 2 P.M. Sharp. Room 208 164 Stuart Street.

SPARE OR FULL TIME WORK
Make excellent income selling hosiery, silk underwear, Christmas cards wholesale prices, large commissions, bonuses. We teach you: Credit plan. ROYAL CROWN, 76 Summer St., Boston.

CHRISTMAS CARD SALESPEOPLE
Big money selling 21 artistic Christmas Folders $1. Gold Sateen, Parchment, Handmade Papers, Mother of Pearl, Suede, Engravings. Smart! Amazing Values! Big commissions. Box on approval. Sunshine Art, 206 Broadway, Dept. 26 New York.

LAUNDRY work done at home by reliable colored woman. Reas. Garrison 2695

COLORED GIRL desires general work in small family, whole or part time. Refs. Comm. 6325

$11,800
CAPE – 2 BATHS
½ ACRE, 2 CAR GARAGE

OVERSIZED Cape, 9 spacious spotless rooms, 2 full baths, 5 bdrms, TV room, sun splashed living room, Holiday dining room. BRIGHT GAY KIT., sep. laundry rm, full base. Prime residential location. BE FIRST TO CALL!

Woods
Rte. 37
BRAINTREE-HOLBROOK LINE
963-7720

NEWTON COLONIAL
6 RMS, 1 ½ BATHS -- $27,500

EXCLUSIVE NEW LISTING
Sparkling young good sized real home in excellent cond, with AS LOW UPKEEP AS AN APT, nr sch, trans, & W. Newton Hill, terrific kit with eating area fine living & dining rms, 3 wonderful bedrms, PLUS PINE DEN OR PLAY RM IN BSMT, fenced private grounds. **A TOP VALUE,** Phone Helen Zimmerman, BI 4-4334 or office LO 6-1343

Dorchester Monthly Tribune

A community newsletter serving the Dorchester neighbourhood, 1930's *Peter Z's Print Shop Bowdoin Street*

EMPLOYMENT

AIRCRAFT MECHANICS
DAY and EVENING Classes Write for catalog. Registration Day and Evening except Sat. and Sun. NEW ENGLAND AIRCRAFT SCHOOL.
Boston airport, East Boston

EMPLOYMENT

MANUFACTURING ENGINEER
$11,000
Must have experience in methods and tooling of small production lots. Machine shop and foundry background preferred. Challenging opportunity with established company. Write giving details of experience.

Attn: M. Alexander, Jr.
HOWE RICHARDSON SCALE CO.
Rutland, Vermont

RENTALS

DORCHESTER – 35 Charlotte St., 2 rms,and a kitchenette, built-in tile bath, shower, installed bar, living and bedroom, extra large, heat, gas, elec. And hot water included $35. COL 6010

DORCHESTER – 6 rm. Heated duplex apt. $40, near cars, buses, stores, etc. Parking space Suitable for lge fam. 119 Southern Ave.

DORCHESTER – Ashmont, 3 to 8 rooms modern, $20 to $30. 1878 Dorchester Ave. Tal 8574

DORCHESTER – 4 large rooms, first floor, all conveniences, Handy location. 15 Euclid St.

APPOINTED – CIVIL SERVICE

PHILLIP B. BORDEN
26 W. Hill Ave., Melrose
ALEXANDER PRUSCINO
306 Hanover St., Boston
LOUIS J. ROBERTS
Bowier St., Fall River
ANDREW SASSVILLE
50 Com Ave Marlboro
CARL JAHNN
Sumer St., Marlboro
PATRIC McCARTHY
18 Lincoln, Marlboro

RESULTS TALK

The above were appointed US Lay Inspectors, Dept. of Agriculture in the past two weeks and make 275 pupils similarly appointed in this ONE BUREAU.

For State Social Worker, State Police, Fish and Game Warden. Post Office – Railway Mail, Customs Inspectors, Police and Fire Depts. Auto Insp, Federal File Clerk.

ENROLL NOW

File by Aug 29th for exam, later; age 25 to 50 salary $2900; lawyers and investigators desired; enroll now for WINNING instruction. Free Catalog. We employ no solicitors. Merit is our magnet.

HERRICK'S INSTITUTE
18 Boylston St. Boston
Also Worcester and Fall River, Mass.
(Don't Envy a Civil Service Employee – Be one!)

Dorchester Monthly Tribune

A community newsletter serving the Dorchester neighbourhood,

1930's

Peter Z's Print Shop
Bowdoin Street

Buys on Bowdoin Street

Dorchester Monthly Tribune

A community newsletter serving the Dorchester neighbourhood,	1930's	*Peter Z's Print Shop Bowdoin Street*

Entertainment in Boston

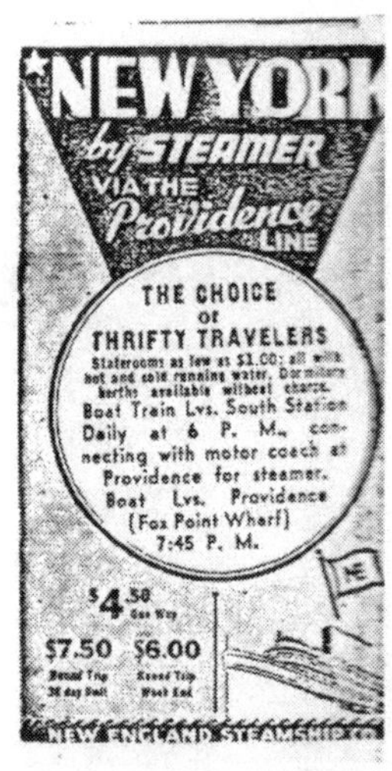

Bill At 36

Who Am I?

January 1, 1936

Ever since I learned to write, I've attempted to keep a diary, a journal of events and personal experiences. Unfortunately, you're either too busy or too lazy. Well, since half a loaf of is better than no loaf, I'll make entries at random—in my own words—no editing, unpolished, crude, but honest. Most important I want to record my strongest feelings and innermost thoughts. Unlike trying to describe my list of characters, I know what goes on inside my head. That's not to say that understanding goes along with knowing. You be the judge. How easy it is to write, "Nancy, I love you." How impossible was it for me to say, "Nancy, I love you." It's too late now because she passed away from the flu on November 7, 1933, and my baby son died a week later. My mother and father, did they really know that I loved them without actually being told? My warm feelings and tender thoughts were never spoken—unknown in the walled restraint of my upbringing. To this very moment I regret my reluctance to express my emotions, especially those which deal with love. "Tough city kids don't weep, or say, "I love you."

Who am I? A strange question to ask one self, especially when I work on my list of Danny's Heroes.

Name: William Paul Flynn

Age: 36

Date of Birth: January 1, 1900—A Century Baby—Reported both in the press and Irish Lore: "Destined for a Special Life" (I sometimes wondered about the definition of "Special") Like the Chinese curse "May you live in changing times"

Family: Widowed, wife and baby boy died in flu epidemic in 1933—Seldom do I write about this tragedy—too painful and I can't really recall the specific details

White, Catholic, Democrat

Occupation: Boiler operator, midnight to eight a.m. shift—Wentworth Institute

Part-time bartender—Danny's Tavern, weekend shift

Education: St. Peter's Grammar School, Dorchester 8 years

Commerce High School, Boston, MA—4 years

Boston University (quit after 2 years, like everyone else, for money reasons. Mother sick, doctor's bills, got married.)

Employment: Boston Book Publishers, 10 years. Because I've always loved writing and literature, I took a job as a clerk. Worked up to proofreader, and editorial assistant. And again, like everybody else, the crash changed our lives. I was terminated.

By a stroke of luck Booker had a contact at Wentworth Institute; I got a job as a fireman in the boiler room night shift; midnight to 8:00 A.M. shift. This schedule suited me fine. My days were free to write and relax. Anyway, a boiler room at night is a great place to read and write when all of the heating, electrical systems, and plumbing systems are humming along fine.

Religion: I am a Catholic, but not likely to be canonized any time soon. I attend Mass only sporadically.

Description: 5'6"-160 lbs.—light red hair, gray eyes, thin nose, small mouth, too small; a 1/2" scar from football cleat curls up one corner of my lip, fair complexion, sort of homely. Always bothered me about my looks; to this day I'm uneasy with women. Maybe it's the slight limp—the result of a foot crushed in a freight elevator—a careless 16 year old kid working his first job in Raymond's Sports Store in Boston. You'd think I would get over the accident. Not so.

Social/Dating: A widow in the South End and I see each other. She's four years older but we get along fine. No serious intentions. It is very difficult to write about sex. Sex will not be a major topic in this history, although for sure, it makes the top of the list in life. But intimacy is not a public conversation in the tavern. Expect no flaming arrows shot into the sky.

Background: Immigrant parents from Admiral's Cove, Newfoundland.

Father, a fisherman, lost at sea in 1920. Mother died four years ago. How God allowed such a kindly woman to suffer so terribly mystifies me. With a fervor that amazed me, I prayed she'd die.

Two brothers and three sisters: Robert and Patricia died in the flu epidemic. My older brother, Danny, died in the War; Dora and her husband moved to Canada. Cathy lives in Roxbury, St. Patrick's Parish. This is the prime reason why I work night shift at Wentworth Institute—time to trolley back and forth during the week days.

Interests: Reading and writing and a few drinks. After a drinking bout, I suffer horrible hangovers—depressed like you'd never believe; therefore, my bouts are few and far between. For me, reading is a great escape with Tom Wolfe, Tolstoy, and Liam O'Flaherty are my favorite authors. Oh yes, and James T. Farrell.

Ambitions: A good life, full of opportunity and achievement, the best I can give. For myself, to write a good novel. If fate had been more favorable, I would have accepted a compromise to be an English teacher. Hopefully Wentworth and Danny's Tavern will set me on my way. A great fear is that my life will pass by without accomplishing anything of value. In these past years I've done nothing. God—where does the time go? A book, a song—a creative accomplishment to let the world know—"Hey! I was here!"

Wait a minute! What a way to begin a New Year, let alone my thirty-sixth birthday. My imagination tells me that the Century Baby moves on to some new adventure—highly unlikely. God, that thought depresses me. I feel that instead of writing a book, I am in fact a character in the book. Should I not be alongside of Shackleton in the Antarctic, plowing through the ocean headed for a small, obscure South Georgia Whaling Station—braving 40 foot waves in an open boat, James Cairde—how ridiculous I am! In all probability I'd be crying because of the cold.

How selfish and insensitive I am. What about Nancy and Jimmy? You know I don't feel like writing. In fact, I don't feel like doing anything except wallow around in self-pity. What is wrong with me? All my life I have accomplished so little. Thirty-six-zero! More wrinkles, aches and pains and peeing problems.

Tom Wolfe was on the top of his mark. Writing "Look Homeward Angel"—a great story but the folks in Ashville, his hometown, would have hung him from a tree because of his description and events in his hometown. Wolfe would be about the same age as I am. And Hemingway another great writer! What have I to show for my labors? A raft of rejection slips. Bill, be tough and stop whining! You sound like a cry baby. One and ½ jobs. Plenty to eat. A roof over your head. A few good friends, including female companionship.

What's wrong? To climb a mountain—to fly off—to reach the moon. Sometimes I debate that I must be totally neurotic or just the blues—the panic that life is passing me by and there is nothing I can do to stop the clock.

Come on, you guys in Danny's—help me out.

Conversations 1936

Heard on the Street and Everywhere

April 1936

No chronicle of a tavern or a neighborhood would be realistic without dwelling upon the Depression. Jobs, jobs, jobs. Each day I hear the conversations: Joe gets fired, Jim hired, Mike tracks down a potential job, Red picks up a couple of days, Bill shuddered at the rumor of lay-off.

Each day the cursing and the conjecture, the whys and the wherefores, the begs and the threats—all related to the day-to-day bread and butter worries: lay-offs, shutdowns, low pay, pay cuts, increased workload, poor conditions, job security, unions, patronage, pay-offs, theft, foreclosures, repossessions, evictions, illness and old age.

Not that everyone lives on the edge of starvation, not that everyone worries about his job, not that everyone loses spirit because of the incessant daily struggles, the most important issue is that anybody who is ready, willing and able, cannot find work. In a country founded on the ethic of labor and opportunity, men and women, unemployed, represent a startling incongruity between theory and fact. If you've been laid off, exploited, evicted, in fact, if only you'd seen the despair on old man Johnson's face when the company fired him, the point is readily thrust home. You ask, "Why did the company fire Johnson?" I mean he worked steadily, diligently, effectively, especially in his younger days. Well, Johnson committed the great American crime: he aged, and worse, he became ill and a trifle slow.

There exists in this country a tragedy; maybe a million tragedies—a betrayal of the spirit, and the belief that we learned as children: in the land of opportunity, labor and energy and diligence will be aptly rewarded. Then why do we have millions of willing able-bodied workers, family men, shuffle idly in the unemployment lines? Can we justifiably say that a country which fails to provide a livelihood lacks something? Change becomes necessity from both a humanitarian as well as a practical point of view. A desperate father, a hungry child owes little allegiance to the hand that starves him. Laws? Religion? To Chico, the laws exist for the banks, the capitalists; and religions keep the poor from murdering the rich (Voltaire). The empty belly says forget the abstractions; give me bread.

Peter Z. the printer says that "Before my kids would go hungry, I would rob and steal—not from the poor but from the banks, the insurance companies, the big monopolies. Never mind my logic or morals; it's the way I feel. "Sin or no sin, my kid'll never go hungry."

Let me descend from the soap box and give you a few typical conversations that I've heard recently. Don't expect verbatim, in fact, some conversations I've only heard second hand. That matters little because you can be damn sure the substance is identical whenever two or three workers meet. Travel from Danny's to any tavern in the city; go to the factories, the stores, the construction sites, the camps—Boston, Philly, Chicago, Mobile, San Francisco; you listen to the talk about jobs. Change the faces, the names, the colors, the religious—white, black, yellow, Mexican, Canadian, Irish; you listen to the talk about jobs. Jobs, jobs, jobs!

Hobo Jungle

P.O'C: "I'll tell ya boys, there just ain't no jobs around. Government don't care 'bout us now. There was plenty of carin' when they needed us guys to fight the War. They was sure sorry when I lost my arm—Gimme another drink . . . oh, who wants a one-arm baso?"

F.R.: "One arm—two arms—who cares? When you got a couple of grey whiskers, no one wants you anyway. Seventeen years at Walter Baker's and you know what. When I got laid off, I felt ashamed or somethin' like I was to blame. Like I couldn't do the work anymore. No one would hire me, or I had some offensive disease or somethin'. But ya

	know the thing that really broke me was my family—they pitied me. Pitied me because I was getting a little old. I just couldn't take that. Started to hit the bottle."
J.S.:	"Pass the bottle, mate. It's the only thing that counts."

Construction Site

M.S.:	"Please, pal. I need this job. Got three kids."
Boss Plumber:	"We ain't hirin'. Sorry, buddy."
M.S.:	"But I know you're hiring. Guy told me. Look, I got seven year's experience and a license. See, look."
Boss Plumber:	"How many times I gotta tell ya, we ain't hirin'."

Shoe Factory

Boss:	"Take it or leave it. No pay for the first week while ya training, an' eighteen cents an hour."
Ed T,:	"Eighteen cents! I gotta take the trolley cross town. I got four kids. It just ain't enough."
Boss:	"Ain't enough? There's lotsa guys would jump at the chance. Do ya want it or not? Eighteen cents an hour and no pay while trainin'."

Printing Company

Manager:	"I have a report that you have been complaining again."
Pressman:	"All I'm doin' is sticking up for my rights. It's dangerous down in the press room. God! Safeties on them machines been broke for a month now. You gotta fix'em before someone loses an arm."
Manager:	"This is the third report on you. What are you, a trouble maker? A red?"
Pressman:	"Can't I complain without being no red?"

Wool Warehouses

Baler:	"Ya hear the latest? We gonna get a pay cut. Ten percent across the line."

Foreman: "Ya, I know. Startin' Friday."
Baler: "Why? Why? We're starving' now—"
Foreman: "For chrissake, don't complain! I'm just a workin' stiff like you. Didn't I tell ya this'd happen when the twenty thousand guys lost the strike in Lawrence—the employers call all the shots now. They got the upper hand. Do anything they damn well please. Didn't I tell ya? So don't bitch to me. It don't do no good, and you might get yourself blackballed. We're both lucky to have a job."

Department Store

Salesman: "I'm laid off? You must be joking! I've been here for twenty-one years, ever since the store opened."
Accountant: "That certainly was a consideration."
Salesman: "A consideration? Doesn't seniority count? Why, I've got more experience that—."
Accountant: "That was also a consideration. To be perfectly candid, the younger men, they are more in tune with the styles. They've got more energy, less sick time."
Salesman: "Jesus Christ! We're back on that again! Could I help it if I got pneumonia? Before that, I never took a sick day in fifteen years. Don't that count?"

Utility Power Plant

Italian: "Mista, I needa da job. You watcha me shovel da coal. You gimme da try."
Watch Engineer: "This is a union shop so get the hell outta here! Ya can't even speak English. Why don't you stick to your own place?

Next thing ya' know the place'll be crawling with boogies and hunkeys. Can't these foreigners realize this is America and we got unions?"

Slaughterhouse

Janitor: "But you were goin' to throw them away. Old bones, crushed and dirty. They ain't no good to meat markets. I wanted'em to make soup, that's all. I ain't no thief."

Boss: "Ya know the rules: no stealing."

Janitor: "All ya do with'em is to feed the pigs. You think more 'bout pigs than people?"

Boss: "I ain't gonna argue with ya. Either you pick up your time or I'm calling the cops."

Sidewalk

G.T.: "Friggin' line must be two blocks long. How long we gotta wait?"

A.B.: "Til ya sure there ain't no work. I been waitin' every day for a month. Got a couple of days last week. Heard there's a big government order comin' so I'm waitin' till noon anyways."

G.T.: "This is my first day, an' I'm a little scared 'cause I ain't done this kinda work before."

A.B.: "Lookit, kid, tell them you're an expert. To survive around here, you gotta lie through ya teeth. Blow a little sunshine up the boss's ass. Tell them you're related to the governor or something. Tell'em or do anythin' that'll get ya the job.

Union Hall

C.I.: "We gotta organize, get tough! Eleven cents an hour—a guy'd starve. We gotta go for more money. We gotta stop the scabs from stealin' our jobs."

B.B.: "Do you wanna get blacklisted?"

C.I.: "I'll take the chance."

B.B.: "It's easy for you to talk. You ain't got a wife and kids. My brother got blacklisted and he ain't worked for seven months steady."

C.I.: "I tell ya this. Next time the cops protect the scabs, I'm gonna bomb the place, no matter where it is. An' I ain't kiddin'! Got nothing to lose."

Outside St. Peter's Church

A.O'C.: "I hear ye goin' home b'y, back to Ireland."

L.M.: "'deed I am. Saved a year for passage."

A.O'C.: "But man, Ireland is no better off. Sure ye see that, for the love of God."

L.M.: "We'll manage the farm somehow—the kids will eat. Anyway I'd rather starve outright with me own kind than die slow of shame and idleness with a pack o'strangers." In fact, I'll become a "Souper." (Change religion to Protestant for a bowl of soup)

Both in Tavern

J.C.: "Ya sure of this? I mean if it blows, if we get caught, we goin' to jail."

C.: "Whadaya, a yellow bastard? I'm telling ya it's a cinch. As soon as the watchman makes his rounds, we sneak in through the window. The truck'll be outside. C'mon, we'll make a bundle of dough, whaddaya say?" Maybe go to Florida for a few weeks.

Firehouse

Fireman: "How do you think I got the job, my looks? Cost me two hundred smakeroos. Gave it to the ward rep. It's a lot of money, but I'm working, ain't I?"

P.J.: "Can you get me one? I'll pay, I'll get it from somewhere. Can you?"

Fireman: "Well I don't know. Let me talk to a guy. He's in with the Ward Democratic Committee. See what he can do for how much."

Collection Agent

Lady: "Repossessing the furniture. What do ya mean?"
Collector: "I got a job to do, lady. You missed the last three payments."
Lady: "But all I owe is thirty-seven dollars. I already paid over a hundred and eighty."
Collector: "Tough, lady. You shoulda paid up. Now ya ain't got nothing."

Navy Yard

Manager (phone): "Yes, Senator, yes sir, I do appreciate all that you have done for me . . . yes, I do realize that he is a cousin of yours . . . yes sir, I'll see what can be done . . . yes, I'll do everything . . . he will be hired. Yes, to a managerial position . . . I will personally see to it . . . yes, sir. Thank you. Good-bye, Senator."
Assistant Manger: "Him again? What is it this time?"
Manager: "A pal, of course. He must have a hundred cousins. It looks as though we'll have to fire Murphy or Pallucci. We've got to make a slot for this man. Here, look at his application—the clown can't even spell 'record'. Damn politics!"
Assistant Manager: "It's too bad we don't have a few Negroes. Let them go."

Apartment Building

Boarder: "What's the padlock doing on my door?"
Landlord: "Because you ain't paid the rent, that's why."
Boarder: "Ya better open that f'n door before I tear it off the hinges. I need my clothes and shaving gear."
Landlord: "You try anything and I'll have you locked up. You just try and I'll ring up the cops on the citizen's alarm."

RECRUITMENT CENTER

Kid: Sergeant, please put me on the roster. I gotta join. Ain't got no one to speak of. Ain't got a job."

Sergeant: "Kid, the roster's all full-up. Seems like these days the Army ain't such a bad place. Three squares a day, place to sack out. Ya know kid, like I says, the roster's full, but maybe I can help—if ya do the right thing. I mean a soldier don't make much pay. Now suppose I was to find an envelope . . . ."

TRUCK ON WHARF

Union Organizer: "There they are guys. Scabs! Work them over with the sticks. Hit 'em hard and fast! Remember it's your job! Your family! If they get away with this, we'll be worse off than slaves."

INVESTMENT OFFICE

Stockbroker: "But Mrs. Gerhardt, you must understand that it was a risk."

H.G.: "Vere is all my saffings? Zis stock, it got to be vorth somezing. You said it vouldn't fail. You said zat."

Stockbroker: "You should have realized the risk."

EMPLOYMENT AGENCY

Agent: "Well miss, let's discuss my fee rate. I get the first month's pay. Of course, we'll spread it over three months so you won't feel the pinch—ha, ha, just a little pun."

Miss: "Ya sure I won't be fired after three months. That's what happened to my brother."

Agent: "Do I look like that type of man? Look into my eyes."

Bank

Banker: "You should have read the terms of the contract. I mean right here it states, "Hereto . . . forwith . . . notwithstanding . . . we are exercising the option to foreclose on the mortgage."

Homeowner: "I can't pay because I haven't got a job. Get me a job, I'll pay."

Banker: "Banks are not employment agencies. I am sorry."

Racetrack

Bettor: "Ya sure? I mean, this is all I got. I gotta pay the rent next week."

Friend: "How many times I gotta tell ya? My brother, my own brother, he knows this jockey. It's a boat race."

Stockroom

Head Stockboy: "No kiddin, you're a lawyer? Why'd you want this lousy job?"

Lawyer: "Because I have to eat, that's the reason. I'm waiting for a civil service appointment."

Head Stockboy: "Don't mind me chuckling, it's just that I never got by the fifth grade, an' here I am, your boss."

Fish Pier

Mate: "By the Lawd Jaysus, a real broker. Six cursed dollars! A family'd starve eatin' gruel. Me gear's near in rags. I'd be better off bein' an angishore."

Lumper: "Look man, at least yer eatin, the finest kind aboard the boat. 'Cept for fish, I ain't had no decent grub for near a week."

Welfare Office

Case Worker: "I believe there has been a mix-up of sorts. Your name was removed from the rolls. But I can assure you, only for a short period. Say three weeks, maximum."
Woman: "How will I eat? The baby."
Case Worker: "Can't you try your family? Surely they will help. Or the Church?"

Pawn Shop

Owner: "Two dollars."
Machinist: "Two dollars for a pair of micrometers? That's crazy! They cost me thirty four. They're precision German—."
Owner: "Vell, sell dem to a German. I got tools, I should be a factory."
Machinist: "Oh, what's the use? What about the calipers—they're Browne and Sharpe's. How much for both?"

Confessional

L.J.: "Bless me Father for I have sinned . . . I stole a case of soap—Father, it's the first time I ever stole anything . . . It was on the back of a truck and no one was around so I took it."
Father B.: "You'll have to return it, my son."
L.J.: "I can't Father. I already sold it for the money. I needed the money, Father, real bad. You see, I've been outta work for . . ."

State House

Senator to new rep: "Your first objective (and only task) is to get elected. Don't waste your time on dead ends. If someone can't or won't help you, drop them."

THE GREAT DEPRESSION

How Does it Feel to Get Fired?
The Boys in Their Own Words

DECEMBER, 1936

Pick up any newspaper: a twisted knot of strikes, unemployment, violence and discontent. Sure, the government promises us that the depression loses momentum each and every day. Possibly that we have seen some improvements, but the gold at the end of the rainbow requires a long painful journey.

When I see an old guy snatch up a butt off the sidewalk, or watch a guy snipe a cigarette and drop it into his pocket, to me, that means that Depression still weighs on us. I've actually seen a fellow punch another because of a pack of Camels left on the bar—in a tavern you just never leave a pack of cigarettes on the bar and expect it to be intact when you return from the toilet. If we concern ourselves with such trivia as cigarettes, there's a a serious problem with the economy.

Let us now spotlight the men themselves. Let each man tell his story—his feelings, his job, his dreams, how the Depression has affected him (for better or worse). Of course, we can expect much comment about work. So much of our lives revolve around our job. We can't eat or drink ten hours a day; or laugh or cry ten hours a day; or make love—too bad—ten hours a day. But we sure can work ten hours a day, six days a week. In fact, when we consider trolley time, lunchtime, etc., work eats up twelve, even fifteen hours, each day. No small wonder people talk about work.

For the past months I interviewed a number of the boys, the regulars from my list. Before we listen to their stories let me state that in the Garden of Eden, many of Danny's boys would complain about paradise. Justifiably, we may muse philosophically; however, the point is vaguely academic; we're the worker ants; life is unfair and imperfect; and our crumbs are heavy to carry. Therefore, many complaints are justifiable. A shroud of frustration and often bitterness hangs over many stories. Not that all of us suffer from the calamity—in fact, some have profited well (used furniture dealers, for one). However, in Danny's, the Depression staggers everyone. The great consolation is that everybody's in the same boat. Maybe some lucky ones do receive a steady paycheck from the city, the state, the feds, but basically everyone in this neighborhood is only one illness or layoff away from economic disaster.

There's something wrong with this work system. No guy's family should be on the brink while in Hollywood people swim in pools of champagne; while the rich sail to Europe, or to the Caribbean. Why should the Fords, the Rockefellers live in luxury while the majority struggle to ultimate defeat? Maybe Chico's right! Because of our fathers were not of the Mayflower stock, does this alone mean that we live our days on a treadmill?

A guy should be given the opportunity to work, to prosper according to his abilities, not his politics or heritage. A country must provide meaningful labor, must provide threads of hope and dreams and victories especially for the offspring. For God's sake, we've got to learn something from this torment! A permanent solution! Some semblance of economic security for the worker. The guy who mixes the batter—so says Chico. Forget the politicians who promise and plead and pledge of "a golden tomorrow". Fair words won't feed the friars. I've got little use for pols. As Booker says," if you squished all the bullshit out of them, they'd fit tidily in a matchbox."

We've got to even out the contrasts; in the midwest they burn wheat while in Boston they bust windows for a loaf of bread; in Brockton, shoe factories shut their doors while in the midwest kids miss school because of a lack of shoes. In California they shoot starving men who attempt to steal burning, rotting fruit. God, I could go on and on.

Jim Martin tells me a cousin in Maine who put out to sea before sun-up. Worked until sunset. Caught a hundred pounds of haddock and got paid four cents a pound—four damn cents! Fuel alone costs $3.00. He earned $1.00 and some change, for a twelve hour day. And yet Henry Ford sermonizes that, "the very poor are recruited solely from the people who refuse to think and therefore refuse to work diligently." And Roger Babson, statistician, pontificates, "Better business will come when the unemployed changes their attitude toward life." Rich men quickly moralize when touching upon the poor.

If you complain, the company blacklists you—a form of torture, a subtle lashing from the whip. Sweet is revenge. Let them agitators squirm and suffer—them Reds'll never work again. Am I paranoid? Look at what happened to Chico. On the West Coast the shipping companies blacklisted him for organizing the unions. For a year he pounded the pavements. Finally, in desperation he came east to a new beginning. Is "Chico" an alias? Who knows? But I do know why he's such a radical—which reminds me of a book that I read a few weeks ago. "In Dubious Battle" by a guy named Steinbeck—I'll have to look for his other books. Good story about the Reds—I'm no Red: America for Americans. But in this story you can understand how guys, especially unemployed and exposed to daily blows, could get involved with Reds—with anyone who promises milk and honey. Steinbeck's characters, Mac and Jim, try to organize the fruit pickers to strike. You catch a glimpse of how the Communists exploit, twist, distort, modify, invert, salvage anyone or anything to their advantage. The book, not only dramatizes the cruel, cold, impersonal side of Communism, but portrays the fury, and the passion, and the bewilderment and the suffering of the workers. Good story. And damn timely.

When a family man loses a job, the knife plunges deep. We see no red blood gushing from a jagged wound. No instead we have a cut, unseen but very painful if not more insidious. For it is a wound of the spirit. How have I failed? You are old, infirm, expendable, ineffective, Black, Jewish, Catholic, Italian, a foreigner, different, without heritage or political pull—that is your failure. With no difficulty I recall my layoff. I felt the shame, the guilt, the despair. For God's sake, mister! I'm healthy, industrious, willing to learn, just give me a break. The lump in my throat, the scum taste of humble pie. The blank stares, the negative shake of the head.

Booker gave me a break. To be perfectly honest I got the job only because I knew Booker. Therefore, I should not toss too many stones in my glass house. A tinge of guilt prompts me to justify my situation. A bartender's job is not all fun and games. Too many Dr. Jekyll and Mr. Hyde's. After a few drinks, the monkey becomes King Kong.

In any case, I completed the job cycle: the layoff, the search, the new job. However, the new job does not result in forgive and forget, especially if you feel overqualified. There remains a scar, implanted deep within you, not easily healed, and probably never fully forgotten. The true meaning of the Depression seethes within me. What about other men?

We can read of unemployment in the newspaper stories written by reporters who have jobs, and in editorials written by the owners. Or we can cast our attention to the obvious. Search no further than Danny's. Interview the workers. Never mind reading about a seaman's strike in San Francisco, 10 killed, 47 injured—listen to Chico swing an ax handle and knock a soldier from his horse. Forget about the staid article about the meat truck robbed by unknown strikers in Field's Corner. Listen to Joe Scarletti describe the overturning the truck and the mob of shoppers emptying the truck within all of ten minutes, and Mrs. O'Toole, baby in arm, wheeling home a leg of a cow in the baby carriage. Listen to a very bright young man say, "To hell with college, to hell with taking chances. Just give me a civil service job: a cop, a fireman, a clerk, a garbage collector—give me my daily bread."

Listen to these men. There is a treasure in these tales. "Tell me, Tom (Dick, Harry) what does the Depression mean to you? What it's really likes to be laid off? Looking for a job? Up against it? Tell me."

The Boys In Their Own Words

Bill Flynn, Bartender

For the past months we've brush-stroked the neighborhood and Danny's. We will sketch a few of the boys and tell stories about them and the three greatest events of their lives (birth, marriage and death.) We will jot the sayings, the jokes, the proverbs; and hopefully, will project the blood and guts, the odds and ends, and customs of tavern life. However, let us now spotlight the men themselves. Let each man tell his story—his feelings, his job, his dreams, how the Depression has affected him (for better or worse). How does a writer describe a person, let me describe some characters in the story, beginning with me.

I worked as an editorial assistant for Boston Book Publishers for six years until my lay off in 1934.

"How did I feel when I got axed? It happened two years ago, but it seems only yesterday. The rumors begin to fly in 1932, around July. I easily remember that date because business was so bad everywhere. It took no genius to know that. Newspapers, radios—a thousand on the bricks here, ten thousand idled over there, shut downs, closings, seventeen percent unemployment in Boston—abstractions which bothered me none. Like a cancer statistic, it'll never happen to me. Anyway, the tragedy of Nancy and the baby occupied all my time and thoughts. In addition, I worked hard at my craft, a solid asset to any firm. So I paid slight attention to the reports, statistics, percentages, bar graphs until, like barbed stakes, they struck home, which means that I was impaled in the thick of it. The rumors became reality. The company laid-off seven men, seven out of a total work force of forty-nine. The rumor of more layoffs persisted. A quiet panic settled over the company. Me? When you think you may get axed, you scour the newspapers, the magazines for stories and articles about economic turn-around, replenishment of jobs, and the shutdowns. You become obsessed with the subject of jobs. In fact, you almost begin to believe the politicians; you applaud those who promise jobs, and actually hate those who preach cut-backs. At night, especially those nights preceding the lay-offs, you lay awake and imagine smashing the faces of those who cut jobs. You, in your wild imagination, armed with great argument, dramatically plead your case before Congress. Gentlemen, learned gentlemen, can you not see this? Can you not feel the torment, the agony? Can you hear the cries of the lost and the forgotten? The country needs jobs. God! The erratic thoughts that zigzag through your head.

On those long, mocking nights, I'm sure the same fantasies swirled through other heads. Everyone wears a tired troubled face. Each morning everyone reports early; each evening everyone yields a little extra effort. No jokes at the water bubbler. Short lunch breaks. No flirting with Mary, the secretary with the cute rump. Nose to the grindstone. The stronger the rumors, the more you justify your existence. You study your co-workers. Who's deadwood? Who is essential? Who can the company do without? Theoretical lay-off lists are constructed. Bill Jones, in proofreading . . . yes, he can be dismissed. Alice, yes . . . she does little. Mr. Cronin, no . . . he's related to the owner. Charlie, yes Charlie . . . drinks too much. And Joe . . . boss hates him. Mickey . . . well he's old, not very productive. Only an imagined list, but morale wise, it buffers you from the dreaded lay-off.

One particular knife that cuts you deep is the passivity. Like a pig on the slaughterhouse ramp, there's nothing you can do. If the company chops, you have nothing to do with the choosing. Democracy fails here. You sit at your desk and wait, and worry and wait. It's Friday, the air is suffocating. Morning coffee tastes stale, acrid, "Whaddaya hear, Ralph?"

"I hear there's gonna be a whopper. Seventeen."

"Seventeen!"

At ten o'clock every worker huddles over his work area. No horseplay. Seventeen! Don't go to the toilet, be inconspicuous. Heads squirreled into collars, pretending to be busy. But inside that head, the thoughts of being axed muffle any constructive work. Inside your gut, the engine whines and races at 100 miles an hour. You actually feel nauseous. Mouth dry, palms wet, bladder full. Look busy.

The bosses' door is shut. Who's in there? Ralph. Charlie hums the taps; gallows humor.

Ralph, head bent, face twisted with disgust, anger, and panic, stomps over to me, "Shit, Bill, I got it! I got the damned hatchet. Son of a bitch!

"Who gave it to you, Mr. Brown?"

"Naw, he's only doing his job. It was that damned Elwin. He finally got rid of me. Listen, help me pack, will you? Gotta be out by tonight."

Have you ever been involved in a lay-off? Have you ever actually seen the crushed, defeated bewildered eyes of a man recently removed from his livelihood? Ralph looked like a puppy punished with a newspaper: afraid and bewildered, unsure of his transgression. I also noticed a trace of bitterness towards me—why didn't I get laid-off and not he? And I'm sure Ralph could sense my feelings; I was glad to have survived—for the time being anyway. Within the hour, Ralph packed, and departed. A statistic. Damn cracker-jack editor, decent family man, friend. Now an indifferent statistic.

I sit at the desk, very quiet. Finally my bladder forces me to the toilet. Jim, from shipping, hides in a stall. Out of sight, out of mind.

"How many?"

"Seventeen," answers Jim, "wiped out the binding department. It's cheaper to farm out the work. Manny, and Joe . . . even Denny—twenty-two years with the place. They didn't even transfer him. What a crummy bunch of bastards! Throw a man out like that. I'd like to slam Elwin right in the choppers."

"Shhh. Keep quiet. You want to lose your job. Now's not the time be mouthing off. Complaining won't bring any jobs back, but it will lose yours."

"But Denny was such a nice guy."

"Who else?" I ask.

"Nelson, Craft, Billy from receiving. Oh yes, Mary, the one with the nice boobs. She was crying. And a couple of guys down in discounting. I don't know who else."

Back to the desk, hoping for time to pass by. Incredible as it may seem, you think you can hear your watch ticking. At five o'clock, you can flee—and still have a job. Safe for another week.

By five o'clock, my shirt is soaked. What a relief! I made it.

For one solid year, I sweated through the lay-off after lay-off. One here, two there. Sure I groped and grappled for a new job, one step ahead of the inevitable ax, but I caught nothing. Initially you search for a better job, then slowly your expectations degenerate from better to equal to finally any job that looks stable. Nothing.

My life sank to ebb tide. My whole world rushed in like a broken vacuum, crushing the guts, and the blood, and the breath from my whole being.

Finally the ax fell, swift and ultimate. Bill Flynn, the great failure. One hot day at the end of June, Mr. Benson called me into his office.

"It's not official, Bill, but next month we're going to terminate you. I really hate to lose you—you're good, damn good—but the company's sales are at rock bottom. Believe me, I did everything possible to keep you, but Elwin gives the orders. I wanted to give you some time to look . . . I mean with all your troubles, it's the least I could do."

I see the embarrassment on his face, and the worry. Worry that I'll lose my temper, or worry about his own job. For a year I dreaded this moment, but now I sense a relief. Let go of the balloon, watch it soar up and up. Free. My head and shoulders feel so light. I now know how a prisoner feels on that first day of release. Within the hour, I jauntily complete my handshakes, and enter into the jobless, nameless, unremembered statistics.

Naturally I saved a few dollars in anticipation; therefore, I felt little panic money wise, at first. In fact, a week home relaxed me. A free agent. Sleep late in the morning; breakfast leisurely; read; browse in the library; contemplate writing a novel. However, as my bankroll dwindled, an uneasiness spread into a ceaseless ache. The solution to my problem was so simple. I wanted a job. I felt worthless. Washed up. A young has-been. Those who had jobs became the center of my envy. Here I was young, healthy, ambitious, capable, but I couldn't find a job. Like a tumor, the envy gnawed within me. I walked and trolleyed and tramped from office to office to store and finally to factory to factory. A beggar in a neat shirt and tie, an unemployed beggar at that. As soon as the personnel man learns you're unemployed, he holds all the trumps. Maybe he has to justify his own job; therefore, he sometimes interviews you, knowing full well that no position exists. I remember one particular interview with Corning Glass; it amounted to a four hour grilling. "What have you accomplished? I see no growth in your career. Why haven't you continued school? Why did you get laid-off?"

He sat there like a well groomed pig, beady eyes and fat face—I all but told him to shove the job. But when you have a family or others who depends on you,—it's groveling time—eating a large piece of humble pie.

For months I explored every lead; newspapers, hearsay from family and friends. I even approached the ward representative, only to learn a political golden rule: politicians throughout the universe help only those who scratch their backs—contributing to campaigns, passing out leaflets, standing at the polls, even bribing. Whoever believes that politicians are servants of the public should be committed to the mental hospital in Mattapan.

I picked up a few days work in a wool factory unloading freights, a couple of days long-shoring; a couple of weeks in a car wash surrounded with Negroes. I landed, finally, a dreary, but steady job as a laborer on a construction site (the MTA tunnel extension on Huntington Avenue). Like John Henry, I laid the tracks. Finally a position opened up as a fireman on a boiler at Wentworth Institute—night watch shift midnight to 8 am. Suited my lifestyle.

When Booker opened Danny's, he hired me for three reasons: Danny was my brother; I needed the job; he trusted me. To this day I'd walk through fire and brimstone for Booker, no matter what, no qualifications whatsoever. So I began to work afternoons, Fridays and Saturday

"The Depression? **I'll** never forget."

Timothy Booker T. Brennan, Owner

37 year old, tavern owner, married with two daughters of his own; he recently adopted his sister's three children when she died. Although everyone believes he's a bookie, actually Frankie Vento is the bookie. Booker has other fish to fry.

Booker is 5'9", 173 lbs; walks as straight and tall as a pine. Two features strike you at once; his flattened nose, via a punch, and his blue eyes, steady, piercing and clear as polar ice. He parts his brown hair off to the side; a few strands stick out like porcupine quills and he wears a large bushy mustache—like a British sergeant major. In fact, he served during the Great War with my brother Danny. They joined at sixteen; Danny was killed, Booker wounded. After his wounds healed, Booker was decorated, and discharged as a sergeant.

His skin is as dark as a ripe berry; therefore, his kids nicknamed him "boogy". Over the years the name adapted itself to his work: Booker. And he so well fits the image—dresses like a dandy, a man about town, easy with money—and the most incredible luck with a deck of cards. With him on a given night you'll meet a newspaper man, a baseball star, a hooker, ex-cons, gamblers, bombers, thieves, a dentist, college professor and maybe a priest. Booker knows everyone. And they trust him. Tell him a secret and be comforted that it's locked in an impregnable vault. Quick to smile (one sees the gap between his two front teeth) Booker constantly hums especially during card games. Philosophically one would place him as a cynic or a fatalist, especially when he shrugs, "What the hell—Who cares?" I love him like a brother.

"I'll tell you this, Bill, this Depression is a real son of a bitch! Not so much for me. I ain't got nothing to moan about. I mean, what the hell, I'm winning a few chips here and there. But if I was up against it like some of these guys, you'd think Chico was a boy scout. Hey look, I wouldn't hump fifty-sixty hours a week in some damn sweatshop in Chinatown. Make only a few bucks—slowly watch ya family go down the drain. And I know what I'm talking about—didn't I see my old man do it? You understand. My Depression was a long time ago down off Dudley Street; wearin' my cousin's hand-me-downs. I never owned a bike. Still pisses me off! Every kid in the world, in the whole wide world, should own a bike."

"But talk is cheap. Me, I ain't hurting none. Course, I feel bad for a lot of these guys. Help 'em out when I can, but I ain't Fort Knox. The Monsignor don't see it that way. Thinks I'm the livin' devil, curse of the neighborhood. But look, I offer a service; never ever forced a guy to drain a beer or make a bet. And Bill, the rule is to shut off guys when they're over their heads. Shut'em off, bag and baggage. I see it this way; the world's a cow an' it's gotta be milked. An if I don't do it, someone else will. Then again my cow could be arrested or stolen tomorrow."

"Depression, huh? Nineteen and eleven, that's when I saw hard times. That dumpy cold water flat in Roxbury, leaky roof distict. Three families using the same toilet, damn thing always leaked. Hadda use newspapers to wipe my ass. Bet I still got newsprint or even a headline inked on my ass.

And cold! Christ, I was always freezing my nuts off. And old coal stove in the kitchen. Get up in the morning and the bowl of water been frozen. I remember me and your brother use to go down to the railroad yard and pick up chunks of coal that fell off the coal cars. One time, that Polack who owned the coal yard caught us said we were stealin'. What a beating he gave me. That's what happened to my honker. So at night I'd sneak in the yard and steal the stuff. But I never forgot that Polack bastard. Coupla years after, I saw him in Roxbury Crossing. I musta punched him all the way to Mass. Ave. Bill, never cross a little kid. They got memories like elephants. A kid don't forget.

"Bill, you remember the time I got evicted. No, I guess you were too young. Worse day in my life. My old man in the hospital, these three big guys with a cop come in the house and move us out onto the sidewalk, bag and baggage. Raining out. Me and Danny minded the stuff while my Ma went for help. It seemed that every kid from here to Timbuktu was teasin' us. I was hurtin' Bill. The last time I ever cried. And it's the last time I'll be evicted. If I had a gun, I'd shot that bastard landlord. And if ever I loved your brother, Danny, it was there and then. He stood tall right with me, and we took on the whole block.

"Jesus, Bill, he was a great kid. If it wasn't for him I'd be planted in a field in France. You was just a little pisscutter when we joined up. Forged our birth certificate using bleach water to erase the ink. Only sixteen, we were. Christ, it was all a joke till we hit the trenches. If we made it, we planned to open a joint. We went through it all. It was awful. Before we'd go over the top, they'd pump us full of booze. Then I got hit, all tangled in the barb wire in a shell hole. Pinned down all day, weaker that all hell. Bill, the only thing that pulled me through was that I knew—I knew—Danny'd come for me. And sure as hell breaks loose—flares and machine guns. That don't stop Danny, he drags me on. He's hit himself, half his leg gone, but he don't say nothing. Gets me into the trench, presses my arm and says, 'See ya pal,' and collapses—Jesus, Bill, I better stop. I'll be bawling all over the place like a school girl.

"Well the rest is old history. After discharge, I went straight for a while. Then Prohibition came; started running booze. Good stuff. I ain't never blinded anyone. What a beautiful place we had, a warehouse down by Andrew Square. Had a still that'd put Schenley's to shame. Good place to cook. I felt like a chemist. Wearin' a white coat and mixing sacks of sugar. No beefs with cops because we had it sewed up way past the captain. We really had the right channels.

Then we opened the speakeasy in town, the El Morrocco on Washington Street. Well, I grew sick of that in-town scene . . . I mean they're all nuts. Killers, machine guns, bombs—I had enough of that shit overseas. So I sold out and started playin' cards for heavy money. One night I made my big score and opened up this joint. Named it after your brother.

"It's a good block, Bill. The people are stand-up. Our kind of people. Got more guts and goodness than the whole of the North Shore. They ain't all saints, I ain't saying that. Sure we got the seamy side, but life's tough and each guy gotta choose his own way of makin' it. When you come down to it, it ain't really no different than the Yankee bankers wheeling and dealing with stocks and interest rates and the electricity. They take care of their own interests, and we gotta take care of ours.

"There's a lot of talent around here. Take Richie Quinn. Great boxer. Shoulda had a shot at the big time, but the big guns said 'nix'. Not a big drawing card. I went to Buckley, the promoter. He's got some good stables. But he done nothing for me. That's life. Just don't expect nothing from me, Buckley.

"This block'll survive this, no bullshit about that. Got the guts. You know who I feel for Bill? Old Dinty. Who'd hire a dummy? Even when there's plenty of jobs. That's why I keep him on. Keeps the place clean. Anyway he useta live on my street. I useta tease the shit outta him. You know how kids are. He musta went through hell. When I opened up, his ma asked my ma to put him on. So why not?"

ENLISTMENT RECORD.

Name: [illegible] Grade: Sgt.
Enlisted, or inducted: [illegible] 1917, at Boston, Mass.
Serving in [illegible] enlistment period at date of discharge.
Prior service: None
Noncommissioned officer: Sgt.
Marksmanship, gunner qualification or rating: None
Horsemanship: Not mounted
Battles, engagements, skirmishes, expeditions: [illegible] July [illegible] to July [illegible] 1918
Following issued by Zone Supply Office, Boston, in accordance [illegible]: 1 [illegible], 1 pr. shoes, 3 prs. socks, 1 shirt, 2 suits underwear, 1 pr. gloves, 1 bag, 1 hat.
Knowledge of any vocation: None
Wounds received in service: [illegible]
Physical condition when discharged: Good
Typhoid prophylaxis completed: Oct [illegible] 1917
Paratyphoid prophylaxis completed: Oct [illegible] 1917
Married or single: Single
Character: Excellent
Remarks: Entitled to travel pay to Boston, Mass. [illegible]
Signature of soldier: [illegible]
[illegible]
Capt. Infantry [illegible]
Commanding [illegible]

Honorable Discharge from The United States Army

TO ALL WHOM IT MAY CONCERN:

This is to Certify, That Timothy [illegible]
[illegible] Sgt. Company C [illegible] Infantry
THE UNITED STATES ARMY, as a Testimonial of Honest and Faithful Service, is hereby Honorably Discharged from the military service of the United States by reason of [illegible]
Said Timothy [illegible] was born in [illegible], in the State of Massachusetts.
When enlisted he was [illegible] years of age and by occupation a [illegible].
He had [illegible] eyes, black hair, dark complexion, and was 5 feet [illegible] inches in height.
Given under my hand at [illegible] Mass. this [illegible] day of July, one thousand nine hundred and nineteen.
[illegible]
Commanding.

Chico, Seaman

33 year old seaman, separated, I think. Never speaks of a family. Not well-liked; word is that he's a Red and this a Catholic neighborhood. Radical, he is an ardent admirer of Joseph Stalin, 5'4", 160 lbs, thin, sinewy, tough.

Arms corded with thick veins. Thin face, a strong thinness. High cheekbones of an Indian. Aquiline nose. Thick black hair, with thin eyebrows that sweep into the bridge of his nose like bird wings. Blue eyes fired with anger, with compassion. His voice is loud, profane, and straight to the point. A wide mouth and stained teeth. A five inch scar runs along his forehead to the corner of his left eye; slightly distorts his eye. Dresses in rough work clothes and a black beret. I have seen him every day for a month; then he'll ship out for months at a time. Very mysterious guy. Tough, energetic, a fighter—a German Shepherd.

"It ain't really bad round here," says Chico. "No ones's out and out starving. It ain't good, but it's better'n the rest of the world. Workin' stiff's starving all over the world. And I've been around; seen it myself. Christ, seen famines and plagues and sufferin' everywhere. Couple of years ago, delivered rice to West Indies. People so hungry there was a riot on the pier. Soldiers set up machine guns. Mowed 'em down. Musta been a hundred bodies. You know how they got rid of them. Poor slobs. Pushed them off the pier. Shark food.

"Something's gotta be done. People gotta have the balls to stand up and be counted. All over the world. Us workin' slobs gotta get a fair share. We do the work. For Christ's sake, in China they're so poor, so exploited a landlord can execute a worker. Just cause he don't like him, have his head chopped off. Everywhere—in Asia, Africa, South America, working guys are breaking their asses for a few cents a day. Meantime all the rich princes, kings, or whatever ya call them, living a life of leisure. Feasting while people grub for garbage. Starving.

"I tell you we gotta have a revolution. World wide. Not just this country, but the whole world. And I want to be part of it. Do my share. Tired of sitting on the sidelines. And now I got my chance—guy I know sent me a letter from New York. They're forming a group to fight in Spain. Abe Lincoln Brigade or something. Guys who feel like me. Sick and tired of seein' people get screwed. So I'm shovin' off in a few weeks and do something that I feel inside. Help the poor of the world. My brothers and sisters.

"It's great when guys join together and fight. Like in May of thirty-four with Harry Bridges; we all went on strike. Longshoremen, teamsters. Jesus, we tied up San Francisco. Ya talk about open warfare. Scabs and strikebreakers, even the cops, tried to bust us. But we stood united. Look at my face, laid up two months by a cop with a billy club as big as a baseball bat. You know, I'm proud of that scar. And I'm proud to go to Spain. Maybe it'll be the spark to set the world on fire. The rise of the workingman. There's so much to done. I get frustrated, I can't sleep nights. This world is so screwed up. I seen it. I know.

"In China, people starving all over the place and it's accepted as natural. No one cares. You know they got death houses and when a guy gets to the end of the line, he pays a yen for a clean bed and maybe a statue of Buddha. He dies in peace. But most chinks don't even have the price of a clean flop. They die in some dirty alley. After workin' fifteen hours a day all their lives, they die in a gutter. It ain't right, Bill. I seen things and worked places you'd never believe. Once worked as a stoker on a coal freighter. Shoveling coal eight-twelve hours. Christ, the fire room was a hundred-ten degrees. Soot and sweat all over ya. You had to wrap rags around your head to keep the sweat outta your eyes. And you get no pay. None to speak of. A dog's better off. Food's nothing but slop. Hunks of fat, they calls beef. If you get hurt, the cook is your doctor. On one trip this darkie-fellow fell and broke his back. The captain wouldn't change course, and the poor guy died. He was only a native, said the captain. I reported it to the embassy, but all that happened was I got sacked.

"I'll send ya a postcard, Bill."

Tarjeta Posta

(UNION POSTAL UNIVER

ESPAÑA

BARCELONA, SPAIN
JULY 19

BILL, BOOKER-
HAVE CARRIED THIS POSTCARD
FOR MONTHS. WE'RE TRAINED
GOOD. MORALE HIGH. I'M
IN CHARGE OF A MACHINE
GUN TEAM. REALLY FEEL
I'M DOING SOMETHING FOR
THE COMRADES, WORKING PEOPLE.
NOW IN BARCELONA. BOMBERS ATTACKING. TOMORROW WE'LL
SEE ACTION.

BEST. CHICO

DANNY'S TAVERN
371 DORCHESTER AVE.
DORCHESTER, MASSACHUSETTS
U.S.A.
C/O BILL BIXTON

Richie Quinn, Meat Packer

21 year old ex-boxer. Single. Works as a loader in a meat packing plant, and on special occasions, as a bouncer in Jack Sharkey's Tavern on Friend Street, under Buckley's Gym. With a few exceptions, the sports buffs rate Richie as the finest athlete to ever come out of this block: boxing, baseball, football, track—the important sports. He weighs a compact 156 lbs., stands 5'8", a middle weight, but he looks much heavier. Proportioned exquisitely; hammered out of a granite block, he shaped like an inverted triangle mounted on a rectangular stand. Heavy shoulders, corded bull neck, muscular ridges from top to bottom. Yet he moves so gracefully, a fluid motion, a ballerina twirling, a cougar capable of lightning thrusts. In the ring, he's something to be seen. The sweat glistens from his back like he was anointed while he slowly bobs and weaves his cobra's dance, coiled like a powerful spring waiting for a shot. Jab—Jab. Hook. Two jabs flash like arrows in flight. Followed by a hook so powerful that when it connects it actually thuds like a sledge. Simultaneously he snorts like a racehorse.

Surprisingly for a fighter, his face is unmarked, even boyish. Skin as smooth and clear as ice except for a few minor scars over his right eye. You'd notice his eyes first: smoky brown and shaped almond as though there were a trace of Asia in his genes. But seventy-one fights has taken a toll: his cauliflower ears feel like thick slabs of liver. But Richie tells me they never ache. His careless brown hair is so curled that you'd think he took to it with a curling iron. But he's too much of a man to do that. It's natural curl. Anyway, who'd press the question?

Richie is tough, but like people who are sure of themselves, he's easy going. Time and time again I've seen the young bucks tempt to try the old gunfighter, test the reputation of just how good, just how fast, just how tough. But Richie walks away from the troubles. Usually Joe Scarletta or Booker warn the young bucks to "Screw off before they get their hats caved in."

Richie says, "The Depression? To tell ya the truth, Bill, I never knew how bad it was 'till I quit the ring. I mean I've been makin' three, four grand a year since I been seventeen. Johnnie Buckley always made sure I hadda coupla bucks in my kick. And I useta make a few in the packing plant. So I ain't never hurt before. I ain't never thought about the future before, but now it bothers the shit outta me. I mean I ain't got nothin' going for me. No real future. Boxings' OK when you're young'n full of piss and vinegar. But after a while you just get hit too many punches. Brains turn into scrambled eggs. Like the story of a veteran and his manager giving an interview to sports writers. The old timer's shadow boxing, flexing, throwing punches left and right. You know, trying to impress the writers."

"He's in great shape," brags the manager, "best shape of his career, physically and mentally,"

A reporter asks, "Who'd you like to fight next, champ?"

"Kid Klondike," snorts the old timer, throwing a few jabs, "I'll murder' em."

The manager pulls him aside, "How many times I gotta tell ya. You are Kid Klondike."

"Well I never want to end up like that. I mean, I still got my marbles. Not that many, but the same as when I begun seven years ago . . . Well, at least I got my high school diploma and that's worth a lot. More'n most guys got.

"I remember I was just a punk kid at Dot High who needed a coupla bucks. You know how it is in the city. Kids're tackling hydrants and punching telephone poles before they's ten years old. Good street fighters. A kid on my street stole a pair of boxing gloves, and we useta take turns. The one with the gloves punched, the other blocked, then we'd swap.

That's how I learned. Jesus, we'd box until your arms fell off. None of this three minute stuff, we'd go for half an hour. My arms felt like sacks of cement. So anyway the coach up at Dot once sees me in a fist fight, and instead of getting me thrown outta school, he connects me with Buckley, the promoter. I'm young, you know and Buckley's handing me all this bullshit about Golden Gloves, and glory and money plus expenses. I mean I lap it up like a cat at the milk saucer—I mean Johnnie Buckley had a good stable. String of thirty guys and he's Jack Sharkey's manager. So there was stars in my eyes.

"My first fight was against a Mick, kid like me . . . Charlestown, I think. Anyway I all but tore his head off in two rounds. This is great, what a great way to make dough, so I says to myself. I ain't a violent guy, just a sports nut. But the roar of the crowd, the screechin' and hollerin', it got me. Christ, it sounds like thunder. Get into ya blood, especially when ya winnin'. Here I am, a senior in high school, makin' more money than my old man. Meeting all kinds of people, politicians, stars, baseball players—Gene Tunney shook my hand once. Yup, they're all with ya when you're winning. No shit, Bill when that crowds screaming, ya get so excited. Almost like being with a girl, you know, I mean, sex. Oh Jesus, the joy! Ya punchin' and blockin', and all ya hear is the roar. And ya know you got this guy on the ropes. Jab, Jab. Whack. To the body, to the head. Then ya see that glassy look in his eyes. He starts to drop. The screams, 'Kill'em, Richie, Deck the bastard!' Finally the climax; he's out. Like being with a girl. I swear ya actually go crazy in the head."

"Every day after school I'd work out at Buckley's gym. Run two-three miles. In great shape. I guess when you come right down to it, I had a good time. I mean, I fought in Dublin, England, New York, and over New England. Portland, Salem, Lowell. But you know I like Boston the best. The Arena, Mechanics Hall. That's where the action is. Maybe's it's you guys, yelling and cheering me on. It made no difference. Do you remember the time I was in the eliminations over at the Arena? Fought four damn fights in one night. Three knockouts and I won that decision from Jimmy McCue from Mission Hill. Tough little bastard."

"Ya, I had my ups and downs, alright. But, you know, I never took a dive for dough. But I did take a dive last year. Was up in Augusta, fighting this

Negro kid. Gave him everything I had, and I mean everything. Couldn't budge the gorilla. The promoter, he wasn't gonna pay me anyway, so I says to myself to hell with it. And I laid down. Made no difference cause my chance for a shot at the big time was gone anyway. But that's the breaks. Like I said, I got out with my marbles. Ya know some of my best friends are the guys I useta fight against. Bill, the old fighters, they're great-hearted guys, loyal as all hell. And they'd work like dogs for ya.

"My toughest fight? Was in New York. The one with Dynamite Jones. Big rangy coon from Harlem. Black, so black, a piece of charcoal makes a white mark. What a tough bastard though! Big thick shoulders. Couldn't get a punch by him. They told me he was a second stringer, straight out of the sticks. I mean the damn liars. Well, no sooner the bell gongs, he faints, suckers me right in. Wham. A right straight from the floor. Right between the eyes. God, I'm wandering around, couldn't even tell ya my name—nothing. Everything's in a fog for the rest of the round. Can't even hear the crowd. Just barely remember Doc massaging the back of my neck. Splashing cold water over my head. Doc stopped the blood coming out of my mouth with Vaseline. Two front teeth cracked. I mean I was mumbling to myself.

"Well, I dunno how I did it but I faked it through the rest of the fight. But the coon, he's hungry. Wants to polish me off in the last round. Knockout, you know. I mean he's got me hands down with a decision. But like I says, he's hungry. He's dancing and weaving, throwing loose rights and lefts. Real cocky. Big smile on his face. Pissed me off so bad I dug up every ounce of strength I had in my body. Like I'm aiming a rifle, I set'em up. He drops his guard. I slug him in the gut, right in the pit. Caught him flat footed. Jesus, his face turned pale. He grabs his gut. I let him have a hook, a roundhouse. No class, all strength. Wham. He dropped like a sack of shit. Legs buckled like spaghetti. Out like a light. Ya I won, but I lost. Hadda headache for three weeks. Even today I still get some bitch of headaches. So I told Buckley I want out. 'OK, kid,' he tells me. Even offers me a job in Sharkey's but I wanna go back to hustlin' crates. Until I find out what I'm gonna do. I mean, feel like an old man at twenty-three. So now I know what the Depression's all about. Lucky I ain't married. Wish't I saved some money though. I mean maybe I coulda bought a little joint or a truck or somethin'. But that's the breaks. Live and learn."

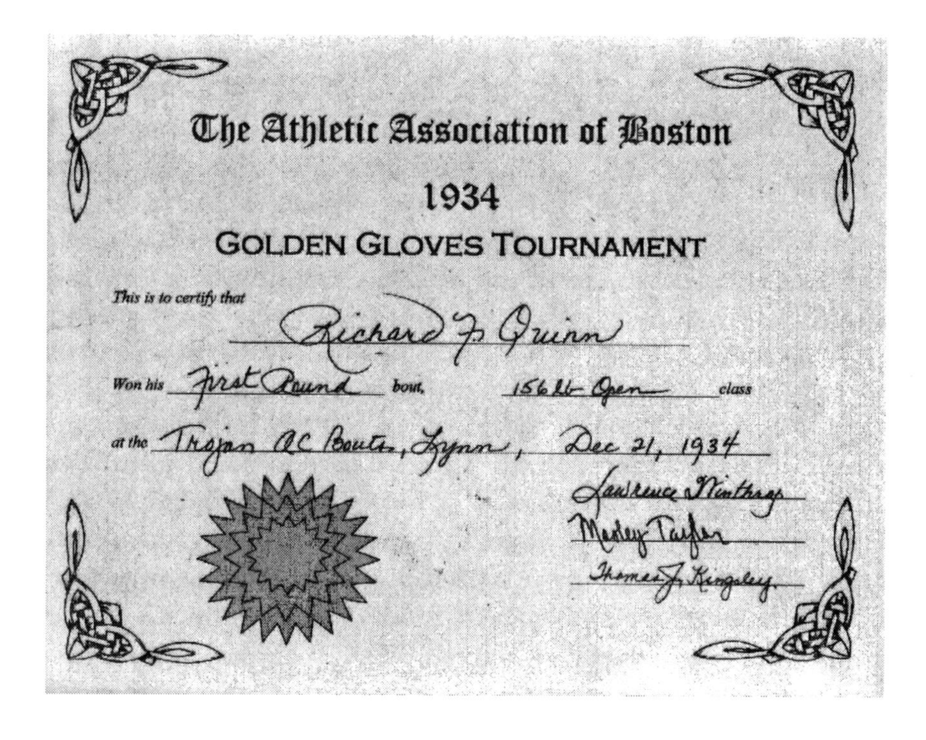
The Athletic Association of Boston

1934

GOLDEN GLOVES TOURNAMENT

This is to certify that

Richard F. Quinn

Won his First Round bout, 156 lb. Open class

at the Trojan AC Bouts, Lynn, Dec 21, 1934

Lawrence Winthrop

Thomas F. Kingsley

Joe Scarletta, Truck Driver

23 year old truck-driver. Born in Salerno, emigrated when four years old. Joe's a chunky 5'6", 175 lbs., barrel chest—too much spaghetti, he claims. His big broad face, and his slightly protruded dark eyes with drooping lids cause him to seem sleepy most of the time. Like a tired dark brown St. Bernard stretching by the stove. His calm and easy nature, his soft unhurried speech adds to the illusion. His cropped brown hair recedes severely; in ten years you know he'll be bald. To combat the baldness, Joe superstitiously wears his hair long on top and especially short on the sides, like a boy's haircut. Therefore he sometimes suffers the kidding "Whaddya makin' ya First Holy Communion?" Usually, however Joe wears a scally cap pulled down to the bridge of his slightly hooked nose. A Saint Christopher medal and a union button ornament the side of his cap. Winter and summer Joe wears his cap and a grayed brown leather jacket. Because of his left arm constantly hanging out the truck window, a large patch mends the hole in the elbow. An inseparable stogie, chewed and often unlit, sticks out of his mouth. I'm sure you'd agree that Joe, indeed, looks like a truck-driver, traveling across the east and west coast—Boston to San Deigo.

"The Depression? Whaddya want to know, Bill? I don't worry about it. Mama Mia, if I did, you'd crack up. There's good and there's bad. I could tell ya about the bad times but, what the hell, you see the bad times everywhere. We got the good times too. Great guys, I work with. Maybe sometimes you're forced to do things that ya ain't proud of. But when a guys gotta family, he'll do 'bout anything. Mama Mia, the things guys'll do when it comes to work and jobs and union. I never listen to Reds, politicians, even Chico; they're all full of shit. But I believe in unions. Thank God, I'm in Local Twenty-Five. Crazy bunch of bastards. That's what ya need if ya wanna protect ya job.

"Did I tell ya 'bout the picket last month—Jesus, you musta heard 'bout the scab meat truck bein rolled over in Field's Corner. All the meat stolen. Damn cops lookin'. A guys gotta be careful 'bout finks. You're solid, Bill, so I'll give you the inside on what happened.

"You remember the cold, cold day last month? Down to zero. Well, we were picketing Northeast Trucking offa Dorchester Avenue. By St. Williams Church in Savin Hill.

"Well, the B.A. sends eight of us outta the union hall to picket the first shift. Butchie Harris, Eddie Sheehan, Lefty DeMato, Swede Jensen, Bobby Joyce and coupla other guys. Freezin our nuts off. Jesus, it was like Siberia. We're marchin' up and down the sidewalk, stomping our feet and swinging our arms. Anything to keep from freezin'. Christ it was cold. Damn scabs inside, nice and warm, are laughin at us. Makin' faces and shit. Just waitin' for us to step outta line so they call the cops and bring in the goon squad. Butchie's fit to be tied. He wants to storm the place, 'Come on out, ya scab bastards!' He's screamin' like a nut. Inside they look scared so they leave the window.

"At lunch, the guys come up here, d'ya remember? Sandwiches and a couple of beers. Well on the way back, Butchie buys a fifth. And Lefty—there's a big house next to the store, with a big picket fence. Lefty sneaks an ash barrel outta the yard. We bust up some orange crates, and get a little fire goin'. It ain't so bad now. And you know how it is when guys get together. One thing leads to another. We stand around the barrel, bullshitting and nipping and telling jokes. Butchie told a couple of pissas.

"Butchie's always kidding Billy Joyce—they grew up in Roxbury together. But instead he turns to Eddie Shehan: Eddie's just a kid, shy and I think a virgin."

"'Hey Eddie," says Butchie, "Let me ask you, do you like fat girls with long dirty hair?"

'Whaddaya kiddin me?' Eddie turns red. Billy laughs because he's not the one being teased.

"Butchie continues, 'With rotten teeth and bad breath. How'd ya like to make out with her?'

"Bill enjoys this.

"'C'mon,' answers Eddie.

"'And with tits that hang down to her knee caps. Do ya like that kinda girl?'

"Bill laughs.

'Butchie says, 'Then how come ya screwing Billy's girlfriend?' We all howled over that one. That Butchie's a funny bastard! A card.

"'We polish the fifth. Buy another. Coupla more pickets are torn from the fence. Inta the fire. By three o'clock we're havin' a f'n—weeney roast. Swede's cookin' hot dogs on a stick. We got beer, vodka, and some potato chips. No one's cold anymore, just stumbling around. Then along comes Cassidy, the BA. Is he bullshit! 'What's this?' he screams, 'An AA meeting? Look at you, the whole lot of you! You useless bastards!'

"By this time, half the picket fence is gone. The flames are twenty damn feet high. Started to burn the branches of this big oak tree. And you shoulda see the barrel, the barrel's so hot it was red. No shit. Christ, we coulda heated half of Savin Hill. Ya, Cassidy was A-one bullshit! Callin us a disgrace to the union. Bunch of screw-ups. He really chewed our ass. Ordered us to put out the fire and get outta there before we were arrested.

"So we screws off. Laughin', and all full up with liquor. Three o'clock. We decides to hit a tavern. So we walks up to Field's Corner. By this time, no one cares about anything. What the hell pulls up outside the Field's Corner Deli, but a meat truck? A scab meat truck? Butchie goes nuts. He's running up the street and by the time he reaches the truck the driver's inside the store. He don't know nothing. Butchie's yanking and pulling the door. Like a dog at an old shoe. But it's locked. So he starts rockin' the truck. We all join in and in two minutes flat we got it on its side.

A whole bunch of shoppers gather around. Swede kicks in the window and opens the doors. Everybody's grabbin' meat. Like it's Dollar Day at Filene's. Like ants all over the truck. Running away with rolls and baloney and cheese—me and Eddie grab half a damn cow. Weighed a ton—half the neighborhood's been eating beef for a coupla weeks. Ya shoulda seen Jimmy O'Toole's old lady, big chunk of a cow in a baby carriage. Makin it up the street.

"So the guy comes out. The look on his puss. Mama Mia! He's yelling and arms going like windmills, trying to stop us. Guy, he can't stop anything. So he bugs it up the street to Station Eleven. But it don't do no good. Within five minutes, the truck was picked clean like vultures. Everybody takes off so it looks like a desert.

"You know, Bill, it ain't right. But there's a Depressions and people do crazy things. Is that the type of story that you wanted, Bill?" Is that OK?"

Casey, Meat Packer

29 year old who claims he was toughened up by his Marine brother; beat him with a "Garry" belt. A loner, lives with his mother on Columbia Road. No means of support but always flush. Very cold, hostile. Something evil or deranged about him. No friends. Doesn't fit in Danny's, or probably anywhere else. Served over ten years in various reform schools and jails.

He's heavy, thick, powerful. Dark scowling face. Black hair, black eyes glowing with dark fury. When he tears at a sandwich with is heavy jaws, it reminds you of a shark tearing and ripping with a savage lust.

Holds everyone, everything in sheer contempt. The only person that I heard him compliment was Dutch Shultz whom he "worked" with a few years ago. Suspicious, seething, totally unpredictable.

I've watched him sit rigid, completely rigid, staring at the mirror. Unblinking. His fists clenched so tight, they shook. The veins tightened out of his forehead like blue strings. He suffers terrible headaches. Every morning he swallows three or four aspirins to prevent their onset. The pain usually stabs in the back of his head, and shoots over to his left temple. I've seen him actually punch the bar in a frenzy of pain.

"Depression, I got a headache, and you ask me about the Depression? Screw the Depression! Whaddya wanna know for anyway? Nosey bastard! Writing all the time. Ya better not write about me. I don't like you—spying for the cops. I'll bust your God damn fingers. Ya hear? You're all alike. The cops trying to get me back in the can."

LANGUAGE IN DANNY'S

"Pahk the Cah in Havahd Yawd"

OCTOBER 1937

Every day I see the boys, hear them speak, curse, sing, whisper. I listen carefully and try to copy what they say. But when I read my writing aloud, something is definitely lacking. All my characters sound alike. They don't look alike in dress, appearance, clothes; gestures, therefore, they shouldn't speak alike. In fact, if there was any place that we'd expect to find a wide disparity in speech, it would be Danny's, or any other city tavern. We'll hear: Mickey Smith with street talk "Ya, he ain't got no brains, but he's happy as a pig in shit."

Danny O'Neill with his brogue, "Deed ye needn't bother yerself lad, ah'm standin the round."

Blackie Hession with his profane laced language, specializing in the "F" word (noun, verb, adjective, adverb . . .)

Jackie Dwyer with his idiom, "Hi, how ya doin?"

Or even me with my boiler room lingo—"condensate, returns, psi, safety valve, #6 fuel"—etc. language of one's trade.

Red Driscoll with roofer's shop talk, "Had a scratcher today . . . 60 square, 3 ply . . . Kid got burnt by the hots . . . Scratch bar . . . shrimp boat full of hots . . . donkey . . ."

And I hear accents from the four corners of the earth. Wide variations. The only commonality I'll find is the swearing. Not that everyone swears, but most do although very few swear obscenely.

Vocabulary is a very important component of any conversation. In Danny's I'll hear the extremes; a vocabulary consistent of skeleton English, grunts, swears, slang and gestures; and a vocabulary of precise diction and pronunciations. It's very curious that some guys speak so well even though they have but a fifth grade education. Tommy O'Hara is a case in point. Although just a janitor at St. Peter's, he's one of the most articulate men in here. Certainly the most well read. It aggravates me that fate gives a man the brains, but not the opportunity. Scotty Burns is another case in point. He learned to read from a Bible, therefore, he speaks with a rich, colorful vocabulary.

Some of the boys use a hundred words when two would suffice. Take Peter Brisk. Ask Pete for the time; he'll tell you a history. "Time?" Sure, Bill, I've got the time. What's the matter with your watch? Broke, huh? Ya know, guy down Uphams Corner, he's a good repairman. The best, and cheap too, ya know. Married to my cousin, and from Germany. Smart guy, those Germans, when it comes to watches and everything. Time? It's quarter past seven . . ."

Sometimes I'd wager that half the boys don't know what a complete sentence is, at least to hear from their speech. They use phrases, incomplete thoughts, dwindling words. Almost like a telephone conversation. Listen to Jackie Dwyer, "Ya, ok. Saturday huh, ok. Small job, well . . . ya know, I'll be there. How much? Ok. you want to call Marty? Good man, ya know. See ya later." Of course each guy has his own unique way of combining words when speaking. For example, Joe Scarletta may say, "I like Ballentine beer," whereas Bob McNamara may rephrase the same though, "Ballentine, that's a beer I like." Or Chico, "Ballentine, I like it."

Although this can be very difficult to show in writing, I sometimes use italics, different sentence structure, underlining and punctuation to show emotions and emphasis. Of course, in the tavern, emphasis and emotion are inextricably tied in with swearing. But then again, it depends on who's doing the swearing, the tone and the accompanying motions. Now, I know that soft spoken Gunny Steele swears seldom. If he were to scream, "Put that damn bottle down!" I could be certain that every man-jack in here would know that he meant business. If Frank Vento screamed the same command, his arms flailing like windmills, he'd receive, "Ah, blow it out your ass!"

Rhythm can be used to emphasize, or de-emphasize. Listen to McNamara, a low monotone sure to hum you to sleep. I can imagine his classes. Vassarian speaks with a clipped rhythm. I sometimes find myself tapping a code with my fingers as he speaks. Try this experiment: as people speak, tap your finger in cadence. Everyone has a special cadence, almost as distinct as one's signature.

These last components of conversation clearly define the speaker. I associate certain phrases, slang expressions and gestures with particular individuals. Casey opens and closes his fist, "Whaddaya lookin' at, shit-head?" Ira Gold moves his hands with soft delicate motions. "As a matter of fact . . ." Booker T. shrugs, "Who cares . . ." And Tommy O'Hara cleans his pipe, scraping away with his knife, "No mistake about it . . ." Tell me the gesture and the phrase, and I'll name you the man.

Suggest, be selective. When I write a speech, I select those words and phrases which not only reveal a person's background and education, but which show the inner depths of his personality. I must show what he says, how he says it. Watch his expressions—his eyes—to indicate the delicate shades of what he thinks. Casey sees a cat get hit by a trolley outside. Screaming with the pain of a broken back, the cat leaps six feet into the air, then five feet, four, two—stillness. Casey chuckles, "Didya see that bastard!" What shades are perceived?

Formally, dialogue in writing must: reveal characters and their motives; give information about what's happening now, and what is about to happen; create an atmosphere; set the tone. I must strip the dialogue to the bone, and structure the words to fit the story requirements. I should avoid overloading with thick dialect and slang; suggest by using a few key words and phrases rather than actual transcript.

Let me digress for a moment. Every time I think of nuns teaching English, it brings to mind the legend of how Booker left Dorchester High School.

An old spinster was teaching sophomore English grammar, specifically the difference between singular and plural.

“Now class,” began the teacher, “if a woman is sitting at a window, that is called singular.” She called upon Booker, “Timothy Brennan, can you answer this question? If many women are sitting at many windows what do you call it?”

Booker paused, “A whorehouse.”

He was expelled.

For the past months I’ve tuned my ears to a number of conversations.

1) Irish

Tommy O’Hara. “Joyce? Why yes, Bill, I have read the man’s writing. A clever chap, keen mind. No mistake about it, Ireland has had a fair share of writers. Yeats, Shaw, Swift, Synge. All good men, honored the world over. That’s history, Bill, fact not fancy. For such a small country, she has given the world some of the greatest literature. Voyage literature, Colloquy of the Ancients, Annals of the Four Masters. In fact, it is said that the Voyage of Brendal gave Dante the idea for his works. No mistake about it, there is more to the Irish than a shamrock and St. Patrick. Pour me a neat one before I go to Confession, will you Bill.”

Jerry Collins. “Casey? You ask me about the man. Ah’ I’ll tell ye, there’s no knowing that one. Half the time mad with drink. ’Deed usen’t he drink half the day and never bother ye atall. Jesus, Mary and Joseph, now the man’s a right nasty fellah. Mean little tinker. Ya could stand the man a pint on two, and all ya’d get is a dog’s abuse. He’s too odd for the likes of me. I like a sniff and then but, I declare to Christ, we’ll never wash the pots together. Well, I’m off for the present “bye.”

2) Street Talk

Booker T. "Gamblin's a sin? Look who cares what the Monsignor says about bookin'? If people wantta bet, they bet. It's as simple as that. What the hell, I provide what a guy wants. I ain't bending his arm. You want smokes, you go to the store; you gotta hot tip, you see Frank Vento. Me, I've lucky. Win a few bucks so I can start this place. I mean, a guy's gotta make a livin'. Hey, look at it this way, if I was around when the police went out on strike, I wouldn't have to work at all."

Bill McBride. "The Depression? Well as a matter of fact, according to the newspapers, it has indeed affected everyone; however I suspect—in fact I see—that again it is the working class that bears the brunt. Not only with regards to money, but more importantly with regards to opportunity. As a matter of fact . . . ."

Chico. "Talk about the Depression. It's God damn rape—a crucifixion of the workin' stiff! I'm tellin' you it's the workers who make the batter but do we get the bread? Like hell! It's the Rockefellers and Fords—got us workin' slobs by the balls. We do the work! Who gets the profits? Well, I'll tell ya who. The banks, insurance companies, the leeches on Wall Street, that's who! Crycifyin' us to a cross of unemployment! Bang the nails up to the flat! And the dummies around here ain't got the balls to strike. Ain't got the sense to fight for themselves. A slave should not die a peaceful death."

Red Driscoll. "Ya know, Riche, I saw the fight and ya know what I think. I think ya got screwed. Ya shoulda won. You shoulda won hands down. An ya know what else I think. Ya know I bet that guinny referee fixed the judges too. They're all alike, those guinnies. I mean that kid ya was fightin; couldna been anythin' but a guinny—not with a honker like that. Ya I woulda told that son of a bitch ref a thing or two. You could bet your sweet ass on that. Ya was winnin' ya know, any dummy could see that. I think you got screwed. That's what I think . . ."

3) Scottish

Scotty Burns. Depression? It's nothing short of shameful. Give me a wee drop to keep out the cold. A man needs work. Ay, there's but a wee bit o'work here but less at home. I'm not fond of goin' home. Canna find work in the shipyards. Ay, it's miserable from what me folks say. Onyway it minds me of some trouble I'm no exactly lookin' pleased to face with. Nay it wouldna pay . . ."

4) Italtian

Tony the shoemaker. "Now Booka, I'm no proud to tell you again. You losesa da ticket, you no getta da shoe. I musta tol' you dis a hundred times. What you tink, I'm run dis place like Charlie da chink uppa da laundry. You bringa da shoe and I'ma remember who da hell da shoe belonga to.

5) Canadian

Jack Walsh. "Bill Morrissey? Know'd em, I have, ever since I been down here. Good mate, e was—a real christer in the old days. Me and em usen't to smuggle kegs o'rum across from St. Pierre. Sure twas the aisiest thing in the wurrold. I did, til one time, we got caught in a starm in the dead o'winter. By the Lawd God, I thought we'd be all carpses. Twas turrible. But I reckon the Lawd takes care of even us divils. Fishing? Sure it takes some bearin', but she does all right by me."

6) German

Blackie Hession's father. "For Got's sake, Bill, I will tell you something. Zat boy of mine, I vas telling him the ozzer day, if you vant to liff a goot life, you vill haff to get a goot education. Neffere mind zat tomato factory. Gottam! He don't effen listen. Vell Bill, ze day vill come, he vill find out I vas right."

Describing A Person

November 8, 1938

For the last few years I've sketched people, but with the words I use they ooze out stiff and wooden. And ironically, my people are real. Every week I see them, hear them, talk with them. But how do you project your senses with words? No easy task.

My eyes see. Jackie Dwyer. Thick neck, round rugged face. A bull. Whereas Vassarian is pencil thin, delicate. A sparrow.

My ears hear. Tommy O'Hara. Soft, pleasant. A melody. "Draw up one for me thirst, Bill." Whereas Red Driscoll croaks, "What a hot damn day. Like to burn my ass off . . . Gimme two beers."

My hand feel. Shake hands with Bill Morrissey. Rough and cracked as an old boot. But Ira Gold. Delicate hands, smooth as baby skin. The hands of a surgeon or pianist.

Unfortunately, at time, my nose sniffs. Invariably Rags Maloney reeks of old clothes, and Blackie Hession smells of tomatoes. Whereas, Chico. A soft fragrance—the butt of many an insults concerning prostitutes. Bob McNamara. Well, a faint trace of peppermint which unsuccessfully hides the alcohol aroma.

My senses succeed; my words fail. Fail to describe a person—a living, felling, vibrant, believable character. In fact, what is a person? What is this volatile enigma that we call personality? To attempt an answer is to sculpture fog. What mysterious process seethes within us? What goes on in a person's head? For example, the other day, Casey bounces in, his face beaming. He tells a few jokes, buys a few rounds. Good time Charley.

Suddenly a metamorphosis. Abrupt as an explosion. His face contorts. Zip—smash! A bottle crashes into the mirror behind the bar. He stomps outside. Was this the result of beatings from his father? An alcoholic mother? How would you describe Casey? You see him, hear him. However, you play a foolish game if you anticipate his thoughts or intentions. The guys leave him alone. Very deep.

Now as another example, take Dinty. Retarded, very simple, a child. But what's really below the surface? An iceberg? Defies an adequate description.

Because I intend to keep this story of Danny's Tavern, I must overcome this lack of ability or understanding. Otherwise, like a defective embryo, the people will be stunted or distorted. A hollow history. Like Tony the shoemaker we must carve out the leather before we sole the shoe. God, it's frustrating.

Basically, I think people are very much the same when we talk of basic motives, drives and ends to which we all strive. We all desire to live, and to avoid pain and suffering. We all want the comforts of mind and body. Rest our heart and soul on a pillow of down. How do we accomplish these ends? Each to his own method, but we're all cast form the same mould. A Greek on a galley ship probably differed little from Red Driscoll, the roofer. A Negro in an African diamond mine works towards similar basic goals as Blackie Hession in the tomato factory. Sure the environment is different, but they all want to live long, to love and be loved, to belong and be respected, and to be secure emotionally and financially.

Let us choose some of these general human tendencies and identify guys which strongly show these traits.

Love and hate. When it comes to children, Danny O'Neill radiates more warmth than a bonfire. And when it comes to the English, you can feel the heat of hatred in Danny O'Neil.

To get or to give. Now, Booker, he likes the fine things. Rings and clothes, and a car and vacations to spring training and a steady growing nest egg.

Scotty Burns, he's generous almost to the point of being a sucker. Always good for a beer, or a donation.

To fight or to retreat. Old Vassarian. A real fighter. Lost every relative—mother, father, sisters, brothers, aunts, uncles—everyone in a massacre in Armenia. Left for dead. No food, no money. Quit? Never. Somehow worked his way to Mexico. Then to Boston.

Frank Vento, Booker's pal. Worked in a wool factory. Got cheated. "Screw work!" Retreated from the mainstream into shady deals.

To accept or to reject. You'd call Jack Walsh the classic Greek stoic. Everything he accepts with the resignation of a philosopher. Grew up under unbelievable hardships. Out to sea at 12. One winter his family ate the dogs to survive. Jack said, at the time they tasted pretty good. Ever since I've known Booker Brennan, he has rejected the rules; he has slammed, banged, finagled his way through life, twisting and distorting and interpreting the rules like they were pieces of rubber. A painful source of frustration to the nuns at St. Peter's, he received many the cuff and blow especially from the pointer stick.

"You'll be no good, you little imp!" Whack, whack! "Go to confession and ask God's forgiveness!" In one door, out the back and to the park for a baseball game.

To join or to withdraw. Gunny Steele joins. Likes to mingle, good fellow. He's the patriarch of Danny's. Sort of a judge. When an argument erupts, or a decision reaches that critical point, the guys look to Gunny for a King Solomon decision. Other than Casey, Chico surpasses anyone for being a loner. A life at sea sits very well with him. Sometimes during a rainstorm, he gazes out the window with a look that takes him far beyond the street scene. What's out there that he so desires?

Environment: Origin, job, education, race, religion, politics. Which one of us can deny the strong effect of our family, our religion, our job, our education, our daily bills and bank account? No great lightening flash. No, slow but sure like the steady drops of water onto the rock. Even granite conforms to its influence. What's that saying? "The apple doesn't fall far from the tree." How many Irish mothers have prayed their sons into the priesthood?

With respect to Danny's guys, 99% are: immigrants or sons of immigrants, working class (or unemployed), minimal education, Irish or Italian or English, Catholic, Democrats, marginal savings. With credentials such as these, opportunity is limited, for this generation anyway. In fact, this environment is like a block chained around a swimmer's neck. No matter how desperately you swim, in time you'll sink. Without bemoaning or cursing the fates I'd bet that many of these guys have the stuff—the talent and the guts, to accomplish something more worthwhile than sweeping floors or throwing boxes or booking numbers.

Award Tommy O'Hara a couple of sheepskins with PhD, and he's be the best teacher in Irish Literature this side of the Atlantic. Only a janitor. But a house full of books, a head full of wisdom and a heart full of Gaelic love.

Booker T. A man of action. A guy to get things done. Give him the authority and he'd manage us out of the Depression. And if he failed, we'd all be satisfied because we would have had a hellava good time.

Psychology: Personality, attitudes, sex life, morals, loves, fears, abilities, intelligence. To me, this is without a doubt a strange territory. Beyond each mountain, in each valley, into each crevice, lie the unexpected, and the mysterious. What's really inside a person's head? What's behind that mask that we call the face? Many the time I take notice of what thoughts and feeling seethe within me. In fact, many times I'm ashamed, and surprised. Thank God, my soul is not a window for observation. I hide many thoughts, deep desires. Love—it's so hard to say "I Love You." Sexual forays—the newly married girl down the street. Sweet, soft with tempting thighs. Anger—wanting to smash one's face. Revenge—getting even for a wrong done. Envious and jealous of even my best friend. Do others have these emotions? Conflicts? Tensions?

All I can say with dubious confidence is that my psychology is result of our physical body and our environment. The mind is so complicated, so difficult to understand. Like a blind man touching an elephant's trunk.

Why are some guys energetic; others bored? Doers and dreamers? Generous and greedy? Proud and humble? Sexually healthy, and prudish?

We all have the basic drives. But what's important is the priority and intensity of these drives. Tommy O'Hara cares little for a million dollars; Sy, the thumb man, would "tear off your balls for a two bitter." Why does Red Driscoll sketch? "What the hell's wrong with you?" asks Frank Vento. "You don't get paid. Why waste ya time?"

Again, because we can't tell all, we must suggest. Pick a dominant trait, an intense quality. Usually we describe a guy very thin. "Gunny, he's a good sport", "Now that Jerry Collin's a funny bastard," "Richie's a tough son of a bitch."

NICKNAMES

DECEMBER 1937

Nicknames and tattoos are both inseparable in city taverns. Every tavern, every block, has a Buddy or Joe, a Murph, and a hundred other variations. In fact, for many guys, the real name might as well be lost or forgotten. Where do nicknames originate? Let's see.

Shortening of a name. I could fill page after page with shortened first names: Joe, Mike, Jack, Chuck. But let's look at some of the last names:

O'B; Okie, Mac; Whitey; Odie; Sully; Balsy (Balsavich); Goggie (Gogan); Mannie (Mann); Perry (Perriera); Hildy (Hildebrand); Burnso (Burns); Murph (Murphy); Nick (Nickerson); Patty (Patterson); Willie (Wilson); Stoney (Stone); Libby (LeBlanc); Jonsey (Jones); Hutchie (Hutchinson); Bucky (Buckley); Brownie (Brown); Blackie (Black)

Jobs. Some nicknames originate with a guy's job. Booker, Cookie; Mickey the plumber; Eddie the carpenter; Karras the tailor; Tony the shoemaker; Charlie the chink; Sailor Jack, Ma and Pa (variety store); Louie the barber; Rags Maloney; Bedbug (exterminator); Garbage Tim; Dick the milkman; Charlie the iceman; Three fingers (a butcher); Doc, Henry Tomatoes (fruit man); Sparky the electrician; Tonto (Indian High Iron Worker).

Places of Origin. Eddie from Southie; Tony the Greek; Arab; Gunny; Joe; Frenchie; Limey; Scotty; Swede; Conuck; Dutchie; the Armenian; the Chink; Newfie (Newfounlander).

Physical Attributes. Many nicknames die with manhood, especially the disparaging ones; however many survive.

- (Color) Whitey; Red; Blackie, Blondie; Darko; Boogey; Black Viani; White Viani.
- (Size) Shorty; Bugga; Tiny; Pee-Wee; Ape; Runt; Skinny; Fats; Bones; Big Denny; Little Denny; Mousie; Gordo; Squeaky; Peanuts; Porky; Four-eyes; little or big preceding a name
- (Looks or Actions) Scarecrow; Bugsy; Hunchie; Bucky; Weasel; Chin; Bulldog; Whimpy; Dinty; Blinkey; Happy; Dapper; Dizzy; Speedie; Curly; Beaver; Fish.

Miscellaenous. Skipper; Mickey; Lefty; Duke; Two-Buck (always bet two dollars); Ace; the Major; Chuck; Spider; Humper; Upstairs O'Hara (Lives on top floor); Downstairs O'Hara (Lives on first floor); Spike; Butch; Froggie; Sandy; Gunny; Kid; Smokey; Hawk (Part Indian); Sparkie (chases fire wagons); Chip; Muzzy; Buddy; vast combinations of initials, Cappy; Rockie; Sonny; Chick; Chuck (Canadian)

PROFANITY

DECEMBER 10, 1937

While I am on the subject of how people speak, I should include what they say: common slang, swears, and sayings because they, too, are an extension of Danny's and tavern life. Every occupation has it's own language and by osmosis this language rubs off onto all of us to some extent. Unfortunately there are so many occupations represented within the confines of these walls, it would take a book, a dictionary, to list shop talk words and jargon. Therefore, I'll address only the extremes of tavern language: profanity.

Profanity:

In the first entry I stated that no apologies would be made because of the rough language. In taverns, most guys swear—not that everyone curses. Tommy O'Hara, Bob MacNamara, and Ira Gold, Iron Mike and a few others rarely curse. However, they are the exception more than the rule.

I'd be surprised if Red Driscoll, and Casey could speak three sentences without a profane word. But with these boys, as with most men in Danny's, the swearing is not obscene. Swearing is simply an emotional expression which may mean many things to different people. Crude, yes; rough, yes; uncouth, yes; obscene, no. Being genteel is difficult in a tavern.

Some swear for emphasis, some swear for lack of adequate vocabulary, others swear for the "tough" image, others swear to conform. In defense we may add that this is the language of the people. No word, per se is "bad." Was it Martin Luther who urged his disciples to speak the language of the marketplace?

Ground Rules for Profanity:

Since this is my story here are some rules: In general, all profanity will be deleted in my writing. If profanity is part of a verbal discussion or if it holds emphasis to a person's expression or style, it may slip through my (on the editor's) review. Otherwise it will not be included. However, it must be admitted that profanity doesn't please your mother. There are times and places that profanity does not add value to the discussion; profanity is not the best way to impress your audience; actually it indicates one's intellect or inability to express oneself in a social setting.

TATOOS

DECEMBER 1937

The other day, Gunny entered wearing a T-shirt, displaying a large tattooed Marine Corps flag emblem on his bicep. Tattoos, they're part of a tavern. Jack Walsh sports a ship on his forearm. Chico wears a large dragon tattooed near his shoulder—Shanghai, I think. Casey displays a crude self-inflicted needle and thread and ink L-O-V-E and H-A-T-E on his fingers.

When you think about it, tattoos are common to all taverns, to city life in general, and certainly to soldiers and sailors. In many circles tattoos are associated with the vulgar, the criminal, and the sexually dubious. I suppose in the same context as saloons, and pool rooms, and carnival crowds. Farmers don't get tattooed, nor cowboys, college graduates, priests, businessmen, Yankees, Republicans or the people with money. But I'll bet you could walk into any city tavern and find three, four guys with a tattoo. And they'd all tell the same story: 'Well, I was with a buddy in . . . and we were so drunk that' . . . That's how it happened to me. I was with Charlie Malloy in Scollay Square. We were both 17, and drunk as skunks, and we pass by a tattoo shop. Before I know it, I'm sitting on a stool with the artist(?) rubbing my arm with alcohol. After he shaves my arm, he lays a stencil of an eagle on my arm and transfers the design with black powder. Then comes the drill, just like a dentist drill. He dips the tip into the dye, and buzzes away, wiping the blood off with a grubby rag. In a few minutes, I'm eagled.

Why did I get tattooed? I'm a man, so I think at that time. Tough guy. Try anything once. One of the gang. Like losing your virginity. Who knows? People have been getting tattooed for 4000 years. The second oldest profession. Here's sketches of various tattoos that you'll find in Danny's. I must admit I've never seen a tattoo on a woman walking down Bowdoin Street.

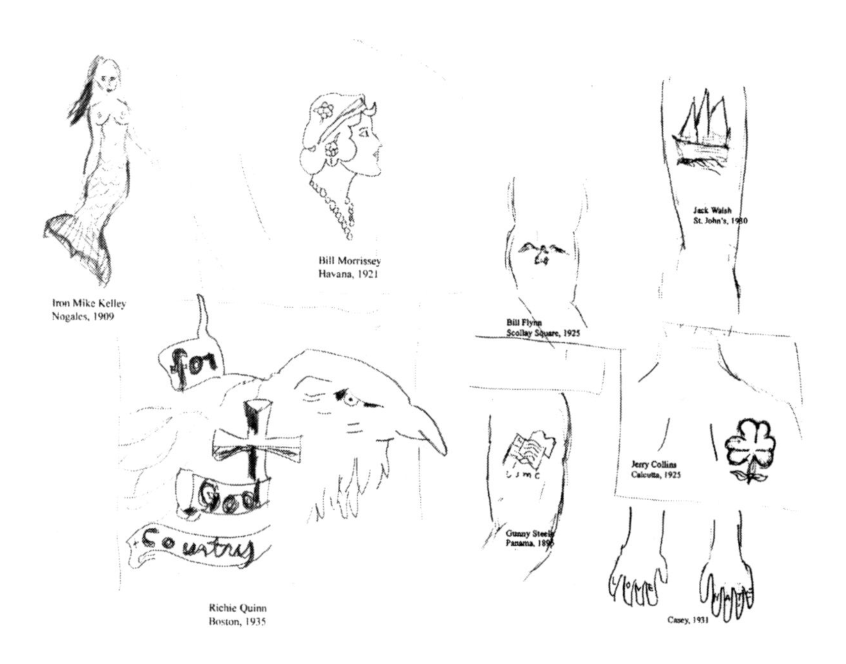

Bill Walks The Neighborhood

Bowdoin Street Businesses—Random Selection

August 1939

Giovanni (Geo), The Singing Barber

Always happy, Geo is blessed with a beautiful voice—often sings Puccini Operas while he cuts hair. And when he sings in church, he'd create tingles, an aura overcomes you as though a spiritual being was contacting you. When St. Peters sponsors the yearly Minstrel Show, he sings all the Jolson tunes.

Of course, not everyone appreciates Puccini or any opera. One time, Casey in the barber chair snapped at him. "Cut out that damn Guinnie music—I got a headache. Anyway this is America! Can't ya sing some Irish songs?" Geo stopped singing but gave Casey a haircut that was suited for a dog who had the mange. Geo muttered, "Revenge is a dish best served cold."

Kelly and Kelly Funeral Home, Twin Brothers (Tall and Short Kelly)

Tall Kelly had no hair to speak of; Short Kelly had the hair of a cave man. With the exception of dropping the casket (including the cadaver) on the icy main stairs of St. Peter's Church, "You're a couple of clowns!" screamed the cadaver's brother, the K & K performed a very professional ceremony at a very reasonable cost. At no cost, the brothers would loan out chairs and furniture for neighborhood functions; weddings, anniversary celebrations, etc. Overall the brothers were well liked on the street. However, the funeral business generates a number of uneasy feelings and superstitions with the boys in Danny's—including me. Casey swears that they steal the jewelry from the cadavers.

Tony Tomato, Dorchester Fruit Market

A very pleasant man wears an old apron and a scally cap. At Christmas, he'll drop into Danny's for a wine or two. Always smiling until he sees a kid trying to steal an apple or other fruit. Don't try to steal; Tommy is very fast on his feet—you'd see his cape flutter like Superman's when he chases down a culprit.

Billy the Butcher (or 3 Fingers) Finest Meat Market

He lost a finger in the grinding machine. But his meat is top quality. A poor joke—long ago worn out, "Say Billy, what are you selling today—fingers? I want to make a hot dog." In the summer months, long spirals of flypaper, like stalagmites, hang from the ceiling with an army of flies pulling and tugging in the desperate attempt for freedom. Every once in a while one would escaped from the glue surface. Frank Vento suggested a new venue for betting.

Louie the Druggist, Bowdoin Drug Store

He looks like the guy who played Louie in the East Side Kid movies. He even speaks with a New York accent. His claim to fame is the gorgeous young lady who monthly enters the store and within earshot of the customers orders, "A package of Trojans, please, the thinnest—they're much more enjoyable." It has been claimed that every young man, especially the bug-eyed soda jerk pops an erection. After the lovely young thing exits, there are hoots and hollers, and sighs of wishful thinking.

Joe Miraglo, Miraglo Ice/Coal Man

Had a horse and wagon rig. In the windows of the 3 decker homes are cards indicating what is required for ice delivery. Joe wears a rubber cape and he flips the ice onto his shoulder with a grapple hook. He disappears down the alley and up the back stairs and on the back piazza carries the block of ice to the ice box. Depending on the size of the box, Joe whips out his ice pick and chips ice for all the imagined lonely housewives on the top floor. Joe and the Hoods milk man—are the topics of many crude sexual jokes. Are the accusations true? I don't know, but Joe always is smiling.

Cohen's Deli Shop

Great cold cuts. Fantastic sandwiches. They hired a young fellow who made the best potato salads and gourmet dishes. The shop could have made millions, but every so often the fellow would disappear on a bender.

Millie's Ice Cream Shop

This was one of the very few businesses on Bowdoin Street that was owned by a woman. Sold sweets, soda, and the most delicious ice cream. The soda fountain had many advantages and some disadvantages, depending on which side of the counter you were positioned. Case in point, the young girl—a very nice young lady was well endowed—certainly a physical attribute that the young (and old) males found most enjoyable. The height of the fountain was relatively high and in order to scoop the ice cream from the chest, the girl had to stretch and lean over. The young (and old) men would be salivating searching for a space between the blouse and some skin. (I'm sure that she was embarrassed.)

St. Peter's Religious Goods/Flowers

This little shop catered to the churches ceremonies. The owner, a small dull fellow with a somewhat dark side, told a potential customer (who was also a Danny's patron). "This statue is so strong that you can beat a nail into a 2x4."

Roma's Italian Bakery

Whenever you walk by Roma's, you are greeted with the sensuous smell of Italian pastry. And if you have the opportunity to observe the backroom—the baking and creaming room, it's like watching the masters at a ballet—sliding the wooden paddle which carries the bread, biscuits, and cupcakes into the oven. Every movement and timing of the baker in completing the task is a joy to watch. And then the finale of the frosting of the cakes—invites the mouth to water in anticipation. The cream—the frosting—the aroma—forget about calories!

Trash Collection

Certainly trash is a critical activity with respect to the health and well being of the Dorchester neighborhood. Unfortunately it is not at the top of the status scale. But think about this: if your cat or dog dies, who takes the remains away—certainly not Kelly and Kelly Funeral Home? The trash man (for a quarter). Because trash collection is such a transient and hard occupation, very few neighbors actually know the trash man on a personal basis. He's simply the "trash man". But if you had to lift barrels full of coal ash everyday, you can understand that a broken back and wrenched shoulders and a hanging hernia are the most causes why the "trash man" may seek an easier line of work.

Sweeping the Streets

With his barrel on wheels and his heavy duty push broom and shovel, this fellow focuses on cleaning the gutters of cigarette and cigar butts, candy wrappers, leaves, sand and grit, and a dead mouse here and there. His name is unknown to me, but the kids call him "The Chomper," because he chews a cigar all day long.

Garbage Man

Although somewhat on the bottom of the social scales on Bowdoin Street, is the garbage man. Most of us in the city of Boston, and certainly along Bowdoin Street have a garbage container set in a hole in our back yard. The steel container is approximately 2' high and 12" in diameter and holds the garbage. It sits in a concrete cylinder which encases the metal "garage can." A cast iron cover provides the lid for the concrete sleeve. As can be imagined the container and the cement holder can become pretty ripe over time. And garbage, especially on a hot summer day can smell very offensive.

So the term "Garbage Man," in this case, is a contradiction between perceived occupation and personal behavior and talents. His name is Thomas Dylan. He stands 6'3", and walks with an even gait—maybe leaning to the left slightly to compensate for the weight that he carries day after day. At work he wears a rubber apron, rough shirt and trousers, and heavy boots. His most noticeable features are his face and eyes—bright and clean his brown eyes convey an inner peace. Although between 35 and forty years old, his skin is flawlessly smooth, and his smile shows perfect teeth.

Generally he is clean shaven and when he removes his wool cap (a black seaman's cap) his hair is always neatly trimmed. His voice is soft and without the Dorchester accent. I believe he was born in Wales. Garbage man or not, Mr. Thomas Dylan is a very handsome man. One could ask, "Why would this Adonis be a garbage man?" Because he truly believes that he has a lovely wife and two young children, and God has provided him with the health and commitment to support his family. This is his calling.

On Sundays, he takes the collections at St. Peter's at the 11:30 Mass. Dressed in an immaculate suit, white shirt and tie, and shined shoes, you could never associate him with the rubber aproned garbage man trudging the smelly bucket down the alleyway of the three decker houses.

His demeanor is graceful. He delights in telling about the woman who approached him concerning her lost wedding ring—"I think it's lost in the garbage," she said. He actually sifted through his container of banana peels, coffee grinds, egg shells, old pieces of toast—but to no avail.

I suspect that many are the ladies who have a wayward thoughts in and out of church confines.

Miscellaneous Stores

Peter's Print Shop
Charlie Loo's Laundry
Karas' Tailor Shop
Pa's Variety

The Thumb Man (Sy)
Tony—The Shoe Repair Shop
Geo's Barber Shop
Fruit Market—Tommy's Tomatoes

Horse and Wagon Businesses
Rag Man
Fruit Man
Milk Delivery
Pony and Camera

Knife Sharpener

Safety and Protection
Police Station 11
Fire Department

Informal_Businesses
Paper Boys
Delivery Boys

Cafes
Walsh's—"The Geek House"
Sportsman Bar—Specializing in Alcohol, Dancing, and Fistfights

Doctors and Hospitals
Dentist "I Drill so Deep Until I Hit China"
City Hospital—Emergency—Babies
Carney Hospital—General
St. Margaret's—Babies
St. Elizabeth's—Babies

Schools
St. Peter's
Mather School
Grover Cleveland
Dorchester High School

B.C. High
Commerce High School
English High School
Wentworth Institute
Hard Knocks—A specialty in Dorchester and in most cities of the world

DOGS OF THE TAVERN

SEPTEMBER 1939

Lunchtime. Gunny enters, "Look". He shows me a large rip in the seat of his trousers. "Half my butt chewed off by that black shepherd dog on Barry Street. Damn block's got more mutts than Chinks in a Shanghai alley. Ought to shoot them all."

Birdie, Frank Vento's dog, stops gnawing on a Slim Jim under the table, growls at Gunny as though she understands.

Young Billy Madden, a meter reader, tells of once breaking a mop handle over the back of an attacking dog.

Then it dawns on me. Like tattoos and nicknames, dogs are part of the tavern and of the block. Most every family owns a dog. What can we say of these city dogs? Certainly no thoroughbreds in this block. No Rin-Tin-Tin, no Buck, no Call of the Wild. No heroic great St. Bernard, fighting a raging blizzard on a mountain side to rescue the lost; at most we have a mongrel fox terrier barking for attention because his drunken master lays sprawled on a snow bank outside the house. In general, the dogs of Danny's are truly American, a rich mixture of breeds, a melting pot of cultures—all depending on the number of males jumping the heated bitch. Of course, some thoroughbreds do live in the block—just like America has it's Mayflower stock, DAR's, Yankees and Republicans—Pekinese or Toys owned by old ladies who clothe them in stylish wooly coats and leashes. However, they'd never survive the raw life in the streets; therefore I'll exclude them from my discussion.

Although our dogs are mongrel, commonplace, even plebeian, most owners brag and boast of fantastic attributes and exploits. Therefore take all dogs stories with a grain of salt. However, there is one dog story—the most famous in Danny's—which I can testify actually happened. Frank Vento's dog, Birdie, sings. Actually carries a tune. At least fifty times I've seen Frank sit Birdie on the bar, and hold a piece of Slim Jim or a hot dog over her head. "Sing, Birdie, Sing!" "O-O-O-O-O," Birdie howls; her neck stretches like a giraffe. Then Frank whistles a few notes. "O-O-O-O-O!" the pitch, goes higher and higher until it pierces your ears. Like someone scratching a blackboard. As Frank changes pitch, the howl changes in tune until it sounds like a strange flute from Persia or India. Frank wins a lot of money betting with strangers about his "singing dog." Great source of pride. It is an established fact in Danny's that if Frank won a million dollars from Birdie's singing (an exaggeration for sure) then he lost twice that much at the dog race track around Boston and Taunton. Or stated another way, the problem that Jerry Collins had with the liquor, Frank had with dogs at the racetrack. He once almost lost his home (or his kneecaps) but was rescued by a timely loan from Booker.

Anyway, Birdie was a great source of pride. So when the Hamilton Theatre held an amateur talent show, Frank entered Birdie, the Singing Dog. Why? Who knows? Maybe he envisioned himself and Birdie as another Ed Bergan—Charlie McCarthy act. Naturally, on show night, with the Hammy only across the street, the boys flooded the theatre to watch the performance. Thunderous ovation, stomping of feet, shouts and whistles when Frank's act came on.

With raised hands, Frank signaled for silence. Quiet, so quiet you could hear the crunch of people eating pop corn.

Birdie sat, afraid and shivering, on a white table, center stage.

Frank pats her gently. "Sing! Birdie Sing!" His voice booms like a cannon, like an orator at a whistle stop.

Silence. Birdie looks forlorn.

A whisper, "C'mon, girl." Loud "Sing! Birdie, Sing!"

Silence. Tittering from the audience. Frank glares. He faces Birdie. His eyes flash with contained rage.

"Sing! Birdie Sing!" His voice sounds like a pleading, a lover's half-crazed begging. As Birdie half-squats, a mesmerized audience sits on the chair's edge. Birdie's neck stretches like a giraffe. But no song. Instead she defecates on the white table cloth.

Never again did Frank urge Birdie to sing, not publicly anyway.

Other than this true famous dog story, we hear few others that we can believe. Sure, every summer we hear of a dog who saves a drowning kid at Malibu or Tenean beach; every winter we read of the dog who wakes up the sleeping family to warn of fire. What's fact or fancy? Most of the dogs in this block do little spectacular. We may ask, just what do dogs do? Let's follow the "typical" life of a "typical" dog, like the 'average' man, the 'average' voter.

As with humans, we must first consider conception, the sex mores of a gang of dogs. Usually when a female heats, we find a pack of leaping, yelping, frustrated dogs ranging in size from a Great Dane to a skinny fox terrier, all chasing a stoic Dashund bitch. A truly ignoble beginning. Sometimes a male will get "caught" in the female. Cries and howls and whimpers from the pits of agony until an irate housewife pours a pot of scalding water on these Siamese connections. Good-bye erection. The last we see is two steaming dogs dashing down the streets.

It sometimes happens that instead of conception, a dog simply appears one day. Lost from another block? Ulysses? A runaway? No collar, no records. High plains drifter, a hobo, a gypsy? Who knows for certain? If lucky, if he wags his tail fast enough, looks sad enough, or licks the right hand, then a family adopts him. He's given a name, a dish from the family dinnerware. A spot to sleep, usually a rug over by the stove or the back piazza. If not, the dog continues his Odyssey.

When a dog gives birth, the litter must be distributed. Some people, with hearts of slate and ash, drown the pups—there's no excuse for that! Usually however the problem of adoption and distribution is accomplished in a few proscribed ways. The most common one is word of mouth. A con-game: "Hey kid, c'mere. See this nice little puppy. See how he licks your hand. He likes ya, kid. How'd ya like to own'em. Here, he's yours. Sure, your Ma and Pa'll love him. G'head." Or in the tavern, "You bet ya ass he's German Shepherd. Look at those paws." It matters little if the dog has paws as big as horse's hooves, or resembles a full grown goat. Let the buyer beware. The final method of distribution is the most desperate, by far the sneakiest, but the most direct. First you locate a three decker full with a flock of kids with no dog. At night, leave the puppy in the hallway, and imagine the next morning. "Hey Ma, look at what I found!" And if the puppy is smart, wags his tail, and faithfully urinates on the newspaper, he's adopted.

Naming a dog. We cold write a vast encyclopedia on the psychology of naming a dog. Without belaboring the point, let it suffice to say, "Beauty is in the eyes of the beholder." For instance, take Tommy O'Hara's mutt, King. King, a collage of colors, a cross between a terrier, a sheep dog, and a bulldog. A face as flat as Raggedy Andy, and a tail like a turtle. His two bottom teeth stick out like crooked yellowed tusks. Always his tongue hangs out, a piece of panting wet baloney drooling spit on the floor. Brown, yellow, and black. His dull coat looks like a shredded rag. Even his ears droop like two worn torn burlap mittens that all but drag along the sidewalk. When he runs, his small sausage legs going a mile a minute, his rear end is almost forward of his front—like a badly misaligned auto. King? We ask sarcastically, King of what? But in a hundred years, we'd fail to persuade Tommy's kids to change the name.

It's curious but when you think of it, some people get stuck with some painfully insulting nicknames: Gimpy, Fat, Pimples, Maggots, Cross-eyes, Snake, etc., yet very few dogs, no matter how grotesque, get insulting names. No, we name them: King, Queenie, Duke, Princess, Caesar—royalty. Or objectively, we name them: Red, Blackie, Spot, Whitey, etc. Or for those who consider a dog part of the family we give them human names: Mike, Charley, Suzie, Mary, etc. We could certainly discuss dog names for a year. Let's move on.

With respect to food, we see here democracy in action. The family eats the same; only the order of food consumption is changed. None of this munchy-crunchy sawdust called dog cereal. No, the dog gets fed soggy left-over Wheaties or Cheerios. Lunch consists of bread crusts, pieces of baloney, or cool soup. And supper, no dog food of waste fats and god-knows-what. Meat scraps and vegetables. On Saturdays, the shopping day, the dog can expect a treat, a meaty bone. Of course, a dog supplements his diet with whatever he can scrounge from garbage cans or steal from another dog's bowl. It's a dog eat dog world. Especially in the area of medical care. On this block, most families do well to keep the kids checked-up, let alone spend money for a dog check-up. A dog's pretty much on his own in this area. Each year, when the dog begins to smell like the elephant house at Franklin Park Zoo, the family drags him into the bathtub, and scrubs him down with brown soap. The dog fights and splashes, but the job gets done. For a week he pouts and avoids everyone. So much for the medical care.

Duties and responsibilities? In every family, since civilization began, every member plays a specific role: the father works and earns the money, the mother cooks and keeps house, the kid—school and play. With one exception: the dog.

In this neighborhood the dogs serve no physically practical role. They watch no herds, nor pull sleds or milk wagons, nor hunt rabbit or raccoon—in fact, most neighborhood mutts wouldn't know one if they saw one. On those frozen wintry mornings, when the old man, sick and sorry, must battle a raging blizzard to reach work, on his way out the back door he usually has to step over the dog sprawled on the warm rug near the stove. And yet we say when times get tough, "It's a dog's world." Then why do we have dogs? The best that I can answer is that they fulfill a psychological need. A dog loves; he makes his masters feel good. A dog is loyal, dedicated, brave—universally respected traits. No small wonder why people so dearly love dogs. Therefore, the smart dog learns at once what pleases and displeases. With the old man, the dog must wag tail, jump happily when he comes home from work. It also helps if the dog rolls over submissively—show the old man he's the boss. With the woman, the dog must absolutely learn early in life, never, never to urinate on the parlor rug. Other than that, a dog should avoid the woman. The less she knows, the better. The dog quickly masters how to please the kids: be a companion, a pal. Give a paw, fetch a stick and a dog's got the purest, most selfless love that God ever created on this earth.

Dangers. Life is not all love and bones and stoic daschunds. In this block, on the streets, travel four wheeled monsters. I bet I've seen at least ten dogs run over in the last few years. Dog, bloody, crippled, whining, laying in the gutter. A kind bowl of water set beside him. "For God's sake, someone call the Animal Rescue League! Stay away, kid, he'll bite ya!" Of course, the kid knows that the Animal Rescue League will uphold the Hippocratic Oath, no matter what the cost. Every effort will be made to maintain a precious life. However, one of the sad realities of adulthood tells us of the needle, the euphemism "put to sleep." The Great Dog House in the Sky. Or a worst fate: the dog catchers who sell innocent dogs to those butchers over at Harvard Research Institute. In the name of 'science" they remove an organ, inject a questionable serum, subject a shock.

Some of the lesser dangers, but dangers none the less, should be mentioned. That weird kid who likes to chase dogs with sticks and rocks. Kids feeding Ex-Lax on Halloween night. Tying cans to tails. Or some clumsy drunk who steps on a tail as the dog dozes on the sunny sidewalk.

When I think of "Call of the Wild," I can't help but wonder about the adventure of a city dog. From a dog's perspective, they face journeys and hazards that'd terrify and wilt the hearts of the Vikings. Strange streets; a hundred honking cars; rattling clanging trolleys; kicking milk wagon horses; snarling dogs protecting their territories; weird kids; and vicious alley cats, the size of cougars and just as fierce. Yes, a city dog needs the stout heart of a workhorse; the courage of a lioness, the tenacity of a tiger and the endurance of a wolverine. Rin-Tin-Tin and Spot (Dick and Jane) would never make it.

Death. When a dog grows feeble and blind and can hardly wobble, some guys drop the dog in a sack off Malibu bridge. But most let the dog silently pass away on the back piazza or on the rug. For $.25, the trash man will carry the dog to the dump. Crude? Yes. Gone? Yes. Forgotten? Never! Cherished in life, mourned in death, a dog lives always in a boy's memory. Tears are shed, unashamed, profuse, tragic. There's not a man-jack in Danny's, in this city, anywhere that couldn't recall his boyhood dog. My dog was named Alley, an old mangy mutt who slept under the covers at my feet. I cried for a month when he got run over.

There we have a "typical" life of a "typical" city dog. Trivial? Meaningless? Depends on how you look at it. As written by Tolstoy, the three greatest things in the world are:

TO LOVE AND BE LOVED

TO CAUSE HAPPINESS

TO REALLY BELIEVE IN GOD

In my book, most city dogs hit two out of three which isn't a bad percentage.

As a final comment, what Danny's lacks in dog hero stories, we make up in dog jokes. As with proverbs or any subject that I ask about, the variety and depth of the responses always impress me.

Booker

"There's this bookie, and he wins about a coupla grand offa this guy. The guy's broke so he offers the bookie a talking dog. The dog can really talk like a parrot. What the hell, the bookie figures he'll make a million bettin'. So for a tryout he takes the dog into a ginmill, and bets a hundred bucks that his dog can talk. Naturally his bet is covered, I mean, what the hell, a talkin' dog?

So the bookie turns to his dog and ask, 'What's your name?' The damn dog says nothing. There goes a hundred bucks.

Well, outside the bookie twists the mutt's ear, "Ya stupid mutt, ya just cost me a hundred bucks! I oughta tear ya head off."

"Don't be a sucker," answers the dog. "Just think of the odds you'll get tomorrow."

(Frank Vento dislikes this joke)

Frank Vento

"This thick mick strolls in a classy restaurant with a scroungy dog. The owner rushes over, points to the sign, "No Dogs Allowed," and shouts "Can't you read?' So by Jaysus,' says the Mick. 'Who's smoking?'"

Jackie Dwyer

"The little boy sees two dogs humping in the park and asks his father what they're doing. 'They're making puppies,' the father answers. That night the boy wanders into his parents' room while they're making' love. Asked what they're doing, the father replies, 'Making you a baby brother.'

"Gee, Pa," the boy begs. "Turn her over—I'd rather have a puppy."

Tommy O'Hara

"This chap is in the movies, and by the Blessed Saints, in front of him is sitting a large dog. The owner has his arm around the dog. God's truth, the dog clearly follows the movie. Snarling, at the villain, laughing at the jokes.

Naturally, this chap leans over and says, "To be sure, but I can't get over your dog's behavior."

"Tis a surprise to me," answers the owner. "He disliked the book!"

Red Driscoll

"This little red-headed kid's sitting on the curb with his dog, a short fat mutt. A priest comes along and ask him. 'What's your name, little boy?"

"Red."

"I bet they call you Red because of your red hair. What's your dog's name?"

"Porky."

"I bet you call him Porky because he's short and fat and has a wiggly tail.

"No," answers the kid, "It's cause he likes to screw pigs."

Red Driscoll

"This kid's walking with his girl. And they see the kid's dog humping. So he says, "Ya know, honey, I'd like to do that."

'Go ahead,' she says, 'It's your dog."

Bill McBride

"A man enters a bar and bets the bartender that his dog can talk. The man asks the dog, "What goes on the top of a house?"

"R-R-Roof," answers the dog.

So to prove the point without any question, he asks, "What does sandpaper feel like?"

"R-R-Rough."

The bartender protests, "Let me ask a question—Who's the greatest baseball player that ever lived?"

The puzzled dog looks a his master, "R-R-Gerhig?"

Casey

"These two mutts are doing it.

So the kid asks his old man, "Whadda they doin, Dad?"

The father thinks awhile, then answers, "Well, the dog on top has two sore paws so the other dog's helping 'em."

"Just goes to show ya," says the kid. "Ya help someone and then they go and shove it up your ass."

Miscellaneous

"My dog lost his tail"

"How do you know when he's happy?"

"He stops biting people."

"My mutt doesn't have a nose."

"How does he smell?"

"Awful."

Red Driscoll Sketches Dinty

April 1938

Rain, rain and more rain. Certainly not a work day, if you're a roofer. Since nine o'clock Red Driscoll sat in a booth, nursing a glass of Pickwick Ale, and sketching. On the floor Red has his roofing tools—claw hammer, cutting knife, Swiss Army knife, leather gloves covered with black tar pitch. Alongside his "work" bag sits his drawing tools—pencils, rulers, pencil sharpener, sketching paper, mounting board and a mirror.

But today's exercise is to sketch himself. Red is using the mirror to sketch a self-portrait—a surprise present for his wife who is expecting their first baby (boy or girl?) in spring sometime.

Red is the acknowledged artist in Danny's and often sketches the patrons on weddings and other special events such as birthdays, anniversaries, baptisms, and the like.

The mirror is propped against the wall, and Red shifts his head in the reflection and his eyes shift back and forth as he quickly records what he sees onto the sketch pad. His tongue sticks out of his mouth and darts back and forth in concert with what he sees and what he sketches. I suppose it is the ballet of the brain. Actually Red studied art at Massachusetts College of Art, but the Depression and liquor ended his formal quest for fame and fortune. "Someday," Red would often say, "I'll return to school. Maybe become another Winslow Homer." Instead Red's propensity is to tell tall tails, especially when he had a few beers under his belt. Not malicious stories—in fact many were comical and harmless. But they earned Red, especially in the roofer's union hall the nickname, "Malarky"—meaning full of bullshit.

Actually, I am very fond of Red. Like all of us, he had his faults but he is a very decent guy who had talents but few opportunities in this economy.

Around 10 AM who is down in a booth near the latrine, but Dinty doing origami with a stack of 3x5 cards—dogs, cats, and birds. He often sells the models to customers for a quarter or a half dollar to earn a few dollars on the side.

Dinty walks to Red's self portrait, "Red," he says "Can you draw a picture of me? Please? I'll swap you for a couple of my models. Huh? I ain't never had someone make a picture of me. Huh? Please?"

I smile at Red—everyone in Danny's knows that Dinty is slow—Dinty the dim—is what the young guys call him. It is a fact that Dinty is not a class A waiter, but Booker made a promise to Dinty's mother to watch over him. And Booker believes a promise nade is a debt unpaid.

Red concedes. In less than 15 minutes he sketches Dinty.

When Dinty sees his sketch, he breaks into a giggle—a tiny drop of spit runs down his lip. "Thanks Red! I'll take it home and nail it on my wall and take care of it—you can bet your life on it." He disappears into the back room.

Red laughs, "All of my customers should be so gleeful. If that were so, I'd be a millionaire!"

"For God's sake," I chastise Red, "you can draw better than that! He looks like Igor from a bad Frankenstein movie, only Dinty is not a hunchback."

"Bill, what the hell do you want? I did it in a couple of minutes, and Dinty ain't no Clark Gable! Anyway look how happy he is, like a pig in shit."

Odds And Ends

Editor's Note:

Because of the copious notes, sketches, comments and somewhat illegible scribbles, I added a section "Odds and Ends" for each of the decades 30's, 40's, 50's 60's and 70's. The intent was to add to the day by day flavor to living in the neighborhood.

The Horrors on the Mary M.

That very morning, Bill Morrissey had settled up at the fish piers. "I tell ye, Bill, this trip was a real Christer—not only did the crew work for nothing with the price of cod so low, but Paddy Ryan, the cook, went into the "Horrors". For ten days, Paddy had hit the bottle—a concoction called "Screech" in Newfoundland. We were off the Grand Banks when he started to scream at the crew as they hauled in the nets. "Snakes! Snakes! That ain't cod! Them's snakes!

The skipper had no choice but to have Paddy tied to his bunk—he swore that a bottle of screech was floating in the water and he would go over the side and fetch it."

It was God awful to listen to him hollering day and night until we landed in Boston. For sure, the taste is a curse."

TB Hospital on Seaver Street, Mattapan

The maintenance crew tells me that the buildings are identified by letters. If you're in G-H building it means "you're going home. But if you're in I-K buildings, it means that you're "in for keeps." "That's the God's honest truth. My pa died in there—shriveled away, he did."

Working Inside the Mental Institution

Mickey Smith is telling the boys about a plumbing project he's working on at the Foxboro State Hospital—the mental institution. "You should hear the noise—everyone is yelling to beat the band."—Well, the chief engineer had a trick to keep the crazies quiet. He tells them that if they keep quiet for an hour, he'll pass out a few cigarettes. Sure enough, they keep quiet."

"Well, you know that working in the trades," offers Jim the electrician, "there are a wide range of odors which would blister your eyeballs! As an apprentice, the first thing I learned is to take Vick's Vapor Rub and run a smidge under my nose, right above the top lip. It works.

Bill, the carpenter, mentions that he tries to avoid touching door knobs with bare hands—"you can never know what a patient will rub on the door knobs. Wear gloves."

The Deaf Beggar

On Friday evenings, a deaf fellow drops into Danny's and goes to each table—he shows the boys a card which reads—"I am deaf, please help me with a donation."

Some of the boys donate a few coins; some nothing at all—and of course, a few of the lads will sneak up behind the poor fellow and shout—Hey!!!

Once in a while the card holder jerked up—a startled response, "He's a fake, I told you so!"

Chico, the Seaman Teaches a Korean Cook How to Play Cribbage

Chico, a hopeless gambler, told me about a Korean cook on the tanker bound for South America. Chico taught him to play cribbage. By the time the trip was ended, the Korean kid won all of Chico's wages—"Wait until the next trip."

Boxing—the "Friday Night Fights" on the Radio

Bill Stern, Announcing

"A left to the head, a jab, another jab to the body, a hook! Got him square on the nose! Blood over his nose" Gong! End of Round 1. Bill Stern is at his most dramatic.

"In the corner they're working on his eye. The Ref comes to look—ok."

Bill Stern is at his best—Pause! Inflection! Volume! The boys huddle at the end of the bar—surrounding this dusty ancient radio—an RCA Model X26. There is much left to the imagination when one listens to a boxing match on the radio. Obviously because of the lack of visual input, much of the "flavors" of the fight depends on the enthusiasm and personality of the announcer—For example, when you hear—a left to the body! A right to the gut. For all you know, the punches could be landing on the boxer's knee-caps.

Eat No Meat on Fridays

"Say, Bill," Casey orders, "Cook me up a hot dog, will ya."

Scotty, sitting on the next stool, says "Casey, today is Friday. You can't eat meat—a mortal sin."

"Shut up!" Casey snaps. "Mind your own business. Who do you think you are, the Pope?" He turns to Bill. "Just for spite, give me two hot dogs."

Scapulars

Joe Scarletta says to Blackie Hession, "I'm telling you, if you wear scapulars and you die, you go to heaven."

Workers Exposed to the Weather

Hands—sometimes hands are used to describe a person or his occupation.

Bill Morrissey's hands were like thick pieces of dried leather or cardboard. The inside ridges of his fingers were cracked raw from cold weather. Freckles on back and rough veined. And in the winter months when the crew is on deck, gutting and dressing the cod, Bill tells me that when it gets too cold you dip your hands in sea water to warm up your hands.

Construction workers also face the elements. When the weather turns nasty too hot or cold, the decimal point in the hourly wage should shift a point or two to the right.

In Danny's this would certainly include the construction tradesman—(carpenter, laborer, mason, iron worker, roofer, electrician, plumber, concrete, commercial fisherman, landscapers, longshoreman, lumpers, car washers, fence installer, truckie . . .)

Study the hands since most men smoke—Camels or Lucky Strike—you can see a permanent nicotine stain was between the first and second finger of his right hand. His nails are yellowed—almost ivory like—thick and curled and unkempt.

The tip of Bill's small finger was missing—he caught in a winch or smashed it with a ripper—I forget—but it was gone—he claimed it would throb in the winter or the coldest of days.

All the trades have their signature injuries. Study the hands, ask them.

Now what does this tell us—we've got a working man—outside—tough—uncaring—a stoic to pain—yet there must be a tenacity or persistence about this man—who else would make a living this way?

These hands certainly aren't the hands of a surgeon or a pianist.

Face—his face is weathered—spotted with freckles and old sunburns. The corner of his eyes look like cracked leather—his eyebrows are blonde—or I should say bleached white.

His hair is fine—thinning.

His eyes are two colors—a sort of dark hazel but somewhat green in the center—from a distance they do look hazel or blue but close—they're unique.

And when he speaks he looks at you—almost penetrating but not questioning—it's his way of speaking the truth.

His lips especially in winter are cracked—usually a split on the lower lip in the center—hardened raw.

His chin is solid—little fat

His top teeth are false—but the bottoms are nicotine stained especially in the ridges—a couple of the back teeth are missing.

However, he's got a pleasant smile—almost philosophical.

On the side of his chin just at the neckline he's got a mole the size of a dime

And he usually wears a scally cap with the union button or a Immaculate Conception Medal.

God bless those who work in the weather.

Bill's Stories Of Danny's Neighborhood

(Published in the Dorchester Monthly Tribune)

1. The Wedding Of Rags Maloney

June 12, 1936

Bright sun, cloudless sky, crisp breeze, 60's. Perfect day for the occasion. Today, Rags Maloney marries Mary Quinn. A wedding long to be remembered in St. Peter's parish. As Booker said later, "Could Charlestown forget the battle of Bunker Hill? Or Lexington forget her Minutemen?" Well, it's unlikely that Danny's Tavern will forget Rags Maloney's reception, the first to be held upstairs in the Dorchester Citizen's Club. Because money's scarce, Booker T, offered the hall for nothing. Rags, never one to pass up anything free, readily accepted the offer. The boys like Rags; therefore, they took up a collection. A few dollars help. Scotty Burns donated seven jugs from his homemade batch. Richie Quinn finagled cold cuts from the meat factory, and Jack Walsh supplied ten pounds of lobster meat. The gallons of dago red wine came from Joe Scarletta's father.

Rags is one of those colorful characters you'll find in most taverns. Not quite a regular, but certainly well known. Hide as thick as a brick. On Saturday's he drives a horse and wagon, and ragpicks. Never one to be keenly interested in clothes, he often wears the pickings. Hence, the nickname, Rags. A more suitable name might have been "scarecrow".

Skinny, tufted crop of read hair, wide eyes, thin face, coat hung on a broomstick. He lacked only the straw. But likeable. Age 37, never kissed a girl. Last year he met Mary Quinn while picking her ash barrel. Wham, bam, he's engaged.

Rags invited five guys from the tavern: Jerry Collins, Jackie Dwyer, McDonough, O'Hara, and Booker. Booker declined, but sent $10.00. All anticipated a good time, especially Jerry. He left Mass early at 10:15 with Jackie for a few to "warm up".

"Give us a couple each." Jerry grinned. "It'll be a corker today," he said emptying the first glass. "I hear Scotty blessed us with some of his poteen. Ah good stuff for a man with a thirst." Round apple face. Blue eyes.

"Who's going?" asked Danny O'Neil sitting with Gunny Steele. Gunny's mailbag lay in the booth.

"Tommy O'Hara and Boss McDonough from this parish," answered Jerry, "and a lot of fellows from Roxbury. Friends of Rags. Do you know Tom Muldoon? He's best man, quite a card."

"No," answered Danny, "but if he's the likes of you two, it be a lively time. Are you going to sing, Jerry?"

"You know me. A few drinks and I'll sing to the lamppost."

"It's that golden voice that gets you invitations . . ." Booker T interrupted, "And that drinking like a camel that gets your thrown out."

"Not this time," promised Jerry, "Just a few drinks, a few stories and songs. And that's it. Did I ever tell you about the time me and Tom were working down in South Boston. Hot day.

On the way home he says to me, "You know, Jerry, we're passing by the best barroom in Boston. Beers as big as a barrel."

"Passing," I said, "Who's passing?" So we have a little taste.

"That night we're weaving down to Andrew Station and we walk by a house with a wreath on the door."

Tom says, "Let's pay our respects. Sure it might be God's comfort if we said a prayer."

Jerry continues, "So I follow him inside this dark house. He stumbles right into a dim room with a piano, a vase of flowers and two candles on top. He's so drunk, he kneels at the piano and blesses himself."

On the way out, Tom says, "You know, it's a shame he died. That corpse had the loveliest teeth I ever saw." Jerry laughs.

"You're full of shit," said Booker T, hiding his grin. "Jerry could talk a dog off the meat wagon."

"That I can," confessed Jerry, a smile as wide as his fictitious piano. "Just a little story to warm up me spirits. Did I tell you about my Uncle Fergus? Years, ago, he's go to funerals over at Beacon Hill. Irish wakes. In those days there'd be songs and eat and drink. Half the night the party'd go on and, Fergus, after a few drinks, would weep. Why'd he's bawl like it was his dear mother who departed. This one time he got lashed up with Protestants funeral. No difference. Their whiskey's as good as ours. Well, he got extra drunk and weepy. He's standing at the grave wailing with tears streaming down his face. And when the minister says solemnly 'The Lord giveth and the Lord taketh away, with that, Fergus lets out with a keening that'd chill ya spine. He stretches out his arms and cries to the minister, "Now what the hell could be fairer than that?"

Again Jerry laughs, another story. A grand storyteller. A Bard in his own right. Laughing, singing, playing, a big-hearted misfit. A happy puppy, full of mischief. Great father—but a damnable husband. Life's a frolic, a romp through the pastures, and the devil may care, but this doesn't pay the rent or buy the food. Nevertheless, Aggie, his wife, still loved him as though he were but a little boy. But Father O'Malley implored separation; therefore, they separated. Danny's became his home.

Drunk or sober, Jerry was a pal to everyone. A stout companion. Through thick and thin. If you needed an ear, he was an elephant. If you needed a drink, he was a St. Bernard. A dime? The golden goose, or whatever his pockets could afford. A laugh, a joke, he always had. And a song. A voice as warm and touching, to melt ice. Loveable misfit Jerry.

"You know who's invited?" asked Jackie. "Widow Quinn. She's Mary's aunt."

"Ah," Jerry shook his head, "I got no use for that one." His face furrowed. "Maybe she's got half the parish scared out of their wits with that widow's curse nonsense. But that's blarney."

Jackie glanced at the clock—11:30.

Jerry continued, "She's got a long tongue. A sword that never rusts. The last time I told her if she yawned, her ears would disappear. I'll pay her no mind." He turned to Jackie, "We'll have us a grand time."

"That we will," answered Jackie, his tongue slightly thick. Tall, strong, handsome, his face a healthy outdoors red, and rugged. Complexion smooth as an infant.

Jerry put his arm around Jackie's shoulder. "You know, my boy, I know for a fact that Noreen Hogan will be there and she takes a fancy to you, lad." Jerry held his hands like he were holding two melons. "She's got such beautiful nellies. As big as pillows. Ah, she's an accommodating lass. "Tis the cow far from home that has the long horns."

"Go along with you, Jerry. She's five years older than me. It's you who'd she fancy. Why, I bet one song . . ."

"I'm a married man." A touch of sadness flushed across Jerry's blue eyes. Tom ordered a round. "Did you hear that O'Reilly fellow is going back to Ireland. Next month. Back to the farm in Kerry."

"Is that the O'Reilly who works on the pier?" asked Jackie.

"No—that's Bill O'Reilly. This one worked in the wool house near South Station. Said there's no work around here. Not enough to keep his family alive. Been out for two months now. And with the price of food. Three tins of evaporated milk, a quarter. Steak, half dollar a pound. Even cigarettes, two packs for a quarter. Who can afford that?

"Enough to make a family man cry," said Jerry, "I can't blame the fellow. If it wasn't for Boss, I'd starved long ago. Pick up a day here and there. Keeps Aggie and the kids in a little money. Good man, McDonough."

Gunny said, "Even the price of fish. Haddock, two pounds for a quarter. And fresh mackerel, five cents a pound. Bill Morrissey said the price may be tops, but he's making none of it. Then again, it's the lucky man to have a job these days . . ."

"That's right," said Jerry, his eyes reddened, his face flushed, "If it wasn't for McDonough, I'd be up against it."

No sooner had he said it, Boss McDonough walked in. "Come on boys," he said, "the reception's about to start."

"Come here, Mac," Jerry said, "let's have one for the bend in the road."

As they left, Jerry weaved slightly. His tie hung outside of his jacket, his shirttail puffed out, his fly rested at half mast.

Booker winks at me, "He's in fine tune. He'll need it when he tangles with Widow Quinn. Like throwing two cocks into the ring."

"Ya," agreed Danny, "It'll be an interesting time upstairs."

As explained, it was the first reception to be held upstairs, and yesterday the Quinn's decorated the hall. Crepe paper, red, white and blue, was draped from table to table and along the walls and ceilings.

Booker said, "It looks more like a boxing ring." In fact, from an objective point of view, the whole layout did indeed resemble a boxing ring, although not quite as square. In the center was the open space; tables lined the perimeter. The three ropes of crepe paper running from table to table added to the illusion. Of course, on occasion the hall had unintentionally served that very purpose. To the perceptive eye, the nicks and chips and out-and-out dents in the plaster and furniture testified to occasional abuse. As Booker says, "Today's sawdust was yesterday's furniture." On the wall a large Irish flag with a collection of shillelaghs covered a large hole in the plaster bashed out by Casey after losing a poker hand.

Where the judges would ordinarily sit, the wedding party table was located along the midside. Directly in the ring center stood a lovely three-decker cake baked by Mrs. Quinn and the Widow. A delicate bride-groom statue perched precariously on top; seemingly they enjoyed the "oooh's and the ahhs's. What a lovely cake." A shaded 100 watt bulb illuminated the cake.

At the inboard end of the ring, one step up to the stage, Charlie O'Rourke, accordion on his knee, perched on a piano stool. Another voice like a songbird. To be frank, he looked like a bird; hooked nose, no chin, thin nervous body, and spindly legs. But a sweet voice. Alongside Charlie sat an old timer with a fiddle and a flute. Good ear and nimble fingers. Music to soothe the savage beast. At the street end of the ring, a makeshift table supported a ton of food: turkey and hams and cold cuts, lobsters and puddings, salads of all variations, breads and puddings and cakes. Rich, aromatic, tasty and enough to literally feed an army of warriors. Near the refreshments Jerry sat in his corner. A duck in the pond. An ashcan full of beer and ice stood next to a table crowded with whiskey, wine, ginger ale, Coke, and of course, Scotty's poteen.

For centuries, weddings have followed certain established customs. We have a bride, a groom, wedding guests, food, song, and drink. From before Cana to the present. Naturally, we would expect little deviation at the wedding of Rags Maloney.

However, there was one blaring deviation from tradition. As we know at Cana, our Lord converted water to wine in a miraculous second. It took Scotty two months to concoct his poteen. A carefully guarded process. On previous occasions, although Scotty complained that Boston water did injustice to the taste, all participants vouched for the potency. As Jerry often said, "It pounded many the head, but blinded no one." And unlike Cana, the poteen was served from start to memorable finish.

Diagonally opposed to Jerry, the Widow sat in her corner. A bulldog face, teeth and tongue ready and willing. She watched each and every drink. In addition to baking the cake, the Widow had donated an enormous ham, laden with frills, that was located at the table's end near Jerry. Therefore, the Widow was possibly insuring that the ham be protected from the likes so Jerry. In any case, corner to corner, they sat like fighters.

One additional characteristic of the hall requires elaboration. Because of the layout and structure, any sound from the hall was clearly audible in the tavern and vice-versa. No secrets. Also, the back room, an open stairway led upstairs. A virtual megaphone. Two months ago some kindly ladies held a shower upstairs. Unfortunately, in the tavern a very loud profane discussion erupted; Yankees, Republicans, Protestants, and how to effectively kill cockroaches. A wide range of unmentionables were shouted loud, clear, and most vivid—a lively topic for the Monsignor's sermon the following Sunday. Then again, the openness and non-confidentiality served a useful purpose; Tommy O'Hara told me that the Irish playwright Synge learned the Irish dialogue because he once lived above a kitchen full of waggish maids. (He drilled a hole through the floor to listen to the chatter)

Although I clearly heard most of the wedding, I feel somewhat like a blind man trying to describe the panoramic mob scene. The Storming of the Bastille. You hear the clamber and the clatter, the hoops and hollers, but you see none of the action.

The wedding had begun. I could imagine the men afloat on the pond, and the women huddled in the corners gossiping. The established customs. More guests arrived.

"A fine couple. Decent girl."

"Not all Irish though."

"Well the mother's German. Only half. But Mary's a fine Catholic and pure as snow. Almost chose the convent."

"By the saints, what more could you ask for?"

A glass of beer for Mrs. Brendon.

"Kinda thin on the meat, ain't he?"

"What odds. They're all the same when the sun goes down."

"Strapping lad. Good worker. In the junk business on the side. Sort of a tinker."

"Honeymoon? New York City. Staying at his Uncle's house."

More ducks to the pond. "Have another little drink will ya."

Charlie O'Rourke announces, "And now lets have a nice welcome for the grand couple."

Claps, hoots and stamping feet.

"Have you tried the poteen? Finest kind."

"Try a little of this for ya thirst."

Tom Muldoon toasts, "Here's to the life we love with those we love."

The accordions play softly. Clinking of glasses. Tinkling of knives and forks. More food. More refreshments. The noises got louder. A dropped glass. A laugh, a whoop. More noise.

Booker looks up from the card game. "Goddamn Irish," he says, "They're like a bunch of bagpipes. The more you fill their belly, the more they make noise."

Charlie O'Rouke, "And now the dance of the bride and groom . . . ."

A lively tune. Accordion, Fiddle, Flute, thumping feet, shouts, laughs, claps and whirling Dervishes.

Noise subsides. Jerry's voice. Beautiful rich tenor. Silver tongue. *I'll take you home again, Kathleen . . .* " His voice tingles your back.

"I bet Tommy requested that," said Danny O'Neil. He lit a Camel, set the wooden match in the ashtray. "When Tommy and she left the farm for Boston, Kathleen's grandmother told her that she'd never seem Ireland again. Not while there was a blush in your cheek or breath in your bosom. Told her that." Breaks a match, "Ya know Gunny, I'd cry too if I thought I'd never go back. Tommy says it's old wives' nonsense. They'll go back together someday when the kids are grown."

Jerry finishes. Claps. "Atta boy Jerry! More!" *Danny Boy. Bold O'Donough. The Gallant Forty TWA.* Guests join in. Sounds good. Claps. Shouts.

"Jerry! Jerry! Sing Kevin Barry!"

In the distant, the flute picks up the plaintive tune. The voice is soft and sad. And sorry about the hanging of Kevin Barry. Your spine tingles up and down.

I'm not Irish, but these words sung by Jerry would melt steel. So quiet. You can hear Dinty sweeping the floor. A few clinking glasses.

Quiet upstairs and downstairs. Not a clink, a sweep. A hushed silence. Respectful silence. Because everyone senses that Danny O'Neil feels more than a tingle. Even Dinty stands mute. Gunny visits the men's room. Danny avoids the eyes, and stares into his beer. His fingertips turn red from the tight grip on the glass.

I'm sure his thoughts flash back to another time, another place. His brother, Liam, killed by the English.

And when Kevin Barry refuses to turn in his comrades, there's not a man-Jack that doesn't, to some measure, feel Denny's pain. A numbness charged with emotion. His eyes water. Cold drizzle on the moor. Run, Liam, run! Gently he sets down his beer, and quietly leaves.

Eerie. Over a hundred people and not a sound. A minute passes. Finally a runt of a guest storms in through the door waving one of the shillelaghs, "Show me an English bastard!" As big as a midget. His speech is thick, his eyes red and menacing, "I'll bash the living shit out of him!" Bark definitely worse than his bite. No John Bull accepts the challenge. However, it breaks the tension.

Talking, a laugh. Now a lively tune. Stomping feet. Shouts. Merry times. Like the roar of the crowd at the main event. Another announcement from Charlie. Good-bye to the bride and groom. "Let's wish the best . . . ." Pats on the back, handshakes, claps. Kisses and hugs. Kisses of happiness from those who dream; kisses of sorrow from those who know. Mr. and Mrs. Rags Maloney leave in a borrowed car.

There's an old saying, "Don't stay until the last dog's hung." However, many of the guests could care less about his or any other saying. They were having a good time. The music became louder and faster. Shouts, swinging, taps and thumps. Joy, merriment and singing. Once I read that only a wisp separates the normal from the insane. Possibly this may be true for an individual. But I'm damn certain it's true for a group of people. A flash of lightning. A choir into a mob. For years I've seen fist fights erupt spontaneously. But this is the first time I've seen lightening strike a wedding. A happy singing party to an angry swinging mob.

In fact, just before the lightning, Gunny mentioned, "It's not the Copley Plaza, but they sure sound like they're enjoying themselves. What the hell, there's plenty to drink and eat. What else is there?"

Booker said, "Maybe a little brawl to top it off." Most prophetic words. The shot heard around the world. It all began with, "Let's throw the garter . . ." Something like that. An uneasy shuffling. Jumps, thumps. "Oh! Oh! That's terrible!" A woman's voice, "Lord preserve us! It's ruined!"

Unintelligible. Another woman's voice—more of a scream, "Hit him Jim . . ." "You clumsy cow!" Crack! (A sledge hits a rock?) Thud! (The body of that rock hits the floor?)

"Hey! Why did you do that?" Whack!

Quick footsteps, shouts. Screams. Curses. Overturning chairs and tables. Bottles shatter. Pieces of the window smash on the sidewalk. "Why you, I'll beat the cursed face off you!"

Cloth rips, "You foolish—I'll mash ya like a bug!"

"Look out! A scream. Many bumps, thumps, crashing off walls. "Mother of Jesus!"

The walls shake. The dart board falls from the wall. A fine snow of plaster drifts from the ceiling. Then chips. Finally, chunks. Everyone looks at Booker playing cards. Excitedly, Dinty tugs at his sleeve. "Screw it!" He shrugs. "Let'em beat each other's heads in. They're having a swell time. Deal the cards."

Clag—clang. Bells. The paddy wagon. Blue uniforms and billy clubs. Stomping up the stairs. Thud—thud. Bodies rolling down the stairs. Abruptly, the fight stops. The wedding concludes and the guests respectfully leave. The main event ends.

"What happened?" Tommy O'Hara gave the most credible account. It seems that Jerry all but drowned in the pond. A manly portion of the poteen. And as expected, words with Widow Quinn were in short coming. As Jerry dug his fork into that gorgeous ham, the Widow said to Jerry, "Don't take that. That's mine . . . for the decent folk . . ."

Jerry held up a forkful of ham and waved it in her face . . . "You call this pig?"

Guests watching, and the wit of the Widow struck, "Which end of the fork are you talking about?"

Jerry spluttered. The goat. He swore.

"You're drunk," said the Widow for all to hear. "Disgustingly drunk!" "And you're ugly" answered Jerry, "Disgustingly ugly! At least tomorrow I'll be sober."

Round one. Back to the corners. On with the reception. A curse? Because Mary Quinn was so shy, she removed the garter while changing to leave. Therefore, the traditional throwing of the garter was delayed until after the Maloney's had gone. Now it so happens that the bouquet was caught by Noreen Hogan. Noreen of the big nellies. Sweet, free Noreen, soft and warm as a rabbit.

If the statues on the cake could see, they would have been amazed at the sight. 15-20 men. Excited. Like hounds howling at the hare. They leaped and snapped. Such big nellies! Up went the garter. Jerry leaped. Shout, shove, push! Of course, Jerry, the misfit stumbled. At best, if he were sober he may have caught his balance. The statues could not hide. They watched in horror. A lumbering drunk; garter in his hand. His arm crushed the underpinning. Buried to the shoulder. Over the statues tilted, approximately the angle of Pisa.

"Oh! Oh!" snarled the widow, "that's terrible!"

Apologetically Jerry tried to straighten the statues, and re-plaster the cake. Worse!

"Hit him, Jim!" cried Widow Quinn.

And Jim did just that. "Ya clumsy cow!" Tearing a shillelagh off the wall he clouted Jerry with a blow that according to Tommy, "Like to split him from his crown to the knob on his gullet." Like Chicken Little, the statues saw the sky fall. Jerry's weight mashed the statues into the cake. Utter destruction. Jackie Dwyer punched Jim. Whack. A cousin punched Jackie. Boss and Jackie joined in. Quickly, energetically, support arrived on both sides. The lightening had struck. The gong had sounded. The main event. Fist, swinging chairs, and bottles. Screams. Half the women scream with fright; the other half with delight.

Encouragement from ringside. "Nothing like a good show of spirit," Mrs. Brandon. "A fitting end."

Widow Quinn was less enthusiastic. A ripped dress. Like the bishops she angrily dispensed with curses left and right. "By the Saints," said Tommy, "I was expecting a plague in Dorchester." But in afterthought he mused, "Her curse worked on Jerry alright. Poor soul. A sight. Covered with blood and cake. Stumbling around like a lost calf. The front tore right off his shirt. Everybody punching him. The mother screaming at him in German."

"If it weren't for Boss, he was in for a terrible beating. Boss dragged him out. Seventeen stitches at the City Hospital. Then they locked him up for the weekend. Ah, poor Jerry. Looked like a stewed witch."

On Sunday Dinty cleaned the hall. An empty battlefield. Smell of stale beer, whiskey and cigarettes. The floor littered with trampled ham and turkey and salads, broken glass, pieces of shirts and a shoe. All broomed and shoveled into three trash barrels. With the front of Jerry's shirt, Dinty washed the floor and cleaned the tables so that very night the boys played cards.

On Monday morning, a mummy stiffly walked up to the bar. The first customer, straight from the cell. Jerry, a painful sight. A large bandage was wrapped around his head. Remnants from his shirt hung out in front like a tattered flag. His jacket was covered with white and pink frosting. Two days stubble. yes red and swollen, especially on the combat side.

"How you feeling?" I asked gingerly. He must be sore.

"Me?" he answers. Puzzled, "Wonderful. A little stiff in me shoulders, but the finest kind." He sips his beer. "Grand wedding. One of the best in St. Peter's."

"And look, Bill" he proudly pulls out a crumpled ruffle of cloth, "I caught the garter."

2. Red's Baby Boy

November 7, 1937

A raw Saturday afternoon, cold and slushy. Danny's is packed with the regulars, young and old, guys coming off drunks, guys going on drunks, shoppers in for a few quick beers, and a drifter or two from other taverns. A typical tavern scene. The men stand two deep at the bar. Small clusters form around the radio, the dart board, and a card game. Coats lay stacked on top of one another in the corner booth along with shopping bundles of fresh bloodied meat and canned food from the First National with eggs, cheese, and milk from Morgan's Dairy Store, fresh fruit and vegetables form Terranti's Fruit Stand. Steam rises from a wet coat hugging the radiator. Dinty sows sawdust which mixes with the crushed butts, spent matchbooks, and coal ashes from the sidewalk. When you walk your feet grind the coal ashes. Crunch-Crunch. A newly pressed suit (Karras' Tailor Shop) hangs from the wall light.

No ashtrays could support a Saturday afternoon; therefore, smoking cigarettes prop along the edge of the bar leaving a regiment of burn scars. Empty bottles and glasses litter the tables. Every half hour or so Dinty swabs them off with a bar rag (Jerry Collins' shirt?)

A little boy meekly enters. "Would you please tell Mr. Dugan that my mother wants him." Little Dugan swiftly leaves. For good reason. To his eternal embarrassment his huge wife, more than once, barged through those doors and literally hauled him, drunk and all, out by the hair of his head.

Like any tavern, you have to shout to be heard. The boys, joke, swear, threaten, promise, talk all at full volume. Sometimes I actually stick a plug of cotton in my ears.

"Hey, buy a round ya cheapskate!"

"Whaddaya got cobwebs in ya wallet?" "He keeps a lock on his garbage can." "Baloney! I got the last round." "Sure and the man has flippers for arms and tunnels for pockets."

"Hey, did ya hear the one about Henry Ford. He dies, see. So there was six pallbearers carrying the coffin. Old Henry pops up and orders his son, "Put four wheels on this coffin and fire five of the pallbearers."

The young guys are the nosiest and without the doubt liveliest. Usually they push, pull, joust, noogie each other, talk sports, boxing and baseball and football and of course, girls. Presently they reminisce about the previous night in town. "Ya should seen this girl. I mean she was there, no kidding. How was the one you were with? Any action?"

"Naw, a beast. One of those holy-holy types. Ya couldna got into her drawers with a crowbar."

The older guys, mostly family men, speak of more mundane matters; jobs, kids, politics, more on jobs, and the cost of meat and bread and coal and oil and shoes, and sports. "My cousin, Al outta work now six months. A stupid thing he did. The company wanted to cut his pay, ya see. So he tells them to shove it. And he's been out ever since."

"Did ya listen to the fight last night? A corker."

Like I said, a typical tavern scene.

Booker sits at a table with Jerry Collins, watching Bill Morrissey and Jack Walsh play a game of checkers. Booker takes a couple of bets on the outcome.

Chico, Danny O'Neil, and Casey flip darts for beers, playing 301; rules—double on, double off and round robin.

Frank Vento, booking the numbers and the races, sits alongside the phone scribbling bets on small bits of paper.

Joe Scarletti and Blackie Hession listen to the races on the radio, "Hey, for chrisake, hold down the noise, will ya? I wanna hear the race."

Taking a periodic break from the tailor shop, Karras comes in for a glass of wine.

Following Karras, a box of Blackstone cigars tucked under his arm, in comes Red Driscoll. Cigar stuck in his grinning mouth. He bellows, "It's a boy!" His face actually beams. Round cherubic cheeks, large white teeth, especially the two front uppers—piano keys, so says Jerry—small mouth, delightful red face—a human chipmunk.

Happily, proudly he passes out the expensive cigars. Sure they cost a couple of bucks, but damn, he's a father. Pats on the back, handshakes, best wishes. His first born—a healthy strapping boy.

"How's the wife and baby?" "Ah, that's grand."

"What's he weigh?" "Seven pounds, three ounces."

"Big boy. A linebacker for the Bears."

Red's chest swells proudly. He walks from table to table, then along the bar.

Red passes out the last cigar. Everyone smokes. Even Dinty lights up. Within a few minutes the place looks like an opium den. Eyes sting.

"Hey, open the door. Smells like a cathouse." Plumes of smoke roll outside. I half expect the fire department to be rung.

Booker calls Red, "Sit down. Let me buy you a beer. It ain't every day you have a boy. And here's the five bucks I owe you. I coulda sworn it'd ne a girl. I mean Ann carried so low. And you know what superstition says: low for a girl, high for a boy. That'll teach me to believe old wives tales."

Red asks, "Ya know the nurse told me. The kid, he was born with a caul over his face. A layer of skin. What does that mean?"

Bill Morrissey's face lights up. Red's question pries open a Pandora's box of superstition about birth. It seems that everyone has a belief or a story, or a list of do's and don'ts either heard from "my ma" or "aunt" or "me old man" or the unspecified "them" or "they." Within the next hours Red hears them all.

Bill Morrissey begins in obvious earnest, "I'd buy the caul, if you mindin" on selling it. I'd see to pay ye ten dollars, b'y."

"Come on," answers Red, "You're slinging the bull."

"No, b'y. Down home they believes it to be powerful luck. Wear it in a pouch around yer neck and ye'll never drown at sea. That's the gospel truth, b'y. Me own grandpa wore one all his life. Went whalin' sealin', fished from a dory, he did. Came through three shipwrecks. Said it was the caul, he did. Lived to be ninety-two. Died when'e took a bad fall whilst patchin a leak on the roof.

"Aye, it's true, b'y," Jack Walsh nods, "Many a times I been in a turrible starm, I wish't to God—I had one. No lies—, down home, a baby born with a caul has the power of healing. God's wonder they say. Not as good as the seventh son of a seventh son but, I've seen 'em stop bleedin'. No bloody lie."

Jerry joins in, "Deed ye listen to them, Red. A caul's a grand thing, and I knocked about a little. Tis said the child will be intelligent. Nonsense ye say, but tis a queer world. There's substance, I believe, to the wife's tales. Me mother always said a child born with an open hand would be generous and a closed fist mean a cheap little devil."

"That's all horse bunk!" Booker shrugs. "You're a bunch of superstitious old ladies. I remember whenever I got in trouble with the cops, my mother would cry that it was her fault 'cause she cut my fingernails before I was a month old. Something about if you cut the nails in the first month, the child would grow up to be a thief . . . then again sometimes, I feel I musta been born without any fingernails."

Dinty brings a round, swabs the table, a few guys leave, a few enter. At three o'clock, Tommy O'Hara walks in, work finished for the day.

Jerry continues. "Birth's an awesome thing. Lot o'beliefs attached to it. Like me first cousin, Ethel. Had a cravin for strawberries, she did. And sure 'nough the baby had a big blotch o'red on his chest. Saw that with me own eyes."

"One't heard of an old woman," says an old timer, slowly puffing on his pipe. "Didn't she warn all the young girls never to touch their face if they got a fright. Seems a girl got scared by a bird, and she touched the side of 'er cheek. Didn't the little one have a brown mole on that very spot."

Jerry asks Red, "Did ya ask the nurse how many lumps was on the cord?"

"Whadaya talkin' about?"

"The number of lumps will tell ye how little babies ye'll have. Don't you know anything?"

Red answered, "I ain't never heard of that one but I know an easier way. Just count the wrinkles on a woman's forehead. That'll tell ya the number of kids. See, I know something. Course I don't believe it, ya know. Like my crazy uncle wanted me to put an ax under Ann's bed in the hospital. Said it would ease the labor pains. I mean, what would it look like? Me brining an ax in the hospital. They'd lock me up in the nut house. I'm with you Booker, it's all baoney!" Red finishes his beer, thanks Booker, joins the younger guys playing cards.

The telephone rings. "Joe Tooley! Is Joe Tooley here?"

Joe Tooley, at the bar, vigorously shakes his head, whispers, "I left an hour ago." No, Mrs. Tooley, Joe ain't here. Left about an hour ago. OK. If I see him I'll tell him. Goodbye Mrs. Tooley."

Red sits with the card players: Jackie Dyer, Richie Quinn, Mickey Smith, Blackie Hessian. Seven card stud, nickel a card, nickel ante. In case the cops come in, they used painted checkers for money.

"You want in, Red?" asks Jackie "Pay for the kids education, or he's gonna be a roofer?"

"He's going to college alright. Ain't gonna be no workin stiff." Red signals Dinty for a round. Did you's guys hear Morrissey and Jerry talk about superstitions?"

“Never mind about that, “says Jackie smiling, “did you fill up that bean pot yet?” Best man at Red’s wedding, Jackie had given Red a bean pot for a wedding present. Jackie had instructed Red to place a bean in the pot every time he made love for the first three years. At the end of three years, Red was instructed to remove a bean for each time he made love. Jackie told Red that he’d never empty the pot. It was a standing joke between them.

“Fill it up, are you kiddin?” scoffs Red, “I got an ash barrel filled up. I’m a bull.”

“Ya,” Mickey looks up from his card hand, “after ten kids you won’t be no bull. It’s tough enough to feed one kid.”

Jackie looks at Mickey, “You can always practice birth control. Can’t you?”

“Like hell,” answers Mickey sarcastically, “Did ya hear the sermon last Sunday about the evils of birth control? You supposed to have seventeen kids.”

Richie Quinn deals the cards. “Whaddya mean? The church has always approved birth control. The woman takes St. Joseph’s aspirin and holds it tightly between her knees. Guaranteed fool-proof.”

“Us single guys” adds Blackie, “we don’t have these problems.”

“Cause ya ain’t getting laid” Mickey finishes his beer.

“Ya, that’s what you think.” Blackie look irritated. “Ya shoulda seen the broad I met last night in town, from Southie, and you know them. All built like bricks. Every one of them. Nice looking too.”

“She was a beast.” Richie jokes, “I wouldna touched her with your dick. In a couple of weeks we’ll see ya in the clap ward.”

“Don’t ya think I used a rubber? What’s I look like, a crazy man?”

Jackie wins the pot, a straight, nine high. "Didya hear about that girl from Upham's Corner? Some swabby got her pregnant, and then took off. Left her high and dry. Only seventeen. I guess she kept it all a secret for a couple of months but what the hell. Was so afraid of her old man she swallowed a bottle of pills or something. Died. Found her in bed stone cold. A shame."

"You ain't kidding," agrees Richie. "I'd hate to be a girl. A guy can tap anything from here to Timbucktu and it's OK. But a girl, she's damned if she does, even just once."

"Let me tell ya this," vows Blackie, "Ill never marry a girl who ain't a virgin. No second hand stuff for me—"

"Cease the crap!" Mickey cuts him off "Deal the cards."

It's past four o'clock. Danny's begins to thin out. Suddenly a table tips over. A disagreement. No fists, just words. "Get outta here, ya son of a bitch!" "Break it up boys, you've both had a little too much."

Vassarian shows up for his two glasses of wine.

Tired of the card game, Red joins in the dart game with Chico and Danny.

"So you've got a kid," Chico points a dart at Red, "Let me give ya a tip. When you leave the hospital, carry the kid upstairs first. It's good luck. Makes sure he'll rise in life. And in this life he'll need all the luck he can get—damn-banks and Rockefellers." Chico shoots a dart.

On another wine break, Karras listens to Chico's tip. He offers his own. "A tip, I'll give you. From my dead mother. Never, never should you name a baby after a dead person. Or it won't live long."

"That's all crazy," Red disagrees. "Morrissey, he wants to buy the caul."

"You mean the kid had a caul over his face."

Chico is very impressed, "It's good luck. Listen, Red, believe this, there's truth to superstitions. Ask around, guys'll tell you."

He pulls out his key chain, "See this piece of rope—A guy hung himself with that rope. Supposed to be good luck. I brought it from a sergeant in the Foreign Legion when I was on a tanker in Port Said. A couple of strikes I was in a riot—the cops charging with clubs. I'd rub it for luck and I ain't never been hurt bad."

Danny cuts him off, "What are ye, a bloody prophet of doom!"

"I'll tell the truth," answers Karras. "You want the kid should have bad life? You think I make this up? Ask Vassarian."

Vassarian hands Red a dime. "Here, put this silver coin in the baby's hand. Make him rich. I hear many things in my life. My father, he believed a baby should see a sunrise before a sunset—for a long life. He did that to me, and I'm 78. It's true. If only I believed him, I would have taken better care of myself. And for good luck, visitors should kiss bottom of baby's feet. First carry baby up a hill—not down hill. It's true."

I ask Tommy, "What do you think? Is it all baloney?"

"To be sure, there must be something there. In the old countries where the people are so close to nature and no communication, you have got to explain the mysterious. Tis probably why woodsman and sailors are so superstitious. I was always told that a child born in the light of the moon would be more intelligent, and a child born on a sunny day would be happy. Rainy days bring tears. If the baby is born on a Saturday, he must work hard for a living.

"Damn, I hope ya wrong." answers Red. "He was born this morning, a Saturday. Looks like he's gotta work for a living."

By seven o'clock the crowd leaves. Six customers remain. Jerry Collins sleeps with head on the table—that's what I most admire about Jerry, he knows when he's had enough. Red feels no pain. "Ya know, Bill, ya know what I think, today when I saw the kid, all red and ugly and when I saw those tiny little toes, I started to cry. He's mine, he needs me. I never really thought about it before. But when I saw him, what a feeling. That's my kid. My kid. Like a piece of me. Like I never gonna die. There'll always be a piece of me on earth.

"Ya know what else I think, Bill, I think a guy misses something if he don't have a kid. I can't explain it. I ain't no good with words like you or Tommy, but whatever's goin on inside is beautiful. Warm and cozy like a shot of whiskey after a cold day on the roof. Now with the kid, it won't be so bad on the roof. I mean now I got someone who needs me."

Red knocks over a glass of beer. I repair the damage.

"But you know, I don't want another kid, not right away. Not just yet. It's been a tough year for everyone. Roofing ain't the steadiest job in the world, ya could bet ya sweet ass on that. And with my ma sick an' everything. Me and my brother gotta pull our weight. Help her out. Can't let her go to the poor farm."

Rubs his sleeve across his nose. "If only I had some dough. Move out in the country. Quincy or Weymouth, somewhere like that . . . then I'd need a car. Ain't life tough? I like to draw and paint but a guy's gotta make a living. I tried to finish art school but ran out of bread. Roofing keeps food on the table."

His head drops; jerks up. "Ya, Bill, that's what I think. No more kids for a while. I guess the only way is to keep it in my pants. You know, Ann is really religious. Wants no part of that birth control business. The church says to have kids, so she believes it. Me, I go to Mass, but I could use a rubber without it bothering me none. It ain't fair. Before I got married I waited and waited. Then all of a sudden you're married and you can do it all ya want. Ya know, the ceremony didn't change me at all. I was just as horny before as aftwerward.

"Say, Bill, ya know what Casey said? Have an abortion." I thought Gunny'd fall through the floor. "That's murder!"

"Well, I'm a lot of things but I ain't a killer, not after seeing my kid today."

He thinks for a while, talks almost as it to himself. "But damn, I don't wanna a kid every year. Ann couldn't take it. She's only ninety pounds soaking wet—How did you handle it, Bill?"

"Nothing to handle Red. We both wanted a kid. It was a bad draw of the cards." I dread the direction of the conversation. Too many painful memories are being uprooted. It's so odd that sometimes you're sure you've outdistanced and unhappy experience only to find a word, a gesture can rasp a raw nerve. I begin to pack the beer chest.

Gripping the bar, Red slides off the bar stool. "I gotta go, I'm shit-faced. Gotta clean up the house tomorrow before she comes home. Well, I'll be seeing you, Bill."

"I don't know how you handled it, Bill. A wife and a little baby. Christ that was a tough break!"

3. The Funeral Of Boss Mcdonough

Construction Worker Killed
Caused by Collapse of Water Trench
New Connection Near Museum of Fine Arts.

December 6, 1936

"Holy Jesus, did ya hear?" Blackie Hession says, "Boss got killed! A cave-in . . . look, it's here in the paper and everything . . . I can't—"

Mickey takes the paper. "Ah damn! Poor Mac. Just had another kid."

Frank Vento huddles around the newspaper. "You sure?"

"There's his name!" Mickey points.

Frank reads, whistles. "Mama mia! I'll be a son-of-a-bitch, I just saw Boss and Jerry going to work yesterday morning. I don't believe it." Everyone finds it hard to believe. You see a guy, talk with him one day, and the next day the newspaper tells you that he's dead.

The article gives only the highlights; Jerry gives the details later that night.

"We were laying a sewer line down by Back Bay, near the Museum—20 inch lines. It was terrible!" His hands shake as he unscrews the cap from a pint of whiskey. After a few long swigs he returns the bottle to his pocket. His eyes are wet, but not the bloodshot wet. His voice is unsteady. I've never seen him so pale, so jiggly.

"We dug this trench, about fifteen feet deep. Good soil, but Boss wanted to shore up the walls, just to be on the safe side. You know, with yesterday's rain and snow and all. Well, the owner was bitching like hell. We're losing money on this job," "the men aren't performing"—the likes of the Yankee bastard. Him in his fine waistcoat and shined shoes. If I had crowned him with my shovel, Boss'd be still alive."

The bar is quiet. Although everyone avoids crowding Jerry, they all want the news. After all, Boss was a fine man, a man's man if you know what I mean. Over six foot, 200 pounds, square face, dark eyes, rugged but temperate.

On Saturday afternoon, or Saturday evening after confession, he'd drink his fill of beer with the best of them. But never did Boss get out of hand. A gentleman to the core.

He respected others; expected likewise in return. At work, Boss demanded a day's labor for a day's pay, and he practiced what he preached. He outworked every man on the crew.

And a family man. Six—no, seven kids, he spoiled them with little toys, trips to Malibu Beach, Franklin Park Zoo, the circus, anywhere, everywhere. He loved his wife; he proved it in the sense that whatever she desired he fulfilled. He was a good church-going Catholic, he was kind to the kids and to her, he was a steady worker, proud to be Irish, and he was a light drinker.

Jerry continues, "We'd just finished packing sand at the bottom . . . the boys and me was over at the truck unloading the pipe. Nico, you know that Italian guy I tell you about," he looks at Booker. "He was down in the trench. I hear sort of a slumpin' sound part of the trench collapsed. I hear Nico yell; then Boss, "Oh God!" And I see him jump into the trench to help. Like a flash the two walls smothered them under! By the Sacred Heart of Jesus, we did everything! Guys crying, digging with shovels, boards, even clawing with their hands. Took two hours to get at them. They didn't have a bloody chance!"

Booker puts his hand on Jerry's shoulder. "I'm sure you did everything you could."

"Ya, that's right, did ya best" everyone agrees.

"It was just terrible. Dirt and blood in his mouth and eyes. Boss's leg busted right under him—ugh!" Another gulp of whiskey. Damn—owner—damn that man to hell!"

"Real shame," says Mickey, "especially with the new baby."

Booker says, "Nora's in some fix now, seven kids. Why does it always happen to good people?" He slams the bar with his fist. "Who broke the news?"

Mickey answers, "Iron Mike Kelly said that the captain down at Station notified Father O'Malley. I'd hate his job. How do you tell a woman that her man's been killed? I heard the nuns at St. Peter's told the kids."

Booker turns to me, "Bill, in the cellar, will you bring up that big jug, the one we use for collections. Set it on the bar."

"What about flowers?"

"Ya, I suppose flowers are a comfort but what she needs is money. Tell Dinty to collect from all the local stores. Boss was a good customer. And make sure Karras donates. What a bad piece of luck."

Luck. Superstition. Then I remember that on my list, Boss was #13. The first to die. All the night I feel uneasy, like I somehow put the hex on him. Sure, it's ridiculous, #13, three on a match, black cat, bird in the house. Nonsense.

But I can't shake the guilt, even when I go to the wake.

Cold wet night, Barry Street, a street of ever enduring 3-decker houses, 30 or 40 of them, probably housing 500 people. Ice slicks the sidewalk at Boss's house, #34, a gray house, dark gray trim. A wreath hangs on the door. Coal ashes are spread on the front steps. Crunch-crunch. Pieces of burlap lay before the door to wipe your feet.

Booker and I edge into the dark outer hallway, headed for the third floor flat. Inside, an un-shaded bulb lights up the hallway. Half way upstairs the wallpaper is old, yellowed, and a flowered design. The upper half had new wallpaper—a bird design. Birds, bad omen! (My mother swore by this.) Ordinarily I would notice none of this, but sometimes guilt makes one sensitive. Unusual smell but not unpleasant. As we ascend I smell cabbage at the second floor landing. Slowly the scent gives way to that sickly sweet smell of roses and carnations and lilies and then cigarettes and coffee and people. The door is open. The hot rush of coal dust from the furnace almost stifles me

Female whispers from the parlor; male voices from the kitchen. We go into the parlor, past the living room (in actuality, a bedroom) which is crowded with wooden chairs borrowed from Kiley, the undertaker.

Near the front windows, the casket. Mrs. McDonough sits alongside, her sisters seated next to her. Boss's brother, John, stands. The oldest daughter is softly crying in the other room. Jerry tries to comfort her.

Booker says, "Sorry for your troubles, Mrs. McDonough. Fine man." "Thank you." Voice hollow, almost an echo. Wide brown eyes tired but strong. Hair tied into a severe bun. Heavy shoulders. Thick broad face, a strong face—a strong woman; a good match for Boss.

"I'm very sorry, Mrs. McDonough," I say taking her hand. Her hand is so cold, so incredibly cold, that I almost jerk away.

"He was a good . . ."

"Thank you," voice hollow.

I feel like apologizing for the #13, but instead I turn to the casket. Flowers and ribbons of all shapes, sizes and colors wall the room. A cross of carnations centers the casket; sprays of roses, sheaves of lilies border the sides. Ribbons, purple white and gold, read: "Rest in Peace," "Our Brother," and "Sons of Erin."

Reflections from a small light play off the shiny wood. A folded Irish flag and a Missal rest on top. Pure white satin and ruffles, so neat and clean, so professional. There lies Boss. Francis J. McDonough. I kneel and bless myself.

"Hail Mary, full of grace . . ."

His large head rests so peacefully on a satin pillow. He looks only asleep, so strange; he always worked so long and hard. I doubt that he's asleep, let alone dead. But there he lies. His eyes seem closed so lightly I expect—I hope—them to flutter. He looks so young and healthy. I get the strange urge to touch him, to see if he's just asleep. Staring at his chest I hope to see a small movement, any indication that he breathes. But there is only stillness.

Number 13.

You know, as I kneel, I realize that I had never looked at his face before—really looked at it. I don't even know the color of his eyes. His eyebrows are bushy and his nose is big, much larger that I had noticed before. Face roughened by the weather, wrinkled and paler than usual, and now waxed. His lips neither smile nor frown. No curse, no message. His brown hair is neatly combed, white at the temples—never noticed that before either. A small patch of hair over his ear had been removed leaving a small bald spot as though the barber had clipped too much (before or after?).

My gaze goes to his hands. Maybe it's the reflection from the silver crucifix. The silver rosary beads look entwined in his big fingers—then I see—two fingernails are gone. His skin on his fingertips are red and raw and ugly. Kiley had probably tried to do a good job trying to hide this—waxing or whatever they do—but he failed.

"I'm sorry, Boss . . . now and the hour of our death, Amen."

As I rise from the kneeler, my legs actually tremble. Whether it's from kneeling or whatever's going on inside me, I don't know. While waiting for Booker to finish his respects, I stand in the living room with the women. The air is strong with smell of perfume. They sit fingering their rosaries. Heavy women. Thick swabs of lipstick, red circles of rouge high on cheeks, nets in the hair, kind gentle eyes. Compassionate. You can almost read their minds. Sorry for Nora, dreadfully sorry, but thankful their men, their kids—ever hopeful and afraid for tomorrow. "Oh Lord Jesus, have mercy on all of us."

Two of the oldest women (grandparents? aunts?), heads bent and lips moving, recite their prayers. Every now and then they begin keening—a soft wail so weird and eerie—so primitive—that it drives me to go into the kitchen without Booker.

In the kitchen are only the men. The smell changes from flowers and perfume to pipes and cigarettes, coffee and whiskey. My eyes sting from the smoke.

There's Jerry, Tommy O'Hara, Jack Walsh—must be half the boys from Danny's.

"Good crowd," says Tommy, "It'll be a comfort. You know, Bill, it's times like these, you see the value in customs and the like."

I nod. Good men. Rough clothes, ill-fitting dark suits. Unfamiliar neckties. Tough lined faces of men who work outside laboring. Scotty Burns sits at the kitchen table, pipe in one hand, a half a water glass of whiskey in the other. His face shines from a close shave; he smells faintly of Bay Rum. Jack Walsh and Red Driscoll talk near the black stove. The coal stove throws so much heat, they must be roasting. A large white coffee pot with green trim sits on the blacktop.

I walk to the table, pour a shot, water chaser. The table is crowded with bottles of whiskey and ginger ale, water glasses, coffee mugs and a platter full of sandwiches. The sandwiches are untouched.

All night long, men, known and unknown pay their respects. Vassarian, old as he is, visits, even takes a whiskey. First time I've seen him do that.

Kiley, the undertaker, walks into the kitchen. Conversation tapers off. A decent man for sure, but what type of chap would go into this line of work?

Father O'Malley refuses a drink. Talks with Tommy O'Hara. Comforts. A rock. Even Booker admits that in times of tragedy where do you turn? To the likes of him—to the Church.

Knock on the door. Mrs. Butler, from the second flat. She sets a fresh hot pot of coffee on the stove; cleans the table and places the platter of sandwiches out of the way in the pantry; takes an ice-pick to the icebox, and chips off a bowl full of ice; washes the glasses of mugs; leaves—all without one word.

Whiskey and words. The next few days see an abundance of both. Insurance man: "I'm sorry Mrs. McDonough but your policy expired months ago . . . The company would have notified you but you didn't inquire. I'm sorry but we have procedures to follow . . . it's not our responsibility . . . Twenty three dollars . . . It's not the amount that is due, it is the fact that it was overdue . . . We had no choice but to cancel. We have our procedures to follow . . . I'm very sorry."

Case worker: "For each child, Mrs. McDonough, you are entitled to an allotment . . . Not much you say . . . Well, I can assure you that it is adequate enough . . . After all, it is charity . . . We are in a depression . . . Many are worse off . . . You should be thankful . . . if your rent is too high, you will have to move elsewhere . . . That is our policy . . . Thank you."

Chico: "We ain't got a friggen chance in this country! Boss was as good as murdered. Where's the damn owner how? Home asleep in a nice soft bed. And Boss, dead, with a wife and seven kids. It just ain't fair . . . Little guys get screwed again . . . Should burn down every goddamn insurance company in the world. Every single one of them! The Government's got to do something to help the working stiff and his family . . . More than just a few crumbs of bread . . . Look at Charlie Polletta, laid up six months with a busted back. Bank took his house, everything but the clothes on his back . . . The politicians gotta wake up. If they don't wanna do somethin' then someone else will!"

Booker T.: "It makes you wonder about God. Why does a guy like him have to die? Seven kids, nice family . . . Here, Bill, give this money to Nora for me . . . Ya' that's right, three hundred sixty four dollars . . . What to you mean we didn't collect that much . . . Just keep quiet and give her the money."

"Father O'Malley's about to begin with the Rosary in the parlor."

"Ad the first sorrowful mystery . . . Agony in the Garden . . . Our Father . . ."

Nora: "Why? Oh God, why? They need a father. Oh God, what's to become of us? Rent due next week. Food. Clothes. Sweet Jesus, they'll never even remember him. Have to move to a new flat."

"And the second sorrowful mystery . . . Scourging at the Pillar . . . Who art in Heaven . . ." Nora's sister. "We'll do something, girl. God will see us through. And don't worry about the kids. They're strong, good stock. Don't cry, girl. You've got little choice; it's the kids that need you now."

"And the third sorrowful mystery . . . Crowning with the Thorns . . . gives us this day . . . ."

John McDonough: "Nora, I'll do whatever needs to be done. There'll always be a roof over your head and food on the table. You can rest as long as my back's strong enough to swing a pick." And turning to Michael he continues, "Son, you're the man of the house now, its time for you to quit school and find a construction job."

"And the fourth sorrowful mystery . . . Carrying of the Cross . . . And forgive us our trespasses . . ."

Father O'Malley: "Your husband was a good Catholic, Nora. I want you to know that he was to Confession this past Saturday, and to Communion every Sunday. I'm sure he's with God. Sure, a man to be deserving."

"And the fifth sorrowful mystery . . . The Crucifixion . . . But deliver us from evil . . ."

The children: "I'll quit school and find work." "So will I . . ." "I don't want to look at Pa. Please Ma, I don't want to sit up all night with him . . ." "Why do we have to go to Uncle John's house?"

Because the funeral is held on Saturday, a number of boys from Danny's attend. Jerry looks dead tired, worse than Nora. Last night he spent at Nico's wake in the North End. Different language; same grief. Four kids.

Murphy arrives with his camera. "Do you want me to take photographs now, John?"

John nods, "It'll be a blessing to my mother."

Six flashes. Various angles. To be sent back home to Ireland.

Before closing, we form a silent procession and shuffle by the coffin. As we leave, I hear the neighbor women busy in the kitchen, preparing the fixings: turkeys and hams and salads and what have you.

The Mass. Father O'Malley in black vestments "Eternal rest give to them, Oh Lord; and let perpetual light shine upon them . . ." the Latin, the pomp and the ceremony that Boss never saw in life, he sees in death.

As the procession rides by Danny's some of the boys come out, heads bent, caps by their side. Even Dinty too ashamed to visit the wake, stands outside, one hand holding his broom, the other crumpling his scally cap. A spontaneous gesture from a man to a man. No race, no creed, no politics—just man to man.

BENEFIT No. 356
For the Family of F.J. "Boss" McDonough
G.E. Radio
To be Drawn on March 6, 1936
$1.00 per ticket

Mrs. McDonough held the winning ticket. No one complained.

GRAFFITI

Through the centuries it seems that human beings have an urge to write their comments regardless of race, creed, or national origin. Some individuals are driven to mark their thoughts on any horizontal or vertical surfaces.

On a whim, Booker mounted a public Bulletin Board near the telephone booth. His objective was to invite the patrons to express themselves—somewhat a "taxation with representation" sense of practice.

For example, Casey is prone to write anything in public on the Bulletin Board—which sometimes causes Booker to cross out the comment—and sometimes a patron will respond to Casey's comment in such a way that Casey becomes infuriated—please note that Casey has a zero sense of humor and does not suffer fools gladly

Every few years or so Booker T. becomes disgusted with the grime and the grease. "Don't wash the walls," he tells Dinty, "paint the damn place." Today Dinty painted the toilet room—battleship grey, thanks to the Navy Yard—walls, ceiling floor, toilet sink and windows. It looks like a grey tomb.

273—good bet—5¢ gives you $30 if you hit 3 numbers
Great number ~~1273~~ 4233
~~408~~ 100 427 642 ~~101~~

"Now I lay me down to sleep and pray the Lord my soul to keep. If I die before I wake, play the number 208."

No credit—Booker T.

Don't throw butts in the trough. They get wet and soggy and hard to light.

Don't throw butts in hopper. We don't piss in your ashtray.

God bless Hoover and the Republicans.

Found—A roll of twenty dollar bills. (Will the owner please form a line at the end of the bar)

Look higher. Higher. Way up! Quick, look down!—Your pissing on your shoes.

The future you hold in your hands.

What has 18 legs, 9 assholes and lives in the cellar? The Boston Braves.

Don't flush toilet. Remember the Johnston Flood.

Jimmy 1936
Rock Dorchester Mohawks

Whitey—Southie Shamrocks
(The best thing to come out of Southie was the Dorchester trolley)

Marx was right!
Who's he?
Groucho's brother, stupid!

Brennan (Owner)
O
X—Good for handout

A penny saved is ridiculous.

Stand close—don't flatter yourself.

It's more fun to be handsome, rich, and healthy than to be ugly, poor, and sick.

The world is flat—Chuck 1491
So is his girlfriend (underneath)

Celebrate the 4th of July—Hang a Yankee.

He who inherits riches shall never know the joy of labor and toil.

Scotchman—Do you realize that sheep are also valued for their wool?

Please refrain from depositing rose petals in the spittoon. They detract from the fragrances of the tavern.

Beware: The strange odor may originate from the fellow sitting beside you.

10% of cops have hemorrhoids—the rest are total assholes—including Kelly—signed Casey (in Casey Script)

For Sale: Granite tombstone—great buy for a man named Caruso

No Admittance to the latrine while the demonstration is in progress.

Don't vote: it only encourages City Hall

Father's Day = Mother's Day on the cheap

Did honest Abe Lincoln get a kick back from Lincoln Logs?

Cherish the pleasant fragrance of the trough

Do not deposit medical waste in the trough

Where's Curley?

The 1940's

Bill At 40 Years Old

January 2, 1940

This New Year's brings a special birthday, my fortieth, certainly unwelcome, pragmatically accepted. The big Four-0, like a milestone in your life, it hangs like a heavy weight chained around your neck. Definitely no longer a young man, that's for sure. Truthfully, both physically and mentally I feel no different than at 30—working at Wentworth and the boiler room, and working one or two days a week at Danny's keeps me busy. However, I keep asking myself, "What have I accomplished?" Very little, I'm afraid. Never published except for a couple of short stories in the Dorchester Monthly Tribune. Like a termite, I gnaw consistently—"Is all my writing, thinking, worth the effort, the hopes, disappointments?" Like shoveling against the tide—never ending. Sure, when I finish a story that I think is good, I experience much satisfaction and expectation. Unfortunately, editors and publishers disagree with my assessment. Obviously my stories lack something. Empty, unbelievable characters? I hope not because they actually do live. Maybe I lack warmth? Poor style? Diction? Interest? Possible my major premise that a tavern is an interesting place leaves the reader cold? Maybe readers desire, not real live people, common in plodding along in life, but desire a fantasy world. Walt Disney, Donald Duck, and Goofy. I guess I can't blame them.

Yesterday I read a magazine story, fiction, about a wealthy young boy, fifteen, vacationing on Nantucket for the summer. Well, the theme of the story was how the boy lost his virginity, and how important sex is to a growing boy (and older ones at that)—feeling girls and dissecting sex manuals and adolescent dirty jokes. The boy meets a pretty young girl, innocent and pure. After dating all summer, on the eve of departure, they make love for the first time on a deserted beach.

The author handles the story with deep gentleness—actually beautiful. The author certainly created a fantasy. But the characters seemed so genuine—how I envied the boy. Why can't my characters generate those emotions? Maybe such a story can exist only in fiction, no matter how intensely we wish otherwise. For instance, how crudely I lost my virginity. I was 17 and drunk with Mickey Smith on dago red wine stolen from Paletti's cellar. It was summer, August, I think, and hotter than hell—at least ninety. Mickey knew this girl over in Roxbury—girl? She was old, probably 30 or 35. Although I was afraid—almost terrified—I agreed to go with him. So we hopped a trolley over to her apartment. She was skinny, with big breasts, and thick glasses, and wore an old fancy robe that you'd expect to see in a Grade B love movie. Anyway we flip a coin to see who goes first. I win. I remember the bed cluttered with Romance magazines and empty cookie boxes, and a hole in her underwear. She wouldn't let me kiss her but furiously wanted me to tell her that I loved her. "Tell me you love me!" she kept whispering. For Pete's sake, I just laid eyes on her fifteen minutes before. But I was a horny, drunk, and nervous—you're only cherry once—so I answered, "Yah, Yah." It was hot. My back and legs ached and Mickey kept thumping on the door to hurry up (I use to kid him about what part of his body he was thumping with). The sweat poured off us; I kept sliding out. Finally she began to rock me from side to side so that I came. Like two firecrackers exploding in my ears. "Oh, you're good," she said, as we both collapsed, and I slid off her like a slippery rock at the quarries.

"C'mon, Bill!" Mickey thumped. "It's my turn!"

In one sense I felt relieved and happy—I'd done it; on the other hand, I felt disappointed, dirty—I never wanted it to happen that way. No matter how Mickey tried to persuade me to return, I refused.

So you see, unlike the young boy in the magazine story, I had my first sex with no tenderness, nor dignity, nor warmth. Then again in real life, kids from this block don't vacation the summers in Nantucket, and you take it where you find it—any port in the storm. But if I had any choice, I would have gladly traded places with that kid. Yes, you know I would've.

Dorchester Monthly Tribune

A community newsletter serving the Dorchester neighbourhood December 7. 1941 *Peter Z's Print Shop Bowdoin Street*

"DAY OF IMFAMY" JAPS BOMB PEARL HARBOR! NO WARNING!

The Battleship Arizona hit by Jap bomb through her stack; became a grave for 1000 men.

SNEAK ATTACK ON PEARL HARBOR

Day of Infamy

DECEMBER 1941-JANUARY 1942
HEARD IN DANNY'S

"The sneaky Jap bastards!—No warning! Why didn't they fight like men?"

"Me and my brother just joined—I'm gonna get me one of those Jap swords."

I want a German Luger!

My uncle is at Pearl—No one's heard any news. He's on the Arizona. No news—no nothing.

Richie Quinn—"Out of my way! I'm joining the Marines—the best!" Semper Fi! (Note: He flunked the physical—too small. Therefore he enlisted in the army paratroopers.)

Did you hear, "Someone threw a brick through Charlie Loo's window—so he placed a sign in the window of his shop—"Chinese".

Blackie Hession and Joe Scarletta:

Joe: "Let's join the Army—you get a warm bunk and three squares a day."

Blackie: "No, let's join the Marines."

"I can't swim—I almost drowned twice at Malibu Beach. Let's do it quietly before people start dumping on me over my folks being German immigrants!"

Joe: "What about the Italian heritage? Same deal, but I'd like the Army. So let's flip a coin."

Blackie suggested, "Heads it's Army and tails it's Marines."

"Right on," said Joe.

They flip a coin—all the boys are cheering. "It's heads! The Army!"

Booker: "Bill, they don't know what's in store for them. But it's a fine thing they do. Defend your country. But you know—I want to go so bad, I can taste it. But my doctor says 'no' and my bones tell me that he's right."

And we hear of children of the original Danny's list—ready to join or be drafted.

Jack Walsh: Two boys joined the Navy.
Danny O'Neil: Two boys waiting to be called.
Bill Morrissey: "I enlisted in the British Navy—I'm from Newfoundland"

Tommy O'Hara: "My boys are waiting for the draft."
Chico: Left a few years ago for the Spanish Civil War—no word concerning his whereabouts.
Casey: "With my record, they don't want me—screw em."
Gunny: "My heart is there but my body says "no."

And as expected—most of the young men waited for the draft.

Engaged Couple: "When I told my girl that I was putting off the wedding plans and joining the Marines, she went ape. 'If you join, you can forget about me waiting.'"

"But you know, I can always get married but the Marines will be a great adventure.

Mother: "My God, dear—join the service—are you insane?"
Daughter: "It's my duty—if I can, I want to enlist in the Marines"
Sign in St. Peter's Church: "For God and For Country"
Sign outside First National: "God Bless America"
Bowdoin Street: Flags hung outside of 3 decker homes and pennants with stars were displayed in the parlor windows.
Police Station 11: Iron Mike is too old—disappointed
Dorchester High School: Seniors can be graduated early; Navy wants them to join.
Army Base: A line a mile long—mostly young kids—all excited about the great adventure.
State House: Senator "If you plan to stay in politics, join the Marines. To put frosting on the cake, go to a top notch college, Harvard, Yale—be a pilot, study law or medicine. The rest of your life will be frosting on the cake."

Flat Feet:

"I got turned down 4F for flat feet. For God's sake, I've run the marathon for two years. And I'm rejected—4F—the doctor's tell me."

His buddy said, "Consider yourself lucky."

"Lucky—like hell—look, I want to serve my country. I want to do my duty as a citizen—and to have an adventure. Instead I'll be 4F and have the neighbors glare at me—call me a coward—a lousy rotten f'n coward—that's what they'll say. What will I tell my grandchildren if I got married and have them—that during the war I shoveled shit on Rebecca's Sunny Brook Farm?"

"Actually I know how he felt. In the World War I was turned down because of my freight elevator accident in Raymond's—damaged my foot. A woman on Clarkson Street called me a coward. Her son was killed in France." 'My Johnnie fought and died for our country. What's wrong with you?'"

Scollay Square Tavern: Two men discussing a deal

Male 1 Early 20's, well groomed, in fact, handsome, and somewhat nervous.

Male 2 Middle aged—wearing a suit which is slightly shabby. Looks like a Scollay Square wheeler dealer, and speaks like a carnival barker.

Male 1 "Look, it ain't my fight. I don't want to be drafted and get my ass shot off. The bottom line is it ain't my war. What can you do for me?"

Male 2 "Well let's say it'll be tough but we can work on a solution to your problem. But it'll cost you."

Male 1 "How much?"

Male 2 "Five thousand bucks—on the table."

Male 1 "You gotta be kidding me!" Highly agitated.

Male 2 "It's a fair price to pay when you figure out the benefits of staying home with a deferral. Think about the available jobs that you can work at—good paying and steady—the Watertown Arsenal, the Navy Yard—Fore River Ship Yard—the auto plants in Framingham. God! Overtime puts big bucks in your pockets—they'll be sagging along the ground so heavy with gold. The country will be pumping out ships and trucks for years. You'll be working all the overtime! While the poor slobs who got drafted will be taking home short money. And furthermore—with all the suckers drafted the place will be overflowing with horny broads. You'll have it knocked. A nice looking young man with pockets bulging with good wages and a harem at your disposal."

Male 1 "Well, suppose I come up with the money, how are you going to guarantee that I fail the physical, and get the deferment?"

Male 2 "I've got a doctor who will work with us—I call him the Blind Man. Think it over. It seems like a great deal to me. Remember money talks and bullshit walks."

Bill Flynn, Wentworth Institute: President addressed the faculty—"Be ready gentlemen, the government has already contacted us about training our soldiers and sailors. We are to start assigning faculty to train students for the military—operate boilers—service machinery—training in flying and aeronautics."

Wentworth had done it before. In fact, after WWI, Wentworth led the training of WWI Veterans who were disabled.

And so I was recruited from the boiler room to a faculty position.

COMMANDER JOHN T. SHEA

Letter to his Son

Commander John T. Shea was on the USS Carrier, WASP sank on September 15, 1942. Below are excerpts from his famous letter that he wrote to his son, Jackie a few months before. This letter was printed in the Boston Post in October of 1942. It shows the feelings of the service men at the time.

June 29, 1942

Dear Jackie,

This is the first letter I have written directly to my little son. I am thrilled to know you can read it all by yourself. If you miss some of the words, mother will help you, I am sure . . .

. . . Meanwhile, take good care of mother, be a good boy and grow up to be a good young man. Study hard at school. Be a leader in everything good in life. Be a good Catholic and you can't help being a good American. Play fair always. Don't ever be a quitter, either in sports or in your work when you grow up. Get all the education you can. Stay close to mother and follow her advice. Obey her in everything, no matter how you may at times disagree. She knows what is best and will never let you down, or lead you away from the right and honorable things in life.

. . . Last of all, don't ever forget daddy. Pray for him to come back, and if it is God's will that he does not, be the kind of boy and man daddy wants you to be. Kiss mother for me every night. Goodbye for now. With all my love and devotion for mother and you,

Your Daddy

Coconut Grove Fire

In 15 Minutes, 492 Die

December 12, 1942

On November 29th, 1942, the Boston Sunday Globe Headline carried the headline. "400 dead in Hub Night Club Fire." The club was the elegant Coconut Grove, which was lined with artificial decorations, a sateen ceiling and lush flammables.

After the injured were rushed to the hospitals and the bodies were recovered, it was determined that 492 people had died in 15 minutes, and hundreds were injured. The club was officially rated for 460 occupants but, in fact, it held 1000 (an obvious code violation) that evening.

For the next several weeks, the tragedy was the topic of discussion in Danny's and every firehouse in the U.S. In Boston, stories of narrow escapes and lucky coincidences. Cancellations at the last moment fascinated and sometimes terrified the eager listeners. "There but the grace of God go I." In fact, the Boston College football team had planned a celebration at the club, but because of a humbling defeat the hands of Holy Cross (55-12 loss) caused the team to cancel.

The cause of the fire focused on the flammable material throughout the building, and the lack of paths of egress, locked doors, absence of effective emergency lighting systems, and unsafe exit signs. The actual cause of the fire was due to a light bulb allegedly unscrewed in the Melody Lounge, via a man looking for privacy with his date at a corner table. A busboy was enticed to put light back on. A match was lit to accomplish this task. Whoosh! Immediately the palm trees, fabric on the ceiling, the furniture—exploded in a burst of fire and gases—as flames rushed up the basement lounge to the main restaurant on the first floor.

Panic—lights went out—more panic—as people clawed for their lives! Within minutes the bar and restaurant were ablaze and or filled with smoke! And in 15 minutes 492 were dead and hundreds injured. Who was to blame?

Everyone had an opinion. Why were doors locked? What were the evacuation plans? Why so crowded? What about fire inspections?

To add insult to injury, a city official charged that some bodies had been robbed of cash and jewelry.

One afternoon, just before Christmas, in comes Scotty Burns, the fireman and his buddy Jack (his last name escapes me). Both were first on the scene that tragic night.

Scotty's hand is bandaged and Jack got a pained look on his face like he had seen something so horrible that it seared into his memory. "I'll never forget," he said.

Quickly a group surrounds: What about the sprinkler system? Why were the doors locked? Why so crowded? What, Why? Who's responsible?

Scotty works the crowd—says, "God, Bill, it was awful, when I first arrived the revolving door was jammed with bodies on the inside of each door leaf! You can see the horror on their faces—mouths wide open trying to catch a clean breath. I'll never forget those folks. Every night it's the same nightmare that I am the one who's trapped!"

"Well, how did it start?" I asked Scotty. A crowd in Danny's throws out a slew of questions.

Scotty answers, "It's still under investigation, but from all indications it started because of the material used to decorate the club, especially the drooping canopy hanging from the ceiling. One of the ceiling lights went out, or was shut off, or was turned off for privacy. The busboy lit a match to replace the bulb. It was like an explosion Whoosh—the ceiling drapes were flammable—it burned like you put a match to a ceiling made of toilet paper—Whoosh—up it went and travelled throughout the room. Of course, the patrons made a rush to the doors.—Especially the revolving doors. Can you imagine 50 or 100 people pushing in on one leaf, of a revolving door and on the other side another 50 are pushing on the opposite direction? Many folks were trapped!" Scotty stopped to compose himself—visibly shaken.

"From what I hear," Scotty continued, "the other doors were locked or hidden so no patrons could leave without paying. You would think that most of the dead were horribly burned but it was the products of gases and the high temperature. It was the gases that killed many of the people."

Jack said "I saw a couple of people seated at a table, dead—not a burn on them. It could have been the panic that froze them at their table. One couple seemed to hiding under the table, hugging each other—at least they died in each other's arms as opposed to being crushed or burnt in the flames."

Bill said, "You know now why people call fireman "leather lungs"—although nothing could protect your body from the conditions in the Grove. Imagine all the oxygen in your body being utilized to feed the fire."

Casey asked, "How long, did the fire last?"

Scotty answered, "Not long—the chief took a guess—an hour max at the most, but the damage was done—of course the interior rooms which were down in the basement level—destroyed in half an hour, tops. Overall with respect to loss of life close to five hundred people died in about fifteen minutes."

Casey said, "You know Scotty, what dumb bastard locked the exit doors—five hundred people dead to stop someone from sneaking out without paying."

"Well—there are many stories going around—"I was going to go but my date cancelled, or my mother was ill. And the strangest of all—BC was to have a party but Holy Cross decked their asses in the football game—so they cancelled out—God works in strange ways."

"You know who died?" asked Frank Vento. He answers his own question, "Buck Jones! I always thought he was a better cowboy than Tom Mix."

Casey chimes in disagreeing, "I hated that Buck Jones, a big phoney." He turns to Scotty, "I heard that some of the bodies were robbed—you know wallets, watches and stuff. Did you get any of the loot?"

Scotty looks shocked, "For God's sake, no!"

"Well, someone made a score," says Casey. "Not as much as the lawyers will make. It's too bad I'm on the wrong side of the law."

Scotty says to the group. "Listen, I want you to cram into your kid's heads and spouses. Whenever you enter a building, especially if it is unfamiliar, always check out the exit signs. Just look around and ask yourself—how would you escape a fire? If you don't see an exit sign, leave. Tell that to your kids, especially if the building is a dance hall or a private club. Where the building occupancy is noted for x and the owners sell x plus y tickets, don't enter the building."

USS DORCHESTER SUNK OFF GREENLAND

FEBRUARY 3, 1943

Approximately 100 miles off the coast of Greenland, a German U Boat torpedoed the Army Troopship, the USS Dorchester carrying over 900 men.

The Dorchester sunk in less than 18 minutes.

The four Chaplains on board, two Protestant pastors, a Catholic priest and a Jewish rabbi, were among the first on deck. They calmed the men and handed out life jackets. When they ran out, they took off their own and placed them on waiting soldiers, without regard to faith or race. They were last to be seen by witnesses; standing arm-in-arm on the hull of the ship, each praying in his own way for the care of the men. Almost 700 died.

The four Chaplains were Father John Washington (Catholic), Reverend Clarl Poling (Dutch Reformed), Rabbi Alexander Goode (Jewish) and Rev. George Fox (Methodist). These four Chaplains were later honored by Congress and President. They were recognized for their selfless acts of courage, compassion, and faith.

Editor's note: In 1960 Congress created a Special Congressional Medal of Valor and awarded it to the families of the Immortal Chaplains.

The USS Dorchester was built as a luxury passenger liner during the roaring 20's. As the economy faltered, the ship was moth balled. After Pearl Harbor, she was brought into service as a troop transport, which carried troops to the Greenland war theatre. The Coast Guard commander responsible for directing the ship through the icepack near Greenland said, "They got no business sending an old liner into the war zone."

Bill's Post Script

March 1943

It has been reported two Dorchester Soldier perished that night along with the 675 other men. Joe Scarletta and Blackie Hessian had both enlisted in the service together right after Pearl Harbor. Their families confirmed the notification.

I can shut my eye and envision Joe and Blackie flipping a coin to determine what branch of the servce that they should join, the Army or the Marines. The Army won. I guess truth is indeed stranger than fiction.

Dorchester Monthly Tribune

A community newsletter serving the Dorchester neighbourhood	1940's	*Peter Z's Print Shop Bowdoin Street*

War Movies

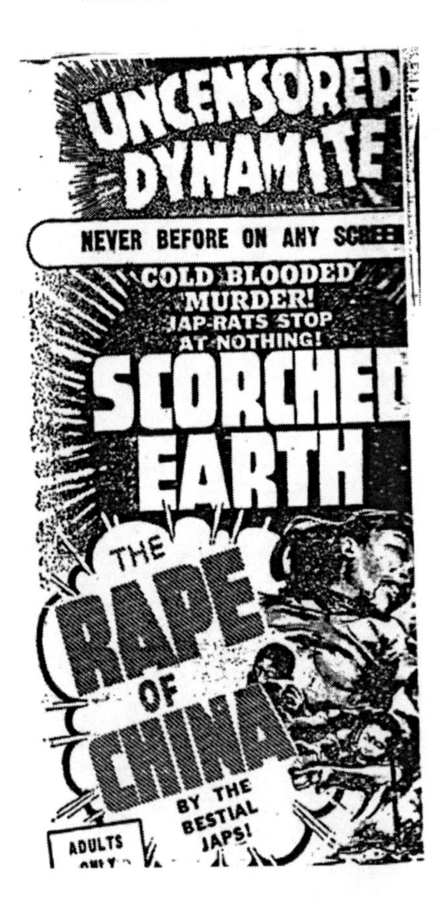

Dorchester Monthly Tribune

A community newsletter serving the Dorchester neighbourhood — 1940's — *Peter Z's Print Shop, Bowdoin Street*

HERE AGAIN! TOMORROW NIGHT
DEFENSE WORKERS
ALL NIGHT SWING SHIFT SHOWS!
ORPHEUM ONLY!
LOEW'S STATE & ORPHEUM

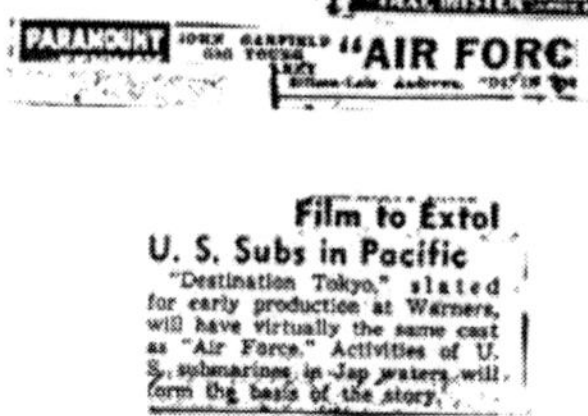

Film to Extol U. S. Subs in Pacific

"Destination Tokyo," slated for early production at Warners, will have virtually the same cast as "Air Force." Activities of U. S. submarines in Jap waters will form the basis of the story.

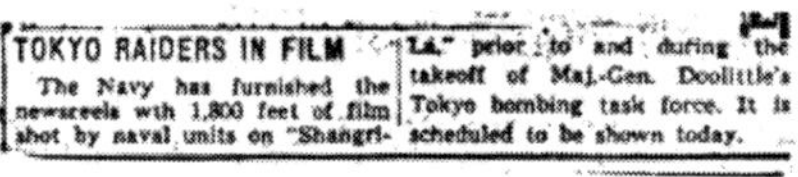

TOKYO RAIDERS IN FILM

The Navy has furnished the newsreels wth 1,800 feet of film shot by naval units on "Shangri-La," prior to and during the takeoff of Maj.-Gen. Doolittle's Tokyo bombing task force. It is scheduled to be shown today.

Dorchester Monthly Tribune

A community newsletter serving the Dorchester neighbourhood.

Peter Z's Print Shop Bowdoin Street

On the home front

NOT Rationed

NO POINTS NECESSARY

Fresh or Frozen Horsemeat

15c Lb.

New York Beef Company

15½ BLACKSTONE STREET

BOSTON—LAF. 4188

Rationing

9

BOSTON EVENING AMERICAN, MONDAY, APRIL 26, 1943

APRIL 30—*Can Goods*

Last day for use of Blue stamps D, E and F in Ration Book No. 2. Blue stamps G, H and J (there is no letter I) now valid until May 31. All six stamps may be combined this week for purchases of canned goods and processed foods—point values must be posted in stores.

APRIL 30—*Meats, etc.*

Red stamps A, B, C, D and E now valid—value 16 points per letter—A, B, C and D expire April 30—E coupon expires May 31—all may be combined this week for purchase of meats, butter, cheese and edible fats, etc.—point values must be posted in stores.

MAY 30—*Coffee*

Last day for purchase of coffee with Coupon No. 23 from Ration Book No. 1—value 1 pound.

MAY 31—*Sugar*

Last day for purchase of Sugar with Coupon No. 12 from Ration Book No. 1—value five pounds.

JUNE 15—*Shoes*

Last day for purchase of shoes with Coupon No. 17 from Ration Book No. 1—value 1 pair.

JULY 22—*Gasoline*

Last day for purchase of gasoline with No. 5 "A" book coupons—value [illegible] gallons for A, B, and C books' coupons.

German prisoners [illegible] were listed as interned in camps as follows:

AT STALAC VIII B

Maine

COOK, Staff Sergt. Vincent—Mrs. Nellie May Cook, mother, 17 Valley rd., Bath, Me.

Massachusetts

CALLERY, Sergt. Philip J.—Harold Allen, uncle, 81 Brooklyn st., North Adams.

AT DULAG LUFT

Massachusetts

DEMARS, Tech. Sergt. Rodney E.—Mrs. Blanche A. Henderson, mother, Cross st., Norwell.

CAMP UNSTATED

Maine

PRATT, 2nd Lieut. Howard H.—Mrs. James L. Pratt, mother, Weeks Mills.

Massachusetts

KENNEDY, First Lieut. Edmond—Mrs. Edith F. Kennedy, mother, 16 Follen st., Cambridge.

MOIR, Second Lieut. David—Mrs. C. F. Moir, mother, 65 South Main st., Natick.

PERRY, Tech. Sergt. Charles E.—Charles E. Perry, father, 111 Pleasant, Rochdale.

RHEAUME, Staff Sergt. Louis W.—Mrs. Helen Rowley, sister, 8 Bungalow rd., West Roxbury.

SALVO, Sergt. Alberto — Joseph Salvo father, 14 Esmond st., Dorchester.

Official WAAC Photo

PROMOTED—Mary F. Connelly of Lindsey st., Dorchester, now wears the bars of first officer, the WAAC equivalent of an Army captain, having been promoted from second officer. She is stationed at the Ft. Des Moines training center.

In the Armed Forces

James E. Coyle, Jr., 84 Radcliffe st., Dorchester, Arthur Hitchings, Jr., 124 Babcock st., Brookline, and Donald W. Neelon, 110 Main st., Waltham, are undergoing training at the U. S. Maritime Service Training Station, Hoffman Island, N. Y.

Quiet Tuesday

1943

It's a quiet Tuesday. I must point out that the boys talk about many subjects: sports, sex, weather, politics, horses, complaints about the beer and the hotdogs and the sandwiches.

"Be Jesus, Booker", grumbles Jerry waving and flapping his salami sandwich. This bread's as stale as a board."

"Ya think you're at a banquet in the Waldorf Astoria? For fifteen cents you're lucky you ain't getting ptomaine poison!" Booker looks up from the Green Sheet. "You damn harps, ya all alike. A couple of years ago you'd be begging for this bread."

"Deed so, but a least it was fresh then."

Booker smiles, returns to the racing sheet.

Quick wit, that Jerry. A character. Most complaints are the petty stupid comments that go on in every tavern—"Joe never buys a round nor parts with a smoke, Charlie wears dirty underwear, Sean gossips, Bill parts his hair different"—same thing, in any tavern.

I look out the window at two young kids punching and skipping and wrestling their way along the sidewalk. Every few steps, they chuck a rock at a trolley stop sign. A mangy old mongrel, probably the result of several fathers, trots faithfully alongside them. The kids stop and pat the dog. Wild hair, bright eyes, loud voices, they speak out of the corner of their mouths, Cagney style. "Tough seamy faces of the city" as Thomas Wolfe writes—he dislikes city kids. I love them: they possess a leathery freshness and courage and a rough honesty. But then again we're colored by our upbringing: never squeal, respect your ma and pa, women, priests and nuns—stand by your pals. Home—it's a place you can always go. As the Jesuits say, 'Give me the boy and I'll give you the man.'

God, there's so much to describe: the block, the characters, the way we live. If only I could write like Wolfe. Then you'd see all the characters in Danny's, the ones I see day in and day out. Oh, when you know them, they're so interesting, so unique, even in conformity. Everyday brings the new, the unexpected.

Gunny Steele, lifting his empty mail sack, plunks down on a stool. Lean, tall, grey hair, dark brown eyes, athletic face, distinguished, looks like a judge or a senator. From years of carrying the sack his left shoulder is drooping. "Ah, Bill, that bag gains about twenty pounds every afternoon. I'm too old for this stuff. So help me God, when I retire in a couple of years, I think I'll get a wheelchair, just to ride the streets." He sips a beer "That's good. Give me a hot dog." He wiggles on the stool, sets his cap and his glasses on the bar. "You know Bill, I've been married to Mary for close to forty years. And do you know, I'll never figure her out. What makes her tick? Last night I'm sound asleep—tough day yesterday.

Well, in the middle of the night, Mary starts shaking me. "Honey, honey, do you still love me?" I'm half asleep so I mumbles "Of course. Now go back to sleep. I gotta go to work tomorrow."

"Remember how you used to nibble my ears, my fingers?" She's sobbing. "Why don't you love me anymore? Why don't you nibble?"

"Well, Bill, I got so angry, I jumps out of bed! All right, all right, for God's sake! Where'd you put my false teeth?"

"You can be sure I got no breakfast this morning." He shakes his head. "Women, you can't figure them out."

I laugh because it's so unexpected of Gunny—of most married guys, to talk about their sex lives. Another taboo of the tavern.

Yes, there's all types of characters in a tavern.

The lunchtime crowd thins; Frank Vento begins calling in bets. Frank tells Booker about the Irish prostitute who was as dumb as she reported for work at a warehouse.

Late afternoon, Jackie Dwyer and Peter Brisk rehash a Saturday night at Moseley's by the Charles. "Great band. Didya hear that drummer?" Their talk shifts to sports: a fight in Lowell, "What a left! The favorite near took his opponent's head off." Or since the baseball season will start in April, "Damn Yankees, the Sox'll murder'em this year."

Around suppertime the tavern fills, two deep at the bar. Jerry tells a "story." Where does he get them?

"The Church is having a large convention for priests. And, to be sure, in the same hotel wasn't there a convention for liquor salesman. Well, the salesman planned to top off the dinner with a "spiked" watermelon, deed a fitting thing. The waiters, the poor beggars, so busy catering to both groups that the spiked watermelon was mistakenly given to the priests.

The maitre d'hotel says, "Ill be run out of town. What did they say? Did the priests like it?"

"I think they liked it, indeed, answered a waiter, "they're all putting the seeds in their pockets."

Jerry repeats his "story" from group to group, receiving responses from laughs to ridicule. How can I tell you about these guys? Booker and Tommy and Jerry and Gunny and the old and young guys? There's so many, so much to tell.

Yes, a tavern certainly has its characters.

THE NEIGBORHOOD

Through the Eyes of Iron Mike Kelly, Cop on the Beat

MARCH 1943

It's a cold wet night, close to quitting time in Danny's. Booker and I are cleaning up—who comes in but Iron Mike Kelly—he shakes off the wet and cold and the shivers.

Sort of reminds me of a polar bear—flexing his muscles. His face is broad and strong, and surprisingly young looking, punctuated by light blue eyes—not a trace of fat on the man.

Booker offers, "Cup of coffee, Mike?"

"Thanks, Timothy," he answers—Mike is the only person in Danny's who addresses Booker by his Christian name.

Is it because booking is illegal? I wonder. Instead I ask, "Mike, Booker and I are curious how you left Ireland and joined the U.S. Calvary."

Mike sips his coffee and emits a sigh, "Good coffee boys. Thanks." He pauses.

"People often ask me how I left Ireland and joined the Calvary—escaped is a more accurate word. Well, it's a long tale but the short of it is that I worked as a wiper on a Norwegian freighter out of London. I must have shoveled a million tons of coal down in the pits of the engine room. I still cough up coal dust. She was a rust bucket with only 2 seaman who could speak English, but she served me well. I jumped ship in Matamoras, Mexico and made my way across the border to Brownsville, Texas. As luck would have it, I met up with a couple of Irish lads who were in the Calvary. Seeing that when I use to work the fields back home, and horses were quite familiar. I joined up. Fought with Black Jack Pershing—a real charger—that one. Straight as a ramrod and twice as strict but fair, and he ran an outfit that was tough as nails. So we chased Pancho Villa and the rest of the Mexican bastards around the mountains for a few years. After I had my discharge, I decided to work my way to Boston."

"So with my records all set, I joined the police force. Good job, secure in one way, but you are never sure if this day will be your last. The Army and Mexico are good training for life—you get a good understanding of life with and without law and order. The working people, the Mexican farmers and the like, are as fine as you can find, but the corruption of the politicians and cruelty of the bandits are beyond belief."

Another coffee—we settle in for a long bull session. Mike is animated by his recollection of the past events. I ask, "What do you think of this neighborhood? What's it like to be a cop?"

"Well," he answers, "Bill, let me tell you, to my way of thinking, it is a decent job. In general the neighborhood—St. Peter's is a good area—a fine Parish—but it has some negatives as only policeman would know. You always run the risk of a danger out there in the streets. A crazy man or a drunk trying to do you in. For the most part, it can be boring, but it can also be very satisfying—helping people—protecting the neighborhood—insuring that the law is respected."

"First and foremost you must be prepared for the unexpected. My wife, Agnes, always gives me a kiss before every shift because she knows that this shift may be my last day on earth. We never discuss this but it's out there."

"Mike, you'll live forever," I joke.

Mike looks me directly in the eyes; Mike is so sincere. "To answer the specifics of your question. America—is the finest kind, lad. This is a great country, mind you, and Boston is a noble city and Dorchester is a fine neighborhood."

"But back home, John Bull really abused the Irish—no jobs, no opportunity. I hear the boys in Danny's complain about in abuse in America—Boyo, you don't know what abuse is! The English not only stole land and food, they cut down all the trees for mansions in London and then they tried to change the Irish language, and the Irish culture. Did you ever hear of the Hedge Master's School in Ireland? It was a secret school held in the woods in Ireland where monks and educators would teach the children Gaelic and the Irish ancestry."

"I was just a young lad when I saw an English officer shoot my uncle—what for? I don't know. But when you have another country acting like a landlord—the law gets arbitrary. And being a youth, you forget caution and try to strike back. So I joined the lads, and as a consequence, I became an Irish soldier. Well, one thing led to another. Let us just say that I hurriedly left the country. A terrible pain to leave the country of my birth, my parents, and my friends, with not a kiss or a farewell to carry me away."

"That's a great story," I say, "but what about walking the beat?"

"Bill, let me explain a typical shift—like last night. Basically, if all is quiet they're similar, it can be boring. It's when a door lock is broken or a store window has been cracked open, or you see shadows moving in a closed store at midnight, your pulse starts to quicken."

"My assignment is Bowdoin Street, midnight shift. Starting at St. Peters—you check every door, front, side and rear. Often the doors are left open at night—people have the comfort of sitting in the pew facing the altar and speaking with the Lord. No problems. Although I suppose no one here would try to steal the Chalice—Jesus, Mary and Joseph! I've never seen that. It's true that such a crime could occur but in this neighborhood if someone did steal from the church or vandalized the altar, then best that the thieves get caught by the police as opposed to the men of the parish who would beat the living stuffing out of them—It would be the same if a woman was attacked or a little kid abused."

"Overall my boy, it's a lonely job walking this beat, especially on the mid to 8 a.m. shift—even a pleasant night. But when it's cold, snow, or a full moon, by God, it tests your patience. Often I sometimes daydream and hum every song sung that I can remember and I think on my old days as a kid, and what life could have been. Of course, I focus on my family now—5 kids. The future—what's to become of them especially in these times with this unemployment? No question about it, if I lose my job, what's to happen with my Agnes and the five little ones. Scary! First and foremost I truly believe in law and order. Without it, we'd be living like the animals in the jungle."

Booker presses him, "Mike, walk the ins and outs for me. Please."

"To get down to specifics, when I start my beat, I report in on the call box, check in with desk sergeant. Then begin making my way down Bowdoin Street. At midnight there are few people—maybe a few young fellas hanging on the corner or leaving the tavern. 'Move on boys, time to go home.' No flip comments, maybe Iron Mike threatens them."

Mike sips on his coffee, "So I check the doors, shake them—if it's locked, that's OK. Of course, generally there's a light inside the front of the store for security. Get a peek inside. The rear door is another kettle of fish. You've got no light and in the rear—dark—and who knows when a cat, dog or even a person leaps out at you, or a kid with a zip gun. Infrequently a door is open, maybe the owner forgot to lock up—or is it being burglarized? Caution—your pulse races. A sound approach is to call into your call box—"I need back-up." The Sergeant calls the wagon and quick on, help will arrive."

"Where there is a signal indicating "Officer in Trouble," a platoon of policeman will be on the scene. Immediately! You always know that it could be you in danger. So you protect your own, even if it cost your life or limb."

He continues, "So you see, lads, the night shift ranges from complete boredom to moments of sheer terror. On the day shift, you really get to meet the neighbors—or direct the school kids across the street, or help old ladies along."

"So, Bill, no great adventure to impress you."

Booker asks, "What about problems in homes?"

"Violence in the home, you say?" asked Mike. "It's definitely not a common experience around here—but let me say no one knows what goes on in any household—it happens—especially if alcohol is involved. But from my experience it is not rampant by any stretch."

"When you get a call to a home, you have to be diligent. Bill, you know that something has happened especially if the kid or the wife has a mark on their face. Otherwise you'd never know unless you are told. Most neighbors keep to themselves—It's none of our business."

"Even when it happens—if the wife or the kids gets beaten to a pulp, she tells the kids—'Don't say anything—we keep our troubles to ourselves.'"

"Maybe a worried neighbor will go to the parish priest—and he may do something. Of course the husband is liable to punch the priest—'It's none of your damn business!'"

He emphasizes, "For all concerned, violence is an ugly business. And it does happen.

"Of course the wedding vows say ' . . . for better or for worse, in sickness and in health.' The man is boss of the family. You have to have someone in charge and it's the man—so teaches the church. Yes, marriage is a partnership, but in this life here in Dorchester and most places, this arrangement is not always perfect. Most guys are in charge or so they think, and the Church preaches—marriage is sacred—no divorce—keep the family together. But, often it is the women who run the show.

"I have officers at the station who say that some wives are holy terrors and deserve a slap every now and then. And the same can be said of a few of the boys in Danny's. Remember that many of the families in this parish are immigrants and back home, across the ocean, you get a slap across the face, or a belt to the rear, so as a kid, you grow up with this model of behavior and you do the same to your kids. Or if the old man gets drunk and beats on the old lady, it is accepted somewhat as long as it never out of proportion. Being a police officer I realize that most men in uniform attract a slew of woman. This never makes marriage more stable.

"The woman is especially the one in an awful situation. Where is she to escape? In fact, where does the woman go—back to Ma and Pa—who may be on the other side of the ocean, a thousand miles away with no money or food to spare? Go to the priest—who is a good man—but he's walking a fine line—the woman is really in a no win situation? Go to her brothers—who beat up the husband—what does that solve? Later on the husband is really angry and he's twice as mad, and he really works her over on the next Saturday night.

"We really need to change our outlook on proper behavior. Even though the Jesuits say a child should be hit but with only a thin twig—this has its drawbacks. Under no circumstances should you injure a child physically or verbally.

"And you know how frustrating family life can be for kids and women and even yourself. Maybe after, a separation is necessary—especially if the man is unstable or alcoholic. I've heard of a case where a guy was so enraged that he poured gasoline over the family's kitten—splashed it with gasoline—burnt it up. Case never solved. Terrible.

Mike pauses and then goes on, "Most people in this neighborhood are living payday to payday. Borrow? How do return a loan? You've got to be kidding me—most families are lucky to have $100 in the bank. It generally ends up that the women in the neighborhood are truly suffering—caught between a man who is an abuser, and children who need protection and money." Thank God there are some women who are as brave and tough as a Marine Gunnery Sergeant who really save the family. And yet they go around with a smile on their face with sorrow eating the inside. God Bless such women!

"I tell my daughters—marry a good man. If he drinks, drop him. If he's violent, drop him. If he's selfish, drop him. Forget the dance routine, or the wavy hair, or the happy jokes he tells. Is he kind? Responsible? Dependable?

"I could tell you, Bill, but there are more than a few lads in Danny's who have caused a sorry situation and pain their home life. I like a drink or two—and I've done things and said things that I regret. But I've never laid a hand on Agnes or belted my kids and I'd never touch my daughters.

"Remember," my mother use to say, "God counts a woman's tears.

"I do believe that women are the better people than the lads. Guys are great as the provider, and protector, and in wars. Women are for the nurturing, and organizing the family unit. Remember that on your deathbed, or on the battlefield the last face that emerges is that of one's mother.

"Thanks, boys." Mike's parting words.

Booker said, "You know, Bill, I heard that cat story about Casey, when he got divorced he burned up the kitten. No conviction. Insufficient evidence. Mike never mentioned that story to me but I do know that over the years, Mike and Casey have had serious run-ins and I mean big-time. Or as Mike once said, "We'll never wash the pots together."

I can envision a fight to the death between a polar bear and a wild animal. Fight of the century.

Booker nods.

THE

Commonwealth of Massachusetts

To CPL. KELLY

'A' TROOP 4th CALVARY

The Commonwealth of Massachusetts honoring the faithful services of her Sons who formed a part of the land and sea forces of the United States employed in the **Mexican Border Service** and maintaining the integrity of the Nation has by a **General Act** of General Court of 1918 directed the undersigned to present you this Testimonial of the people's gratitude for your patriotism.

Given at Boston this 5/4 in the year of our Lord One thousand nine hundred and 19

By His Excellency the Governor

OBITUARIES

Gunny and Vassarian

MAY 29, 1943

Gunny Steel

This month, both Gunny Steel—Marine Gunnery Sergeant, and a U.S. Mailman, and Vassarian died. Great old timers. Vassarian passed away in his sleep, poor old guy. Gunny died from diabetes. I'll miss them—sort of disbelieve they're gone. In fact, I half expect each to walk through the door; Gunny, leaning with a 10 degree list toward his old leather mail sack, in for his beer and a hot dog; Vassarian, silent, proud, in for his two glasses of wine. It's unfortunate. Good people; kind, honest, proud, loyal, courageous, solid to the core, and contrary to the brevity of the obits, legends within the tavern.

Let me tell you what the obit failed to say of "Vassairan, Nicholi, died suddenly." His son, Buddy, told me this story of how Vassarian immigrated to this country. Born in 1860 in Armenia, he grew up in a small village near Aliverdi which is close to the Turkish border. Well, since time began, Armenia has been ravaged by bloodbaths, wars, pograms, either from the Turks to the south, or the Russians from the north. In 1871 or 1872—Vassarian was about twelve—the Turks raided his village one dawn. A virtual massacre. Luckily his mother had time to hide the boy in a small cave no bigger than a trash barrel buried in the ground. Twelve years old, and he witnessed his mother and sisters raped and disemboweled. He saw his father strung from a tree, the flesh torn from his body, and finally dismembered. What the raiders couldn't carry, they burned, so that by nightfall all that remained was a pile of ashes, and searing memories scorched into the heart of a twelve year old Vassarian. It's said that the fire that melts the butter also hardens the egg. In this situation the egg hardened to the tenacity of blue steel. With only a vague address of his older brother somewhere in a place called Boston on the other side of the world, the boy headed north and east. A journey that would last many years and would easily outdo Marco Polo—Polo had maps; equipment and money. Vassarian had nothing but heart. Joining a caravan, first he traversed the Caucasus Mountains. Around the Caspian Sea, crossed lakes and across the Steppes, he labored at a village here, a farm there. Farmer hand, laborer, fisherman, and sometimes a thief. He sowed the seed in one field; harvested fruit in another. Into the interior he wandered, through such remote villages and outposts named: Sibay, Tara, Barzas, Zina, Ulan Ude, Chihsi; he crossed raging rivers, and the mighty mountains and godforsaken deserts with unfamiliar mystic names such as: Lisitsa, Ket, Kan, Kaxakh Uplands, Ural Mountains, Yenisey River. Seasons came, seasons passed. He labored, hunted, fished, planted—whatever was necessary for life and limb. Slowly, doggedly he caravanned eastward in an incredible trek across the West Siberian Plain, and Central Siberian Plateau, across the lands of jeering cold and furious blizzards and a raw frosted isolation where no sane man nor beast would dare to explore; a land where that abrupt span of spring and moderation and green vegetation fleeted by, a brief pause in the long year of ice and snow. Because of a broken hip, he mended a year at a Lake Bykal fishing village.

Turning southward he traveled through the strange land of the Mongolians; then eastward through China. Finally he reached Vladisvostok—the sea. 4000 miles. Seven years. Boston: that vague address, his only living relative drove him on. Signing on a Russian square-rigger, he sailed the world until he reached the North American continent. He jumped ship on Mexico. For two years he shoveled and sifted in a silver mine until he had saved enough to smuggle across the border. Then on to that sought after city called Boston. He never found his brother; however, since all Armenians seem to be cousins, Vassarian did find his own kind. A girl to his liking. Married. Sired eleven children. Must have a hundred grandchildren.

Worked as a baker all his life. Never attended school, but he could speak four or five languages fluently. Every one of his children graduated from high school; two graduated from college.

I first met Vassarian when Danny's opened; I regret not having known him as a young man. Even with age, he walked erect, proud with and agility and determination. Sporting his wide bushy mustache, he often looked at you with a steady gaze so that you knew here was that stuff from the era of wooden ships and iron men.

Last month, Doctor Holly, warned him to avoid his wine or he'd die. His son Buddy, now middle aged himself, told me that Vassarian looked at the Doc with that steady gaze and said that for seventy years he had lived on borrowed time. Each day alive was an extra. Therefore, he'd drink his wine, live the life he wanted, and the next be damned.

And Gunny. Wise, stout Gunny. Lunchtime companion for years. A beer and a hot dog, except on Friday's and Lent; then tuna. Because the diabetes had worsened, of late he drinks only water. Whereas, Vassarian kept generally silent, Gunny could converse on any subject. God, I'll miss him.

Last week on his return from a check-up at the Boston City Hospital, he said, "To heck with it, Bill, gimme a beer. What difference does it make?"

He looked pale as a ghost like he was down with the flu or something. He rubbed his ankles and kicked his foot against the bar. "Can't feel a darn thing in my feet. Oddest thing. Can't walk, my eyes bad, sleep all the time. Bill, I think this old dog's had it—never make it through the winter. Doctor wants me back for more tests. I told him I'd think it over." Sighing, he kneads his forehead and eyes between his thumb and fingers. "Oh boy. You know, Bill, I made my peace. Confession, Communion, ready as I'll ever be. The doctors all but tell me it's a matter of time. Amputate my legs? I say for what? But you know, you're never ready for it. I suppose when your time's up there's nothing to do but lay back and drift with it. But you're never ready. There's always a person, a memory, a hope—a something—anything to make you want to stay. Damn! I'd love to be twenty-one again. Back in the Corps. In China maybe. Best days of your life but you're too stupid or crazy to know it. Seems like a guy spends most of his life wishing he were twenty-one. When you're ten you want to be grown up. Twenty-one. And when you're my age you sure as hell want to be twenty-one. Don't pay attention to me, Bill. The old dog's seeing some tough days."

Another beer. Sits in the booth with a newspaper. Almost immediately he dozes off, his head gently bobbing off his chest like a buoy in a soft swell. His right index finger twitches spasmodically as though he's Morse coding a message. Red Driscoll enters, slams the door. With a start, Gunny snaps us. Rubs his eyes.

"See you Bill," he says with a wave. I never saw him alive again.

The obits tell nothing about Gunny. Born in Roxbury, oldest of seven children, Gunny left home "to see the world." After hoboing out west for a few years, he joined the Marines, an outfit to his liking. He served a few hitches. Whatever the country that had a marine contingent, he, at one time or another, served a tour. In 1989, fought in Cuba. Survived all the battles without a scratch. Ironically when the shooting stopped, just before coming home, Gunny got bitten by a snake, a fer de Lance. Really poisonous. His sergeant all but hacked the leg off him. But it saved his life. You should see the scars. And in the summer of 1900, when the Boxers and the Chinese Imperial Army besieged the American legation, Gunny's outfit drew the bloody rescue mission. Near Chein Men—some name like that, Gunny took shrapnel in his shoulder; he continued fighting. Finally, the Americans broke the siege. There's a famous picture taken near the gate to the Imperial City. A picture of an Army Captain killed in action, laying under any American Flag and surrounded by soldiers and Marines. Gunny is the third on the left.

Gunny mustered out of the Corps 1912. Of course, he tried to re-up during the War but age and mild diabetes caused rejection.

Sometime later, he became a postman, and settled down. He had seen the world. Now for a guy who served in the Marines, it's really amazing that he seldom swore. You'd expect a rough, tough, profane gunny. But no, he was more or less reserved. Minded his P's and Q's. Still he looked like a Marine, that certain straight-back walk, with a slight swagger. Strong features. The guys all respected him so that he, by an accepted unspoken consensus, became the patriarch, the judge, the peacemaker of Danny's. When there occurred a beef, a lopsided fist fight that required a verdict, and action, all the guys looked to him for a decision. He was that type of guy. Yes, the obits tell little about the men.

THE THUMB MAN

(Or Sy's Variety Store)

JUNE 1943

Down from the intersection of Bowdoin Street and Quincy Street one can find a cinder block building—Sy's Variety—probably 30' by 30'—which houses more food products and home necessities than the First National Warehouse. The block house is attached to a 2 story wood frame building which includes the family establishment. The owner is named Sy—no one knows or could pronounce his last name—Maybe an Armenian family who escaped the terrors of the Great War and lived to tell the tale. Sy lives in the store and the house with his wife and two boys—seldom seen outside—both play violin.

From a practical perspective the home/business is a very efficient business model. The store is open 12-15 hours a day, 7 days a week. Sy handles the busy hours and his wife takes up the slack. One must admit that the commuting time is nil. Yes, this set-up has many advantages. One obvious one is that Sy has the unique edge to improve his profits and squeeze out every dollar he can. Forget all but the money is his motto. In the neighborhood Sy is commonly referred to as the "Thumb Man", or sometimes the "Broom Man", or simply damn, thief!

Whatever his name, his physical features are certainly unique, a large spherical balloon supported by very short legs and topped by a smoother smaller head. He has no hair except for several tufts sticking out of his nose and ears that jump up and down, especially when Sy is animated which is often. Stand close to him and you can feel the energy in his every movement in his search for gold in America.

A static radio in the corner plays belly dancer music, and the store generally smells of food, actually a sweet fragrance that would tempt your mouth to water, even cause Pavlov's dog to drool.

Inside the store, wall to wall, ceiling to floor, the interior was packed with goods, from bologna to bubble gum to quartered pickles in a moldy glass dish which appeals to the younger children who are not concerned in their taste and health. Let the buyer beware—why else was he in business? It may have looked like a disordered pile of everything on the shelves, but Sy knew the profit margin of each item and exactly where they were located. Many were some young ruffian who would slip a Hostess Cupcake under his jacket. Whap! Caught and tugged out to the street. "Don't come back, you little thief!"

It is well known that the cast iron kettle should not call the frying pan black, but Sy was not up in his proverbs. It was commonly accepted in the neighborhood that Sy engaged in some devious tactics himself. Such as when weighing a pound of bologna, or other weighable vegetables or deli meat his thumb (which had a large wart on it's side) would suspiciously hold onto the scale system such that an extra ounce or two were added to the total weight of the meat—hence the name "Thumb Man."

Another subtle play was as follows: on the counter where the customers would place their items—milk, bread, Wheaties, etc. there was a broom nonchalantly laying near the tally field. As Sy was hunched over the brown paper bag, listing the goods: Milk 20¢, Bread 15¢ etc, somehow an unsuspecting customer would find "broom" 50¢ written on the tally sheet. Of course, if caught, Sy would claim that it was just a mistake. It was estimated that over the years, Sy sold that particular broom, fifty times.

Another common scheme involved the game of chance using a product that was manufactured in New York City—Sy had a large cylindrical flat box—very colorful—very enticing to win $5.00 per chance! Only a nickel! On the flat side were a series of holes which contained a tiny roll of paper which indicated what you would win. Pay your nickel, use the pen provided by Sy and punch out your choice. "Almost! Try again?" Did anyone win? I doubt it, unless it was Sy.

Let's say that Sy was not well liked in the neighborhood.

As Peter Z told me, "When I was a kid probably about 10 years old, my mother use to buy on credit, Sy kept track of the bills with one of those grey-black covered teacher grade books." Well every week or so, my mother would give me a few dollars to pay down the total—I mean, for God's sake, my old man was out of steady work and all for a couple of years. Anyway, when I put $2.00 or $3.00 down, Sy would rant and rave "Two Dollars!—Is that all you have! You owe me $15.00! I'm running a business here kid, not a charity."

"'Now you go home and tell your mother to keep up or else—I cut you off!' Here I was a little kid and this bald headed freak is degrading me. I never told my parents—my old man would punch him out."

"But you know, when I think about it—and be assured—never beat up on a little kid—they have memories—actually pains—that never leave you. Although in retrospect the Thumb Man did me a favor—I promised myself that I would start a business and make something of myself. And I ain't getting rich with my print shop but I'm doing ok without beating on little kids. And I try to treat people with respect."

Young Casey's Halloween

Trick or Treat

November 1943

A customer comes in for a beer, and complains that a kid busted the lamppost outside his house. "I'd like to kick his ass!"

Busy night outside of Danny's. It's Halloween where the little kids dress in costumes and march down the street with their parents. Generally, the smaller tots invade the side streets carrying a bucket for "Trick or Treat". Because every Dorchester Street is crowded with 3 decker houses and a large Catholic population, many kids are a consequence.

It's all fun—kids with their orange faces and wigs and ingenious witch and ghoul outfits give a lot of pleasure to the parents and neighbors. There are many in-house parties with a tub full of water and floating apples and kids drooling in the water. The kids have to stick their face into the bucket and bite the apples—all in good fun—plenty of candy—marshmallows, fruit, and apples.

However as the age of the trick or treaters gets into the teenage years, the rules of the road, so to speak, change. Instead of eating apples, teenagers use them as weapons—missiles thrown at cars, windows, and pedestrians.

There's also the soap the windows of cars—store front windows—a pain but generally harmless fun.

So this night begins with a patron saying, "If I catch any little punks soaping my windows I'll punch him. Don't pull trick or treat on me."

Charlie, a customer, says, "When I was a kid, me and five other kids used to hang around Bellevue Street because of girls and all that stuff. Anyway there was this new guy, Mr. Greene, he was big as a gorilla as mean as a tiger with piles, who owned a 3-decker with an alley way that sloped down to the back yard. There were about four or five ash barrels because the tenants heated the house with coal.

"So my buddy, Vinny Blacke challenges one of the dumber kids who we called him Huntzy, after the East Side kids. "I trick or treat you to roll old Greene's barrels down the driveway. In a flash, Huntzy rolls two or three barrels down the driveway, hell—What a racket! What a mess!

"All of a sudden—a huge figure bolts out of the front door! A maniac! You should have seen his face—man was crazy! In a flash all six of us take off down Bellevue Hill. I'm the slowest so I know I'll be the one to be caught and get my ass beaten. I didn't look behind—I heard the thud-thud of his boots and him huffing and puffing and the weird high pitched sounds coming out of his throat. 'Son of a bitch! Little Bastard,' gurgling he keeps repeating, 'I'll beat him to a pulp!'

"Now you know where Bellevue crosses Hamilton Street which is a very busy street—I didn't look south, east, or west—I charged across the street—just missed by a car. But Greene stumbles and falls—he must of slid on the blacktop about 20 feet. I didn't look back—I turned the next corner, dashed down the alleyway and made it off to my house—all in one piece.

Everybody laughs at the story.

Another patron, Jackie Dwyer, pops up, "On my street I had this crabby old neighbor, Fatso Brown. Whenever we play football tag in the streets, you know you roll up a newspaper and tie it with twine. That was our football. Fatso hated us—and if the football was badly thrown in his yard, he'd keep it.

"So at Halloween we decided to get even. You know how the horses from the ice man or the junk man would dump into the street. On the days before Halloween we walked the streets and collected a paper bag full with horse manure. Then we'd pack the sack with toilet paper and tissues.

"When it was dark out, we lit the sack on fire on his porch, rang the bell and took off. Fatso runs out of his house and immediately begins to stomp out the fire. Of course his shoes were then covered in horse shit."

Other guys talk about stealing underwear off the clotheslines and tying it to some dog's tail.

Now Casey, down at the end of the bar is listening to these stories. He pops out, "Did you fellas break the lampposts on Halloween?"

The Boston lampposts were heavy cast iron decorative, circular poles with a delicate clean glass covering the gas element—a thin coiled membrane somehow gave off the flame. In Dorchester and many other areas of Boston, the lampposts were inviting targets to vandals.

My four friends and I were about fourteen years old. "Well," continued Casey with a weird look in his eye, chuckles and says, "Down my cellar I found an empty gallon jug used to hold bleach water. I figured I would do a double header—break the lamppost with the gallon jug. Casey explains, "The other kids saved rocks and sidewalk bricks for the occasion. So about 10 o'clock, the boys are walking down Hamilton Street right off Clarkson Street. A quiet street of nice 3-decker houses."

"All the little goblins are in their beds, and the street is quiet. You know to hit a lamppost with an empty gallon jug is like throwing a 100 yard pass—it ain't easy. I whipped the jug into the air—bull-eye!

"It was like an explosion! The noise—the lamp glass shattering and the jug breaking. The noise of the glass shattering on the sidewalk! How joyful I was!

"Until who comes out of the alley between two houses but Big Sid, the cop. He grabbed up the hair on my head and near lifts me off the ground. 'You little punk!' You goina pay for this! And I'm taking you to the station.' He drags me up to the corner call box on Bowdoin Street and calls into the police station. 'Sergeant,' he reports. 'I've got this perpetrator who just broke a lamp with a jug.'

"Of course down at station 11, the sergeant wanted to know the names of my friends. I don't know their names. No tell—I figure like I'm Jimmy Cagney.

"Well, my old man came to the station, he didn't ask for any names—he just slammed me into the back wall. If it weren't for the police, my old man would have killed me, especially when he figured out that he would pay for the damages.

"Even though the cop suggested that I go to reform school, the judge figures it was a dumb prank and I was put on parole. Of course the next time I got in trouble—I stole a car—I did go to reform school. But he says, that's another story—let's save it for Christmas."

BERNIE

The Beginning

DECEMBER, 1943

I'm in love and I'm hurting. Happy and sad. Simultaneously, I'm gloriously ecstatic and damn tormented. Why must every pleasure in life demand a painful price? Each morning the shout of delight bursts in my chest, but is blocked by the cry of despair in my throat. Yes, I'm in love, but with a married woman. A beautiful dream but an impossible dilemma. Bernie. Bernadette! What a wonderful woman! Since we met, no longer am I depressed and lonely. Off the heavy booze. Again I find myself enthusiastic about writing. It's been a while since I picked up a pen and let my thoughts flow; the furious words gliding across the page like a puck on ice. Bernie, ah sweet Bernie—a cool cloth to a burning forehead, a frosted drink to a lost nomad. Because of her kind, intelligent, understanding personality I feel like Lazarus resurrected. She's magic. God, but I love her so! No longer does the pain of Nancy and the baby haunt me every wakened hour. No, Bernie has caressed and dulled those tragedies to a livable level. In time all pain subsides somewhat, but as long as you have an active memory the scars seldom disappear.

I do feel guilty with respect to my wife, Nancy, and of course, I would give my present life up if she and Jimmy would return. But that won't happen, and life is for the living.

Bernie, all my thoughts center around her. Morning, noon, and night. If we're separated, I think only of our next meeting; even when we are together. Half the time I'm planning when to see her again. When I wake up, when I work, when I eat, when I'm ready for bed—I love her and want to be with her all the time. And it shows.

Red Driscoll, "Hey, Bill, wake up! Whadaya damn deaf? Gimme a beer!"

And Booker, "What the hell's wrong with you, you in love or something?" Little does he know.

Never have I experienced an emotion with such an intensity, and a tenacity; it's like an electric craving permeates my whole body as though I were an overcharged battery. Have other people loved like this? It's like a love from a great novel, a love like Cyrano's. Do I feel this love because I'm lonely? Surely I'm lonely—I've been a truly solitary man all of my life. Not so now. All day long as I sit in front of the boiler at Wentworth's power plant, I carry on imaginary conversations with her. When shopping I search for gifts or trinkets that she might appreciate. I scour the newspapers for theaters and plays and movies and books that she might enjoy. Is this love—striving to make someone happy? She certainly brings out the best in me. And the more I do for her, the happier it makes me. How I enjoy walking with her, talking with her, making love to her. She has blessed me with a new meaning to life. How odd of me to write of love, of my innermost thoughts—it's not congruent with city breeding, where expressions of love and gentleness are reserved exclusively for mothers and girlfriends and maybe a sister. Once I wrote, "tough city kids don't cry or say I love you." Still true, but I no longer care.

Never have I met a woman so compatible. Sometimes in a man's life, he fantasizes about a perfect woman, a secret love of tender arms and sweet lips and true heart. Is there not a weary man who on a lonely summer night has cried and prayed to that vast universe of dark and diamond pollen, pleased with a someone, somewhere out there to bless him with a trusted friend, a magic lover who would soothe and knead away the pain and diminished the losses and the fears?

Sure, you cynically claim it's a foolish goal, never to be attained except in fairyland—but it came true for me! Bernie is fantasy. A magic. A trusted friend, a lover, a stout heart, my fantasy in the real flesh.

Let me try to describe her. Figuratively you'd first notice her soft blue eyes. She looks at you straight on, honest, open and somehow almost challenging. Honey light clipped curls frame her small face, delicate and smooth textured with jolly apple cheeks and a merry little mouth that frequently laughs, reminding you of a frolicking puppy. A few, almost imperceptible freckles dot the tip of her nose. She has a gentle smile that mysteriously has the effect of calming me down even when I'm angry or upset.

Bernie is 34 years old, a small woman of 5'2" and a delicate frame fragile, like Harvard University's glass flowers—even a light touch might break her. Yes, small, but well proportioned; in fact, because of very modest dress one would seldom notice how well formed were her breasts. Easily she could do without the support of a bra. Her clothes, her hair, her whole being is always immaculate, so clean and fresh-blown like a light fragrance from a rare perfume.

When we are alone, she has a habit of fingering my hair, my ears, or softly caressing my arm or back, and although this habit is so natural, almost involuntarily on her part, it moves me so. I construe the non-verbal gesture as her way of saying "I love you so."

At times she says little but it's always a comfortable silence. Generally she speaks in a voice so light and distinct you'd be reminded of the tinkling of wind bells in a Chinese garden. I swear that her voice is incapable of rising in anger or profanity.

I could write on and on. Easily I could bore you to sleep. Never could you understand how I feel about this wonderful woman. As I re-read my words, how inadequately do I express my feelings. My words seem so empty, even corny. But let me tell you, the feeling inside of me is so strong that I actually ache! Have you ever loved someone that intense? I hope so. And if you could imagine the happiness that her love has brought to me, you'd grind your teeth with envy. For only 3 months I've known Bernie, yet these 3 months seem like 3 years, even 3 centuries. Trying to remember life before meeting her is like trying to remember how you lived as a child of five years old. Yes, you recall some events but life in general is distant and hazy to recall. Three months ago. And of all places, in the Upham's Corner Library.

One afternoon in November, as I was browsing through the stacks, I was so engrossed that as I rounded the corner, I solidly bumped into a young woman.

"Look Homeward Angel," dropped to the floor, and as both of us bent to retrieve the book, we knocked heads.

I blushed, she laughed. So pretty, so warm, that my ordinary defenses disappeared, my usual uneasiness vanished. I held the book motionless.

"May I have my book, please?" she asked, her eyes staring at me straight on with that curious look of hers.

"You like Wolfe?"

"Very much so, in fact, this will be the third time I've read it."

Vaguely I can recall the comments and remarks swapped back and forth, then the awkward silence, real or imagined, that ended the conversation. We both continued our bookshelf odyssey.

As luck would have it, we left together, both headed towards Upham's Corner. We walked and talked, introducing ourselves and our addresses via parishes, and do-you-know-who and she mentioned that she was married, her husband overseas in the Pacific—at that time I detected that something was amiss. In general, we had a friendly conversation about books and authors and philosophies, obviously subjects of mutual interest. I chatted like a woodpecker until we reached the corner. I regretted to see her go—I enjoyed her so much, so much so that I had to see her again. But being married and all, I avoided insulting her position. I doubted if I'd see her again.

But as luck would have it, two weeks later as I shopped in Boston, I met her in Filenes Basement.

"Hi," I pause. Stupid as it sounds, for an instant I had forgotten her name. "Hi, Bernie, how are you?"

"Fine," she smiles, her eyes crinkling, almost mischievous. "At least this time you didn't knock me over."

I laugh. We swap a few comments, pleasant conventional chatter. I almost panic as she gestures to say good-bye, and since I'm hung-over from the previous night—when I'm hung-over most inhibitions disappear, I ask, "Care for a drink?"

Surprisingly, she smiles bright and wide, "Sure, no harm."

In the Statler Lounge we pass away an hour or so over a few drinks. Just a congenial conversation I tell myself, but she's so pretty, so intelligent, such a warm gentle woman that it strikes me how much I care for her. Did you ever meet a person that you liked instantly? No sooner did you lay eyes on her, you get the feeling, that intuition—call it just a hunch—but she's for you. You searched for so long this girl. Let her not slip away.

Although I can now remember that I had a great time simply talking with her, for the life of me, none of the specifics come to recall—with one exception; again she repeated that she's married, her husband, Gregory, being overseas in the Pacific, Army G-2 Intelligence or some support group. Bill, you lowly cad. Some poor damn G.I. slob in a foxhole getting his butt shot off by the Japs while you make time with his wife. Bill, you 4-F low-life! Another drink. It's casual, Bill, one drink causes no grief. Strictly platonic. And in many ways it is a platonic afternoon.

We discuss books and ideas with both of us pleased and receptive in the give and take of forging a friendship. She listens as I bore her with my writings. She even makes suggestions on how I should revise my stories. And as my attraction for her grows, I feel the defenses peal off layer upon layer like you'd peel an onion. So trusting of her, briefly I mention Nancy and Jimmy—very few people hear these thoughts.

She lightly touches my hand, "Oh, that must have been painful. I'm so sorry." Her sympathy is so genuine that I fight the urge to embrace her with gratitude. Like I said, that hunch tells you this is the girl. Hang on, Bill, the flicker of light reflecting off her wedding ring catches my eye—oh balls!

Another drink, my third, her second.

"This is the last," she says.

I change the subject, no mention of farewell. "How did you become so interested in books?"

She answered, "Well, when I was a child my dad had me read a few pages every night before bedtime; in fact, every week he'd take me to the library. I guess with that environment you'd either love books or hate them. I worked out well for me. I graduated from college but the war and marriage caught up. Now I'm a plain old working girl."

"Do you feel awkward with me—I mean, you're married?

"No, of course not, especially in my situation"—she abruptly stops, she says, "There's nothing wrong with talking. I can't live in a vacuum. It's difficult to find a person with mutual interests. Books and theatre. Things that interest me."

"Yes, sometimes in Danny's, when everybody's ranting and raving about baseball or football for three or four hours, I feel like screaming," I respond.

She finishes her drink. "I think it's time to go." She extends her hand. "Thank you very much. I really enjoyed myself."

Hang on, Bill, "Maybe another time?"

She hesitates. I blush. "I think I'd like that."

I push the issue. "Friday night? Eight o'clock?"

"Sure. But only casual, Bill. You understand."

I nod. Butterflies. So lighthearted I'd walk on air but a ton of guilt pulls at my leg. A husband G.I. in the fox hole. It's OK Bill. Ya, sure, you low life!

In fact, how easily we deceive ourselves when it's to our advantage.

All week long I anticipate the date as a kid would yearn for Christmas Eve or a circus. I borrow Booker's car, buy a new shirt, get a haircut, shine my shoes—only intellectual. I tell myself to be perfectly honest, a platonic evening is what I actually expected. Never did I expect the evening to turn out as it did.

A cool breeze and low clouds indicated rain or possible snow as I wait on the corner. Nervously, I check my watch—8:20—she's forgotten. Changed her mind? She's married. I stare down the street.

"Hi," a voice behind me. Her face, lightly flushed from the wind, beams at me. "Sorry I'm late. Had a few errands."

My relief breaks into a smile, that sensation you get when you take a risk and you win.

We go to a nightclub, Blinstibs over in Southie. A dance routine is top billing. Fairly good show, excellent food and an exceptionally enjoyable evening. Only one problem; time moves so quickly. At midnight Bernie lays her had on my forearm, squeezes softly. "Thank you, Bill."

The tone, the inflection, the gentle squeeze is so genuine. "It's been so long—so long since I've had such a delightful evening."

Her voice betrayed such a rooted sadness that for a moment, I thought she'd cry. Beneath her usually happy exterior, a serious problem pains her deeply, a problem I suspect that relates to her husband. The reason that I say this is because a few other times during the evening whenever she spoke of him, I detected a note of resignation—make the best out of a bad situation with the fatalistic acceptance of a stoic Roman senator. Duty first.

She sighs, "Is it my imagination, Bill, but why is it when you're enjoying yourself the hours fly like minutes, but when you're bored the minutes drag into hours?"

"I know what you mean." Meanwhile I ask myself what's bothering her? "Bernie, I sort of sense that something's bothering you. Is it us being out tonight?"

Somewhat surprised. "You're very sensitive, Bill. Very perceptive. I hadn't realized that it showed. Yes, there's a very serious situation that I have to live with. Possibly sometime I'll explain more, but not now Bill, please. You've been so nice to me and I've had such a wonderful evening, let's not discuss anything somber. OK?"

"OK by me."

A light covering of snow greets us as we cross the street, and when I see speeding headlights I encircle my arm around her shoulders to direct her. She responded by slipping my arm around her waist giving me a playful hug. We laugh, both high, full stomach, happy. Compulsively I lean over and kiss her. Soft moist lips, warm and tasting faintly of sweet fruit. She pushes against me hard and darts her tongue into my mouth. A car honks his horn. We pull away laughing. What a delicious free feeling euphoria. A wild joy rushes through your whole body; you ache, a happy ache—it's so hard to describe, but you know what I mean. It's so good you ask yourself, "Is this really happening?" Like a kid at Christmas overawed with a sparkling new bike. A squeal of joy. Flakes of wet snow melting on your face, a pleasant gust, you hold a magic girl, a comfortable buzz in your head—why must times like these end?

In the car, she snuggles close to the driver's side, staring at me straight on. Her hand rests on my shoulder, her fingers giving tiny massages. I kiss her lightly and she's warm and receptive and her coat is unbuttoned and this excites me. I smell a trace of perfume—sensuous. My hands run over her body, along her back at first, then her breasts and finally along her legs and under her dress to the top of her stockings—flesh. She rubs my thigh, presses against me as she gives me French kisses. Soft rustling of shifting clothes. No girdle and the pleasing touch of soft hair beneath her panties.

We ease down onto the seat and something in my head tells me this is unreal, an illusion, a dream! But she moans very quietly, and her tongue flicks in my ear. It's real! My pulse pounds in my head. My breath, fast and hot. Damn belt buckle. Easy zipper. No condom. Deep and full—so moist. Her leg wrap around and slowly we undulate. It's beautiful, incredibly beautiful. And no one could convince me otherwise. Two people enjoying love. And it's not just physical—in fact, I had too much to drink to orgasm, but it is still enjoyable. For those brief minutes there exists no such thing on earth as sorrow or pain or hurt; nothing but love and pleasure. I reach no physical orgasm but mentally, yes. Someone as wonderful as Bernie thinks enough of me to share love. The highest form of non verbal communication. And to know that she enjoys me, this excites me. Let's face it, I love sex any way I can get it. I'm only human. But when you have sex with someone you really care for, the joy, the orgasm, the thrill is increased ten fold. Sex is always good but with someone you love, it's another dimension like two parallel lines meeting at infinity.

"Feels so good," she whispers, almost a slight peek of delight.

A shudder, our breaths slow until there is no movement, no sound except for a periodic passing car. How tranquil. How peaceful, like all tension and cares were drained from your whole being. An empty bottle, a deflated balloon. Five minutes, ten minutes. A little chilly. The heat of the moment has been banked and with the cool solitude in my conscious a sense of guilt pervades. He husband overseas. Bill, you 4-F cad. A claw of responsibility grips you; no condom, no protection. Maybe a stiff dick has no conscience, but a soft one does. We rearrange ourselves. The silence produces friction.

"Bernie," I whisper, "In a way I'm sorry this happened. I mean I don't want to cause you problems . . ."

She interrupts, "Be happy, Bill, I am. And you can't cause me problems. Not with my husband. You see, this is the first sex I've had in years; in fact even if he were home we're not intimate. I've only made love with him a couple of times during our first year of marriage. Since then it's only been a marriage for show. We're both Catholics, so divorce is out of the question. And anyway it'll kill my parents if they knew it my marriage was sham. It's failed, Bill, even before it started but they're unaware."

"What do you mean, even before it started?"

"Except for my priest, I've never told anyone this story."

"What?" She tucks her head into the crook of my shoulder. Twice she begins to tell and twice she stops. My curiosity runs full peak.

"When I married Gregory, I was a very naive college graduate and he was a prince charming. A brilliant college professor, a few years older than me and very sophisticated. He was everything a girl dreams of; young, intelligent, kind, affluent—his father is a famous patent attorney in Washington. If anyone had the world by the ears, it was certainly Gregory. What a fine man. And it seemed that every interest I had, even he was so compatible—almost like a girlfriend. I guess, Bill, you'd say he was effeminate. He is probably the most gentle person I have ever met in my whole life. Even to this day. His face, even his hands were so gentle—his voice was soft and soothing. We'd joke about what a fine nurse or mother he would have made—little did I suspect." She looked up at me, ran her tongue nervously over her lips. "On our wedding night, naturally being both virgins, a couple would be somewhat apprehensive. Well if I were nervous, he was petrified, shaking all over. He was so afraid that he actually became ill. Vomit and all. I assumed that most of his condition was due to the excitement of the ceremony. But it wasn't. He was afraid of me—sexually. He felt so guilty. Even disgusted. It was horrible! If you could have seen the pain, the nausea all over his face as he went through the motions—Oh God!" She actually shivered. "I tried to understand. I begged with him to let me help him, overcome whatever was bothering him. We had a lifetime to live. But he said nothing. He slammed his eyes shut and froze in the fetal position until the next morning. Finally he tried to explain that somehow he was different from most men. As a little boy he seldom played rough sports; he preferred being with girls with whom he felt comfortable. And as he unfolded the stories about bullies picking on him and being afraid to undress in gym, I began to piece together a puzzle.

Slowly the realization sunk in. At first I wanted to die, shrivel up and disappear from the face of the earth. Then I told myself it couldn't be true. In fact, no matter what my ears heard I refused—absolutely refused—to believe what he hinted. You read about the Greeks and Spartans and Caesar but never . . ." She was crying now and shivering so much I wrapped my topcoat around her.

"Why did he marry you?"

"Because he thought he could overcome his fears. After all, all of this was in the latent stage. I forced myself to believe it was a phobia that could be treated. I was like a girl who knowingly marries an alcoholic thinking that she'll change him. I learned the hard way. Never did I realize how deep Gregory's problem was. He tried. God knows I tried. Sex became a terrible ordeal for both of us, but I prayed he'd overcome his fears. And there were actually times when I thought he enjoyed me. But he was pretending. The final realization occurred one day that I left work early. I discovered him in bed with a young student—a male. Oh God, it was awful!" She continued, "I tried to understand why? Was it me? Was I less of a woman? It was like trying to understand "infinity" or the concept "God always was." Finally I had to speak with someone no matter how embarrassing for me. So I went to a priest, a thin Scottish priest with the compassion of a Calvinist. Never divorce, he told me, or you'll be damned to the fires of eternal damnation. It was obvious he knew less about homosexuality than I did, because he scolded me and told me I was to blame. It was my fault and I couldn't perform my duties. If I were understanding and helpful, then there would be no problem. Of course I ran from the rectory in tears."

I asked, "Why didn't you separate?"

"My parents, his parents. Outwardly our marriage seemed perfect. How do you explain your husband is homosexual, especially to his father, an all-American tackle? No, the only solution seemed to be a compromise. We lived as brother and sister."

"Oh!" I say, almost a groan.

"No, it worked out. We both lead our own lives. Gregory's a good companion, a good provider, a wonderful husband in everything except sex. I accept him for what he is, and he reciprocates.

Often he's told me to date men if I wished. Every letter he mentions that I should enjoy myself. But, until tonight, I've been faithful. Whoever said that truth is stranger than fiction was certainly right. So you see Bill, you won't cause any problems for me. If I were truly married, we could be friends, but we wouldn't have gone out for a date."

I say little. "I'm sorry, I'm . . ." I stammer. "You should get a divorce. It's not fair."

"It is not possible. How could I ever explain? It would destroy everyone. Excommunication. I just can't."

As I said, I never expected the evening to end with this for a ending.

A week passes and I still doubt what happened. Making love and listening to her incredible story and living with my conscience. Bill, how low can you be?

A nice girl. You pump her full of liquor then make love to her in the car. And her husband, queer or not, stuck in a godforsaken jungle. You 4-F so and so! Do the right thing. Cross her off. Vow never to see her again. Have respect for her and her reputation. Sooner or later you'd cause her heartache. If you really care for her, you'll drop her. Send her a note, explain that you think she's a beautiful person but termination is the wisest approach.

All week a cloak of depression hangs over me. Forget the guilt, I've got to see her again! I can't call, she has no phone. Can't contact work, too suspicious. I'll leave a note in her mailbox.

The phone rings in Danny's the next morning.

"Hi." A tingle. It's her!

We meet for lunch and another lunch and a movie and a number of walks that blend into a full blown affair. Even though I hurt with guilt, I love her. How can you stop with such an emotion? When you love someone you love them regardless of the circumstances, and it's so easy to rationalize. It's oh so simple to dismiss her marriage because her husband is homosexual. Well maybe not quite so simple, but attainable. My logic tells me that only heartache and hurt wait downstream. Even so, I love her and I plunge headlong, forget about tomorrow. The guilt subsides. And with each date, I love her more, like a drug addict who builds up a tolerance and then requires a higher dosage of morphine. Without her, I suffer withdrawal—and with her—I can't get enough. Yes, I'm in love and I'm hurting.

A Year With Bernie

December 1944

For over a year, Bernie and I have all but lived together and if I loved her before, now scarcely could I imagine life without her—like my limbs or even my breathing so much is she a part of me. I tell myself that, I'd love to marry her—I will never give her up! But I must, someday. But not today. Yes, today she's mine.

My feelings are probably less passionate but definitely more tenacious like the roots of a tree nurturing, gaining strength and stability. No hour passes that I don't think of her, ache for her. Yes, like being sucked into a welcomed whirlpool, down deeper into the vortex of my innermost thoughts, I live in my solitary world—Jerry Collins talks to me for fifteen minutes—my part of the conversation is a collage of "Yahs—you don't say—really—is that right?" He might as well be speaking to the wall.

Forget about nightclubbing with Booker, or the ballgames, or the prizefights with the guys from Danny's, or the 'tracks. I'd choose her delightful company any day of the week. Every free hour belongs to her. Plays, movies, dinners, the beaches on Cape Cod, the White Mountains of New Hampshire—with Bernie I've enjoyed some of the happiest moments of my life. I'd confess that this past year has been the happiest of my life. Maybe it's the contrast with previous years, when I felt secluded or trapped, like a shaded plant dying because of lack of light. And she appeared as the warm May sun. Her smallest gestures touch me so. When she greets me, her smile and bright eyes, and the way she tells me she'd missed me—a thrill buzzes through me from head to toe. A happy boy greeted by his frolicking pup. If you could only feel the joy that she radiates, you'd be green with envy. No guy should be this lucky.

With Bernie the sex is beautiful, but in she's also a great friend—in the same category with Booker and Tommy O'Hara. I claim no other friends of this caliber. Sure there're plenty of acquaintances, including fine solid people, but scarce new friends, and Bernie leads the list. And that unfortunately, is a rare combination, a lover who's a good pal. A My Gal Sal—incidentally Sal was, in fact, a madam who aided the brother of Theodore Drieser (An American Tragedy). In gratitude, the brother wrote that song. Bernie told me that gem of trivia.

We can meet at 8:30 a.m. drive to New Hampshire, backpack to Cannon Mountain, picnic all afternoon, watch the sunset, and at midnight back to her apartment. I hate to see her leave. Time as swift as a flash of light, becomes a curse. I'm insatiable for more hours with her. She's magic. Sometimes I disbelieve that a woman, so pretty and intelligent, enjoys my company. In any case, Bernie is a treasure—a truly wonderful person. It's so pleasant to walk with her along a deserted beach at dawn listening to the tumbling waves slapping the sand. The taste of salt in your mouth and the tingle of dried salt on your skin we walk hand-in-hand and few words need be spoken. Or on a cliff, to watch the setting sun play a chord of blue-black shadows across the mountains, the erratic wind blasting and buffeting your body, your hair blowing furiously free, and your gasping breath challenging the gusts, arm around her waist and laughing. If only there was a machine or a sixth or seventh sense that could transform feelings into words! Metaphors frustrate me. Can you imagine what I feel?

And if the mountains and beaches are majestic, to be in bed with her is sheer ecstasy—and that word is by no means misused. Gentle, tender, sweet, soft, warm, moist, whisper—words to describe our love. How inadequate! How could I possibly explain making love, especially after the indescribable joy of climax when we embrace. Her head nested on my chest and in the vast sweet silence of true intimacy. If the genie would bless me one wish, it would be to stop time. Let me enjoy an infinity of peace and secrecy devoid of defenses and loneliness and masks of society's design, and all the accompanying tensions, prejudices, and fears. Yes genie, let me blend with this woman as though our flesh were a timeless exotic vapor. Why, genie, are you fantasy? A phantom who haunts my mind.

As we lay together, I explore the me of inside, the me of my childhood, and like unshelling the defenses of my upbringing, I discover, and because Bernie is the woman that she is, I tell her my thoughts, my deepest dreams and fears and glories—words that no one else has ever heard. And she smiles—she understands. A tiny squeeze of my arm, yes she understands. And she reciprocates and the soft words or the heart lead to whispers and kisses and love and whispers and love—for hours on end.

Sex is tender. Not only physical but mental. To think a woman would offer herself totally, so loving, so innocent and open. You try so hard to please her, and damn it excites me to see a glaze come over her eyes, to see her bite her bottom lip and tense her body until it actually quivers and "Oh, that feels so good." The outside world ceases to exist.

Two people escaping from an earth of war and hate and suffering. Two grains on a desert enjoying a fantastically precious moment in the agony of time in motion. How could this be wrong? Sure, by rule books, by the Church; by the vast herd jeering with uncompromising morality, we stand condemned. But I ask myself, is it sinful for two frail souls, to love each other, to gift each other with a joy and sweetness and a peace that neither could imagine possible?

I feel so wrong! Does a parchment, a ceremony really make the difference? I truly love her so. I see no wrong. But I feel guilty! And frustrated because I see no solution to my dilemma. Divorce? She'd never consent. And I too am a product of a Catholic upbringing. Excommunication and eternal damnation! But thankfully, the day of resolution has not yet arrived.

As Bernie so often says, "Love me now and let the river flow." But when she mentions plans for next year, I shudder. What will next year bring?

If only things were different. I'd marry her before the sun set. Whenever she mentions Gregory, I flush with a vague uneasiness—no, call it as you see it—guilt is what I experience. Bill! She's married! Skip the excuses. But the man's sick, a homosexual. A damn degenerate! The marriage is a sham! Please listen, Church bend the rules. Let her be free. I love her and my love is true. Never have I known such happiness—and equal misery. Never have I known such joy—and jealousy. Imagine me, dating a young married woman, me with no claims whatsoever, experiencing twinges of jealousy whenever Bernie mentions another man—how must Gregory feel? Does every Garden of Eden have a forbidden fruit? What is love? Does it always include hurt and worry and anguish and jealousy and possessiveness? The ambivalence of the anxious mother watching her child off for the first time, or the tearful father bidding farewell to his soldier son to a faraway war, or the pain of parents witnessing the dissolution of a daughter's marriage—Bernie's parents. Another source of guilt.

If I could care less for her, I could do the right thing; stop seeing her. But I love her. No letting go and even though pain waits for me around the corner I continue along, knowing damn well I'm going to be crushed. A helpless bystander tensing that instant before the hammer blow shatters the glass.

Well, as Bernie says, "Love me now, and let the river flow."

BERNIE

The End

AUGUST, 1945

I am stunned! I knew it would end! At least in the sense of a vague abstraction. But now a reality, so abrupt. Whack! A hammer smashes the glass and my life shatters into a jigsaw of fragments. Next week Bernie leaves. Gregory is going blind, a rare eye disease, his only hope is treatments at the Walter Reed Hospital. In any case at week's end, Bernie and her parents move to Washington, D.C. to be near him. I understand the situation; of course, I wholeheartedly agree that she must go. But understanding and agreeing takes away none of the pain. I actually feel sick to my stomach—that queasiness like you've been punched in the gut.

Damn! I'm so restless, so frustrated, like a caged panther at the zoo on a scorching hot day, pacing back and forth in his small cubicle and periodically roaring for the miles of free open land that you once had. I think of nothing but her—twenty-four hours a day. It's unreal. Nancy and Jimmy were so painful—beyond words. Their deaths had a permanency that forced me to accept the situation. With Bernie something could be done, but what? No easy answers. Indecision. No sleep. My insides feel overblown, packed tight, so over-pressured that I feel like I'll explode like a balloon. All because of one telephone call.

Bernie hits me straight on, "Bill, it's awful—Greg's going blind! Oh God—what a terrible thing—poor Greg! And me, me carrying on. Oh Bill, I love you," her voice cracked and I well imagined the tears, and her hands outstretched with emotion, "You know I love you Bill, but Greg needs me." Pause. "He's coming home next week. To Washington D.C.

The Army's got specialists there, the finest in the world. I've got to be with him. He'll need me now, more than ever."

A strange numbness shrouded me. And yet, I also felt somewhat of a relief, as though what I had dreaded for the past year had finally happened. It was over. Like the patient who fears an operation only to discover afterwards the anticipation is worse than the fact. What could I say? "Don't go because I love you?" Sure I loved her. I fail to imagine life without her but what other acceptable solution do we have? You tell me.

I feel so guilty—here I am living with a soldier's wife, and meanwhile he contracts an eye disease in Australia. The Army ships him home to the best medical treatment in the world. Naturally Bernie belongs at his side. Forget that he's homosexual—he's blind and he needs her. The situation is hopeless. I mean between Bernie and me. How often has she's told me, "Love me and let the river flow?"

And by the way, the river flows makes me believe that truth is certainly stranger than fiction. As I sit here writing, sometimes I panic, flushed face, wet palms and all. Other times I sit emotionless, a Roman stoic, a yoga dispassionately observing the events around him. Emotions or not, I'm losing the girl at the wrong time.

On Friday, she leaves. So little precious time remains. A few nights to be together. I shrink time, no longer in terms of weeks or months but in terms of hours, minutes, seconds. A condemned man gagging on a last meal and eternal hope of reprieve. No doubt about it, I'll miss her—the most compatible human being that I've ever known. So many things remain to be said and to be done. Books and walks and dates and conversations and even silence. There is so little time.

Tonight we rendezvous for the last time. A quiet dinner, that's all. The last time! Is it all a mirage? And worse, last night we made love for the last time. I measure everything in terms of the "last!" How awful a terminal patient or a condemned prisoner must feel; the last day, the last meal, the last visit, the last embrace, the last sunset, the last prayer, and finally last thought. Sure my situation is not a true death but, it hurts!

A quiet dinner. I forget what we ordered. Later, a silent walk along the Charles River. I doubt if either of us spoke two sentences. The sun set too quickly and I drive her home. Outside her apartment, I look into her sad but steady eyes.

"Bernie, I'll miss you. I'll miss you like I—" I never finished the sentence.

Her lips, compressed almost bloodless, move ever so slight as though she forced control. A few tears washed out of the corner of her eyes. Silently she squeezed my arm, still staring straight ahead, and saying nothing. A few tears, a million metaphors. I fill up.

"Don't—don't cry," I whisper, afraid my own voice would crack. "It's bad enough that you've got to leave but don't cry. Please." And even as I speak I feel my own tears. To cry in front of anyone else I'd cringe with embarrassment but with Bernie, it's OK. I love her so; anything was all right with her.

Bernie says nothing. More tears. The light from the lamp-posts reflect off the tears streaming down her face.

"Go Bernie! Go for our sake! You're killing me." I cry like a kid. "Go, will you. Please!" I actually push her away and she opens the door. I pull her back to me—half of me wants to let go, the other half just can't.

Damn.

Her face is wet, her nose is running and our kisses are a mixture of wetness and cries.

She holds me for a few seconds, her arms bear hugged around me, "I love you Bill. Goodbye, dear sweet, heart."

She disappears.

Dorchester Monthly Tribune

A community newsletter serving the Dorchester neighbourhood,

Peter Z's Print Shop
Bowdoin Street

Nagasaki – Second Atomic Bomb, August 9, 1945

JAPAN SURRENDERS

World War II Is Over

AUGUST 1945

It was officially announced—Japan surrendered, unconditionally.

Booker: "Bill, set up the house—all day! When the boys can't stand, then shut them off. Only local guys are welcomed. If the Charlestown or the

Mission Hill boys get word of this offer, they'll move down Bowdoin Street like a swarm of locusts chomping through the bounty. The bar would be dry within an hour."

Obviously, Booker was a little high, probably from the total excitement, pride, and happiness. He drank very little as a rule but today was very special. He clinked his glass with me, and said, "We beat the bastards—the Krauts and the Japs!"

Someone at the fire station at the Mather School set off the siren. God, what a racket! And of course, fireworks started in the late evening. Kids marching up and down the streets waving flags.

Iron Mike said that there would be a bonfire in Ronan Park tonight. It's odd but I am unhappy that I was not in the service. If I had served on guard duty at Commonwealth Pier, I would feel that I had done my share.

All along Bowdoin Street, the flags are waving—the mothers and fathers and wives—the faces all happy—their loved ones would return. "Thank you, Lord for returning my children." And on the radio, you can hear Kate Smith singing—"There'll be Blue Birds over the White Cliffs of Dover" and "Don't Sit Under the Apple Tree with Anyone Else But Me."

Iron Mike Kelly: "Isn't it great, Bill? I have my youngest one who is in the Navy. It'll be great to see him. Encourage him to go to college, or even maybe to join the force.

Bob McNamara: "None of my own kids are overseas, but I might l have 20 or 30 older students serving but I've lost track of them.

LEGENDS

The Boys We Know

SEPTEMBER 1946

"The Legend of Jesse James" plays at the Hamilton Theatre this week. Odd because during this past month, out of curiosity, I read about legends and myths and folktales. The folklorists define a legend as an oral story which is believed to be true by the teller. Length, language, or setting matter little. In fact, legendary touches upon all countries and cultures, and involve such disparate topics as religion and outlawry, actual heroics and the supernatural, greatness and the superfluous. Of course, we all know of Robin Hood, and Roland, and the Spartans—the more universal folktales. But we need no travel no further than our own shore line.

I'm sure that most of us who've attended St. Peter's Grammar School remember the religious legend which tells us that the Gypsies are cursed to roam the earth forever because one of them stole the nail, forged specifically to pierce the body of Christ during Crucifixion. Or which of us could forget the legends of how a boy or girl "heard" his (her) call to a vocation?

Show me a youngster who's never heard of the outlaws, Billy the Kid, Pretty Boy Floyd, Jesse James. (It seems that legendary outlaws are always kind to the old and infirm, always generous to the poor, always chivalrous to the female, always driven to crime by external factors beyond their control, and more often than not, betrayed by friends.)

And on foggy nights, do we sometimes recall the superstitious tale of the mother's ghost returned from the raging fire (runaway truck, swirling waters, collapsing roofs)? Or which city block is without a "haunted" house inhabited by that demented hag with a chin like an old slipper and a mystical black shawl, who mysteriously prowls the back yards at midnight?

And Hollywood propagates the heroic legend of that stout, loyal dog who unflinchingly sacrifices his life for the boy master.

Which of us has not seen pictures of the great Babe Ruth pointing to the centerfield bleaches—for all those wide-eyed crippled kids in the hospital? And how many times have we passed a massive construction site only to be informed, "There's a workman's body buried in that concrete piling?"

Yes, each section of the country, each neighborhood, and even each tavern claims their own special legends, Danny's being no exception. Sometimes there is raised a question about veracity, but then again I've heard particular stories repeated so often and so fervently that I'm confused about what's fact and what's fiction. However, because we're attempting to present a loose history, the legends below are undoubtedly true, and questionably Danny's is origin.

Other trivia involve Jerry Collins chug-a-lugging 2 quarts of beer in 3 minutes or the inspired tale of Booker hitting the numbers pool 3 days in a row—He also bet the lead number 3 which failed to run—for 143 consecutive days, a definite statistical freak.

But some of our legends challenge the best of them. When you read those documents about Danny Flynn and Iron Mike Kelly—these are real men! Each commendation is more than a sheet of paper; it represents an adventure, a legend. Danny's can boast not only physical heroics, but also legends of Bob McNamara and his intellect in engineering (before his alcohol problem). The physical bravery of Booker and Richie Quinn. And finally Chico's postcard—the subject of hours of discussion and guessing about his whereabouts, his reasons, his commitments.

Yes, Danny's can certainly brag of many unique individuals. Not all of their trials and tribulations are documented, but true nonetheless. And this holds true for groups of fellows too. Every tavern has certain cliques, trades, occupations: construction workers, police, firemen, truckies, etc. A great source of pride and cohesion for the individual members. A great well spring of legend—the old veterans ventilating to the rookie-apprentices about how tough the weather (the conditions, the men, the exposure) was 10-30-30—years ago. The old veterans reminiscing about "Big Joe" or "Tough Tom" or "Jack the Jaw"—"Those were real men in those days, son."

Let's look at some of these group legends. The roofers brag of the giant, Hawk Metz who shoveled 10 or 20 tons of gravel in 2 to 3 hours. Or Jake's crew who scratched, 4-plyed, and graveled 10,000 square of room in 101 degree F. (The numbers, in this particular case, vary dramatically in direct proportion to the beer consumed).

A favorite high-iron legend tells of Tonto, the MicMac Indian from Maine who, just before the lunch whistle, tumbled off an I-bean 120 feet above a slab on grade. Luckily he landed on packages of insulation which were stacked on the slab. Shaken but unbroken, he sauntered over to the Waldorf.

The fireman, good source of heroic folktales, boast of Joe Wilson, Engine 4, shimmying up a scorching piazza column to rescue a little girl from a flaming 3-decker—to this day, the crust of scar tissue prevents Joe from clenching his fists. Or Scotty who arrived first on the scene at the Coconut Grove disaster.

We could ramble on and on. The mailman repeat the legend of the lost checks; the taxi-drivers swear to God of the numerous propositions (always long, lean, lovely, and infinitely wealthy); Boston City Hall workers shed a tear when re-telling of James Michael Curley draping his expensive cashmere overcoat around the fragile shoulders of the City Hall scrub woman; the truckies speak of the crazed hitchhikers, escapees from prison (insane asylum, hospital). The MTA trolleyman recall the third rail legends or "jumpers"—people who jump/get pushed/fall into the train pit. Even the teacher's ponder about that legendary student Einstein who hung himself after exams. Yes, each group lays claim to their legends, big and small.

As Booker often remembers that many of the boys are exceptional—out in the work world when a danger is often a second away—police and fireman are obvious examples. But anyone in construction or who work around machinery or the public arena are at risk from a punch press crushing an arm, or shock from an exploding transformer, a burst high pressure steam line or an exploding boiler, a bucket of hot tar splash onto you from the roof or you trip and plummet ten stories, a brick or a beam falling from a roof could happen at any given moment. Going into a trench to lay a pipe has been the last act for some—Boss McDonough being a case in point. Even a safe clerk's job in a bank can have it's dangerous episodes—an angry customer with a weapon. Many times these situations form the topic of humor at the bar—as we all joke about our little bouts with fate—sad but true, sometimes they become reality.

They are all exceptional, claims Booker. All of Danny's boys are brave, loyal, committed to their family and friends, the backbone of a neighborhood.

But there is one group in Danny's that stands apart, I suppose in the way that cowboys differ from townspeople or farmers are as different as a diamond is from a rock. That group; the fisherman. The only ones in this block which deal exclusively with nature. There are no farmer's in Danny's. Even the Bible honors these men, "They that go down to the sea in ships, that do business in great waters. These see the works of the Lord, his wonders in the deep."

I would guess that more legends surround the fishermen, both individually and collectively than all occupations in Danny's taken together. Bill Morrissey's father grew up with the famed Howard Blackburn who was lost in a blizzard with his dory mate and rowed across miles of ocean under incredibly harsh conditions. Lashing winds and freezing waves smashed both men and boat. Weather so cold and treacherous that Blackburn froze his hands to the oars while his dory mate silently iced into a marble statue on the bow. He landed in Newfoundland, senseless and half-dead. However, under the care of an outport family he survived, but lost his fingers. After all of that, he later rowed the Atlantic Ocean in an open dory—twice—with only a big Newfoundland dog as his companion.

Yes, the fisherman stand a breed apart. I'm proud to know such fine men as Jack Walsh (one of the original names on the honor roll), Bernard Reilly, Kevin Hoban, Bill Morrissey, Herb Whitten, Jess Piercy, Roland Antle, and Bill Cuff. Solitary, provincial almost to the point of being unfriendly toward those who work ashore. Abrupt, coarse, rough, but honest, generous, proud and brave describe these souls. We see an individual man who strikes us as mean, petty, and tainted. One who in many a drunken stupor, take a header off the bar stool, but he's the exception. As a group, I respect the fisherman. Maybe because I've never shipped on a liner, let alone fished from a rusted tub. I hold them in awe. Certainly I must confess that my prejudice reveals itself because my father fished for our livelihood. I remember him as a big-strapping giant; gruff, severe, strict, no pal to a boy, but fair, decent and responsible. I suppose I respected him more than I loved him—no, that's not true—I did love him. He had gentle eyes, clear and deep as burnished glass a roughened face and hands, lean and grizzled as tough as crusted leather. He had a heavy voice, almost unnoticed because he spoke such few words. A series of grunts highlighted his diction. Vividly, I recall him hunched over the kitchen table, pipe in hand, patiently waiting for my mother to cook supper. I can smell the slabs of fried haddock, delicately browned in a frying pan full of crisp toasted blocks of salt pork. I hear the sizzling sound of frying fish—tiny furious splattering of fat. Ma cooks in one of those enormous black pans, and uses silver pot covers to mute the splatters. Gobs of butter, salt and pepper brown the fresh fish. My mouth waters.

I listen to Pa tell Ma about the "trip," Old Jim McDuff caught his arm in the winch—"tore it off right to the stump. Blood gushed out like a Joe-Jesus chicken with no head." He went on to explain with a collage of grunts and gestures how the Paddy Ryan, the cook, strapped a sack of flour to Jim's shoulder, thus stopping the bleeding. One day's voyage to a St. John's Hospital and Jim survived. The story concluded with "Mind ye, he'll be ashore for good now. With one flipper gone." Harsh, abrupt, unfair, but nonetheless a fact.

Or if the trip was a "broker," he'd swear, "By the Lawd God, I hope to see the day they'll pay a cursed dollar for a photograph of a cod."

Or after a merciless winter storm—"In a gale o'wind,"—his face wind burnt to a firehouse red, his knuckles and lips cracked from the frost, he'd talk of being routed at 2:00 a.m. to chop ice from the bridge with axes to prevent the trawlers from capsizing. "I tell ye, woman, took a bit o'bearin."

No wonder I held him in awe. And then one spring morning he "went out"—just another trip. He never returned. Like his father, lost at sea.

Each of these fishing men face the same uncertainties, the same brutal exposures. What motivates a man to fish, to freeze, to endure half the night on an icy deck, trawling, and hauling, and chopping? What type of man sets out to sea in the dead of January in a rusted boat that most people would consider less than worthy to cross the Charles River in June?

Let us analyze groups who work as fishermen and construction workers. What characteristics might we expect? With objectivity, we could guess; individuality, courage, pride, loyalty, generosity and uniqueness which apply to most of the tradesman who work in the elements.

Individuality. On a fishing boat, formal discipline and authority are virtually non-existent. Each man understands why he's there—to catch fish. Feast or famine, you're on your own. No walls, no clock, no 8:00 to 6:00. When it's time to haul in the nets, you haul in the nets. Typical comments that I've heard, "I'm me own man." "If'm I don't like the skipper, I'll catch me a site aboard 'nother boat." "Who needs a union, b'y? As long as a man does his job." "For the love of God, it's the only thing I know how to do. A man's bloody foolish to do this for a livin'. Mind ye, a life at sea is a life wasted." However, you sense a pride in their eyes—they are their own man.

Courage. Many occupations involve uncertainties; cops, fisherman, high iron, even bookies. But none face these uncertainties so consistently, so intensely as the fisherman. An icy deck, a missed footing and you're tumbled into the sea weighted down by oilskins. A buckled hull plate, a busted piston, a freak squall and the ship sinks. Even the pay remains an uncertainty. Only a brave man, one with faith, would dare take such risks to gamble with the tempest of the sea.

Pride. A quiet, fierce ingrained pride lives within them as though it were physical, like an arm, leg, or heart. Proud of their heritage of Newfoundland, Nova Scotia, Norway or Ireland. Proud of their skills, their endurance, their manner of harvesting bread, the challenge of the elements. Who else could coin a work, "angishore," to derisively describe those who work ashore (hang ashore). Although seldom braggarts, a fisherman walk with his his head high.

Loyalty. On a trip, each man has a job to do, each has a stake in the "catch", and each has responsibility for the success or failure. More importantly, a slacker, a coward, a misfit could cost the life of a mate. Trust and loyalty mean the same to the men, to the boat. These men eat, sleep, work, live, endure, challenge, suffer, rejoice, weep, even sometimes die together. Therefore loyalty and trust must be synonymous. And there's no one tighter than a shipmate; if he states **it is so**, you can be sure **it is so.**

Generosity. An absolute rule. If one comes up short, whether gear, cigarettes, or money, one would expect a shipmate to assist. It has been said that a mate never refused to help unless he wanted to insult someone.

Uniqueness. In looks, speech, sayings and songs, origin, work equipment, superstitions, fisherman are unique. On the coldest days, look for men with open jackets and rough gloveless hands, men with reddened faces, and that certain strut. Whereas policeman and fireman dresses in uniforms and badges, the fisherman wears his uniform of oilskins, and rippers (knives to gut the fish). Listen for words like "turrible, worrold, catched, lops, squish, truck." Listen for the sayings such as "a red dawn is a sign of rain, b'y." Or "When the gulls fly high, expect a storm." Listen for the songs, "I's the b'y, or Jack was Every Inch a Sailor" or the tap-dancing McNulty's. Find men from such places like Misery Point, Bread Island, Ha-Ha Bay, Fogo Island, and Cape Broyle. Seek out not roofers who use "scratch bars" and "hots", but men who work with "rippers, dories, nets, helms, gripes and cod, and haddock, and useless skates and dogfish." Search, not for men who ride the trucks, Fords or Buick's, but men who ride draggers named, "The Breeze," "The Ripple," The Spray," to places like "George's Bank," and "Sable Island," (the Graveyard of the Atlantic). These are fishermen.

And where the boys of Danny's tell folktales, the fisherman outdo all legends. On a warm day, William Lee fell out of his dory, and under the weight of his oilskins, sunk like a rock. Luckily he grabbed his trawl line and hauled himself hand over hand from fifteen feet underwater. What went through his mind? "Well, by Jaysus, I froze all winter, I'll be darned if I'd drown in summer."

There's also the story of Bill Cuff who upon first seeing the bunks on a new boat remarked that they looked like coffins. On the first trip, the ship disappeared—lost with all hands.

Jess Piercy turned down a berth on a ship because his mother dreamt that she saw him dead on ice. That ship?—the Titanic.

Roland Antle, while fishing off George's Banks, picked up a dog swimming, the crew all but mutinied; they swore the dog was a bad omen. However, on the following night in a wall of fog, Roland stood watch at the helm. The fog was so thick he couldn't see the bow. For horns echoed from all directions. Suddenly the dog barked, and pulled at his arm. Roland wheeled to port barely in time to miss a large freighter.

Yes, the fisherman stands alone, and their stories compete with the best. But for sheer savagery, for the ultimate of human courage and endurance against the cruelties and calamities of a roaring blizzard on a remote ice float, the greatest legend concerns Jack Walsh who, at nineteen, survived a sealing disaster in 1916. I was privileged to hear his account first hand.

Our legends range from the minute and the ridiculous, to the great, possibly gallant enough to challenge an epic.

Jerry Leaves Danny's

July 18, 1948

It all began with Jerry's comments as he stumbled out of the lavatory. He had snoozed away the night in the under the shrubs in the side alley.

His clothes were filthy and his flannel shirt was covered with burrs and dirt. His body gave off an odor of stale beer and body odor. His face is crimson—he'd been vomiting until his eyes protruded unnaturally. For a moment I thought he would faint. So help me, he reminded me of the character from a carnival in a low budget 1940's movie starring Tyrone Power.

Unshaven and shaking he pleads to Booker and me, "I've had it guys, my whole life feels like nothing but dust. Meaningless. My time in India with the British Army—did I really live it or is was it a dream? I don't know what's up or down. My marriage to Aggie who stuck by me all those years—now gone. Poof! My kids, my job—all gone because of booze. I'm at the end. I need a bottle of the hard stuff. No beer for me."

I answer, "You know, Jerry, I love you like a brother. But don't you agree that the hair of the dog that's biting you is now consuming you?"

Booker adds, "For God's sake man, we're really worried about you! Goddammit, Jerry, you're not a kid anymore. You got to start taking care of yourself. Why are you sleeping out in the alley? If you need money—tell me—we'll take care of you!"

A look of raw anger crosses Jerry's face. "Hold on, guys! Don't judge me or condemn me yet."

Booker puts his hand on Jerry's shoulder. "Jerry, if I didn't care for you, I'd be quiet. But I do care for you—both of us want to help." Jerry pulls away as if Booker's hand was charged with electricity.

"Jerry, I've had my battle with the booze as you well know—with Nancy's death and the baby. I didn't see the light but I felt the heat I got help from AA—look man, you can too."

Booker pipes up. "I know a fellow in Charlestown who can help you out. This guy is a priest and an AA member. A good man. Let me give him a shout. All I ask is that you listen to what he has to say. OK?"

In a huff, Jerry left the bar, "Screw you—both of you! I don't need no Alcoholics Anonymous baloney. I need a drink."

He slammed the front door so hard the window in the center of the door broke and shattered to the floor.

In the corner of the bar, Dinty hid under the table.

Later I speak with Booker, "Jerry's all screwed up.You know Booker, you have a knack of helping people see the light. I swear that you would have been a great gospel preacher. You have that magic to show people the way. For God's sake, you set me straight! I just didn't care about anything except alcohol. One drink is too many and 10,000 isn't enough. Jerry's a good guy. He's a great comic and maybe it's true that comedians are really suffering inside. See what you do for him."

I don't know what exactly Booker did, but I knew he did his utmost to put Jerry on the right path. Jerry stopped coming to the bar. First a day, then a week, a month, six months—no Jerry. Many of the boys asked if he was drinking in another bar.

God, I missed Jerry and his jokes at Danny's. And so the years pass on.

PRINTER—A FATHER'S LAMENT

1948 World Series of the Century
Boston Red Sox versus Boston Braves—almost

Boston Baseball fans were in a state of ecstasy!

The Braves had locked up the National League Pennant title. On the last day of the American League season the Red Sox beat the Yankees, and the Cleveland Indians lost to the Detroit Tigers. The result—a playoff game in Boston between the Sox and the Indians would determine who would battle the Braves in the World Series. Imagine two Boston teams in the World Series!

The game: Denny Galehouse would pitch for the Red Sox; Gene Beardon, a knuckleballer, would pitch for the Indians.

Booker: The night before asks, "I wonder how much the scalpers will get for a couple of tickets?"

Peter Z: "A pretty penny, I bet. You know Booker, I've been a Red Sox fan all of my life and to have a World Series between the two Boston teams would be a lifelong dream. We'll never have an opportunity like this in 100 years. But there is always a fly in the ointment. My youngest son is an avid Indians fan—how this came to be is a mystery to me. The boy, Tom, is thirteen and being an outcast with respect to his choice of cheering for the Indians has set him up to brutal teasing from his friends in St. Peter's. God, I've had groups of kids knocking on the door teasing him. Tommy is in his room crying. Well, I don't know what the outcome will be, but tomorrow, I'll be up and about Fenway to score a couple of tickets—scalpers or not. Of course, I'd love to see the Red Sox win, but my kid's happiness counts more. Whatever happens, I'll make sure that my kid and his older sister at least see the game.

The Game Results: Indians beat the Red Sox 8 to 3.

Lou Boudreau hit 2 homers and Kenny Keltner smacked the ball all around Fenway Park. A solid Indian win.

Next day Peter Z's down in the dumps. But his kid, Tom was overjoyed. When he walked into St. Peter's schoolyard the next day, all of his teaser friends were silent. "I felt like Caesar returning to Rome after his victory in Gaul," was Tom's response.

Peter smiled and shook his head. "It ain't easy being a father."

WHERE IS RICHIE QUINN?

Names from the Past: Richie Quinn, Chico, and Bill Morrissey

MARCH 17, 1947

Shouts, swears, drunks, fights—"Ye narrowback bastard, take that!" Another St. Patrick's Day in Danny's. My head splits as the bar is swamped by a mob of misfits wearing green hats and shamrocks, and shouting "Erin Go Bragh" and "Bold O'Donahue." I may seem overly caustic, but when you tend bar your enthusiasm quickly attenuates during holiday celebrations especially when you must endure the festivities as a sober spectator. I mean, how much baloney can a bartender endure? For example, propped at the bar, old man Mulrooney who looks like Abe Lincoln with DT's, sighs philosophically as though the world breathlessly awaits his message, "An Irishman is many things." Without sounding unduly critical I'm sure that my definition of "many things" differs dramatically than Mulrooney's.

However, this year provided a special treat; Richie Quinn rode the lead limousine in the St. Patrick's Parade over in Southie. Decorated paratrooper, 82nd Airborne Division, 3 combat jumps, Bronze Star, Purple Heart with an oak leaf cluster—a hero by any measure. But dearly did Richie pay the price.

"Useta be a great fighter, that Richie," Red tells young Bob Hall. "But he's all shot now, his nerves you know. Caught a piece of shrapnel in the squash." Red taps his head. "You know what I hear? I hear that he got it on the left side of his head, and because of it, he drags his right leg. Sounds crazy, don't it but that's what I hear. The docs at the V.A. been working on Richie for over two years but he ain't never gonna be the same. His hands are so shaky he can't even hold a glass of water. Damn shakes, he's worse than Jerry Collins."

Poor Richie. The best boxer, great baseball pitcher by far the greatest athlete the block ever produced. A legend, come and gone.

Well, anyway the mob fizzles out until at supper-time only a few of the regulars remain. It's been a long day so I break a self-imposed rule (draw a beer) and join in the bull session, reminiscing about Richie, Joe Scarletta, and Blackie Hession and all the different guys that come and go in tavern legendary.

"Hey, Bill," asks Red, "Ya remember that sailor, Chico? Ya ever hear from him?"

Chico—that's surely a name from the past. Chico. A red? A savior? Soldier of Fortune? Who can read motives?" A real nomad.

"No," I answer, "Last I heard was that postcard from Spain. Something about he was a machine gunner with the Lincoln Brigade. That must be ten years ago."

Obviously Chico was committed to the peasants of the world—the oppressed. But he had two consuming passions—booze and probably more so, gambling. Every year he shipped out for six or seven months. And it seemed like the summer was the proper time to blow it all—good times with drinking, horses at Suffolk, and dogs at Wonderland or anywhere else there was a race or something to bet on. Maybe women was another passion but Chico never discussed that with me.

One time Chico told me that he met a Korean deckhand who could not speak English very well. So Chico taught him some English and how to play poker. Before the trip was over the Korean won all of Chico's pay.

"Say, what ever happened to that Bill Morrissey?" asked Red Driscoll, the artist in Danny's. Ya remember he wanted to buy the caul when my kid was born? Said that if a seamen wears it around his neck, he'll never drown. What a lot of crap! Them Newfoundlanders are sure a superstitious bunch."

Bill Morrissey, another name from the past. In fact, it was Bill who brought in the giant lobster claw which decorates the wall. The last I saw of Bill was during the War when he returned to Newfoundland to help out at home and to join the Canadian Navy. Yes, Bill Morrissey, a warm gentle man and the perfect stoic.

At the mention of Morrissey's name, Booker chimed in, and told the story of Bill, drunk as a skunk staggering out onto the street and getting knocked ass over teakettle by a car, causing a deep gash on the crown of his head. Booker drove him to the emergency room in the City Hospital.

The intern who examined Bill prepared a shot of Novocain. Then Bill saw the needle he said. "No bye! Get that thing outta me sight—just sew me up."

Booker never saw the likes of it. Bill shut his eyes and did not utter a sound. "If I didn't see it myself, I never would have believed it."

APRIL 1, 1947

Speak of the devil and soon he appears. Today who should amble in through the doors, but none other than Bill Morrissey.

"How's the bye, Mr. Flynn," he greets as though his absence were but a few days let alone a five year odyssey.

He changed little, maybe a few more wrinkles but I can seldom guess the ages of men exposed to wind and sun. Actually he remains as I remember him. light brown hair, parted in the center, and very dry as though it were dusted with a fine powder. His skin probably sensitive and light in youth, now is leathery and speckled with the long-ago freckles camouflaged into the roughened texture. And as we shake, I remember his hard hands, almost as tough as the claw on the wall. Years of smoking Camels have browned and yellowed his fingers. Whenever Billy drank too much, first he'd laugh into his hands and utter incoherent words then he'd just fall asleep.

"I see me lobster claw's still on the bulkhead. Let's have us byes a round of beers. C'mon Booker."

"What the hell, where've ya been?"

As Bill explains, he's certainly "knocked about." First he returned to Newfoundland to help out "me ol'man. As a reward for his assistance "me ol'man gave me the four God forsaken compass points of the earth to earn a livin'. He fished, lumberjacked, "tramped about the wurrold and all that truck." When the war broke out, he joined the British Navy "took the shillings as me uncle useta say" and made the Mermansk Run on a Limey minesweeper."

"I'm back to stay this time, byes. Ye can bet yer bottom dollar on that. Gonna get me papers in the Fisherman's Union, I am, and me citizen's papers right off. This country, tis a grand place fer a feller to make a livin' north, south, east and west—It's all yours son. Let me tell ya buckos I was on that run up to Russia, a place called Archangel. God that's a right pitiful place. Cold and as bleak as ever a man laid his eyes on. And them poor Ruskie devils, woman and all unloadin' the cargo and eatin' nothing but turnips. Terrible place, no lie. As soon as we'd unload, we'd fly the hell out of there. No bye, I know'd a good place when I sees it, and Boston's the finest kind.

Bill empties a few beers; sits on the chair reversed; jaws with Booker and me and some of the older guys. So much does the scene, the comradery remind me of Red's sketch, 1936 or thereabouts. Over ten years ago. Where does time go? And Bill drinks and laughs incoherently into his hands. He gets warm and peacefully falls asleep. Another lost soul returned. Do things really change or do we live in cycles? I wonder if Chico will return?

ODDS AND ENDS

War is Over—1945
Heard at the Bar

A Navy veteran from Ohio, Joe Lesh, USN: "I've spent 3 years down around the fish pier—near Castle Island. It was my duty for three years—sort of a waste. I want to move on with my life. Go to college—get a trade—anything that moves me forward. Get married, have kids, raise a family . . .

Ira Gold—Attorney: "It's a great time for the veterans—well deserved for sure. For those who are so motivated, this is a great opportunity for the folks who served—the G.I. Bill. Go to college—get a profession—Doctors, lawyers; business owners.

"For the Boston labor population before the war, college was out of reach for most workers. But in the future, thousands of workers will use college degrees as launching points into professional activities. Of course the government will have many benefits to offer—buying homes, veteran's benefits, Civil Service competitive exams will have veteran's preferences—police, fire, city, state and federal careers. Dorchester will change. I'm sure veterans will spread out north, south, east and west to the suburbs. Houses will need to be constructed—whole tracts of homes. Roads and railroad tracks will be built. Autos and trains will become a necessity. The world is changing—pay attention—and plan and invest wisely."

Shot Gun Wedding

"Well, I'll tell you, Bill. That Mary Smith is pregnant—at least that's what her father told me. And you can bet a gold doubloon that the old man and her brothers are trying to catch up with the snake to make him do the right thing. Father O'Brien is supporting the decent responsibility."

20 Minute Hero
June 6, 1949

The roofers are acting up—it's been raining off and on all day. So the boys knocked off work early. Half the crew head to a bar—in this case, Danny's is the prime destination. It's early enough so that the boys get home in time for supper—if it was a really nasty day the crew would hit the bar at 10:00 a.m. Then boys would be crawling up the stairs at suppertime. If the weather is bad for days, they'd be sleeping in the weeds in the alley.

When the boys knock-off early in the morning, it will be a rough day all around. As only a bartender can know, where the beer flows, common sense takes a vacation. I've seen a dart game start at 10 a.m. or 11a.m and by 4:00 p.m., the roofers will be chasing one another around the place, using each other as the dart board.

On this particular morning it was the 5th anniversary of D-Day at Normandy, the crew foreman is a veteran of D-Day. One look at him—a big block of muscle—walks with a limp—reminds you of Lon Chaney in the Frankenstein movies. Definitely no one to mess with.

Now my curiosity got the best of me, especially where I have a "mildly" crushed foot from an elevator accident in Raymond's Sports Store in downtown Boston. I call to one of the younger fellows who frequent the place, "What's the story with the limp—roofing is not a trade that is compatible with an unsteady gait."

"You mean, Mackey, he was in Normandy, 2nd wave, stepped on a landmine and boom! Lost his foot. Trained with his outfit for 2 years and was in combat 20 minutes. Stepped on a mine but he didn't give up on life. He could outwork the whole union hall. As a foreman, he can be a son of a bitch but he can do the work and then some."

Some of his friends call him the "20 minute hero." Me, I really respect the man. He knows the business.

Gold Star

Down at Kane Square there is a small single family home near the trolley stop. The prominent feature of the home was a pennant hanging on the parlor window which indicated a person serving in the military. Of course there were quite a few pennants in windows throughout the city. Most of them had a blue star, a few had the gold star. This serviceman gave his life for his country. Whenever, I rode to trolley to Andrew Square, I would pass that home. I would think about the story behind the gold star. How many poor souls were affected? The mothers, the fathers, a curse to have an offspring die before you do. And to the mates and the children, a star to define words of grief. And the brothers and sisters. No benefits, that's for sure.

Dedication

Walsh Post 369
Dorchester, Massachusetts

William G. Walsh
Marine Gunnery Sergeant
Received the Medal of Honor Posthumously
For Sacrificing his life to save fellow Marines, during the Battle of Iwo Jima, 27 February, 1945.

Born: April 7, 1922
Roxbury, Massachusetts

Died: February 2, 1945 (age 22)
KIA on Iwo Jima
Place of Burial: Arlington National Cemetery

Letter from Jackie Dwyer from Hiroshima

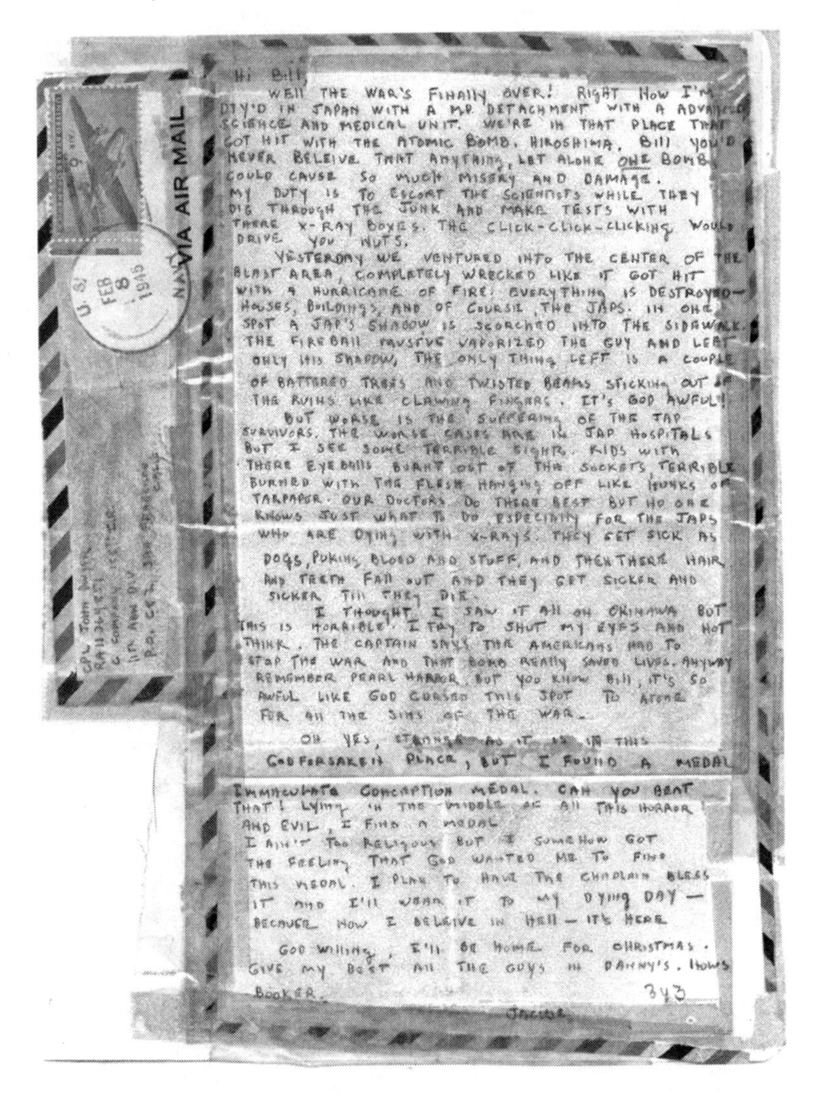

VIA AIR MAIL

NAVY

U.S. FEB 8 1946

HI BILL,

WELL THE WAR'S FINALLY OVER! RIGHT NOW I'M DTY'D IN JAPAN WITH A MP DETACHMENT WITH A ADVANCED SCIENCE AND MEDICAL UNIT. WE'RE IN THAT PLACE THAT GOT HIT WITH THE ATOMIC BOMB. HIROSHIMA. BILL YOU'D NEVER BELEIVE THAT ANYTHING, LET ALONE ONE BOMB COULD CAUSE SO MUCH MISERY AND DAMAGE.

MY DUTY IS TO ESCORT THE SCIENTISTS WHILE THEY DIG THROUGH THE JUNK AND MAKE TESTS WITH THERE X-RAY BOXES. THE CLICK-CLICK-CLICKING WOULD DRIVE YOU NUTS.

YESTERDAY WE VENTURED INTO THE CENTER OF THE BLAST AREA, COMPLETELY WRECKED LIKE IT GOT HIT WITH A HURRICANE OF FIRE. EVERYTHING IS DESTROYED— HOUSES, BUILDINGS, AND OF COURSE, THE JAPS. IN ONE SPOT A JAP'S SHADOW IS SCORCHED INTO THE SIDEWALK. THE FIREBALL MUSTVE VAPORIZED THE GUY AND LEFT ONLY HIS SHADOW, THE ONLY THING LEFT IS A COUPLE OF BATTERED TREES AND TWISTED BEAMS STICKING OUT OF THE RUINS LIKE CLAWING FINGERS. IT'S GOD AWFUL!

BUT WORSE IS THE SUFFERING OF THE JAP SURVIVORS. THE WORSE CASES ARE IN JAP HOSPITALS BUT I SEE SOME TERRIBLE SIGHTS. KIDS WITH THERE EYEBALLS BURNT OUT OF THE SOCKETS, TERRIBLE BURNED WITH THE FLESH HANGING OFF LIKE HUNKS OF TARPAPER. OUR DOCTORS DO THERE BEST BUT NO ONE KNOWS JUST WHAT TO DO ESPECIALLY FOR THE JAPS WHO ARE DYING WITH X-RAYS. THEY GET SICK AS DOGS, PUKING BLOOD AND STUFF, AND THEN THERE HAIR AND TEETH FALL OUT AND THEY GET SICKER AND SICKER TILL THEY DIE.

I THOUGHT I SAW IT ALL ON OKINAWA BUT THIS IS HORRIBLE. I TRY TO SHUT MY EYES AND NOT THINK. THE CAPTAIN SAYS THE AMERICANS HAD TO STOP THE WAR AND THAT BOMB REALLY SAVED LIVES. ANYWAY REMEMBER PEARL HARBOR, BUT YOU KNOW BILL, IT'S SO AWFUL LIKE GOD CURSED THIS SPOT TO ATONE FOR ALL THE SINS OF THE WAR.

OH YES, STRANGE AS IT IS IN THIS GODFORSAKEN PLACE, BUT I FOUND A MEDAL IMMACULATE CONCEPTION MEDAL. CAN YOU BEAT THAT! LYING IN THE MIDDLE OF ALL THIS HORROR AND EVIL, I FIND A MEDAL

I AIN'T TOO RELIGOUS BUT I SOMEHOW GOT THE FEELING THAT GOD WANTED ME TO FIND THIS MEDAL. I PLAN TO HAVE THE CHAPLAIN BLESS IT AND I'LL WEAR IT TO MY DYING DAY— BECAUSE NOW I BELEIVE IN HELL— IT'S HERE

GOD WILLING, I'LL BE HOME FOR CHRISTMAS. GIVE MY BEST ALL THE GUYS IN DANNY'S. HOWS BOOKER.

343

JACKIE

Bill's Stories Of Danny's Neighborhood

(Published in the Dorchester Monthly Tribune)

1. The Lesson From Charlie Loo, Laundryman

1942

Saturday is my best day. There's no school and I have a lot of fun playing kick the can or tag in the tree across the street. Old man Reilly owns the tree but most of the time he's too drunk to care. That's good because it's the only tree on the whole street.

In the afternoon Ma yells from the 3rd floor piazza, "Jackie! Bring Pa's shirts up to the Chink's!"

I'm in the tree and she can't see me. But she calls anyways. Her yell sounds all over the place so I can't make believe I don't hear her.

Billy Keough is on another branch and he asks, "What did you mother say?" It's funny but Billy can't understand Ma. He says she talks different. But I never notice it.

Ma spots me. "Come on now, boy" she calls. "Come down out of that tree, and get going."

When I'm on the sidewalk, Ma drops down Pa's dirty shirts, then a dollar wadded up with a pink laundry ticket. Most Saturdays I bring home a couple of clean shirts—Pa always wears a white shirt for Mass on Sunday. And most Saturdays Ma lets me keep a dime for myself. So I don't really mind going. But this Saturday even five dollars ain't enough. I'm scared to go near the Chink's—not after what Billy Keough did yesterday. Billy lives on the second floor in my house and he's in the second grade with me. On the way home from school yesterday, he wants to have some fun teasing the Chink. Billy don't go into Charlie Loo's laundry so he can tease him. Billy stops outside the window.

Inside Charlie is bent over, ironing a shirt, going a mile a minute and never stopping for nothing. Work. Work. Work. Charlie never stops working. Even once when Ma took me shopping late one Friday night, Charlie was still ironing and wrapping white shirts in brown paper—how come he never gets the shirts mixed up? That always puzzles me. They all look the same except for the marks on the collar. "P" goes on Pa's shirts—I don't see what the mark stands for. Well anyway, back to Billy. He stops outside and knocks on the plate glass. When Charlie looks up, Billy scrapes his front teeth with his fingernails. This is supposed to be a real bad swear in Chinese. Not like "ass" or "bitch" in American but a real bad one—like—well, never mind. I got mad at Billy. He knows I got to get Pa's shirts on Saturdays. And another thing I was mad about was that I sort of like Charlie. He don't bother anyone. He's all alone and he ain't got any friends to laugh with. Work. Work. Work. I feel sorry for him. Charlie looks away from us, and goes back to ironing. Then Billy really bangs the window. It almost broke. Now Charlie comes running outside. His face looks mean—and I'm not sure, I can never tell if he's mad or glad. We take off down the street. Charlie doesn't chase us even though Billy keeps yelling. "Chinkie-Chinkie Chinaman! Charlie Loo's the laundryman!"

Now you can see why I'm so scared to bring Pa's shirts up to the Chink's. He's going to blame me for what Billy did. It's a real hot day and I'm already sweating all over. All the way up to the laundry, Charlie's face sticks in my mind. Charlie's sort of old and he always had that kind of a grin on his face—not glad or sad, just in between. He looks just like one of those wise Chinese kings in pictures, only he ain't got a beard and he speaks good American—as good as me anyways. His eyes are just like two black aggies I use to own—jet black and glassy as a mirror. I never got close enough, but I bet I could see my face in his eyes. His hair is just as black but not shiny like licorice. And his skin is smooth, not wrinkly like Pa's. I don't know why people say Charlie is yellow. His color is more like butterscotch pudding. I can picture his smooth face crinkling up like a squash when I got into the laundry. Yelling at me. Yanking my hair like the Sisters in school—all because of that Billy Keough.

When I get near the laundry, my heart is banging like a drum. I have to go to the bathroom so bad my stomach hurts. I look at the laundry. The door is wide open because it's so hot and the Chink is alone, ironing away. I'm too scared to go in alone so I wait for a customer to go in first. Next to the store is a small field, full of broken bottles, cans, boxes and junk—nothing else. This is where I wait. Pretty soon who comes along but old man Reilly, drunk and weaving all over the sidewalk. He goes inside the laundry. What luck! I rush in after him.

Inside I can smell sweet meats and vegetables cooking in the back room. And the clean smell of starch and steam. The store is always so clean and neat. The smooth white shirts look like new snow. The clean brown paper packages are just like washed rocks on the beach. They're stacked on the shelves, and the paper is crisp and unwrinkled. Even the string is white and clean. Gold, pink, and orange laundry tickets are stuffed under the string.

I'm pretty nervous but Charlie doesn't even see me. He's watching Reilly who's ripped open a brown package and looking at his shirt.

"By the Lord Jesus!" Old man Reilly yells that when he's mad. "You lost my new shirt, you did! This ain't my shirt."

A dumb look comes over the Chink's face like he don't understand American. He shrugs and jabbers, "Hung-ching-koo-chuck," or something like that. It sounds real deep in his throat like he was trying to cough up a fishbone. I guess it must be Chinese but it's the first time I heard him speak it. But then again maybe Charlie didn't speak American when a shirt is lost.

"By the Lord Jesus!" Reilly swears again. "I've worn that new shirt just once. This ain't my shirt!"

Charlie points to the laundry mark. "Hung wing-koo-chuck."

Old man Reilly crushes up the shirt and goes to leave.

"Hi Mister Reilly," I say, then to Charlie, "Can I have Pa's shirts?" I throw the pink ticket and dollar. Back to Reilly, "How are you?" I try to keep Reilly inside until I can leave.

Old man Reilly doesn't answer me. Instead, he stumbles against the open door and almost falls on his face on the sidewalk. Now I'm alone with the Chink. I get ready to run if he tries to grab me.

But instead of yelling or tearing my hair Charlie hands me the shirts and change.

"So you know Mr. Reilly?"

"Ya," I answer, "He lives across the street from me." Since the door is open and since Charlie ain't mad, I ain't scared anymore. So I ask, "You lost Reilly's new shirt?"

Charlie shakes his head no. "Your neighbor seems to lose a new shirt every month. Maybe he should find a new laundry.

Charlie opens his hands. "Hung-wing-koo-chunk." Then he smiles—a real happy smile that I can understand. I can even see his gold tooth. Right away I feel bad for what Billy did.

"Charlie," I look down at the floor. My face gets hot but I don't have to go to the bathroom anymore. "I'm sorry about yesterday."

"You did nothing."

I finally peek at Charlie's face but it's the same puzzle as ever. He wraps P's dirty shirts into a ball and throws them into the dirty laundry basket which was almost full.

"How come," I ask, "you never get Pa's shirts mixed up?"

"The mark on the collar tells me who's shirt it is. It's a name that I can understand."

I walk outside. Charlie follows me.

"A beautiful day," he says, as he squints his eyes in the sun. The slits are no bigger than pencil lines. Then he looks at me.

"But all days are beautiful when you are young."

"Not rainy days," I say.

"Even then." His voice is low and far away I can hardly hear him.

I'm ready to leave when Charlie points to the small field, "Tell me what you see in the field."

I didn't see anything. For a minute I think he was just joking me with me. But his face was too serious. I look again.

"Tell me everything you see."

"Nothing," I said, "except for the busted glass, and those cardboard boxes, and them oil cans. That's all."

"Anything else?" Charlie took a couple steps until one foot was on the sidewalk and the other on the dirt, "look closely."

I looked and looked. "Some more cans and them clumps of grass. That's all I see."

"You see but you do not see," answered Charlie as he squatted down, and barely touched a flower—one of those yellow buttercups.

"Oh, that. That's only a buttercup. There's thousands of them all over the park."

"It is beautiful, is it not?"

"Ya, I guess so."

Charlie looks at me and his eyes are really glassy, almost like he was crying. But I know he wasn't. I don't think so, anyway. Then he whispers just loud enough so I can hear, "To be able to see beauty even in the ugly is a great gift. It takes years of work and patience. But to see beauty in the everyday common things is the greatest of all gifts. It requires a lifetime." Charlie straightens up. He stares into my eyes until I look away but I can't. "You are just a little boy and many years are before you. Maybe you do not understand my words now but someday you will. Each morning look for a small piece of beauty from things that are familiar to you, even if they are ugly. Look not only with your eyes but your ears and nose and hands. And if you do, everyday you will grow more and more into a man. This I tell you."

Without another work Charlie walked away.

All week long I looked. I don't see a buttercup the way that Charlie does. But I try and I see other things. The smell and feel of clean underwear, Pa's hands when he cuts the meat, even baby Mike laughing when Ma changes him. I still can't see a buttercup. But someday I will. I know I will.

Then on Saturday when I'm up in the tree I hear Ma. "Jackie!" "Jackie!" Bring Pa's shirt up to the Chink's!"

"He ain't a Chink, Ma! He's my friend, Charlie!"

2. A New Shop For Old Tony

1949

Even the oldest of the cronies in the cellar barber shop were unable to remember Old Tony ever to be a young man. It seemed as though the old shoemaker had been forever wrinkled, white-haired, and as permanent as the ancient red-brick tenement which housed his shoe shop. A gentle man at peace with himself, content with his craft, he sat hunched over his work bench near the window and painstakingly tapped tiny nails into an inverted shoe. His black-striped apron, pregnant with paraphernalia, sagged between his knees. Although none cared to notice, the scene was a magnificent example of a true craftsman at labor. His soft hair disheveled with the carelessness of concentration. His skin browned and toughened as the leather of his shoes. His hands, veined and steady as sure as a surgeons. His intense brown eyes reflecting his seventy-three years of life and faith.

Every now and then he glanced out at the passing faces, eager to greet a friend with a warm smile, "Alloo! Whay you say?" But today he saw no friends, only young strangers. Forty-two years ago he knew all the faces but not now. The young faces, hard, hurried and uncaring, drove nails into his loneliness. Nobody cared about him anymore, he told himself. Except for his big dog, he was alone. For many years now Rosa and Tony Jr. were dead, and so were most of his friends. He felt isolated from the people, insignificant as a hydrant. He was here and no one really noticed or cared until they needed his skills.

He stared at the empty tenements across the street. A year-old rumor claimed that the City Redevelopment Commission planned to tear down the block and build a six lane highway—directly through his shoe shop. That rumor had encouraged many families to move. He hoped that the rumor was false he had cemented himself and the shop to the sidewalk.

As the first rays of the morning sun shafted through the window, Old Tony notice the think layer of overnight dust on the display.

"You stupid. You forget to clean window," he criticized himself. "You forget everything these days." He limped into the back room which served as his living quarters, and returning with a ragged feather duster. He began his morning ritual, dusting the window display. First he carelessly fluffed that half of the window junk; stacked Cat's Paw soles and heels, overturned cans of shoe polish, entwined boot laces, and a remarkable array of abandoned shoes of varying fashions. Then to the other half of the display, Old Tony took special pains. Slowly and surely he dusted, first two pairs of beautifully polished boots followed by the stands on which they stood. Every Sunday, after his visit to Rosa's grave, he polished both pairs of boots.

Finished with his morning chores, the old shoemaker settled down to work—only two pairs of shoes to replace their soles and heels. Business was extremely poor these last few years. He adjusted the bench close to the window to get the light of the sun, and humming as soft tune, he shaved the leather.

The door opened. "Ting-Ting," the wine-glass bell rung. Gronquist, the owner of the tenement block, entered his heavy body filling the doorway.

Old Tony greeted him warmly, "Alloo! What you say?"

"Bad news, Tony," answered Gronquist, his voice as dingy and black as his outlook on life. His religion was money and nothing else. Deep in his black eyes glared the thoughts of rents and eviction notices. Yet, even though he and Old Tony were opposites, they got along very well, mostly because the shoemaker had something that Gronquist hoped was contagious—faith and peace of mind.

"You've got to give up the shop, Tony," said the owner leaning against the shoe-shine stand. "The Redevelopment Commission notified me this morning. If the mayor approves the plans today, I've got ninety days to clear out my buildings. Later on this morning we'll know for sure."

Old Tony set the shoe on the counter. For a few minutes he said nothing. The news was no shock, he felt the agony and fear of the dispossessed. No longer was he a young man easily adaptable to change. No, he was old and alone and very, very tired.

"Ninety day," he muttered and though it was ninety seconds. "That'sa too soon." Suddenly a comforting thought crossed his mind, and he said, "God will take care of Tony."

Gronquist stared into the old man's trusting eyes. Such blind faith, he thought. And although Gronquist was a cynic he could have wept for Old Tony's plight. Strange people, these old Catholics. The roof caves in and still they trust God. If only some religion could give me what he's got. Quickly he pushed the thoughts from his mind—they made his fierce monied life too sterile and barren.

"Listen Tony, have you ever thought of retiring? You could get by on Social Security. Anyway you're not making money here. On a pair of shoes you spend two or three hours, and then charge only three dollars. You lose money." From the acid expression on old Tony's face, Gronquist knew his words fell on deaf ears.

The old shoemaker was stubborn and proud, and even worse, the shop was all he had—his sole source of independence was his work. He knew no other life. "I like my work. No good for me lay around." Although he dreaded the future, he stubbornly announced, "I find new shop somewhere!"

Gronquist became irritated at the stubbornness. "But the repair business is dead now! Machines have seen to that. Anyway, people earn more now. When shoes get worn, they throw them away and buy a new pair."

"The olda the shoe, the better the fix," he answered with a truth from his trade. "Tony fix any shoe better than new."

"I know you're the best," agreed Gronquist. "I can remember when people came across town just to have you fix their shoes." His tone turned cold and logical. "But that was during the depression and the war—thirty and forty years ago. You've got to change with the times."

"You don't teach olda dogs new ways. I no retire!" He shook his raggy head with finality. No words would convince him to retire.

"Alright Tony, have it your way." Gronquist rested his hand on the old shoemakers's frail curved shoulder, and the sorrow he felt, he could not aptly into words. So he said, "I hope you don't lose your shop. I really hope the Mayor disapproves the plans, for your sake, not mine." He squeezed the shoulder slightly, wishing that the gesture would describe his emotion. Without another word Gronquist quickly walked out of the shop.

"Thanksa, John," old Tony mumbled after him. More than ever he appreciated the gesture, the concern—for too long he had lived alone in the rear of the shop with only his dog, Romeo, for a companion.

Old Tony returned to the shoe he was working on. Tip-tip-tip! His tiny hammer buried the nails into the leather, after which he brailled his fingers along the inside checking for burrs. As if solely by instinct he tapped and brailed, yet his mind was ninety days away. Dispossessed, jobless, homeless, because of a new highway. He felt like an old shoe at Easter, thrown aside for the new. He consoled himself that God would take care of him, and that change was life. The young replaced the old. New machines outdid nimbled men. Yes, change was the law of life, even so, change was what he wanted least, for age mellows not only the wine but also the spirit. Why must he lose his shop, he asked himself? Highways were no use to him.

The warmth of the sun lolled old Tony into a slight doze; these past weeks he was so lifeless and tired. His eyes stung slightly until the lids shaded down; his head bobbed lazily up and down. He dreamt that Rosa and Tony Jr. stood far away on a highway, and excitedly beckoned to him but he was barefoot and unable to move no matter how hard he struggled. The shoe slipped through his flexing fingers. Thud! The noise started him out of the frustrating dream. After shaking and stretching the sleepiness from his body, he finished repairing the shoe. Again the muffled dread of losing the shop drummed through him. To the Redevelopment Commission the shop meant little or nothing, but to him—he and his shop were fused one and inseparable.

In the window stood his most treasured possessions; a glittering pair of Army boots which had belonged to his son Tony Jr., killed on an unpronounceable Pacific atoll. How many thousands of sad evenings had he caressed those boots?

Alongside the Army boots stood the apex of Tony's craftsmanship. A strong solid pair of boots hand-made to rigid specifications for an explorer. Forty-two years before, on the very day he opened his shop, a stranger had paid in advance to have them made. These boots, the stranger explained, were needed for a long journey. With the infinite patience and skill of an artist, old Tony created a masterpiece. But for some unknown reason, the stranger never returned. So the old shoemaker displayed them—an example of Tony's quality workmanship. And through the years the shop he gave nothing but quality—all those years. In ninety days, the shop would be gone. Bulldozed. Why? Why!

Like a lost wet dog, the old shoemaker looked at his shop, now dark and dingy and idle. But in the old days, he remembered, scraps of leather and rubber and bent worn nails littered the floor; the air hung with the sweet smell of new leather and polishes; the shop hummed with tip-tip of his hammer, and the bir-r-r-r of the sewing machine. How happy he was—so long ago.

He ran his hand across the gnarled oily counter, and the two were so alike they were indistinguishable—grooved and worn smooth by a lifetime's labor. He reached up to the shelf and lightly touched the stack of repaired shoes; work boots and baby shoes. Old Tony always felt a deep pride when he repaired work boots. They had a sense of life and labor; they were tangible as a block of unsculptured granite. For children's shoes, the old shoemaker reserved a special spot. With the facility of a surgeon, he cut and sewed and molded them for comfort, for toughness and durability, yet with ample room for growth—young feet had such a long road to travel.

To Old Tony, shoes were not inanimate hunks of leather and glue and stitching. No, shoes had life. Shoes were like men; they were born, they were worn, and when they grew old and out-fashioned, they were sentenced to a forgotten box in the closet. Shoes had eyes which looked up to man, a tongue which comforted, and a soul which became a mirror of the owner's life. Shoes showed the equality of men but also their inherent individuality, and were often the mark of a man's character. Old Tony had spent a lifetime with shoes, and what had he to show for it? Nothing but a doomed shop, an unwanted trade, and a host of memories—mostly memories of Rosa and Tony Jr., a sharp ache of loneliness bit into him and for a minute he stood motionless, his mind prodding the past.

A scratching at the back door broke his reverie. Two more scratches, followed by an impatient bark. Opening the door, Old Tony smiled at the mongrel, a shaggy brown-black wanderer. Furiously whipping his tail, Romeo jumped and rebounded off the old shoemaker's thighs.

"Where you been for three day? You mal cane," mildly he scolded.

Romeo lowered his head, and rubbed an apology against Old Tony's weak legs.

"I know where you been, you little Romeo. Chasing all the lady dogs."

Romeo rubbed harder; whined lowly.

"When you are tired out and hungry, you come back to Tony for something to eat. But pretty soon there's no gonna be place to go. We both get thrown out into the street." Old Tony opened a can of Rival, and filled a saucer full of wine. No sooner had he set the food down, Romeo burrowed his nose in the meat, and wolfed it down.

"You musta have good time with the ladies. You don't find time to eat."

Finishing the meat with a lick of his chops, Romeo nuzzled up against the old man. Old Tony ruffled the dog's head tenderly, scratched behind his ears and under his neck and finally along his back and sides until Romeo's hind leg flexed in phase with the scratching.

"You poor dog. Don't worry. Tony always have food for you. Even out in the street. But maybe the Mayor no tear down my shop. Now you go to sleep in the corner. You looka tired."

Romeo snuggled into the corner, wedged his nose between his paws, and within a minute fell fast asleep.

Leaving the peaceful dog, Old Tony returned to his work bench where again he sunk into reveries. He thought of Rosa and their quick happy years of marriage and of their fine son. The proudest day of his life when he saw young Tony step up to the podium and receive his law degree. Old Tony's son was a lawyer—how the shoemaker bragged! Then came Pearl Harbor. Young Tony's first and last furlough was cut short, and in his hurry to report back to camp, he left his Army boots behind. Of course Old Tony repaired them to new. But no use. Even now his eyes watered as he remembered that terse telegram. A piece of him had died, not blood, bone or sinew, but within him. For any man who lives to see a son die also dies, but in the heart which is much crueler.

Shortly after the telegram Rosa became sick, a lingering painful illness of two years. Which pained her more, the cancer or her dead son, he often wondered. He did his best to save her, the finest of specialists, hospitals, day nurses, medicines. Money was no object so that quickly the savings dwindled. He sold their house; that money quickly disappeared. He borrowed and borrowed himself into a deep, deep pit until that night when Rosa quickly died. More of Old Tony died within. He was left alone with an enormous debt, yet he never complained, he never soured. God's will be done.

For five years he scrimped and scrounged until he paid off his debt. But once the debt was paid, his loneliness began to ache all the more. The loneliness was like a decayed tooth; some days it ached and tormented, other days nothing. But always the decayed tooth was present.

His business dwindled but not his magnificence. Life, he believed, had been good to him; he had loved and had known love. He had known contentment. And he accepted that all things born must come to pass. The aged would die, only to be replaced by babies. Yes, the new replaced the old. The highway would replace his shop. But fiercely did he wish his shop could be saved.

Finished with the shoe repairs, Old Tony searched for some job needing to be done. He disliked idleness. He swept the floor, oiled the machinery, arranged the polishes and laces. After which, he decided to soften and polish the explorer's boots. A quick strength came into his hands as he worked on them. How often had he wondered what had happened to that stranger who had ordered them? Where was he? Had he made the long journey?

"Ting-ting,' the bell toned the message.

Old Tony looked up at the young pink-faced man with insincere eyes.

"You Anthony Bacco?" he asked with a note of disdain.

"Thatsa me."

"Here." The man plopped a state-sealed document onto the counter. "It's a foreclosure notice. You've got ninety days."

"I don't want no paper! I want my shop!" it all seemed like a dream. They couldn't take his shop. Where would he go?

"Listen Pop, whether you like it or not, the highway's coming through here." He studied the meager ship and acidly said, "No one's going to miss this dump."

"You no take my shop!" shouted old Tony, his voice cracked.

Romeo darted from the back room, and for the first time since Old Tony found him, snarled. His ears lowered, his body crouched, his teeth menaced.

The young man ran out.

Thankfully, the old shoemaker patted the dog's head, then remorsefully stared out through the window. Forty-two years, six days a week, he had worked in this neighborhood. Another piece within him died.

Again he returned to the boots, softening and polishing until he became lost in a numbed panic. The work, the warm sun sapped his energy. The finished boots lay on his lap. He was so tired. So slowly he drifted from reality. His chin weakly nested on his chest, his mouth dried, his breath became short and soft. At first he was aware that Romeo tugged at his cuffs, but soon all awareness faded. In the far distance he heard a whine but that too faded. The sun darkened, and a wonderful sense of security overcame him. Suddenly an electric shock shot through him and before he realized what happened he was walking down a long road. Somehow the boots were on his feet. It was then he understood. With a smile, he journeyed to Rosa, to young Tony, to his new shop.

GRAFITTI

World War II is the most common theme of this decade

Men with short bats, stand close to the plate.

Kilroy was here.

This place is so cruddy that Kilroy wouldn't dare come in here.

What did the Englishmen say when he got circumcised
Good-bye old top.

I'll never get drunk again
Oh my head's full of pain
And it grieves me to think
That because of a drink
I slept with Betty Grable in vain

Remember Pearl Harbor (and Wake Island)

Marines at Wake Island in response to the query "Can we send you anything?" Send us more Japs!

Hang Tojo and Hitler

Scollay Square Sweethearts (TAL-44216)

What are you laughing for? The joke is in your hand.

A bird in the hand can be messy.

Bataan—Never Forget

Jim Morris
Army Air Corps
Brooklyn 1943

7/2/44 Dracula Drafted

Love thy neighbor, but don't get caught

No matter how you shake and dance, the last few drops go down your pants

What's the first thing the eskimos learn?
Don't eat yellow snow.

Eddie loves Mary
(*underneath*)
So doesn't Mary

A thing that should never be done at all
Is write your name on the shit house wall.

Free toilet paper. Compliments of Acme Sandpaper Company

Why take two, when one will do?
(*underneath*)
For gracious living

This is where Napoleon tore his Bonapante.

Death before Dishonor

Danny's—you don't buy the beer, you only rent it.

Bob Horgan eats meat on Friday

Please flush urinal, Germany needs the water

This is a teepee
For you to peepee
Not a wigwam
To beat your Tomtom

Mayor Kerrigan couldn't clean up the snow.
You expect him to clean up Boston's trash?

Number Play 207 101 1100 368 3/4/43
347

Harry's our Boy!

Why do humming birds hum?—Cuz they don't know the words.

New lollipop Lifesaver flavors—"Fruit of the Loom"

St. Patrick's Day Special: You can retrieve your personal effects at the police station.

Don't get depressed: you're not invited.

Did anyone leave their finger in the telephone coin return?

You know—"clean air smells funny"

Unleash Father Coughlin

I want to come back to Earth as a bug and bite everyone in the ass—Casey

(*underneath: Casey went to public school*)

The mirror in here lies.

Emily Dickenson needs a date for the Dorchester High School Prom—Suggestions? u*nderneath*: Rags Maloney u*nderneath*: Casey would be a great escort.

Kilroy was Queer—he wouldn't come in here.

The 1950's

Bill At 50 Years Old

Adjunct Teacher at Wentworth
Part-Time Bartender

January 3, 1950

This birthday brings the half century mark, 50 years old. Where did the years go? 50 years! How do I feel? Well, don't I feel different than I did at 40. Maybe it's because you age so gradually you seldom notice the slow down and new wrinkles. But when you see your friends, especially after a long absence, you perceive the results of the fleeting years. And now everyone seems so young; the rookie cops and fireman, the apprentices, the college kids—another reminder of my age. At times, I detect in some kids a resentment of me, because I'm "old." Like I can't follow a conversation or joke. I'm too old to appreciate life, love or what-have-you. Like a stranger to earth, a newly arrived Martian. Then again some young folks respect me, as though my years have nurtured worthwhile wisdom.

There are little clues tel me that I'm getting old. I now need my glasses to read the clock at the bar and after a busy day, the back of my right knee aches And a tell-tale sign, I have to get up many times in the night to urinate. And each winter, cold weather bothers me a little more. I sleep with another blanket on the bed at night.

Mentally, I feel as sharp as ever, my mind is always going. I'm not unhappy, but not ecstatic either. I am more accepting of things as they are. But I still want to fight the system. I still write, going for the big score, someday. That vague someday. But my somedays are now dwindling. I am 50 years old. I'm over the 2/3 mark with no chick or child. No family. That bothers the hell out of me. A few good friends like Booker. I tell myself not to think of Nancy and Jimmy. I get too depressed. Bernie. I wonder where she is now? Is she happy? Why do I think of her today? You know, every time I hear the song, "As Time Goes By" I think of her.

If only I could meet another woman like her. One that I'd be comfortable with, to pass the times with, do things together. Sure, Cathy's a good woman, a good date and the sex is good. But to live with? No. We're too set in our ways. She's too moody, too demanding.

Don't misinterpret this, Cathy's a fine woman, but I need a Bernie. A warm, quiet, loving woman who'd touch me and really show concern. Maybe I'm an insecure guy. I have to be reassured. Insecure, aren't we all?

I go to Copley Square but I don't feel like writing today. No urge. As though I'm coming off a bender.

Here I am, in one of the greatest libraries in the world, the Boston Public Library, surrounded by a million books and I don't feel like reading or writing. I browse the shelves, half-heartedly, and select a few books. I sit at a table and just stare out the window. Hot and humid inside. People look uncomfortable as their heavy winter clothes weigh them down.

My mind wanders. Think—do something! 50 years. 2/3 mark. Write something, even if it's gibberish. Rough out a story, a sketch, a conversation, a philosophy. Nothing comes to me.

You know, I use to love books about philosophy. Now they are too difficult to read. I use up too much energy when I have to concentrate. Plato? Philosophy, Faulkner, with his 213 word sentences—no way? I'm over the hill. You can't teach an old dog new tricks. That's stupid. As you age, philosophy should be all the more relevant.

Think of a good book. Quick. Of Mice and Men. Why did I choose that book? Cyrano de Bergerac. Moby Dick, 1984, Studs Lonigen—how I loved that story in my younger days. Farrell at his best.

Can't concentrate today. I let my thoughts float into a stream of consciousness.

If only I were a published author with loads of money. If I were rich I could do as I wished!

Which is . . . ?

I would travel. Over the years, I have traveled extensively. With summers off from school and my work at the bar is flexible.

I would go to Greece, Ireland, China, Australia. I'd go on safari. Form an expedition. Ship out, like O'Neil, "Bound East of Cardiff." See the world, the seas and mountains and peoples. Caress beautiful women with inviting white thighs, laughing eyes, and full moist lips. Or as many authors say, sparkling eyes and cherry lips and milky smooth skin and soft melon breasts. Drink the sweetest of wines. Feast and, most of all, laugh and be happy. Live.

Live? What do you mean?

Live! You know, be happy and content.

Bill, happiness is in your head. It's all in your head—tending to your own garden and not envying another's. An aborigine in a godforsaken desert, gnawing on a raw lizard may be happier than J.P. Getty consuming a ten course dinner. Yes, Bill, happiness and contentment are in your head.

Sure I know the grass is always greener. But some men live such full lives. That's happiness!

Is it? You want to travel Bill? Well for God's sake, go ahead! Take off! You're free, white and over twenty one! Got twelve hundred dollars in the bank. Quit work. Booker'd take you back. Hike in Greece and Ireland. Hobo around for a year. Join the Merchant Marine.

I can't.

What's stopping you?

Because, because I'm afraid. You see, I'm a dreamer. Wait a few minutes and I'll give you a better, a more rational answer.

To hell with baloney reasons, Bill! Whatever's inside your head is your own creation. Only you can change it—or accept it. One or the other. An eternal malcontent. The solution is in your head. Inside—certainly not outside. Outside you live in the greatest country in history. Secure, plenty to eat, good job, a bank account, a few solid friends. Why this discontent? What do you want from life?

Everything, Everything! The wine, women, and song! The glory, the immortality, the adventure—I've worked so damn hard, writing at two and three in the morning. So damn hard. Didn't the Sisters at St. Peter's tell me that hard work would be rewarded.

Bill, Bill, that's nonsense! If you born a Rothschild you could buy a publishing company and print up a million copies. But you're not a Rothschild. You're a Flynn. A guy with little talent and unrealistic goals and that combination equals misery. Shoot for the moon only if you've got the goods that sell. Real life is full of inequities. There are rocks and hard places, and the school of hard knocks. Editors could care less about labor pains; they want to see the baby. If you truly possessed the gift, you'd already be rich and famous. So lower you goals. Lay back and enjoy the years. Why always fight life and the system? Turn on the ball game. Stop thinking about it all.

No! The goals remain the same. Even if I fail, even it hurts, I'll still try to reach my ring—maybe in the final analysis that's what life's all about. Stop!

Why is it every time I write an entry, I go philosophical? If only I could accept things like Booker. He lives each day at a time. No great hassles for him. Yeah, periodically he gets angry, but generally he maintains the aura of an Epicurean. Fun and games. Life's short so live it up. Good old Booker. Here's a joke he told me yesterday:

"This big mouth is in a bar, bragging about how he can identify any drink in the joint.

Naturally people are bettin' money left and right.

And every drink the bartender sets up, the big mouth rolls around in his tongue and correctly names the brand. Not once wrong.

Well, during it all, there's a drunk down the end of the bar, who lays a shot before the guy, "Alright big mouth, see if you can identify this drink."

Big mouth sips the drink, swishes it around, and quickly spits it out and shouts, "That's piss!"

"Well, of course," answers the drunk, "But whose?"

BRINKS ROBBERY

Some of the Boys Discuss What to do with a Million Dollars

JANUARY 17, 1950

The morning began with Booker sliding the Globe across the bar, "Did you hear about the Brink's Robbery last night?"

A few fellows huddled around the paper.

"Look, did ya see in the paper. Brink's got hit for $1,000,000. A gang of guys tied up the night crew, and got away."

"It was a beautiful job, no one got hurt. What a sweetheart of a job. Man, I'd like to make a hit like that."

"Yea, but if you miss, your balls'll be nailed to a tree."

"And it's a sin." They all laugh.

"Imagine a million bucks!—how many guys did it take? Ten? That's over a hundred thousand a piece. Not bad for one night of work."

And so began the topic for the day; "What would you do with a million dollars?"

"First I'd fly down to Havana and buy me a hooker for a month."

"Me? I'd go to California or maybe Vegas. I hear there's all kinds of broads there."

Frank Vento, "I'd travel the tracks. Take me up to Rockingham—eat the good foods, the best drinks—what have you. I'd live like a king! Maybe I'd buy a barroom—one like this. Set up a nice bookie business. Sit back and live it easy."

Booker said, "You know, if you had a million bucks I bet you wouldn't have even a dollar in your pocket in a year from now."

Casey concluded the robbery with his assessment, "One thing wrong with a deal like that—too many guys—the best deal you can make is with one or two guys—or even better if you can do it yourself. Then keep your mouth shut. No one to squeal, no one trying to beat you. That's what will screw the job up."

NORTH KOREA ATTACKS SOUTH KOREA

Heard at the Bar

JUNE 1950

"Where is Korea? What business does the U.S. have in this war?

"Truman says that we have to stop the communist taking over in Asia.

"My brother is stationed in Japan. His outfit is shipping off to Korea."

"Out of my way! I'm joining the Corps—the Best! Semper Fi!"

And we hear of children of the original Danny's list—ready to join or be drafted.

Jack Walsh: Two boys joined the Navy.

Danny O'Neill: Two boys waiting to be called.

Tommy O'Hara: My boys are reactivated for the draft.

And as expected—most of the young men waited for the draft.

Job Deferments: "I'm a machinist at the Navy yard."

Bowdoin Street: Very few flags hung outside of 3 decker homes

Dorchester High School: Seniors can be graduated early if they wanted to join.

Army Base: Mostly young kids—all excited about the great time.

State House: Stay in college, get a deferment.

Danny's Tavern: Very little interest unless you were involved in enlisting or being drafted.

Dorchester Monthly Tribune

A community newsletter serving the Dorchester neighbourhood

April 3, 1951

Peter Z's Print Shop
Bowdoin Street

KOREAN WAR UPDATE! YANKS CROSS 38TH ON 10-MILE FRONT

General MacArthur inspects South Korean line within 500 yards of North Korea position of East Coast

HOUSE OPENS DEBATE ON UNIVERSAL TRAINING

Proposed to conscript young men age 18 to 25 for universal military training and service. Highly Controversial.

POISON GAS DEFENDED BY CAMBRIGE CHEMIAL ENGINEER AS WAR WEAPON

Claims that poison gas is suitable in the present world crisis

FRENCH OPEN ATTACK

French Troops have counter attacked northeast of Hanoi after successfully withstanding incessant assaults by Communist-led Vietminh guerrillas.

Dorchester Monthly Tribune

A community newsletter serving the Dorchester neighbourhood — 1950's — *Peter Z's Print Shop, Bowdoin Street*

Today's TV Stars

CHANNEL 7

3:15 – Bride and Groom – John Nelson, Dick Foran
8:30 – Billy Rose Show – "Farewell Appearance" starring Judith Anderson
9:00 – Vaughan Monroe Show – with Ziggy Talent and Shaye Cogan
10:00 – Danger —"The Undefeated" starring Walter Slezak.
10:30 – Starlight Theater – "The Flaxen Haired Mannequin" starring Gil Lamb

CHANNEL 4

3:15 – Vacation Wonderland – with Edgar Guest.
4:00 -- Kate Smith Hour – the john Butler Ballet group featuring Sono Ostate, Fleeta Brownell Woodroffe, the herman Chittison Trio and Richard Himber.
8:00 – Star Theater – Jackie Gleason, m.c., Patti Page and Stang.
9:00 – Fireside Theater – "The Gentleman from La Porte"with Eve Miller, Warren Douglas and Sheb Wooley.
10:00 – Original Amateur Hour – Ted Mack

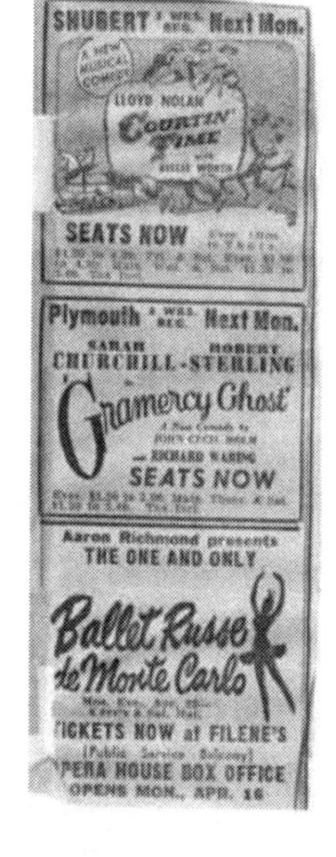

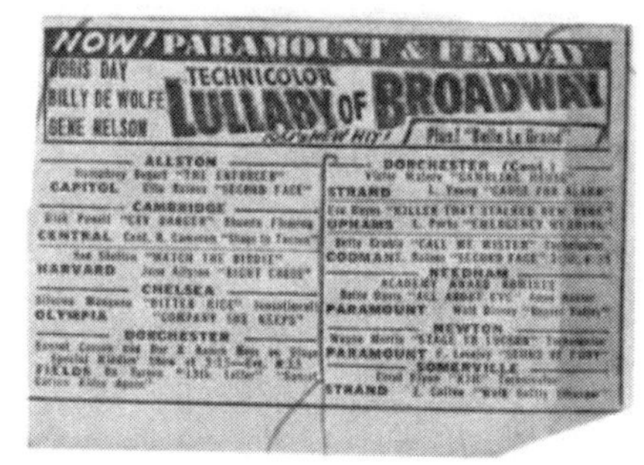

Dorchester Monthly Tribune

A community newsletter serving the Dorchester neighbourhood 1950's *Peter Z's Print Shop Bowdoin Street*

Dorchester Monthly Tribune

A community newsletter serving the Dorchester neighbourhood 1950's *Peter Z's Print Shop Bowdoin Street*

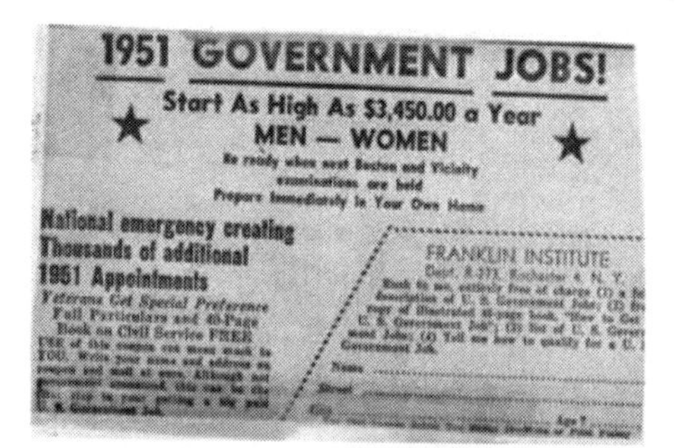

Dorchester Monthly Tribune

A community newsletter serving the Dorchester neighbourhood | 1950's | *Peter Z's Print Shop Bowdoin Street*

RED SOX - YANKEES
BASEBALL SPECIAL

$34.50 — $35.50

MORRISON TRAVEL BUREAU, INC.

Dorchester Monthly Tribune

A community newsletter serving the Dorchester neighbourhood 1950's *Peter Z's Print Shop Bowdoin Street*

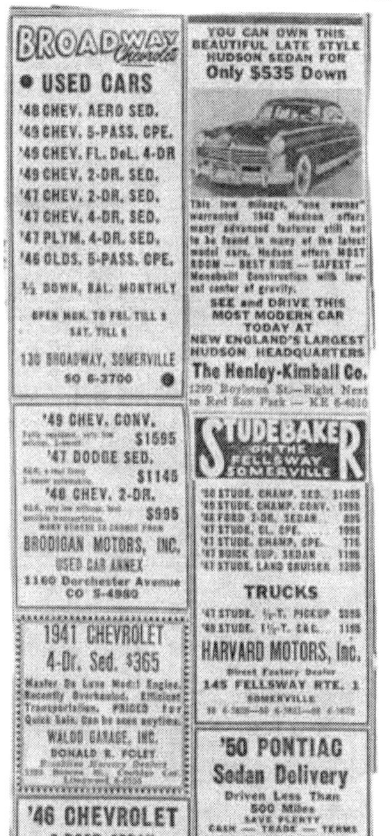

MICKEY'S KID

Home from Korea

JULY 1952

Mickey Smith leans on the bar, "Bill, I'd like you to meet my son, Jimmy. Just home from Korea. Fourteen months with the 1st Cav.

Bill shakes hands with Jimmy, "Welcome home. What's your pleasure?"

"Coupla beers," Mickey lays $20.00 on the bar. Bill pushes the money back at him. "No charge—that's Booker's rule. Anyone who serves gets a free ride. At least until they get squared away at home. Cheers."

Bill walks away.

Mickey turns to his son, "Well, Jimmy, I know that you saw sights over there that you don't want to talk about—just as well not to say anything at home. Your mother and sisters are sensitive. They've worn out a couple of sets of Rosary Beads. When you're at home, the less said the better. But I'd like to hear how you received your two decorations."

"Now, Pa, there's not much to say. I did what I was supposed to—just like everyone else."

"You must have done more—what did you do to get those the medals, the Purple Heart and the Bronze Star?" Jimmy answered, "The Army was awarding them to many soldiers. My best buddy, Moe, was shot in the chest—so I got out of my foxhole and dragged him to safety. Moe would have done it for me. In fact later that afternoon, the gooks hit us with a mortar attack—Ping! I got a piece of shrapnel in my leg and my platoon sergeant carried me back to the aid station. That's the way it is. The 1st Cav takes care of its own."

"You know son, you're just like your brother John. Can't wait to get in and get it over. Why just last week I asked him what he was going to do when he graduated from high school. You know what he said? He was going to join up—join up and get it over with. Pete Malloy, Jim Malloy's kid, wants to join up with him. I thought he'd wait to get a job at the Gas Company. Speak to Paul Malloy—he's a foreman—knows the guy in personnel—good advice for your brother—but no, he's got his mind made up."

"See Pa, why not get it over with? Why take a job and then get drafted? To hell with that—I'm glad I done it the way I did. One more year and I'll be out. Then I'll have the G.I. Bill—maybe I'll go to college or voke school. I agree that the Gas Company is a good steady job. By the time John graduates maybe the war will be over."

They have a few more beers at the bar. Well wishers are flooding the bar with empty upside down glasses (a signal that denotes a free drink). Mickey is getting buzzed—he looks so wistful. "You know Jimmy, your mother, all of us, were really worried about you. You put a few gray hairs on our heads. But thank God you have a life now. You survived and we all owe a debt to those who got killed. We need to live a good life for them."

"We love you—I love you," Mickey's voice cracked, "This is so difficult to say Jim—someday you'll see for yourself but it's a hard to say how much you love someone. I found it hard to ever say it to your mother and she's a wonderful woman." Tears come to his eyes. "I've had a bit too much to drink. You go talk to your buddies, they're waiting down the end of the bar—I'll be along. Early shift tomorrow." Mickey goes home.

Jimmy shoots the bull with his buddies—many laughs while they rehash stories from the old street corner. Jimmy had to be carried out of the bar and Bill drove him home.

Bill At 53 Years Old

Middle Age

Friday 13, 1953

Today has been an unusual day.

After class at Wentworth the provost informed me that I have been promoted to an Associate Professor, a full time faculty position. Out of the boiler room as an operator and into the classroom. The courses that I will teach are Building Systems; Heating, Air Conditioning; Ventilation, Plumbing; Electrical and Facilities Management courses. Because Wentworth offers three semesters of course work, I could have my summers free if I want. Actually it is a very good deal. I'd be teaching 3 courses in the fall and spring semester and teaching 3 days a week. I must admit that teaching college is prime job. Teaching high school in a tough city neighborhood is no bargain. Wentworth, being a no-nonsense school, has few disciplinarian problems.

When I emter Danny's for my shift on Friday night, I am in a very good mood—mentally planning a few summer hikes and a trip overseas. As I set up the bar—washing off the bar and cleaning the shelves, Booker asks me, "Bill, how long have you been here at Danny's—twenty years?"

"Actually, eighteen" I answer. "I started here in nineteen thirty five."

He nods, "How old are you now? Fifty two?"

"Fifty three. Why are you asking me all of this? Am I getting canned?"

"No, of course not. I told you years ago, it's your choice. Stay as long as it suits you." He pauses, "I'm pushing 60 and every day I feel new aches and pains. Maybe it's time for me to think about slowing down. What about you? God—you're teaching at Wentworth; hiking and traveling all over; impressing the ladies. And yet you continue working here one or two shifts. And on top of all of that you are still writing. Where do you get the energy?"

"I feel fine, Booker. I only work part-time here because it keeps me in touch with the Dorchester scene. And now that I've been appointed associate faculty, I'll be required to prepare lectures. But I'll still make the time to write and travel. There are still places that I'd like to go and more adventures to experience. In fact, maybe you and I can take a trip next summer. What about China or New Zealand?"

"No, I'm too old. Anyway I've got six years on you—I'm slowing down. You think you can hike all over the place up until you're 100 years old. What the hell motivates you?

I almost answer, "Growing up poor as a church mouse," but I let it pass.

Booker sighs, "I've been thinking about moving down to the Cape. The wife and kids want me to sell my businesses including Danny's. Maybe you should knock off writing for a while—you've been at it so long you've got the backroom beer locker loaded with notebooks, papers, books, newspapers. I can't find room for the beer and wine."

"Not yet, Booker—in fact why not visit Europe this summer—visit where you were with Danny. Remember we had a great time visiting the cemetery. Let's see the whole countryside."

"Like hell, I lost a piece of my ass from shrapnel, it's probably buried on some hill in France."

"OK, Booker, you've got your plans and I have my dreams. But I'll make you a promise. When you retire down to the Cape, and I decide to pack it all in—retire from Wentworth, quit Danny's, store away all of my writings, and burn my hiking boots, I'll move down to the Cape too. We'll sit on the beach all day and stare at all the old ladies. Is that a deal?"

"Bill, I promise you that I will find someone who knows the book business to get your writing published, even if I have to pay for it myself."

"OK—it's a deal," I answer.

Eye to eye, we shake.

School Boy Parade

1953

It's a warm spring day in Dorchester. We're watching the boys heading to high school and catching the trolley. Today is special—it's the school boy parade. When all the public high schools in Boston march down Commonwealth Avenue in competition for the best marching band in Boston. They've been practicing a year of military drills for one or two hours a week.

"Here, look at my kid," Red hands me a sketch of Commerce High School boys doing close order drills in the armory, "He's a cadet non-commissioned officer." He points to one boy in the picture, "That's my boy. In a few years he'll go to college. No roofing for him. He's a good boy. He studies hard, no smoking and no swearing."

"But you know Bill sometimes, especially when I come home after a day on the roof, dirty and sweating, and maybe have a couple of beers under my belt, he avoids me. Like he's ashamed of me. Especially since someone told him of my nickname—Malarkey—a bullshit artist.

"Bill, you're a writer, so you know that words can hurt, maybe more than a bullet."

"Come on Red," I answer. "Your kid knows that you love him. In a few years when he has his own family, he'll think of you as a genius and a great artist."

It's not surprising that Latin School that takes the honors for the best marching band. But English High did well. The H.S. patches on their arms—all dressed in starched khaki uniforms with their school colors—Commerce High—my alma mater was blue and grey. Led by the student officers and flags and the drum and bugle corps—which unfortunately sounded like the remnants of the Charge of Light Brigade.

Unfortunately this competition ended in the late 1950's due to lots of reasons, but one reason is because sometimes school spirit got carried away after the competion and sometimes fights would break out. No more military training in high school with a major retired Army major acting as instructor.

After The Discharge

Then what?

1953

Korean Vet, Rick Smith—recently discharged and two old timers; (Bob McNamara, School Teacher, and Ira Gold, Attorney)

Bob asks, "Well Smitty, now that you're ready for discharge, what are your plans?"

"I dunno, get a job I guess."

Bob suggests, "Go to college, young man. It's the best investment that you'll ever make. Shoot for the moon. Take one of those interest surveys and aptitude tests. Determine your strengths and interests. Then find a college or voke school that can prepare you. Get as much useful education that you can afford. The world will be your oyster."

Ira Gold suggests, "Get a government job and take night classes. The old timers in Danny's—especially the survivors of the depression have always preached public sector jobs—Teachers, Fireman, Police, Civil Service positions. Go for the pension, boyos."

Bob, "You were in Korea—and were wounded—you know that being a disabled vet really helps. The Civil Service gives considerable benefits to DAV's."

"They gotta take a disabled vet over the others," says Ira. "For heavens sake—you top the fireman exam or the police exam. And if you get sick as a public employee—you take your body to a V.A. hospital and tell them—here fix me up. That's an exaggeration but not by much. And you can get a pension with the state, it may not pay the best but it's secure."

Ira concludes, "Public employment has defects but overall, the benefits outweigh them. Certainly civil service is worth consideration."

POLIO EPIDEMIC IN DORCHESTER

1954

"Bill, did you hear about Iron Mike's kid?" asked Peter Z. "He's over at City Hospital—they think he's got polio."

"What happened?" I asked.

"He went swimming down at Tinean Beach, last Tuesday—real hot day. Came home, complained of a headache—then he went to bed—woke up sicker than all hell—called Dr. Moore—one look—said to take him to the City. He's been there ever since—Mike and his wife crying and everything. Worried like hell," Peter explained.

"How old's the kid?"

"Thirteen."

"Jesus, hope he don't end up in an iron lung."

"Man, I'd rather die."

"You say that now, Peter, but if you had it you'd want to hang on."

"What a terrible thing to be crippled like that, especially a young kid. I think about the disease, Polio—what a terrible scourge—what a worry too. There's been three or four cases in the parish already."

"You know another bad thing? Everybody is terrified for their kids." Tommy O'Hara joined in. "Mike's kids are like outcasts now. All the neighbors are afraid they got the polio bug or whatever it is. No one says it outright but they don't want their kids playing with his kids. It's like they're lepers."

"You can't blame them," I answer. I mean I don't have kids but if I did, I'd do anything to protect them. To Hell what the neighbors think!"

"I guess it's time to tell the kids not to go swimming at Tenean, that place is a swamp." Tommy suggests.

"Try Carson Beach, it's just as bad—anyway all those clowns over in Southie think they own the ocean."

"You know you gotta give Roosevelt credit, I mean crippled and all of that. With all his money he still got it. It don't know no boundaries."

Peter Z adds, "I'm glad I live in the city, I hear it's worse out in the suburbs. I wonder how you get it, get bit by a mosquito?"

"That's yellow fever and malaria—not polio."

"Blessed be the day that they get a cure for this." says Tommy. "You think if they could build an atomic bomb or win a war they'd come up with a cure for Polio."

I added, "Did you know that the Iron Lung was developed at Wentworth Institute of Technology?"

THE HARDWARE STORE

Herman the German (AKA Eddie Edison), Owner

1955

In Dorchester, as in most cities, towns, and villages everywhere, when a home owner decides to do a repair task around the house, he does the work himself. Call it a guy thing. Or just a fact that it is too expensive to hire outside labor. If the resulting job is sreally screwed up, you probably had a friend or relative helping you. Who amongst us has not suffered the loud mouth know-it-all. "Sure I know all about installing a second hand gas stove or I can rewire your fire alarm system," he'll claim.

But when the fire department arrives at your house, followed closely by the peering eyes of the neighborhood, you find yourself at a unable to adequately expain what happened.

Who comes to the rescue?

Enter the Hardware Man, an unsung hero of the neighborhood. Located on Bowdoin Street, owned and operated by the smartest, most practical man that I ever met. His name is Herman Stolz but he was addressed as either Herman the German or Eddie Edison, Dorchester's version of Thomas Edison.

You explain your problem and he's the go-to guy at a fair cost. Born to German immigrants—his father was a cracker-jack machinist. Eddie studied the trades at Boston Trade High School. With an unbounded energy level and commitment to success, he enrolled at Wentworth

Institute in the two year program to advance his skills and he worked as a carpenter's apprentice at the same time.

He excelled in the courses—mechanics, boiler design and operation, machine shop techniques, electricity and lighting, small motor repair, and tool design. Upon graduation he was presented with the prestigious Arioch Wentworth Award for commitment to the school values as reflected on the Wentworth logo, "Honesty—Energy—Economy—System." For sure, Eddie possessed those qualities and then some. Of course, his detractors would say that Eddie wasn't very friendly, nor was he a glad hander. I would counter with the question, "What do you want—the smile or the service?" Suffice to say that Eddie did not suffer fools.

He was small in stature but solid and straight. Not an ounce of fat. Day or night he wore a Navy black watch cap, a habit that he picked up in the engine room. Why, I don't know. His hair was full and black as tar. His face was strong and featured a solid chin. His eyes were very attentive. He never missed anything or event that was purposeful. Even though he carried a micrometer in his belt, I swear he could estimate any dimension from a distance. He also carried a scale, a slide rule and a table of math formulas at all times.

At the outbreak of World War II Eddie joined the submarine service. This was the same time I was giving classes on boiler operations at Wentworth Institute. The country called on Wentworth to train future sailors to man the engine rooms on its vast fleet: destroyers, cruisers, battleships and aircraft carriers. After working in the boiler room since 1935, I earned my first class fireman's license. But Eddie, even as a student, knew more than I about building and repairing things.

I must admit that with tools I am all fumble, stumble, and trip. I have a lot of talents, but don't ask me to hang the picture level. But if you need the solution of a second order quadratic differential equation, I'm your guy.

You might be asking why I am mentioning the hardware store and its owner? Because like many other businesses in a neighborhood, they provide a life line to the well being of all. Sure we appreciate Doctor Cronin up the street, Louie the pharmacist, Iron Mike the policeman, Scotty the fireman, and of course the all the priests and nuns, but Eddie and the hardware store brought an important value to the neighborhood.

And what about Geo the barber, Charlie Loo the laundryman, Tony the cobbler and so on. Each and all provide a valuable service. If for one reason or another, the business closed down life in the neighborhood would be a little less efficient. No short work days for a business owners like these. It took dedication. And no doubt it was the lifeline of the wealth that surrounded us. The Bible it says it all, "You reap what you sow."

In 1953, Bowdoin Hardware closed down because of owner illness. Eddie weighed the risks and took his chance at owning a business. At the time he was working for a union carpenter shop where he froze in the winter erecting building frames and roasted in the summer banging out forms for concrete work. Good pay for a young man but hard on your body when you reach your forties. So he bought the hardware store. And he devoted all his energy to the task. In the early morning he would be involved in new house construction or a repair project; in the afternoon and evening he'd be tending the store, fielding the customer questions, such how to fix the following:

1) Leaks—Roof/Windows/Foundation/Pipes/Ducts/Doors/Toilets
2) My house/Bedroom/Cellar/Attic is too hot/too cold/unventilated.
3) Place concrete/Mix concrete/What is a slump test?
4) Paints: Oil/Water Base/Best outside temperature
5) Select a heating unit: Hot water/Hot air/ Fuel/Electric/Gas/Oil/ Wood/Economy
6) Squeak—Table—Chair—Door
7) I tightened too hard and broke the screw in the manifold. Tap a hole.
8) Clean up stains/Remove rust/Preventing Drafts/Determine the efficiency of My boiler/Clogged Drains/Install insulation/Asbestos Issues/Lead Paint—Little Children
9) Sizes: Nuts/Bolts/Metric/Gauges/Material
10) Re-roof/Types of siding
11) Screws/Nuts/Bolts/Fasteners
12) Lighting issues

If you think about it, you could do this same exercise with the tailor, the tinker and the fruit man. They all have their expertise and they were your neighbors.

By 1963, Eddie had built a beautiful home in Wellesley, owned a few three deckers and did a little consulting on the side. But something was missing in his life. To fill a void, he began teaching at Wentworth in the evening. We became good friends, Eddie and me. Sometimes I would sit in class and marvel at Eddie's approach. He taught about life.

He would begin his course with a question. "Do you know the book *Message to Garcia*? It was written over a hundred years ago. It's a story about president McKinley who needed to get a message to General Garcia who was located somewhere in the jungles of Cuba. Who should he send?"

"Rowen" said his advisor.

So he gave the message to Rowen who said only, "Yes sir." He didn't ask, "Why me? Or where are the maps?" He tucked the letter in his shirt and left. Several weeks later he returned from the jungles of Cuba after completing the task.

"It is a good story, gentleman, about hard work and commitment to the task at hand. Don't complain—I don't want to hear about the labor pains—just show me the baby.

His message was about working hard. Anyone born in this U.S. can succeed according to his ability. He talked abut his immigrant father who was a machinist—the most underpaid, under appreciated trade in the world. Machinists, God bless them, one wrong cut and the piece is ruined!

"Someday you will own a house for your family. Look at the structure as a living breathing system. You'll need to heat it, and paint it, keep it clean. It will need repairs for the broken windows or the cracked stairs inside and out. If you don't do that, your house will get sick with mold, bugs, or rats."

When he lectured he would instruct the students with what to do. Then watch them do it, making sure no one fell behind. He was always asking them all to participate.

"Make a design! Do your layout! Give me a sketch! A picture is worth a thousand words!"

"Check your numbers! Measure twice and cut once! Build a cardboard model first."

His lecture on the last day would be inspiring for his students, "When you get out in the work world, be proud of Arioch Wentworth, the founder of Wentworth and it's motto, 'Honesty—Energy—Economy—System.' And most of all, deliver your message to Garcia."

"If you are ever in my neighborhood in Dorchester, please visit me at Hamilton Hardware. We'll talk shop. And when you are old enough visit Mr. Flynn at Danny's Tavern down the street. Good luck, boys."

CAMPAINGNING FOR WARD 15

Dorchester Style

1956

In his younger days, Angelo Coletti, had won the Golden Gloves Heavy Weight Championship in Lawrence. His boxing name was "Banger Burke." He was a hulk of a man, standing 6'4" and pushing 240 pounds. Of course this was twenty years ago. He joined the work world as an administrative clerk with the Department of Corrections down at the Walpole State Prison. He had a successful career and as he neared his retirement, he decided to enter politics. He ran to be the representative in the St. Peter's Parish.

Saturdays were good days for campaigning. Angelo, or "Banger" as most of us knew him, decided to hit the taverns to make his pitch. He had a flashy card with a photo of his family, his lovely wife and three young children. It included a list of his accomplishments; Dorchester High Graduate, U.S. Army Veteran, graduate of Boston State College, etc.

Now it so happened that Jackie Dwyer and the Gas Company street gang, was having an afternoon get together with his co-workers at Danny's. The beer flowed freely and as Jackie opened the door to leave, Banger was just coming in.

A trailer truck of a man, 6'4", 240 pounds meets a Volkswagon 5'2", 152 pounds. Just like Robin Hood and Little John on the narrow bridge.

"The Banger" pushed his card into Jackie's chest. Jackie glared at the "Vote for Coletti" card and said, "Coletti—huh! I wouldn't vote for you if you were the last son of a bitch on the face of the earth!"

"The Banger" barely moved his arm with a hook that landed on Jackie's face. Poor Jackie hit the deck like a sack of bricks. Angelo made a quick political decision; this Irish tavern was an unlikely source of votes so he wheeled around and exited.

Jackie was dragged to a booth to patch up his split lip.

I wondered how Mayor James Michael Curley would have handled the situation?

THE ESSAY PROJECT

The Beginning

JANUARY 1952

Life certainly has many surprises; for example, Bob McNamara, the math teacher at Dorchester High School, walks into Danny's Tavern and says "Bill, a colleague of mine, Paul Conroy, an English teacher at Commerce High School has a student from this neighborhood—up on Barry Street. Paul tells me that the boy has considerable writing ability. He graduated from St. Peter's a few years ago, but like a lot of kids, college seems out of touch—no money. So he, is going into the service—the paratroopers, instead of applying to college."

"What is he, soft in the head?"

"No, a good kid, name is Thomas Melvin, he just wants to sow his oats, join up for a couple of years and then get the G.I. Bill. But during this past year or two, Conroy asked the boy to write some brief essays and compositions about growing up in Dorchester. You know, family life, going to St. Peter's with the nuns—stuff like that. And after graduation, he signed for Commerce High instead of Cathedral High. Not a very bright move, but kids will be kids—and immigrant parents are not the best judges of the Boston School System.

I ask, "So why tell me?

"You're a writer—and from what the Paul tells me, the lad has some talent. So maybe you can review what the kid writes and mentor him along."

I respond, "I'm sure he can find better mentors than me."

"Look, all I'm asking is that you review his stories and Tom's essay project. So the kid can use it for his college application. You know you could be encouraging another Thomas Wolfe. You got contacts."

"OK," agrees Bill, "Here are the ground rules—I will read what the kid writes. If he's good, then I will make a suggestion—you know I've never made a score writing myself. Nada! People have a great misconception about success in the field—best sellers are few and far between. But send me the his stories and the essay. Really Bob, couldn't you find a more suitable mentor? I'm a bartender and an engineer not a poet laureate."

Bob answers, "But you are also an instructor at Wentworth Institute—one of the best teaching schools in the country. But most important, you love this neighborhood. And we're dealing with one of our own—the kid needs a break and some guidance—a noogie in the head."

I agreed—what else could I do?

ESSAY PROJECT

1940-1958

GROWING UP IN DORCHESTER, MASSACHUSETTS

By Tom Melvin

To: Mr. P. Conroy
English Department
Commerce High School
Louis Pasteur Avenue
Boston, MA

Re: The Essay Project
Submitted by: Thomas Melvin, Senior Class of 1953

cc: Mr. William Flynn, Instructor
Wentworth Institute
Huntington Ave, Boston, MA

Dear Mr. Conroy,

Submitted for your review is The Essay Project, a series of writings, observations, and reflections related to my time in St. Peter's School, Commerce High School and my activities and misadventures along the way. You have been my shepherd and have guided me through my four years of Commerce High. No student could ask for more.

On a personal note, I would like to extend my appreciation to Mr. William Flynn, Instructor at Wentworth Institute, and fellow writer. Mr. Flynn generously provided many hours of review of the essay.

Yours truly,
Thomas Melvin

P.S. As we discussed, instead of going on to college immediately I plan to join the paratroopers for a 3 year enlistment. I then hope to attend college using the G.I. Bill. Although both you and Mr. Flynn have expressed reservations concerning my enlistment in the paratroopers, to me my enlistment was predetermined 10 years ago. Attached is a sketch of me, circa 1943, wearing a necktie with a picture of a paratrooper floating to the earth? Strange, isn't it?

Sincerely,
Thomas Melvin

Red the

Essay Project

Student Years in the Boston School System and Other Experiences
(1940-1956)
St. Peter's Parochial School (1940-1948)
Commerce High School (1948-1953)
U.S. Army Paratrooper (1953-1956)
By Thomas Melvin
22 Barry Street
Dorchester, MA

Objective of The Essay Project

Mr. Conroy, my English teacher at Commerce High has suggested that I write an Essay of my personal experiences in Dorchester's St. Peter Parrish and neighborhood. Under the auspices of Mr. Conroy and Mr. Flynn, an instructor at Wentworth Institute of Technology, I hope to use this essay in the future when I apply for College Admission. This essay will serve as an example of my writing style and maturity. The plan is that the following stories will demonstrate my ability to pursue a research project, as I describe the neighborhood of my childhood and youth.

Family Background

My mother, father, and stepfather were immigrants from Newfoundland; they made their livelihood from the sea, fishing from dories, and trawlers.

My mother, Mary, emigrated with three possessions; a pair of rosary beads, a change of underwear and a curling iron. The only other thing was she had a few dollars which were required of the government entrance rules.

My father, David, a Newfoundland fisherman, died of TB in 1943, leaving my mother with 6 children, the oldest being thirteen and the youngest a new born. At the age of eight I was unaware, and even now at 17, I really cannot fathom how my father and mother handled the TB. In those days, the outcome for survival was bleak. I do vividly recall my mother and father standing in the middle of the kitchen crying the day he had been diagnosed with advanced stages of TB.

Never had I witnessed either of my parents cry. It is all so strange, the three of us standing in the kitchen. Two crying adults and one paralyzed young boy standing witness. To this day, I close my eyes and I relive the scene in puzzlement of the future consequences.

No idea of the outcome did I ponder. All I know is that the father had a portrait taken so that his children would know what he looked like. The picture was located on the mantle in the parlor for many years.

At the end of WWII, my future stepfather, John Joseph Walsh (Jack), also a Newfoundland fisherman and a family friend, returned from the Army in the Pacific Theater, and married my widowed mother, six kids and all. Jack was a wonderful man and an excellent provider.

School Days In St. Peter's School

Hooking School with Sandy Cotter
1st Grade 1941

It seems odd that I vividly recall my 1st Grade experiences 12 years after the actual events occurred on the first day of class. My prime memory is of Sister Adele taping Kevin Foley's mouth shut with a roll of white bandage. There he was with a mop of curly dark hair and his face swathed with cloth like a mummy. His eyes, popping out of his face reminded me of a baby deer ready to be shot by the hunter in the Disney movie, Bambi. This nun was not one to fool with—a female Edward G. Robinson.

Actually, Sister Adele was a tiny thing—that's all I remember. But I do have one weird memory in grammar school. It was standard practice on school nights to go to bed at 7:30. (Note: the Lone Ranger was on the radio at this time. However, being a good boy I tried to comply.) One night I had this dream as clear as can be. I was riding a horse and Sister Adele needed a ride to escape the bad guys. She was in danger so she jumped on my horse and we rode away. My God, what made me think of that? Am I growing up to be a pervert? In any case I saved her and we escaped harm's way.

But let us get back to the story "Hooking School with Sandy Cotter." (Digression—Please bear with me as I reminisce—I possessed reddish blonde hair and a happy face—to my mother I was her "golden boy" and I never stopped running up and down the hallway on the 2nd floor of a 3 decker on Barry St., a very active young lad. Today I would be filled with some psychoanalytic drug or smothered in a vicious fluid to slow me down.)

Back again to my introduction to the first grade, with 30 of my male classmates. Kevin sat beside me. He was a real chatter box. In fact he never shut up. He reminded me of a squirrel or a pigeon, constantly in motion. Of course, squirrels and pigeons don't talk. But this was Kevin's downfall. He did make sounds. Finally after two hours of the constant drivel Sister Adele called him into the "Coat Room" where nothing good ever happens. He emerged looking like a mummy—of course a silent mummy. After this Kevin became quiet, in fact the quietest kid in school. Years later, before I graduated from Commerce High School I went on a field trip to the Museum of Fine Arts—The Egyptian Exhibit. Lo and Behold! Kevin was there. He still had nothing to say to me. Proverb: "Still waters run deep." Very quiet kid.

Being a neighborhood school, it was customary to go home for lunch—eat tomato soup and a baloney sandwich—and return to class for the afternoon. As fate would have it, I met Sandy Cotter, a neighborhood kid, who was not a St. Peter's student—a public school kid who went to Mather School. Even at this young age there was the element of elitism. He may have even been a Protestant!

It was a beautiful, fine day—when Sandy asked, "Why go back to school, let's go up to Ronan Park and play."

Great idea, Sandy!

This afternoon should be fun! Little did I know of the proverb, "The road to hell is paved with good intentions."

Yes, the road to hell was paved with good intentions that day. A pleasant, healthy afternoon in Ronan Park rolling down the grassy hills. What road to hell? Well for one—if one is absent from St. Peter's you must bring a note in to school which would be no big deal, if you knew how to write a note and could forge your mother's name. And so another proverb comes to mind, "Oh what a tangled web we weave when first we start to deceive."

At supper, Ma asked me about my first day at school. "Fine," I mumbled and sat in limbo—no words—no eye contact. I ate the rest of my supper in silence. Later from my older sister's notebook I rifled a piece of low grade paper, the kind that smudges when you try to erase an error. On my second day as a refugee, I avoided the classroom again in favor of "Cat Alley"—a filthy place behind rows of brick apartments filled with garbage and a gang of smelly old alley cats as my companions.

This went on for a few days—one of the days was very wet. I stood sopping wet with my smelly cat friends. I'd come home and give my mother a paper I had done with a few x's, a couple of squares. There were no conversations like, "Ma, do you know the philosopher Thoreau? Or Sister Adele showed us how to bisect a 45 degree angle in Geometry today."

A few days into my miserable physical and mentally existence, I walked into the house and heard my mother running down the hallway. The ironing cord whistling over her head, "No Ma!" and into the bed room I dove, squeezing between the mattress and the wall. I wiggled under the bed to avoid the terror coming at me with a strong Newfoundland accent. Her yells subsided, but the horrified looks of my older sibling's expressions told the tale, "The Golden Boy" now became "The Kucka Kid."

"Tomorrow," she yelled, "I have to take you to school to see the Mother Superior! Mother Superior!" She gasped. Ma had gone to only the 4th grade in Newfoundland so what could she say in my defense?

"It wasn't my fault, Ma—It's Sandy's fault—he made me do it!" Yes it definitely was a situation that we came to bury Caesar not praise him. Mother Superior! I almost wet myself at the thought.

The next morning as Ma and I stood before the Mother Superior's office door, Ma actually shook. The solid oak door was as large as a wall. I had expected shackles to be mounted on the wood, where I would be hung and beaten.

The door slowly opened and there she was—Mother Superior. David versus Goliath, Ma with her 4th grade education and Mother Superior with a Master's Degree from Boston College. Ma left home at eleven years old to take care of Grandma Johnson who lived on the other side of the village in Newfoundland.

Mother Superior was dressed in black and white. She spoke in whispers but her words hung in the air with an aura of condemnation. Her face was old beyond years, like Father Perrault in the movie "Lost Horizons" and I was little Ronald Coleman, ready to pee his pants.

A fine tap on the bell on her desk and Sister Adele appeared silent as a ghost passing through the door. I looked to see is she had her scotch tape or a club in her hands. Neither. She led me to an audience of thirty boys who stared at me, a vile specimen who hooked school. She directed me to the center of the classroom, facing the fury. If I had read the Tale of Two Cities." I would have claimed "It is a far, far better place I go now then I have ever known."

I searched their faces—my classmates—for a sign of support, understanding, or awareness—No! I was Quasimodo hanging on my tolling bell. Even worse I was definitely the Kucka Kid.

Silence. Painful silence.

My classmates, the urchins, salivated for a condemnation. It was thumb's down for the gladiator. And Sister Adele dropped the bomb, "Class, isn't he a bad boy?"

The chorus called out loud and clear, "Yes Sister!" with a whiny lispy "S." You could never imagine two little words dripping with more venom "Yes sister!" the chorus chanted.

I saw one runt mouth the words "Bad Boy" the way you'd tell your dog, "Bad Dog!" after he tore a hole in the mailman's leg. His name was Bartholemew "Chubby" Fenton. In the land of Joes, Mikes or Bills who had a name like Bartholemew? His face was round and full like the moon. He reminded me of a boy Charles Laughton in Mutiny on the Bounty as he silently mouthed the words "Bad Boy" accentuating his lips and even leaning towards me! God, it was terrible! I had such an urge to punch him. All I could do was cement that "Bad Boy" into my brain.

You traitors! I thought. You weasel faced cowards! A bunch of rats! Thank God that I was too young to have learned juicy Dorchester street swears.

To this day I still here those words, "Yes Sister!"

Later in life when a few of the boys had troubles and behaved like rascals, Chubby led the pack of rascals. In the fourth grade he was caught stealing girl's underwear off the piazza clotheslines. I would imagine Sister Adele saying to me, "Isn't he a bad boy?" And I would respond, "You bet your ass, Sister, he's a real bad boy!"

The Paint Rags Saga
2nd Grade 1942

In the spring of second grade, on Friday afternoons, Sister Maria George would treat us to a paint session. It was a strategy to enhance our appreciation of the arts. The school would provide water and paints and a well used container of various colors and brushes of varried quality. Of course the paint days were always on Fridays—tan or green shirt days.

In order to protect our clothes, especially the tan or green shirts, we were instructed to bring paint rags from home, such as a sleeve of an old t-shirt, or even a piece of a diaper.

Of course, after my "hooking" crime I obeyed every order or rule imposed one me. I endeavored to erase the "Bad Boy" image that was probably noted in a large black journal locked up in Mother Superior's desk. "Kucka Boy" was probably noted with red ink and marked as a bad apple who hated school. No more demerits for me. Like General MacArthur, I vowed would graduate from St. Peter's with an *almost* perfect record.

Well, on this particular Friday, I was running late returning to school after lunch. This is not an excuse but Ma was slow with the soup and sandwich. As with Sandy, I was to take the heat for someone else's mistake.

Anyway I rushed along and no sooner had I sat down in class I realized that I forgot my paint rag! Oh no! My face flushed. Even though the room was cool, I began to perspire. Think! I need a solution. I look around at my classmates but they must have known that I forgot my paint rag. They all gripped their cloths like they were the Shroud of Turin.

Sister Maria George went into the cabinet and brought out the paint and the brushes.

I am trembling in anticipation of what she will say, "All right, everyone show their paint rags."

Think! Think! Automatically I have a solution—a possible solution anyway. I reach down in my pants and fish around my body parts like a mountain climber on a rock face in Yosemite. My fingers search for a small rip to insert a finger near a seam. I find an opening! I grab a piece of the cloth and yank! It really hurt as the cloth was pulled hard onto parts of my body that were sensitive to pain. I pulled and I tugged and finally the cloth ripped silently. The cloth that was now in my hand was about 3"x3" and the rest of the garment was something like a loin cloth. Tom Tarzan, the boy who paints in the jungle.

In fact, later Ma asked me how I ripped my underwear, "Climbing over a fence, Ma."

I did not explain the pride that I felt when Sister asked about the paint cloths, "Has everyone got their paint cloths?" I had my paint cloth, even though it almost cost me my balls in the process.

The "Kucka Kid" would not get any demerits today.

An Act of Kindness
3rd Grade 1943

Early one fall day at recess time, Sister Bernadette (Bernie to the kids), called me aside, "Thomas, may I speak with you, please?"

Out to the coat room we went. "What did I do?"

Her voice was soft, almost inaudible, "I am afraid that I bring you bad news, your father has died." She paused, "I am sure that he is in Heaven with God."

For an instant, her message did not register. I knew that Pa was in the TB hospital in Mattapan being cured, certainly not dying. Several months before, he ran away from the hospital and made his way home. I had arrived home from school for lunch, and lo and behold, Pa was on the back piazza. He smiled and hugged me, no kisses of course. I remember that so clearly. In retrospect, I guess he didn't want to spread his germs.

My mother was beside herself. "Dave," she whispered frantically to my father, "You have to go back!" You can't stay here. Think about the kids and the neighbors."

"Thomas," Bernie brought me back to reality, "Every day I will say a prayer for your father."

It was recess time and as this bad scene took root, I walked to the edge of the school yard and thought about Pa being dead and Ma and the rest of us all alone. The tears started, slowly at first. The more I thought about the whole situation the more tears followed, even thought couldn't really understand what was happening.

"Why are you crying?" asked one of the older boys.

Jimmy Cully, a friend who was several years older than I, shooed the group away, "His father just died. Get outta here and leave him alone," Jimmy was somewhat of a protective big brother who lived close to my house. It is odd, but I can still hear Jimmy's words as he tried to shield me in my solitude. Tears are on the brink.

After the wake and funeral I returned to school and Sister announced to the class that after recess that I would be the "General of the Line." My job was to maintain order and decorum in the line—which is like being assigned to herd a group of cats. To make it worse, I was small in stature and many of my classmates were as big as water buffaloes with the disposition of wolverines. I was told more than once, "Beat it you little runt before I stuff you into a trash barrel" when I told the other kids to keep in a straight line. But lucky for me, it was all words but and no action.

If there is one endearing memory that I carry from St. Peter's it was the act of pure kindness of Sister Bernadette. To this day, dear Sister, you have my gratitude.

Cooties Invade St. Peter's
4th Grade 1944

Obviously the subject of cooties (bee nuts) is not generally the most common topic in polite society. But it has it's place in the discussion of growing up in Dorchester. Please be advised that cooties have many myths associated with them like only "dirty" people have cooties. This of course is not true. They are simply a fact of life and and cause the mothers of the world much distress.

I forget the exact year that I first encountered cooties in school. But I do remember my first cooties of record. I was in the fourth grade. Bruno Colletto sat in front of me. He was almost a foot taller than me—in fact he was huge. From my perspective behind him, he looked like he was wearing shoulder pads. He had curly black hair, and because I of my vantage point I could not help but notice the frayed collar on his clothing and the fact that it looked like he always needed a haircut. I knew the shirt dress code—white shirt on Monday and Wednesday, blue shirt on Tuesday and Thursday and Friday you had a choice of a tan or green shirt. It was long after grammar school that my sister clued me in about the "shirt code." She told me that it was a way to make sure that the kids changed their clothes. Otherwise a few students would wear the same shirt for eight years or until the material rotted off their backs—which ever came first.

Anyway, I was looking at the blackboard trying to follow the Sister's lessons when I could not help but notice a tiny, tiny movement on Bruno's hair. A mirage? One cootie? Bruno leaned back and scratched—lo and behold, one of the little cooties fell on to my desk—right into the ink well. Certainly an inglorious ending for the cootie. Then another one. At first I thought it was a light colored ant. But it was shaped different from any ant I had ever seen. I took my pencil and batted him off my desk to the floor.

What should I do? Touch one of Bruno's massive shoulders and tell him, "Excuse me, you have cooties" or start chanting "Bruno has cooties—Bruno has cooties!" I think not. One reason was that Bruno was a great kid. A good calm guy who seldom got angry. However, I doubt if he'd stay that way if I announced his cooties to the world.

Later at home, I mentioned the incident to Ma. "Oh Lord," she responded, "I hope it is not lice."

Within a week, whether by tom-toms or some smoke signals from the schools in Boston, the word was out. "Down with the cooties." Of course, it is automatically assumed that the cootie plague originated from the Mather School or some other public school. Catholic School kids never got cooties.

My mother is proactive. It may be that she felt that Mother Superior had already carried the belief that little Tommy's a private cootie-carrier. After all, if he can hook school and hang around "Cat Alley" he probably brought the cooties into St. Peter's.

I realize that this revelation in my essay may cause me to be rejected into any college. Maybe Harvard University doesn't accept applicants who have had cooties. Or have cockroaches in their houses. I wonder if there is a question on the SAT about how often one should change his/her underwear or take a bath.

All of these are somewhat indelicate subjects in most families. Not to be discussed at the parent-teacher conference. But this is my essay, and the truth must be told. As a general comment, I change my underwear at least once a week, and my father killed off the roaches long ago. But I have seen roaches in Sy's Variety Store, scurrying around the vegetable bin. And Molly, our huge cat has long rid the house of any mice or rats. My mother's odyssey, like General Patton's 3rd Army was to eliminate all the lice in the family. How she treated all the kids one at a time remained a mystery. I wonder if she ever had lice? I never asked her.

She had me sleep with my hair saturated with oil from the old burner in the kitchen. My head was turbaned like King Tut as I slept. Thank God I didn't smoke or play with matches. Yes, the fireman would exclaim "The kid looked like a flaming torch" as he ran down Barry Street.

The second step in the annihilation of the bugs was more direct. Lice actually prefer clean heads. The nit comb is like a series of metal teeth with very little space between them. My mother would run this through my hair while my head was hanging over in the sink. When she finished the stroke and get the little culprit. She would nudge the cootie to the flat side of the nit comb—then roll her thumb nail like a street roller paving the street and crush them like a tank rolling over the Japs in the WWII movies! You could all but hear their screams. Then, Ma would tap the mashed remains in the drain.

It may have seemed awkward but Ma with all of her children had considerable experience. Actually as she performed the beastly task she'd be humming a soft Newfoundland sea song. Of course my small head was fine but my sisters had long hair, somewhat of an apartment for cooties, so my mother cut their hair short. After only 2 treatments the population of lice had decreased to zero.

And so this concludes the tale of the cooties attacking St. Peter's School. Boys and girls with cooties is no reflection on the school. It's not easy to be a little kid with or without lice. All in all. I survived the cootie experience. But sometimes I wonder if nuns got cooties.

Long after graduating from St. Peter's I met Bruno again. He had a job with his uncle who owned a demolition company, "I love the work," he said, "It feels great to have someone order me to take a sledge hammer and demolish a building."

Saving Teeth at Forsythe Dental Institute
5th Grade 1945

Although not an official part of school, one cannot deny that dental hygiene is an essential aspect of overall health. From a kid's perspective it is part of the school experience. A good percentage of the population of Dorchester are immigrants who came from poor countries. Many of the families back home did not have sufficient food. Dental care was simple, if you have a severe tooth ache your tooth was extracted—sometimes in a kitchen with a bottle of whiskey and a pair of pliers, and Uncle Mike or Grandpa was the resident dentist.

It is only natural that city schools, public and private, have adopted a program that addressed the dental health of its student population. The Forsythe Dental Institute became part of the St. Peter's experience. However, as with many things in life, the situation is a double edged sword. In order to function the Forsythe requires patients—little kids or crudely stated "guinea pigs" to practice the art.

Of course all of my experiences were in the early 40's when you didn't have a shyster lawyer to chaperone you to the check up on the quality of care, such as wrong tooth removed or half of your tongue paralyzed. And there was a baptism of fire involved when you're a little kid. The buzz of the drill, especially when it hits a nerve—aghh! Or the extraction—some stranger sticking a pair of pliers in your mouth while you suffer the crunch, crunch of a tooth being yanked. Your face stuffed with rolls of gauze! Yes, the response ran the spectrum. Some kids toughed it out; others wet their pants. For a few, such trauma, caused them to avoid a dentist for the remainder of their life and there are those gummy parents with ill fitting dentures that fall out when one laughs or chews steak.

However, all things being equal, dental care—free dental care—was a blessing. And the quality of the dental students, in fact, was exceptional. Of course those dental trainees who have a goofy look and wore glasses several inches thick would frighten even the toughest kid. And who wants to spend an afternoon with a strangers hand stuffed into their mouth?

Let me brace myself and relive my first trip to the Forsythe Dental Institute. Now my first trip I viewed as a vacation day from school. One of the joys, as a kid, is the cancellation of school because of snow. However in St. Peter's, there were essentially no such possibility that school would be cancelled for snow. Holy Day, yes—Snow no! But in the scheme of things at St. Peter's there were practices whereby certain grades were transported to the Forsythe Dental Institute for free dental work. No school in the afternoon and a free bus ride! Of course free dental care is obviously a good thing. But little kids never reflect on the meaning of a double edged sword. Dental students in the Forsythe need live specimens to practice their dentistry; cleaning, drilling, and extracting.

The city sights were exciting as we bumped along on the hard seats of the bus. When we arrived we could see the Museum of Fine Arts, an imposing structure. The Forsythe, adjacent to the Museum was also impressive, especially to a group of kids who lived on streets of 3 decker wooden houses.

We pass down unfamiliar streets past the tall buildings. We stop in a large parking lot surrounded by white granite buildings. The bus stops.

"Out!" cries, Sister Maria George—the chaperone first sergeant; she blows the whistle and we tumble out and head for the entrance. The first impression—an overpowering smell of alcohol. When you live in a three decker house, there are distinct smells in the entryway as you enter—cabbage—spaghetti—fish or onions.

But alcohol is definitely not the aroma in my mother's kitchen. And the size of the rooms 15 feet square with 20 foot high ceilings. We march like lemmings into a large room full of chairs, small squirmy boys with frightened eyes. Suddenly you hear a sharp cry, "Oh—Oh—Agh!" And you see a little boy trying to escape the chair. "Sister, where's the toilet?" As we enter the waiting room, we see a boy with a mouth full of gauze—red bloody gauze. Brave Heart or not—get me out of here!

"Sit down," calls the 1st Sergeant. "Alphabetically; A's sit here—B's—Line up!" Those who think quickly shift down to the far end of the seats. Maybe the doctors will get tired of doing teeth and let us go home early. But no such luck. It's like being in the room with the Wizard of Oz—only he's not worried about the Lion, Scarecrow or Tinman. No! he's into teeth—my teeth! Finally, after scrunching in the chair, my name is called. The dental students move in sticking me with the little needle. Does that hurt? How could they expect an answer? The dentists fingers are in my mouth and half way down my throat like baloney rolls.

He said, "My name is Dr. Frankenstein. I am here to examine your teeth and to guide you to the path of good oral hygiene. Are you OK with that?"

"Yes, doctor," I answer with my British soldier stiff upper lip. Actually my dentist was a warm, bright and gentle smile and smelled of tuna fish. He asked, "Do you brush your teeth after every meal?"

I mentioned that with 6 kids in the family, I'm unsure of who's toothbrush is mine. And do you clean between your teeth—with a pick? No—floss. What's floss? Do you brush before bedtime? Then like a flash, I revert to the Proverb, "An ounce of prevention is work a pound of cure." You don't brush, then you lose teeth

He continued, "Ah-ah—hmm—good, oh, no not so good."

When he had finished the exam, he told me I had a small cavity. He drilled a small hole in my tooth and mixed up a compound, and filled the hole he made in my tooth. Next he polished my teeth with a fine powder. After he told me I could rinse my mouth I rolled my tongue across my choppers, my teeth felt smooth and clean.

"How's that?"

"Fine Doctor—can I go now?"

He had his supervisor check the work he had done on my teeth.

"Thank you, Sir." I was extra polite in case I had to come back. My ordeal was ended. The bus ride back to St. Peter's was quiet. There were a few moans when the bus hit an especially big bump, but generally quiet, each of us reflecting on this new experience.

Sister Proverbs
6th thru 8th Grades 1946-1948

As part of the essay project, I was to review my writings with Mr. Flynn, an instructor at Wentworth Institute of Technology. Mr. Flynn was a writer of short stories and he often quoted proverbs in his stories. His love of proverbs and my experience with Sister Elizabeth (aka Sister Proverbs, my nickname for her), created a warm bond between us. This led me to add a brief explanation of my first time going to a speech clinic.

In Commerce High School, Mr. Conroy, my English teacher suggested that I explore elocution lessons in a speech clinic affiliated with Cathedral High School. I was assigned to a nun who was in a doctoral program specializing in speech pathology. Not that I had a serious impediment, I did not stutter like King George of England, or have a tongue as large as a beef steak. No, I had a nasal problem of speaking through my nose; excessive nasal assimilation is the technical term. Actually, the result is that I sounded stupid, like Lenny in Steinbeck's story of *Mice and Men.*

Her name was Sister Elizabeth, or it could have been Sergeant Elizabeth. Her approach to education centered around a practical application for everyday living above and beyond the development of a solid Catholic citizen. At our initial meeting she gave me a copy of *A Message to Garcia* by Hubbard. She instructed me to read the book for the next week and to tell her my thoughts at our next meeting. She gave me the assignment with the demeanor of a Marine drill instructor. Nun or not, she was a no nonsense, tough lady.

I would learn later how appropriate proverbs were everyday life. Next she asked me to explain the proverb, "He that would have the fruit must first climb the tree."

I fumbled something about Newton watching the apple to fall to the earth. Her eyes rolled—suggesting but not saying, "Wrong you dummy, Thomas."

She explained, "My task, is to improve your verbal skills. A resonant voice, proper pronunciation and good diction are skills that will reward you all of your life. I see from your background that your parents are immigrants. I also see that you have picked up an accent, a combination of Dorchester and Boston. In terms of professional careers, speaking deficiencies will not serve you well in life."

"Furthermore if I hear you use profanity, I will ask you to withdraw from the program. Do you understand?"

I nod. I think that maybe the nun will be good training for when I join the paratroopers. I have a great respect for teachers, especially the nuns at St. Peters

Sister Elizabeth was a young woman, tall and thin. Not a wrinkle on her smooth face, almost baby like skin. Her cheeks were high and she wore rimless glasses. Her voice was soft, but firm, and always perfectly professional. In fact, I imagined that she had a beautiful singing voice.

We met once a week for two hours during my senior year at Commerce High. Most of the practice sessions were in standard diaphragmatic breathing, project your voice, use your optimal pitch and correct pronunciation. "Do not—I repeat—do not drop your r's and g's at the end of a word." a—e—i—o—u. Correct tongue placement."

Every week she would hand out lessons for me to practice for one hour a day on a variety of elocution exercises. During each class we would practice them. During the last twenty minutes of class she would hand out a list of proverbs and ask for an explanation of the proverb and we would consider the wisdom and the wit of them.

Below are my favorite twenty-five proverbs:

1) When poverty comes in at the door, love creeps out at the window.
2) He who plants trees loves others besides himself.
3) A hunk of bread today is better than cake tomorrow.
4) Death is the poor man's doctor.
5) Hope is a good breakfast but a bad supper.
6) Don't kick a man when he is down.
7) Pity is a poor plaster.
8) Experience is the best teacher.
9) A soft word never broke a tooth yet.
10) The eye of a friend is a good looking glass.
11) Sweet is wine, bitter its payment.
12) Don't kill the goose that lays the golden egg.

13) Half a loaf is better than no bread.
14) Forgetting one's debts does not pay them.
15) If you believe all you hear, you can eat all you see.
16) Better come empty than with bad news.
17) One cockroach knows another.
18) An apple never falls far from the tree.
19) Oh what a tangled web we weave, when first we start to deceive.
20) Two wrongs don't make a right.
21) Don't bite more than you can chew.
22) It's the squeaky wheel that gets the grease.
23) Live and let live.
24) Better be idle than working for nothing.
25) Three without rule! A boy, a pig and a mule.

I all but cried when the year of our lessons ended. I guess you could say that I loved Sister Proverbs. On the last day she gave me a little present. It was a trophy that read "Tom Melvin, Master of Proverbs." And a note that said, "Good Luck, Tom. Should I refer to you as the originator of me being 'Sister Proverbs?' P.S. There are no secrets in any organization—High School or a Speech Clinic. Best Wishes, Sister Elizabeth."

My Passage Through The Neighborhood

Saturday mornings: 6-8 years old climbing fences, trees, garages, rock walls

Early Saturday morning, Jimmy and Jack—two of my kid friends, would start at the rock formation at Barry and Quincy Street. We became very proficient scaling the walls as though they were the North Face of the mountain. Then we proceeded down the alleys—climbing all in route: fences, trees, and garages. Good practice for future second story men when we reached adulthood.

Saturday afternoons: 6-10 years old at the toy store owned by 2 Syrian brothers

Zarkie and Ruben—a classic ying and yang pair—Zarkie smiled and Ruben frowned. The store was located next to the Hammy Theatre—providing a large window area which showed hundreds of toys, trains, dolls, games, trucks, soldiers and a host of cheap toys (manufactured in Japan—guaranteed to last at least a few hours) on Saturday afternoons. As the kids waited in line for the movie to open, a hundred boys and kids, drooled over the vast array of toys available for their delight—as long as you had money—which most kids did not have. Inside the store, the walls were stacked with toys, and also edibles—one prominent edible was a small tray of sliced pickles which upon inspection was covered with dust, a few dead flies (and other unidentifiable bugs) and a misplaced green crayon at the bottom.

Alongside was the candy case: it was during certain war-time periods of rationing food or bubble gum. Yes, the Hammy Spa rationed the bubble gum. Kids learned early that if you were a good customer, bubble gum would be available for sale. For the rest of the kids, it was you're SOL. At the exit there was a display of goodies adjacent to the door—the temptation was too great for many kids (Sister School or not)—a whole rack of Hostess Chocolate Cupcakes would disappear and into their jacket pockets—(only a venal sin). Anyway Syrians are not Catholics.

The Hamilton Theatre—(Hammy)

I would suspect that most neighborhoods in Boston have one or multiple theatres or "shows" but Danny's lays claim to the "Hammy" especially as it relates to a Saturday afternoon for the kid's show. If you have only one dime to your name, an afternoon in a toy store is no fun—unless you happen to be the world's greatest shop lifter—a very unlikely successful activity with 2 sets of Hindu eyes watching your every move.

But in the Hammy your dime pays for an afternoon of two movies, a Tom and Jerry Cartoon, a bouncing ball sing-a-long (which is somewhat stupid because most of the kids there can't read, dislike singing, and frankly, just want action—the Cowboys and Indian movie.) All of this is capped off with a Buck Rogers Serial which probably has a hundred episodes at a slow pace of one per week. I know of no one who actually saw the last episode.

Typical movies involve the Long Ranger and Tonto, or Roy Rogers, Trigger and Dale Evans or even better Leo Gorcey and the East Side Kids meet Dracula and Frankenstein. At the conclusion of an East Side Kid movie when the older girl is kidnapped by the "bad guys", Leo Gorcey led his troops running like hell down the street and over the fence to rescue the girl in danger. The audience would go wild with hollering and stamping their feet on the floor and sometimes banging the chairs. The old Hammy building actually shook. From the street level the building reminded one of a volcano ready to erupt. But the girl was always rescued, the lava cooled, and the little kids exited the building fully satiated. One thin dime certainly brought undue pleasure.

However, if you were a third grader from St. Peters' and there were older kids from the Mather School, (a public school known for is bullies) there could be trouble. A noogie here and an elbow there; of course if you had a high school brother, you would be safe.

As you got older, the ushers had the upper hand. If you talked or laughed loud, or ran around, the usher could have you ejected. If you pulled the hair of the girl in front of you, or stuck a wad of gum to the seat then you could be banned for a month or longer.

The older you got, cleverer you would become in your harassing of the usher and other fellow patrons. You might eat pistachio nuts all day and save the shells and when the theatre became dark, you surreptitiously deposited the shells onto the aisle floor. As the usher "walked his beat" he would crunch-crunch the shells. There was much merriment.

Friday Nights: Teenage Years—Alcohol and Sex

This was the era of alcohol and sex—the anticipated phase of life's precocious joys. Our first obstacle of the night was to get an adult to buy us beer. Usually the purchaser was someone's older brother, or possibly a neighborhood cretin with a very low IQ who charged a few dollars for his services. As we got older we faked our own ID's by going to City Hall and getting a birth certificate. The paper was a parchment which would turn white if you put bleach on it. So we'd dip the entire document in the tray of bleach and with a bit o flight rubbing, the ink would disappear. When the paper dried, we'd fill out the doctored information with a ball point pen. With our own ID's we could purchase our own booze, generally Pickwick Ale. One problem solved.

One New Year's Eve with the temperature plummeting to 15 degrees below zero, we trudged up to Ronan Park and huddled like a group of buffalo on the plains in a blizzard. We would drink the beers, get little buzz on, vomit a few times and go home looking like we were returning from a trip to the North Pole. The next day we would brag about what a great night we had, as no one had succumbed to hypothermia.

With respect to sex, I ask what sex? I would truthfully say that in my teens I was more celibate than the Indian mounted outside of the Museum of Fine Arts. I suspect most teenagers, if not all of my friends, were likewise. The 50's were not the decade of teenage "action"—at least not in Dorchester. The highlight of my sexual experience occurred when I was in the Waldoff Cafeteria in Upham's Corner. I would sit at a table, in the low lighted section of the place, pretending to be reading a magazine and catch a peek up the dresses of the young unsuspecting girls. Not old ladies who sat with their legs spread at 48 degree angles. No, my targets were the teenage girls who were sitting with their legs slightly parted. I would sneak a peek. If I caught a glance of underwear, that was boyo! What of the 6th

Commandment? It was my rule that if I stared for only 5 seconds it was a venial sin; but anything over an hour was a little more serious.

COMMERCE HIGH SCHOOL

In its heyday, Commerce emphasized business courses; accounting, business math, typing, economics, business methods, etc. Courses which would prepare the student for jobs with banks, insurance companies, major and minor corporations.

In that time many high schools had specialties. For example Trade High School taught auto mechanics, Charlestown taught electrical, Dorchester taught carpentry.

The 1950's began a transition period throughout the Boston High Schools. I enjoyed my friends and that period of my life. Because we had to take the trackless trolley or bus to school, it was our first experience away from Dorchester. The school was located on Louis Pasteur Avenue, across the street from Boston Latin School.

The teachers were committed to their profession, if you were willing to learn, they would make sure you achieved your goal. I could not ask for a better English teacher than Mr. Conroy, nor math teacher like Mr. Marsh.

Commerce was a school for only boys. Being shy and insecure, I missed the opportunity to socialize with girls. As a wallflower, I did not date, learn to dance or attend prom. The school had a dress code—no blue jeans—period. Boys who disobeyed were sent home.

The school was adjacent to the Harvard Medical School, and because there was very little security we would go into the Medical Museum and stare at the body pats in jars and the antique medical instruments that were used hundreds of years ago. Actually, it was a prime experience for a young boy to be exposed to such an incredible example of quality education.

One day as Bobby and I walked across the Harvard Medical School Quad on our way home, we walked past an abandoned paint can and brush which offered too much temptation to pass by. On a beautiful stone wall, Bobby painted "SULLY" in four foot letters. I can well imagine the curses from the maintenance people and the administrators.

In my freshman year, one of the students stole a bunch of blank report cards. That year there was an abundance of students on the Honor Roll. This continued until a mother was called to the school and the jig was up. No longer could Commerce boast a 99% student body who were on the honor roll and destined to graduate suma cum laude.

School Of Hard Knocks

Trips to the City Hospital and Other Medically Memorable Events

Dislocated Elbow—Horseback Fight (Age 8)

My first broken bone happened during a horseback fight on Barry Street. I rode on my brother's back (piggy back style) and our opponents were likewise. The object of this crude "Knights of the Round Table" clash was to knock the rider off of his "horse". My brother made a quick turn and I was propelled to the streets—my elbow knocking the granite curb and dislocating the bone. The first words out of brother was, "Oh my God! Don't tell Ma that I did it!" My family and most neighbors did not own automobiles so we walked to Bowdoin Street to catch a trolley. A passing motorist saw the commotion, and drove me to the emergency room. I vividly remember his words as he saw the bone displaced and said, "Well, kid, you won't be swimming very much this summer."

I stayed in the hospital two weeks. During that stay, I developed a strong dislike for milk—every day the milk served in a thick mug—was warm and smelled sour. For years I shied way from milk at home until we got refrigeration and the milk was cold.

Inserting My Hand into the Washing Machine Ringer

I was visiting my aunt when she was washing clothes. The ringer on top of the machine was used to squeeze out the water of the washed clothes.

I wondered what would happen if I inserted my fingers into the ringer. I discovered the answer immediately. A paddy wagon took me to the emergency room. No broken bones.

Fractured Ankle—Run over by Auto (Age 10 years)

I was in the 5th grade approximately and I was on the running board of a parked auto on Barry Street. Down the street came Phil, a kid who was "after" me. I jumped from the running board and when a box type Ford ran over my ankle, fracturing the ankle bone. The kid who lived on the 3rd floor said to the driver—"It's OK mista he's laughing." What a jerk! Via the MTA, my cousin who was about my age took the wrong train and I had to limp a long way to the emergency room of the Boston City Hospital. Finding a stick, I hobbled to the emergency room like one of those Chinese refugees.

Broken Wrist—Sandlot Football (15 years old)

Sandlot football was my thing. Our sandlot was Ronan Park. During this week we played at Garvey Field in Neponset which was unfamiliar to us. We were punting; the kick was blocked—I caught the football got turned around, and ran the wrong way—just like Wrong Way Corrigan. Then in a heroic attempt to erase the blunder, I broke my wrist. Someone gave me a ride to the Boston City Hospital. As Shakespeare wrote, "The evil men do live long after them, the good are oft interred with their bones." This was considered a "bad" day.

Tonsils

As with most kids, the time arrived when the tonsils had to be removed. My mother deposits me, so there I was in my Johnny with my ass hanging out for all the girl nurses to see.

I was with a fairly large group of kids whose asses were also hanging out. Even though I was leery concerning the future tonsillectomy, I was truly impressed with the wide diversity of asses—shapes, colors and textures. Naturally you are afraid, especially when several nurses bring us into room adjacent to the latrine. There is a gurney with tubes and what not. Here she says, lay on your stomach. Very business like the nurse lifts up my Johnny and inserts a tube inside me. The warm fluid really runs its course like it's held by a fireman. Wow! Do I have to go! I take off to the toilet. And as Sister Proverb would say, "He who hesitates is lost!" The second part of this process is the removal of the tonsils which are on the opposite end of my body. Compared to Forsythe, this tonsil ordeal is big time. It sort of reminds you of an execution of twenty people—who goes first?

It is often said that the pigs who are climbing the ramp to be executed know that their fate is coming to a head. I swear that little kids have that uncanny sense that all is not well. It's the "Twilight Zone."

A nurse, dressed in green including a green mask—reminds me of a gecko—points to one boy—"your turn." The kid starts to take off—crying at the top of his voice. The others try to calm him down as he pees all over his Johnny. She makes eye contact with me—"What about you? I bet you're a tough kid from Dorchester" I clench my jaw and shake my head more from fear than acquiescence and walk through the door (just like the little piggies). I'm too scared to cry or run. Will it be worse than what was stuck in my bum? I lay on the table face up thinking that my bum is safe. This giant of a man with the green mask and a pair of lenses on his glasses that would challenge a coke bottle. They put a spaghetti strainer over my face. I am motionless, but when they pour the ether and I start to spin, with all of my energy, I yell Ma! Ma! Ma-a-a—off into oblivion.

The only redeeming part of the experience is the Aspirin Gum.

Dumb Move Category—Rubber Water Pistol Filled with Lighter Fluid

I filled the rubber water pistol with Ronson lighter fluid—like Tom the Torch in the circus, I expect to bring the lit match to the nozzle, squeeze—and hooray—a flaming whoosh. Unfortunately the only thing that caught fire was my hand.

To alleviate the pain that night I hang my hand off the bed into a bucket of water. Big blisters. Another kid, Frankie—a few years older filled his mouth with lighter fluid—lit a match—whoosh—successful like in the circus. Thank God, I'd look like the Elephant Man.

Sucker Punched (No trip to the City Hospital)

Carnival time in St. Peter's School yard, I was exiting the activity. A young man—never seen—chose me at random and slammed me in the side of my face with his fist. All I remember as I lay on the blacktop driveway is a non-existent referee counting 1, 2, . . . and if I stayed down for the count, I would die. Somehow I beat the count and did not expire. But what a shiner I had. It was a strange experience to say the least and to this day, every once in a while, I descend to the cellar, take my voodoo dolls who represent the clown who punched me. I coolly drive a 10 penny nail through his eyeballs and other unequivocal parts of his body.

US PARATROOPERS

Enlisted, July 6, 1953

Why did you join, you ask? Because, maybe it was preordained that I make this decision. Attached is a photo of me taken in the 2nd or 3rd grade. Please focus on my necktie—a paratrooper floating down to earth with his parachute.

Transition

As a measure of how serious this decision—my exit from kid-hood to manhood was illuminated by my father's parting words spoken with tears in his eyes, "If you get a dishonorable discharge, you can't come home."

My first ride in an airplane was after I joined the paratroopers. This action was a direct violation of the important proverb, "Look before you leap"—no pun intended. The flight was from Boston to Ft. Campbell, KY on an airplane which had many rattles and vibrations.

My first meal at Fort Campbell was lima beans and liver—God, this is going to be a long ordeal!

Highlights of Basic Training

1st Sergeant Brick emphasized "Never point a rifle at a man unless you plan to shoot him." Farewell to make believe fun games such as cowboys and Indians and cops and robbers.

As part of basic training, the company would pull "Prison Chaser"—guarding stockade prisoners as they cleaned the roads, landscaped the grounds, visiting the hospital for examinations, etc. All guards received adequate training, and all were armed with a shotgun and the warning, "If the prisoner escapes, you take his place in the stockade, no ifs, ands, or buts!" A fellow, Pvt. Ellis in my platoon, allowed his prisoner to go into the latrine while Ellis waited outside. The prisoner bolted out the window. That evening Ellis did not return to our barracks—he was in the stockade. A hard lesson, indeed!

During the next prison chaser duty, a month later, a young and very small soldier, "Shorty Wilson" was out in the woods with his prisoners, clearing brush. Shorty's prisoner took off! "Halt! Halt or I'll shoot!" Shorty blew his head off. Shorty was transferred to another camp. I never saw him again.

Combat Experience—Mottley

In the Army, on Friday nights, there is a GI Party, during which the platoon cleans the barracks, top to bottom. Like most group tasks, there is the element of "Goof off time." In this case, a station wagon with a sign selling tonic, chocolate milk, sandwiches, etc. stops by the barracks. During the break, I observed the acting corporal drinking a coke. He was probably in the army a week longer than most of the platoon. He was a big lanky black boy from Alabama named Mottley.

I purchased a chocolate milk and when Mottley saw me, he began to yell at me. Then he knocked the milk out of my hand—I charged him. (During the previous week the platoon had been on the rifle range in the raging sun. Therefore, my lips were blistered—touch the blisters and they bleed. Well, there was blood all over the barracks; unfortunately it was all of my blood. Mottley knocked me down and as I tried to get on my feet, he kicked me in the forehead—a solid hit that would have been a 50 yard goal. Enraged—my face soaked with blood, I charged him again. Frightened of my bloody face and my scream he ran between 2 bunks. There was a disassembled M1 rifle on a bunk. I made a grab for the barrel assembly to use as a club.—Then the Platoon Sergeant broke up the fight. I lost the battle, for sure. But I won the war. For the remainder of Basic Training, all hands in the whole company, gave me considerable leeway, especially Mottley.

Combat Experience—Potter

For paratroopers, the boots have special significance. Corcoran Brothers in Stoughton manufacture these boots which sell for $50.00. Each soldier is responsible to purchase his own boots. I loved spit shining my boots to a bright glow. One Saturday night, I set my boots under my bunk.

In the morning the boots were missing, stolen! I was livid. I scoured the barracks (Fox Company) with my friend Mitchell, a rancher from Iowa. Later that morning a soldier from Easy Company walks through the barracks and asks, "Where's Potter, the fellow who wants to sell the jump boots?" Potter's bunk was on the second level. I confronted him. He was a very fat man—unusual for Airborne Training. He denied the theft passionately. As the day passed, I was getting nowhere until Mitchell screamed at me—and sic'd me on Potter as though I was a German Shepard "Get Him!" We punched each other and on the ground Potter got on top of me. I was trapped like I was smothered by an elephant. Mitchell rolled me on top. After a few waps, Potter ran to the Orderly Room for protection. The long and the short of it was that I never saw my boots again. Lesson learned! Hide your valuables.

Another case in point, one weekend we were allowed to swim in Kentucky Lake. They had open crate lockers in the changing room and someone stole my whole Army Kit, shirt, pants, underwear, watch, HS ring from Commerce High School. In order to return to camp I stole someone's uniform except for boots which looked like size 18. Thank God, I was not caught by the owner. He must have been a very big man! I looked like one of the seven dwarfs the way the clothes hung from my body. To this day, whenever I go to a gym I always carry all of my valuables on my person.

Major Events of My Military Experience

During a parachute jump at Yamota Drop Zone at Fort Campbell, this exercise involved the drop of the whole regiment jumping from 1200 feet, including jeeps and heavy equipment across the drop zone.

I was in the first wave. After I landed, I was running to my designated assembly point where I would join my company. I looked up to see another wave of C-119's coming—troops began to parachute out. Therefore I began running out of harm's way—a loose helmet, rifle, piece of equipment might drop on my head.

As I ran about 70 to 100 yards away, over a little rise, I caught a quick blur and heard a dull thump like a duffle bag hitting the ground. I rmoved to the sound. It was a soldier who plummeted to the ground from 1000-1500 feet. Later I found out he was a private from Medical Company whose static line had broken. He failed to deploy his emergency chute. Someone said that he hit the ground face first. Although I was the first to his body, all I can remember was that his chin pointed at right angles to the direction that it should have pointed.

This was the first and only time I witnessed a violent death, and hopefully the last.

Bobby Bazooka

There was an older fellow in my platoon from Tennessee, and his name was Robert Lee, affectionately known as Bobby Bazooa to the platoon. In the Airborne, the recruits are generally 17, 18 and 19. But he was about 24 which is old for a recruit; however he was very intelligent and worldly—a product of a southern military family and The Tennessee Military Academy. Unfortunately he was expelled from this academy—I suspect with his gentle voice and engaging manner and his drop dead good looks that his transgression(s) somehow involved a woman.

One weekend Bobby and I had a weekend pass in the Town Pump, a soldier's bar in Clarksville Tennessee. I thought Bobby was a great guy and we became good buddies. We had great conversations about the North and South. But with guys, especially, young soldiers, the subject of women came up. Now I went into the service at 17 and now I'm about 19, and still a virgin. After a few beers with Bobby, I came to the conclusion, that if I screwed off the top of his head, all I would find is a giant penis. Bobby liked his women, "good old girls" is how be referred to them, with not the slightest hint of irreverence. And he was well equipped both with his soft pleasant voice, a southern charm and a body part that caused the boys in the platoon to call him Bobby the Bazooka.

Bobbie would often shake his head and exclaim "I don't know how the North won the war, you all with your little Yankee weenies."

Anyway, we're at the bar and Bobby is talking about his first sexual experience. "Let me tell you all about this old girl, a real beauty. We were having a picnic in the woods. It was a real nice day, the ground is covered with small wildflowers and we are sittin' right by a small stream. We spread out the blanket . . ." He pauses, looks out the tavern window at the cloudless sky. Closing his eyes his face is so peaceful and reflective as though he is recalling a beautiful scene.

"She undresses and lays down in those little flowerbed." He sighs. "I'll tell you this, Muzzy, my eyes all but popped out of my head. I can still see that image right now."

"She lays in those flowers and I stare at her hard. Lordy, Lordy, that has got to be the most beautiful thing I ever saw. You ain't got to believe it but there was even a couple of them lady bugs flying around."

"Bobby, you're full of bullshit! Actually I am impressed.

"Maybe a little bit, but not by much" Bobbie says, "Let me tell you, Muzzy, when we graduate from jump school, I'm going to take you down to Nashville and fix you up with a nice gal."

And in fact, he did. There no wildflowers or lady bugs. But it was glorious experience.

Jail in Clarksville

On another weekend pass several buddies and I were arrested for disturbing the peace. We spent the night in jail. A virtual dungeon with "Soldiers Home" chalked on the wall. At that time Webb Pierce had a hit song, "We're in the Jailhouse Now!" We sang that song until our voices became hoarse.

All along the walls was a seat probably 18" wide, barely enough to lay down sideways. There was a toilet in the corner. Another cell held the local town dregs and criminals.

At dawn, which seemed like a month's time in Alcatraz, we were fed breakfast. An aluminum container of macaroni and a large raw onion. Southern hospitality at it's finest. (See receipt attached $25.00 fine.)

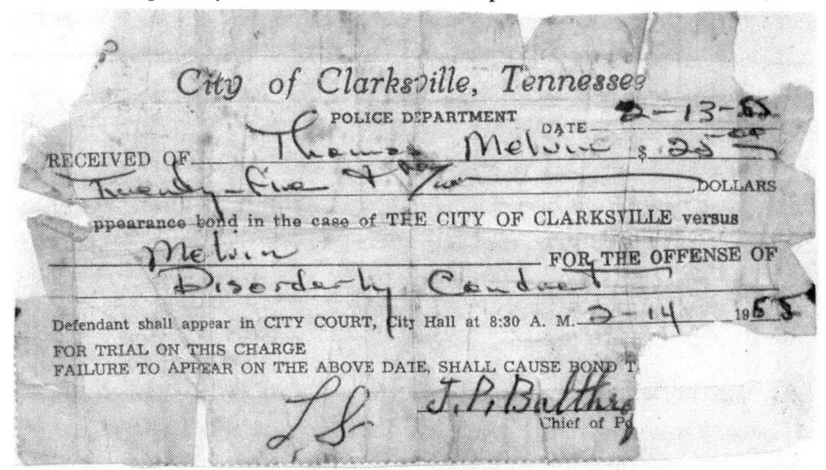
City of Clarksville, Tennessee

POLICE DEPARTMENT DATE 2-13-55

RECEIVED OF Thomas Melvin $ 25.00

Twenty-Five & no/100 DOLLARS

ppearance bond in the case of THE CITY OF CLARKSVILLE versus

Melvin FOR THE OFFENSE OF

Disorderly Conduct

Defendant shall appear in CITY COURT, City Hall at 8:30 A. M. 2-14 1955

FOR TRIAL ON THIS CHARGE

FAILURE TO APPEAR ON THE ABOVE DATE, SHALL CAUSE BOND T

J. P. Balthr

Chief of P

Automobile Accident Rte. 41A Fayetteville, NC (1955)

Several buddies and I made the rounds of Fayetville, NC outside of Fort Bragg. On the return trip to Fort Bragg I sat beside the driver who drove off the road and down an embankment. I broke my upper arm on the steering wheel. In the hospital, the doctors operated and a rod was inserted into the middle of my bone between the elbow and the shoulder. After six months of healing, the doctor removed the rod. I made a bracelet out of the rod, which I wear on my left wrist to this day, certainly a solid remembrance of my time in the Airborne.

Lousy jobs

Employment as a teenager through my early 20's

Car Wash—I worked for a short time at the car wash in Neponset Circle. You have to be thick skinned to survive in the car wash, "Hey boy! There's a little dirt on my wheel! (The car looked like it participated in the Normandy Invasion) Move! Move!

Tomato Factory—I worked a few weeks, 7 AM to 7 PM, 6 days a week. Sunday morning 7 AM to Noon, a ½ hour lunch, and 2-15 minute breaks. My job was to stand at the conveyor belt and sort tomatoes. Ripe tomatoes were transferred down a sloped platform to a fellow who packs them in a box. Green tomatoes went to the end and went into refrigerators to ripen. Rotten tomatoes went in a barrel. After an hour the tomatoes began to look like apples, oranges, and peppers. A fellow worker next to me said, "This is a great job!" "Bullshit," I said.

Roofing—learned how to work hard in the weather and take abuse in a job that is, in fact, dangerous. Good people to work with. The diversity of workers was extensive—from Crazy Charlie who one work day, when a hearse rode by, said, "That's my father. He's a no good prick."

The foreman, Mickey V was rather profane and somewhat erratic. He had lost a foot on the Normandy Beachhead and he was trying to impress a state inspector on the roof as he looked into the shrimp boat full of hot bubbling roof pitch, "That must be hot." "Nah," he muttered as he stuck his artificial foot into the bucket. Another time, on a very, very hot day, the workers wanted to quit early and go home. In response, Mickey picked up a metal scratch bar and held it like a baseball bat. "Anyone who tries to leave, I'll bash in his head." No one left.

Tug Boat—I worked on a tug boat for Mass Tow on Four Point Channel towing Esso Oil Barges around the New England Coast. On one shift we were off the Nantasket Beach with storm clouds ready to break. I was on watch on the bridge with Ray, the first mate. I saw what I thought was a buoy, but it was one of four fellows—drunk as skunks—fooling around in a small outboard boat. The boat had capsized. We could not go directly to them because we were towing a huge oil barge. We had to slowly circle around. Two of the boaters panicked and tried to swim to the tug—risking their lives because the oil barge could not stop. In any case we called the Coast Guard who arrived just before a thunderstorm. I often wonder if those drunk clowns realized how close they were to meeting their maker. One interesting character, the cook named "Plab" on the tug had a blind eye which was all white. He'd wear a pair of sunglasses with eye piece missing over the white eye.

Coat Factory—Herbie and I got a job in a coat factory one Friday in the summer. His job was to press the buttons into leather pockets; my job was to steam press the wrinkles out of winter coats. At this lunchtime, the boss told us that we had to work on Saturday. We quit, got our $3.00 paid for our morning hours and drank beer that night.

Pulling Weeds in Texaco Oil Yard—Because the oil tanks in the yard on Chelsea Creek were huge and combustible, our jobs was to pull out the weeds. If someone flipped a cigarette over the wall and ignited the weeds—BOOM! We would place the weeds in cardboard boxes and launched them into Chelsea Creek, a Viking Funeral. A great job for kids.

Hat Store—I worked in a Millinery Store town in Boston. Because I was not a good employee, the boss thought I moped around the store. He decided to sack me. I overheard his telephone call to the agency: He was loud: He needed to get rid of the "mope (me)." So I called my pal, Jack, who applied for the job. Then I was fired. Of course, Jack never showed up. Screw the boss. The "Mope" wins this time

Mowing Lawns at Cedar Grove Cemetery—I mowed lawns one summer. No electric mowers. It was tough work. One kid worked with me, Smitty was his nickname. Of course in a cemetery, when you had to urinate, you just found an isolated area. But he always went to the headstone of John Churchill. "Why do you do that?" I asked. He answered "That's my landlord's headstone. I hate the bastard! Always yelling at me!"

Happiest Years Of My Life

Quincy Quarries

Quincy, Massachusetts, home of the 2nd and 7th presidents, both named John Adams, is also home to the Quincy Quarries. There are a number of quarries, Cashman's, Goldies, Green Tank and several others. Imagine a hole drilled in this massive block of granite, say 500 feet by 1000 feet, and no bottom—not true but certainly deep enough to sink old cars, stolen cars, and junk, and possibly a few bodies. Actually his deep hole was the result of quarrying valuable granite used world wide in monumental buildings, statues, rich lobbies in banks, and more plebian—curbs for sidewalks. The actual stone work was terminated when water springs were encountered, and consequently filled up the excavations to the point that it was economically move viable to relocate the excavation operations to another site. And as the saying goes one man's problem is another man's joy—hence we have swimming locations scattered around the Blue Hills which invite boys and men to swim. There is only one ground rule: Only swimmers can survive in the quarries because once you step off the ledge, the water depth may be 10-50-100 feet deep. Only guys swam in the quarries because we all swam bare ass. In the 1950-60's women did not participate in such activities. In fact most guys, myself included, did not own a bathing suit.

It is said that happiness is the ambrosia that you ingest as food and nectar is the drink that you sip as you attempt to escape your present situation. Without doubt swimming in Cashman's Quarry with my buddies was the happiest and most carefree days of my teenage years and early twenties. At least that is how I remember these times.

Why? Because there was no Ma or Pa, no lifeguards, no cops, no rules, no teachers, no homework, it was like "Lord of the Flies" with your buddies. It was a day of adventure jumping off the cliffs, Lewis and Clark climbing another mountain—not quite as dramatic but fun. Diving for coke caps, playing baseball using the frogs as the softballs, and branches as the bats. And the adventure of hitchhiking.

Because most of my buddies are first generation Americans, the parents come from Ireland, England, Canada, Sweden, Poland, Norway—generally Europe. Most parents had no idea of what we were up to. "Where you off to, boy?" asked my mother. "Going to the quarries, Ma." She had no visions of me jumping off cliffs, or drowning or being picked up a drunk driver.

In fact, when I was a teenager, hitchhiking was the only way to get to Cashman's. generally, we'd walk past Field's Corner, stand by a traffic light, and stick our thumb out. "Ride, Mister?" we'd call through an open window. More often than not we'd hitch a ride, especially if the driver was an ex-quarry rat himself.

On this one day, I'm hitching with Jimmy Cully and Herbie Whitten. A car stops—another little adventure.

"Sometimes, you'd hear an interesting story. A burly guy in his 30's or 40's, driving a new Buick "You know, when I was your age, I'd go to Goldies. After high school I joined the Marines and fought on Iwo. When I got discharged I went to BU on the G.I. Bill. Now I own my own business selling mechanical machinery. Got a great family too."

"But I look at you three and my heart breaks." He continues, "To be your age and hitching to the quarries. It's crazy. I've got the world by the balls and yet I'm so envious of you kids. We pull up at the variety store. This the place?" he asks, "You still dive for bottle caps?"

I nod, "Yes."

"Listen, kids, you take care—remember that time passes so quick. Enjoy yourselves."

We stop in the store, buy three Hershy bars and some soda, and look around for bottle caps. On the way to Cashman's, we reach a block of granite probably 3 feet by 3 feet and 4 feet high. It was a superstition for travelers along this path to pick up a piece of granite from the trail and place it on the granite block. On the return trip one was to remove the piece of granite and toss it back on the ground for luck.

The quarries can be dangerous. If someone was killed, it was generally from a leap from the cliff and hitting rocks just under the waters surface or hitting the telephone pole floating in the water. Of course during daylight you could see the culprit under the surface. Swimming or jumping off the cliffs at night was another activity that was even more dangerous. And a few unfortunate boys died. Another cause of death was drinking alcohol. Last but not least was drowning. I include myself, a lousy swimmer, but most of my friends were good swimmers, so my chances of a rescue is much improved.

It was more likely that the boys would bring beer to the quarries at night. The combination of beer, darkness, and boys with risky natures is a recipe for disaster. It is a proven physiological fact that many boys and adult males are missing chunks of brains.

Obviously, it was very dangerous if one were to jump from the top of the side wall—which ranged from 20 to 70 feet. A rocky dirt road ran around the perimeter of the vertical walls. From this road, the most adventurous ran barefoot and leapt into the water below. These high points were named descriptively, Suicide, The Roof, The Point and the notorious Black Harry.

Jimmy Cully and I would often make the jump from The Point. He would dive head first, and I would jump and hit the water with my feet. I'm no dummy.

Painted on the face of the walls was the graffiti: *Joe, U.S. Marines, Bobby, U.S. Navy, Charlie, Southie Shamrocks, Mary and Bill, Red Raiders, Rockets, Chippewas.*

Stolen Clothes

Actually having your clothes stolen is not a physical danger but an embarrassing possibility. Generally you rolled up your clothes in a cylindrical bundle and tucked it near a boulder close by. Because you swam naked, it seemed prudent to guard your clothes with the eye of an eagle. Why? For one, if you had a new pair of levis, an expensive pair of sneakers, your high school graduation watch and a "Marine Garry Belt" you would be valued over $100.00. My prime concern was, "Can you hear the roar of your old man!"

To every kid in the quarries, I warn, if a culprit steals your bundle, you face this dilemma, you are naked and 20-30 miles from home. You now have two choices; hitch hike home naked, or steal someone else's clothes. First and foremost be cautious of those kids from Southie, Charlestown, and Roxbury, they'll swipe anything; 10 year old sneakers with holes in the toes, or ripped underpants that are more like a loin cloth with a crosshatch of skid marks.

Final warning: Don't bother to steal their clothes. Better you should hitchhike naked.

The Flat Rock

After hours of swimming, diving for bottle caps, jumping from cliffs, hitting frogs for home runs, it's time to wind down. My favorite place is the Flat Rock, actually a horizontal granite slab, 3x5 feet and it sits about 3 feet above the water. i splash water on the surface to cool down the granite, and I lay down using my bundle of clothing as my pillow and light up a Camel. Nothing like a smoke after a swim. So enjoyable. I feel like Ted Williams after he hits a grand slam. Time to rest and meditate.

Here I am, age 21, recently discharged after 3 years in the Airborne, ready to go to college. I choose Aeronautical Engineering as my major. I worry if I can complete the program. I need lots of prep courses, algebra, geometry, physics and what else? Money? I have the G.I. Bill. $110 per month for 4 years. Tuition at B.U. is about $900 per year. I figure if I run short I can work part-time and earn spending money for beer. It's a can do situation.

The quarries have been a part of my life since I was 16. Upon a little reflection, my time at the quarries has been some of the happiest times of my life. Not Ha-Ha funny but definitely peaceful, enjoyable, and productive. What am I going to do with my life? Ideas buzz through my brain. I guess the stream of consciousness is the passage to creativity. Let go and flow, I tell myself. It is so peaceful, I begin to doze off. Quickly, I catch myself before I fall asleep and cover my privates with my shorts.

Sometimes in this state, impure thoughts from the testosterone factory enter my head. But they must quickly extinguished before my buddies start throwing insults and possibly frogs or rocks at me.

All this seems like a dream; the noise, the splashing, the laughing. Am I here?

In general, I am more of a dreamer than a doer. In my stomach there is that panic feeling of doubt and possibly failure. It's odd but my friends from Dorchester view the job market with little fear. "Go public, boy—City, State, the Feds, Cop, Fireman, Gas, Edison—go for the pension!"

Is that what I want? The security? I really don't think so. I guess only time will tell.

The Trip Home

Herbie wakes me, "Hey, Muzzy! Time to go. Jimmy already got a ride from one of the guys. He's got union class tonight!"

So we dress and conclude a very good day; the adventure of hitchhiking, excitement of cliff jumping, no stolen clothing. We hike the trail to the "monolith" and remove our stones in respect to the gods for our future of surviving and having a great day.

Now maybe it may be my imagination but a massive black cloud blocked the sun so that the trail became darkened. At the bottom of the trail were about seven boys—strangers to us—but several wore "Quincy" on their t-shirts. "Hey!' called out the biggest fellow, "You from Quincy."

"No, Dorchester." I answered.

Another boy who had a very large nose—an aardvark I thought, the biggest of the group, asked Herbie, "Do ya have a smoke?"

Before Herbie could answer, he punched him in the stomach, a real solid and surprising hit! Herbie dropped like a stone!

Without even thinking, I blurted out, "You shouldn't have done that, kid! He just got released from the hospital with an appendix operation!"

Aardvark's face turned ashen. He backed away from Herbie.

Herbie held his stomach tightly and issued a moan that would have curdled the hair on Frankenstein's head, "AHHHOOOOH!"

I was hoping that blood would start gushing from Herb's eyes and ears and really scare the shit out of Aardvark and his gang.

No blood came, so I knelt by Herb and took his pulse—probably on the wrong side of his wrist.

"Is he ok?" asked one of the gang.

"Only time will tell." Again Herb emits a guttural sound. "Only time will tell. Get out of here before I get the police."

"Thank you," one said to me.

As they scurried away, I thought, "Quincy may have produced two presidents but their current offspring need some improvement."

Retaliation is Swift

On the following day, Herbie told Jimmy Cully, a very tough young man. Although I was not present, a few days later, at Cashman's, Jimmy was shown Aardvark. "Hey, You!" Jimmy shouted. You bothering my friends? Then he slammed a wet bathing suit across Aardvark's face.

"I'll be back with a closed fist if you ever bother them again!"

Proverb, "All's well that ends well."

Dorchester Citizen's Club

There is a proverb that says, "Give a beggar a horse and he will ride it to death." The Club upstairs had a steadily shrinking number of members, primarily old timers, many of whom were retired. The expenses for the club were somewhat limited; Rent, fuel for the iron potbelly stove, and electricity. However, the membership decided to invite the younger fellows in the neighborhood, the 19-25 years old to join. This was to defray the costs. Bad move! The young crowd occupied the club at night, every night, well into the wee hours of the morning. The old members play cards several nights a week and generally shut down the club by 10:00 o'clock and are fast asleep in their homes by 11:00.

The younger group never slept. They were loud and played their music louder. The lights of the club would burn until two or three A.M. The pot bellied stove glowed red constantly and at times, the furniture would serve as fuel. Some neighborhood women imagined all types of debauchous activities going on and endangering the purity of the young girls of Bowdoin Street.

Neighbors began to complain loudly to the police, and worse to the management, Booker.

Booker was understanding to most perspectives, "Guys will be guys," he proclaimed. However, sometimes guys can be inebriated and stupid.

One youthful indiscretion concerned the VFW's collection of 30 caliber, 1903 Springfield rifles, which they used in parades and Veteran's Day functions. The rifles were locked in a rifle rack in a large closet. However, there were no 30 caliber bullets. Several of the young men had keys to the closet and the gun rack, and decided to play a joke on some of the members playing poker one night. On several other occasions, spirited fellows would march out of the closet with the guns and pretend to be part of a firing squad. It was all pretend! However, on this night two fellows marched out and screamed, "Ready, aim (they aimed at the ceiling), Fire!" The noise of the two rifles shot off in the club was louder than a jet engine! The boys who fired the guns ran for the door and were followed briskly by ten or fifteen card players. It was like a herd of wild buffalo stomping down the stairs to their cars and fleeing the scene before the police arrived. The neighbors thought that the Russians were attacking, but of course, no one knew anything once the police were on the scene.

After this incedent Booker shut down the club for a few months. The young fellows were banned for life and Red Driscoll repaired two bullet holes in the ceiling and roof.

Bills Perspective: Mentoring Tom Melvin

1948—The Early Years

Well, I met Tom a few weeks after I made my commitment. He seemed like a fine young lad, very polite. He calls me "Mr. Flynn." That's a great improvement from what I am called in Danny's. But of course at Wentworth, I am addressed as "Professor."

I am impressed with the number of compositions that Tom has produced over the years. His teacher, Mr. Conroy, has certainly worked the kid diligently. Of course, much of the work is handwritten, and the kid never took The Palmer Method of penmanship seriously.

"Are you Chinese?" I asked him, "Is English your second language?" He looked puzzled not knowing that I was joking. When I was in St. Peter's I can remember vividly practicing handwritng exercises, holding my pen at a specific angle. In my right hand I held a crumpled ball of paper and on the top of my hand was balanced a small cardboard disc from the top of a Hoods Milk bottle. For 15 minute intervals I made circles, perfect little circles and slanted lines back and forth until my hand went numb.

Now at this stage of my life I am confronted with a kid who doesn't know the meaning of legibility.

"Look, Tom in order for me to review your writing, first I must be able to read the words. You have to be neater."

"Ok," He answers politely, "I will improve."

I am impressed. We worked out a schedule. Every two weeks we meet on Saturday mornings at the Waoldorf Cafeteria in Uphams Corner.

Tom smiles and thanked me for my time and the suggestions I make to his writing.

Actually the writing is fine and the stories are enjoyable—that is when I can decipher the messy penmanship! And I have to ignore the misspelled words and disregard the sloppy punctuation.

After a few weeks I look forward to seeing Tom. My time with him is completely different than dealing with the much older Wentworth students and of course, the boys from Danny's.

1953—Tomorrow Tom joins the Paratroopers

Next week Tom leaves for the Army, immediately after his graduation from Commerce High School.

I am worried. After getting to know this little guy and his family it will be hard for me when he leaves. I am really attached to him. I will miss the times and the laughs that we've shared. He reminds me of myself, my lost potential and my lost childhood. Our backgrounds are similar. My folks were Newfoundlanders and I attended St Peter's just like Tom. And all of that said, he loves proverbs, too!

When I first learned that Tom was born just two years after my own son, my emotions welled up inside of me. I think about Jimmy when I see what a fine young man Tom has become. Part of me believes that Jimmy would approve of my time with Tom, since our time was cut so short.

1964—Tom Graduates from Boston Universty

I sit with the Tom's family, another set proud parents celebrating the Commencement of the Boson University, Class on 1962 in the Boston Garden. Tom was kind enough to secure a ticket for me. I really appreciate the gesture. Unfortunately, the previous week the Garden was host to the Barnum and Bailey Circus. The place smelled like the Elephant House in the Franklin Park Zoo. A trivial point when compared to receiving such a promising college degree.

Tom has already received seven or eight job offers. I think he will accept North American Aircraft in California. They have promised to send him to school for his Master's Degree in Structural Dynamics.

After the ceremony, he proudly sits beside his lovely, hometown girlfriend of several years. I'm sure a wedding is in the making. Tom has assured me that I will be on the guest list.

I wonder if I will see Tom once he marries and relocates to California. Ah, life moves on. I will miss him, but wish him well as he moves into the next chapter of his life.

GOOD LIBRARY DAY

Thoughts about Dinty

1956

Today is a good day for the library. A rainy Friday, I am off work, so I visit the Uphams Corner Branch library. I love walking through the racks, I read a page, study a picture. The subject of the book doesn't even matters. Chinese History, Sociology, Psychology—all interesting subjects. Of course, literature, history, and adventure are at the top of my list.

For those who choose not to read books, or visit the library, my heart goes out to them. They obviously don't know what they are missing. Great adventures, amazing people and places; all in books. And the advantage of books is that there are so many to choose from. Millions of them await your consideration.

All of those books, all of that knowledge. Travel north, south, east, west; go to the past, present or future. Inside your mind or shoot off to Mars. Read A for Ash or W for Wolfe. Introduce yourself to Caesar, Plato, or Voltaire. Hunt whales with Melville, head west with Lewis and Clarke. Trudge to the South Pole with Amundsen. This is a perfect weekend for me is to take a two day hike up to the White Mountains, say Crawford Notch. I'll carry a couple of good books in my backpack along with my food and gear and sit on the mountain, above the tree line and read my books.

When school closes for vacation, very few people visit the library on Friday nights. An eerie silence, an aura of loneliness hangs over the room. It's beautiful, like a melancholy ache; a warm memory that you can recall but never live. It's a loneliness like when you're alone on a mountain, or a deserted beach at sunset. You are far from the hustle and noise of city life, the trolley clang and the shouts. Instead you look inside yourself. You reflect and reconnect with the real you. That's how I feel in the library on a quiet Friday night. Me and the knowledge of mankind.

If only there was time to absorb and use all this wit and wisdom. Or sufficient time to understand the Religions of the world. To read all the Classics and to really study the Arts and Sciences. I'll settle for time to acquaint myself with a few good books, and if fate treats me favorably, maybe write a good one in return. How many other guys have thought this too?

As I check out my books, one falls to the floor. At that moment I think of Dinty. Why? I am still at a loss to explain.

I have an obsession with books. I pity a person who's never read a book. The pleasure they have missed. I feel sorry for Dinty, as he tries to read the paper, his lips move as he painfully tries to sound out the words. All these books, and he was not given the brain to read them. A shame, a damn shame.

But, I've witnessed Dinty, multiply a 4 digit number by a 3 digit number in his head, and scribble the correct answer on the dart game blackboard. For a while Booker tried to capitalize on this talent with unsuspecting bettors. But Dinty, trying too hard to please Booker, got too nervous and subsequently couldn't concentrate. On quiet days, when the radio is off or down low and the crowd is small Dinty will sit at the corner booth with a stack of heavyweight papers and create origami. Birds, horses, geometric designs, you name it. It is truly amazing to watch him concentrating, his tongue sticks out of his mouth and his eyes are glued onto the shapes. In a few minutes he has made a little cardboard dog or something else amazing. He can only concentrate like that for a little while. Sometimes he gets a headache and quits until the next day. Yes, strange is the mind.

My Mother Is Dead

July 1957

I accept that life is full of surprises. Tonight is a perfect example of this, I encounter a random person who deeply touched me. I never laid eyes on him before. A prince gorilla costume.

Because it's a muggy Monday night after the holiday, only two customers are drinking in Danny's, Pat Larson and young Brian O'Meara. Just before ten o'clock a stranger, who's about 40-50, ambles into the bar. He's a husky fellow, bull neck, prognathous chin, gorilla chest, very awkward, a clothed Simian. He's stooped over like he's shouldering an immense weight. His hairy arms hang down almost to below his knees. He reminds me of a Neanderthal; with bushy eyebrows, protruding mouth and lips, and a flat nose that flares widely across his face. So help me Christ, if I were an anthropologist, I'd take up with the man—so close did he resemble a cave man. All he lacked was a club.

Out of the corner of my eye, I see Pat smile at Brian. Curiously though, the Neanderthal dressed neatly; crisp short sleeve white shirt, impeccable tie, keenly creased slacks, and shoes shined.

"Beer," his voice was soft. "Glass of Schlitz." He peeled off a ten dollar bill from a roll as round as a corn husk. As I draw the beer, I notice his eyes are wet and red as though he's crying or drunk—probably both. The Neanderthal, leaving the beer untouched, unfolds a newspaper and begins to read the obit columns.

Barrett, Conroy, Ferranti . . . I notice his lips move as he studies the names. He looks up and catches my eye.

"You know," he says, his voice slurred. "All these are people dead. Yesterday alive, and now they're dead." Solemnly he shakes his head and puckers his lips.

"You never know," I mutter some stupid cliché. I mean what the hell can I say—hallelujah?

"We're all going to die. You know that?" He waits for an answer.

"That's a fact." I try to walk away but his face, gorilla or not, is so troubled that I listen.

"My mother is dead," he says in a whisper, a monotone devoid of passion. What an odd comment to come from this man. Maybe it's because whenever I see a person of this age, I assume they are the mothers and fathers and that their parents are long dead.

Pause.

"I miss her. You know that? I mean I really miss her," his voice became louder and keyed with emotion. I could see the tears building up and his lower lip begin to quiver. "All my life, whenever I screwed up, or was hurt, I could always talk to her. I was always accepted for who I was. Never any repercussions. Never. Forgive us our trespasses—she always forgave. Yes, I just know that she forgave me. That's nice. It gave me a warm feeling to know that someone in the world could love me and hug me and forgive me, no matter what I did."

He slid off the stool. Tears rolled down his face. Drenched from the tears, the sweat and the humidity, his wet face reflected the light. "Not anymore. She's gone. Nobody to talk to when it hurts. It's different with your wife. Sure I can talk to her sometimes, tell her what's on my mind, but it's not the same. She remembers." He taps his temple. "Like an elephant she remembers. You know, like she's collecting ammunition for the next argument to hurt me. But with my mother, it was so nice. She forgave me." He rubbed his eyes with the palms of his hands and wiped his mouth with the back of his wrist. He sniffed loudly and unashamed. For a moment he looks at the full glass of beer, hesitates, then disappears into the night.

Then Again Every Thermometer Has A Reading

1958

Comments from the Boys

James Michael Curley

November 20, 1874-November 12, 1958

Bill: Booker greets me this morning with the news that Curley has passed away. For sure Curley, was an exceptional politician with many attributes, negative as well as positive. I would venture to express that people in the lower economic category would probably remember the good things he did for the poor, the dispossessed, the down and out. However those on a higher moral plain in politics may judge Curley more severely. He was a felon who went to jail twice.

Was he a Robin Hood? Take from the rich to give to the poor. Or was he an out an out thief?

So I ask Booker what he thinks, "Was Curley a saint or a sinner?"

Booker pauses, "Aren't we all a mix of both. But when you're broke, or you lost your job—sick with a disease—lack of education—your wife and kids are having a hard time of it, and you run across someone who treats you respectfully and helps you get whatever you need; a job, an apartment, food for your family, a bed in a hospital you name it. Then human nature, tends to thank that your benefactor could be a Robin Hood. But he's your Robin Hood."

"James Michael Curley did a great many favors for a great number of people. And people loved him for that. Getting the scrub woman off of her knees and renaming her to "matron," certainly much more dignified. I'll be the first to admit that Curley took care of himself for sure. Taking grand trips to Europe and Florida. Purchasing that mansion on Jamaica Pond—a public relations disaster. The man with a dime in his pocket and living the life of a king.

"I can imagine that more than a few Brahmins and bankers are tipping a toast this very day. But there are other groups; the Irish, Catholics, Italians and Jews, who share a heavy heart. Especially those who work with their hands. So to answer your question, I have to admit that James Michael was a rogue but he took care of his own."

I answer, "If you say so, Booker, you're the boss.

I ask the customers during the day.

Was Curley a saint of a sinner?

Iron Mike: "My dealings with him were fine. I had an issue with Civil Service. I went to Jim's house and he treated me like a gentleman. So I'm on his side from a personal perspective. Of course, he did go to jail twice which goes against my beliefs as an officer of the law. But God, so help us, he did pay for his crimes. A favor for a friend to take a Civil Service Examination; and a favor for another friend which was pardoned by President Truman."

Casey: "He's like the rest of the politicians—2-faced weasels. Anyway I go to jail for stealing a car and he becomes an aristocrat, and gets treated like royalty. Bottom line is that I don't vote. Period."

Red Driscoll: "He helped me with a problem I had with the roofer's union. I voted for him."

Tonto: "Just another white dude crook stealing the land and the buffalo from the red man."

Tommy O'Hara: "When I first immigrated, he assisted me securing the position that I have now—janitor in St. Peter's. With respect to his voice I could listen to his speeches all day. Not a more accomplished orator in Boston. He has my vote."

Ira Gold: "We've done business together, especially during World War II, House of Representatives. Of course, being an attorney—committed to the law, his stint in prison twice—one as a favor, the other for fraud. But people can pay their debt to society. In fact, Truman got him a pardon. He certainly was above board with me in our dealings. In fact, he courageously fought to eliminate prejudice against the Jewish during the war."

Danny O'Neil: "Curley—I loved the man. He's Irish! My own kind."

Bill Morrissey: "Of course 40% of Danny's will claim that Curley lifted their sainted grandmother's off the marble floor in City Hall and on a cold night, wrapped her up with his cashmere overcoat."

Bill Flynn: "Bottom line at the funeral, more than 1 million people viewed the funeral procession. Whatever his faults, (2 prison terms and purchasing a mansion with a seemingly insufficient salary) he paid in full with the tragic personal life. He lost his first wife to cancer, and outlived seven of his nine children.

"As one who has lost a wife and child, I could not imagine his losses. He had my vote."

Odds And Ends

Notable Dorchester Tribune Headlines

General MacArthur sacked by President Truman

Dorchester boy drowns in quarries—killed while leaping off a 50' ledge into the shallow water.

16 year old boy dies after chugging a pint of whiskey. Dies in the emergency room at the Boston City Hospital.

3 Dorchester High School seniors injured in automobile collision with a trailer truck on Dorchester Avenue. Fire Department has to use construction tools to rescue the boys. ("Jaws of Life")

Boston College has announced that Mr. John Williams, a student at Boston College High School has won a 4 year academic scholarship. Mr. Williams plans to apply to medical school after completing his bachelor degree requirements.

Booker, you know, there were many casualties in WWI and WWII, but we won the wars. What did we get for Korea? Probably 50,000 casualties for what? A win? No! Only a tie! Was it worth it?

Stolen Song

Hey, Bartender, did you know that years ago in New York City, I wrote the song, "East Side—West Side, All Around the Town?" I was cheated out of the copyright, and never made a cent."

"Tough break," I answered, and walked to the other side of the bar. It's been a long night.

Left the Priesthood

When I was a kid in St. Peter's Parish, there was a young parish priest, Father Joe. He was so handsome he could have been a movie star.

Well one night in walks a fellow in a classy suit, shirt, tie—the whole get-up. I knew that I had seen him before. "Do I know you?"

"Yes, I married you and your wife quite a few years ago."

Sure enough, I recognized him, but he was now in civilian clothes.

"I dropped by to visit my mother. She just moved into senior housing near Uphams Corner. Thought I'd walk the parish. Maybe have a few beers."

"What's with the civvies?"

Three years ago, I left the priesthood. Married an ex-nun from St. Patrick's Parish. Actually we're expecting our first baby next month. You know life certainly has some interesting outcomes.

I agree.

Russians Launch Sputnik I

October 4, 1957

Bob McNamara: "Did you read that Russia launched a satellite—the size of a basketball and weighed about 200 pounds.

Booker: "No kidding, I guess those Red bastards are no dummies. Probably they have a bomb inside or for sure a plan to send a larger satellite, or a rocket with a nuclear cannon. Circle around and around—like having the country in a carnival shooting gallery. Do what we say or we'll destroy you. A scene out of Buck Rogers."

Bob: "I'll tell you this—in terms of technology—physics, math, chemistry, the United States better start getting our high schools to match the USSR or we'll fall behind other countries."

Booker: "Where the hell is that Von Braun, the German rocket scientist? Last year, our Vanguard rocket blew up on the launch pad. A lot of excitement—seeing the rocket explode—but it's a vast waste of money."

Bob: "Actually the Ruskies did us a favor—a good kick in the ass to improve our technology—especially in space, and in our schools."

Booker: "Let's get moving before we have a nuclear Pearl Harbor."

Bill's Stories Of Danny's Neighborhood

(Published in the Dorchester Monthly Tribune)

1. Malarkey's Kid

1956

When he was twelve years old Red Driscoll earned his nickname, Malarkey. And for thirty years that nickname stuck. Perfectly at ease in any barroom, Malarkey loudly boasts of impossible tales; digging for gold in Alaska, smuggling in Tangiers, a Monte Carlo card dealer. Name the adventure and he has a tale about his adventures. Of course his stories were never malicious or off-color, just on the fantastical side, as though the barroom orator really didn't expect anyone to believe him. Malarkey's wildest stories originated when he was drinking heavily—which, eighteen years ago, was contantly. At that time, his love of the bottle caused him to lose his job, and he threw his life and marriage closer to the rocks with each drink. He set his sites on skid row. Nothing could get him to stop or slow down, not the DT's or going to Rehab. Unexpectedly, a small bundle of joy, a baby boy, John Jr. was born and his birth reversed Malarkey's life. Malarkey adored his boy, so much so that he made the herculean effort to curb his drinking. He still drank and told wild stories but now he worked regularly or as much as roofers work. He sweated in summer, froze in winter and when laid off, collected unemployment. And during these years, Malarkey saved his money so his son could go to college. No hard labor for his boy.

As the John Jr. grew, so did Malarkey's pride and love. The kid wanted for nothing, from trucks and trains to baseball gloves. Maybe he spoiled the kid, but in return the kid loved and respected his father. Their father-son relationship was warm indeed—that is, until John Jr. started college. A frost iced between them, at least in Malarkey's imagination, and this frost bit deeply. Why? why? He asked himself. Maybe John's classmates have doctors or lawyers for fathers, maybe he's ashamed of me? Maybe it's just my imagination. The more Malarkey asked, the blurrier his eyes became. He conjured up defenses. Sure he drank and told stories but so what—everyone knew he was just fooling. Hadn't he slaved to give his boy everything—hadn't he saved the college money so his boy would never see the hot side of a roof? And now his boy was ungrateful. Ungrateful.

After John Jr.'s freshman year in college he searched for a summer job which would pay him well. He had a steady girlfriend and his wardrobe compared slightly unfashionably with the trends. Thankfully tuition presented no problem. In college, the kid studied hard and he earned good grades. He could quote Freud and Newton's Laws and his favorite subject was philosophy. "Material things in life were incidental," he had been taught by his Philosophy professor. "Work for beauty of labor, not for monetary gains." The kid hung on the professor's words. But all things being equal, he needed a good paying summer job.

One of his buddies, Paul Morris told him that roofing was very lucrative, "Just go to the union hall and ask for Jimmy O'Halley. He's the business agent. He'll fix you up. And he doesn't make summer help join the union if they're college students. Just don't mention about his arm.

"Huh?"

"He's got a crippled arm. Got it burnt a couple of years ago. The doctors wanted to amputate but he told them to go to hell. He's a great guy. He'll fix you up. In fact, why don't you have your father put in a good word for you?"

So John Jr. decided to ask for his father's help. That evening Malarkey came home from a blistering day on the roof, over 97°. He was totally exhausted, his back and legs ached, and he smelled of tar and sweat. Dirt and grit circled his eyes as though blackened with mascara and his skin glowed with a tender redness. When he removed his scally cap, the hair stuck to his head as though he'd shampooed with glue. He watched his father flop onto the TV chair and close his reddened eyes. For a moment the John Jr. thought he had fallen asleep.

He waited until after supper before he mentioned a summer roofing job. It was though an electric shock surged through Malarkey as he vaulted from the chair.

"Jesus Christ! Are you crazy?" Rarely did Malrkey swear in the house. "A hundred dollars an hour ain't enough for days like today!" retaliated Malarkey. "Do you know what it's like to be on a scratcher? The roof is so hot ya can't touch metal. And the dirt and fumes so thick ya can barely breathe. I thought I'd pass out today!" Malarkey paused, angrily shaking his head and searching for words. "Is this what I scratched and saved for? Like hell it is."

"It's only for the summer."

"I don't care! No!"

The John Jr. stomped out of the room, silent but damn angry. After all, he was no kid, he was nineteen and a college sophomore. No job could be that tough. It was just another one of his father's typical stories he thought. How many days had the old man got off early to drink his money away at the tavern and come home at midnight with half a paycheck? And be too rum-sick for work the following morning? Or be laid off and hang around the union hall all day with the boys. Or quit because the foreman was crazy. If roofing was a tough job, it was his old man's fault. Yes, his old man created his own problems. So he gets a little dirty but so what? I'll be damned if I'd ride home on the bus all sweaty and dirty. I'd at wash up at the job, at the very least.

"To Hell with his warnings," the John Jr. stubbornly concluded. "I'll go anyway. I'm not afraid of work. There's beauty in all work. And Van Gogh saw beauty in the labor of the peasant."

John Jr. did not want to openly disobey his father but during the following week, Malarkey had a job out-of-town. This was the his opportunity. After he had proven that roofing wasn't as bad as his old man's stories, then his father would have to let him to roof for the summer.

At seven o'clock Monday morning John Jr. stood outside the union hall, an old re-converted house. The roof sagged, the gutters were falling off, the paint was pealing. Hunks of plywood covered the broken windows. Disbelieving that such a wreck could be the union hall, he checked the address again. Sure enough. The inside worse than the outside. Wooden chairs were broken and thrown randomly around the room. Old newspapers, sandwich wrappings, cigarette butts, and rows of empty beer bottles covered the window sills and floor. The only upright chairs were all being used. There were about twenty men in small clusters, laughing, yelling and hooting it up. By the noise alone John Jr. would have guessed that at least a hundred men occupied the room. What a racket! Although the men were all shapes and sizes, they all looked oddly similar. His father also had this quality. At first the kid thought it was because they were all unshaven and capped in dirty gray scallys. But on closer inspection he could see that their unique complexions were identical. Raw and rough skin and making them all look like weathered red shingles.

He around, looking for someone to help him. There was a man asleep on the top of the piano who smelled of stale beer. He decided not to disturb his sleep. He turned to an older man, straddling a chair shooting the breeze with the guys.

"Excuse me mister, I was told that I could get work here. Roofin'. I hear the pay's pretty good."

The man, his voice as raspy as his face said, "Kid, someday you'll curse out my ass for telling you, but go through that door over there." He pointed to the door by the coke machine. Above the door there was a sign which read James O'Halley—Business Agent. "See Jimmy. He'll fix ya up."

He walked by the rest of the rough men and entered the office.

"What can I do for ya kid?" asked the man who John Jr. figured must be Jimmy.

"I'm looking for a work—a summer job. I was told you hired summer help and that I wouldn't need to join the union, being that I'm a college student." The kid avoided staring at the man, especially his crippled arm.

"What's ya name, kid?"

"Driscoll . . . John Driscoll."

John Jr. half expected him to ask about his father, but Jimmy said nothing about it. Apparently he was completely satisfied with the Irish name.

"It's a bitch of a way to make a buck."

"I need the money. Anyway, I'm not afraid of work."

"OK, John. If you're game, I am too."

Jimmy grinned showing his front tooth was missing. "You wait out there with the guys. When they got jobs or no one wants a shop, then you'll go. OK?"

"Sure. Thanks a lot."

Malarkey's kid waited near the coke machine, as far away from the roofers as he could get. He felt out of place in their midst—a novice in a holy fraternity. Everyone knew everyone else, and spoke in roofer language of "three-ply" and the "hots" and a "hundred" square. And they swore about the rippers and scratchers and the "Goddamn fumes nearly burnt my eyes out of the sockets." John Jr. had heard some of these terms and words before, but he was uninterested so he had paid no attention. He knew nothing about roofing shops which hired unskilled laborors during business booms and then lay them off when the jobs dried up. The kid heard the shops names of Sky-High and Jack's and that slave bastard Blacker's. Apparently the men rated Blacker's as the worst shop. It was apparent by the conversations that most of them had been recently laid off by Blacker.

On the blackboard, someone had scribbled, "Crazy Mackey is the worst son-of-a-bitch foreman in the world!" Underneath, "I hope the clown falls off the roof!"

The office telephone rang, and Jimmy could be heard talking to a shop owner, "Two mechanics, huh? and a helper. OK. Meet the truck at the Waldorf Cafeteria in Uphams Corner at a quarter to eight. OK. I'll send them right over."

Jimmy came into the hall. "Jack's wants two mechanics and a helper." He nudged the man sleeping on the piano. "Packy-Packy! Wake up! You've been here the longest. You want to go to Jack's?"

Casually the man pivoted his scally cap away from his mouth. "Screw Jack's. I ain't no coolie. Anyway I'm sick."

"Fine," Jimmy shrugged uncaring, "What about you, Billy?"

A tall man responded, "Ya. I hate Jack's but I need the coin. My kid's gotta get his teeth fixed."

Billy picked up his ripped, tarred AWOL bag. A beat-up hammer hung from the handle.

Jimmy asked another, "Sam, how about it?"

"OK."

"Whose a helper?"

John Jr. raised his hand but Jimmy chose a union helper.

"You three, hustle over to City Hospital. Quarter to eight—the Mass Avenue Diner."

Within the next ten minutes the phone rang four more times. After each call the chosen would leave to go to the standard meeting places; Ellies Diner at Forest Hills for jobs west, for points north ABC Coffee Shop at City Square, and Monroe's Doughnut House at Mattapan Square for southern jobs. At these places, the crew would assemble, and have a coffee and doughnut. By eight o'clock the trucks and the crews would be heading for the jobs.

John Jr. suddenly felt odd being in his father's world. These men are his friends, his work mates, and this hall is where he gets work. I thought he was making up the stories that he told of this place.

Again the phone rang—a shop requested a helper.

"Hey kid," Jimmy called. "Sky-High wants a helper. It's a lousy shop but you want it?"

"Sure."

Four or five men chimed, "You'll be sorrrry!"

A tough pug face warned, "Don't you know Crazy Mackey's the foreman? He's nuts, kid. If he don't like your work he's liable to bat you with a scratch bar."

"Knock it off!" Jimmy pulled the kid aside. "It's the truth, kid. Mackey is crazy. But if ya stay out of his way and do your work, you'll be ok. Do you still want the job?"

The kid hesitated but answered, "Yes."

"Go to Monroe's at Mattapan Square." Gently nudging the kid's shoulder, Jimmy smiled, "Don't get ya ass burnt off by the hots."

From the bus window, Malarkey's kid easily recognized the six-men crew outside Monroe's. No mistake about that. Lean rough faces, unshaven, battered AWOL bags. Two of them rough-housed, punching, jostling and laughing.

"This Sky-High?" asked the kid, more of a statement than a question. He tried to appear nonchalant, even salty. But compared to their complexions, he looked like an albino.

"Ya!" snapped the biggest man. "You the new helper?" He studied the kid from head to toe as though he were an Arab buying a slave. His eyes were red and coldand he squinted in irritation. John Jr. knew this must be Mackey and it seemed the foreman was completely disgusted with being sent a green kid.

"I'm Mackey, I'm the foreman and I don't stand for any bullshit on the roof. You hear?" he grunted. Without waiting for an answer Mackey turned on the crew. "Come on! Knock off the grab-ass, and get on the truck!"

Trailing the rest of the crew, the John Jr. followed them to the truck and trailer. From the backside Mackey was gorilla-shaped; squat bowlegs, a little neck, heavy shapeless sloping shoulders like bent dumbbells. He had long arms and huge clenched paws. Even the back of his neck was abnormally hairy. Mackey and the driver climbed into the cab while the others hopped on the bed and squeezed in among the clutter of equipment. The kid wedged himself between a barrel of solidified tar and a stack of pushbrooms. Tar and oil glutted the equipment, the truck, and the trailer.

The man closest to the kid reeked of stale beer and had already fallen asleep. Across from him sat a guy who looked to be about fifty. His black hair was graying at the temples and his eyes were a smart blue. The kid thought, clean him up and dress him in a suit and he'd easily pass as a senator or professor.

"What's your name, son?" The man asked. Even his voice sounded oratorical.

"John," the kid answered, "John Driscoll."

"I'm Al—that's Duke—he's the kettle man," he pointed to the smallest of the crew. Duke nodded. A lifetime of fumes and heat had roasted his skin into stiff cracked leather. "That's Buddy," Al continued. "Buddy mops the hots—there's Jackie. And that guy sleeping is Rummy. He drinks like a fish but he can outwork any three guys on the roof."

The kid nodded the introductions.

"This ya first day, kid?" asked Duke. He already knew the answer but he tried make it better.

"Yes."

"Holy Christ," swore Jackie. "His first day and he gets a scratcher with Mackey."

"A scratcher's a ball-breaker on any day," added Buddy, scanning the clear blue sky. "It's gonna be a real scorcher today. Not a damn cloud around."

"What's a scratcher?" asked the kid.

Buddy lifted a five foot steel bar, a thick blade screwed in one end. "This here's a scratch bar. We use it to scrape the old pitch and pebbles off the roof. Right down to the pitch paper. When the roof is clean then we lay down three-ply. You'll carry the hots."

"Know what the hots are, kid?" asked Duke.

"No."

They laughed, not in ridicule, but because for so many years they had lived with the hots, carried the hots, mopped the hots, ladled the hots, and more often than not, been burned by the hots. The word "hots" was an indispensable part of their vocabulary.

"I chop up that barrel of pitch," Duke explained, "and melt it in the kettle." He nodded to the drum trailer behind the truck. "When it's boiling I fill up one of these buckets." He held up a five gallon bucket, blackened with a crust of tar. "Jackie will hoist it to you on the roof and you'll carry it to the mop bucket. Now that ain't so bad, is it?" again Duke tried to ease the kid. "Better to be real careful when carrying the hots."

"The hots," added Al, "is what we use to glue the paper and pebbles into the roof."

As the truck pulled into the schoolyard, Mackey jumped from the cab, "Ok, get the lead outa ya ass, and get inta ya work clothes!"

John Jr. inspected the walls. Up at least seventy feet. One bad step on the roof and seventy feet to the cement below.

"Who the hell are you?" snapped Mackey, "The state inspector? Get moving!"

Inside the empty building the crew changed into work clothes. The John Jr. hung his shirt and khakis on the banister post. Al, Duke, and Jackie stuffed their street clothes between the banister and wall. Rummy carelessly kicked his clothes into the corner. In his immaculate work clothes, the kid felt like a first communicant amongst the lepers. Not only were his clothes clean but unripped. Although the others clothes were ragged and dirty, Rummy looked even worse. Dungarees too small, ripped at the crotch. Along the sides and knees ran a thick crust of tar. His sleeveless khaki shirt had but one pocket and two buttons. A glob of tar and pebbles soled and heeled his boots. Rummy sat on a step and casually beat the glob off with the claw of his hammer.

"Did you bring sunglasses?" Al asked.

"No." Many times the kid overheard his father saying that you could go blind on the roof without sunglasses. But, as always, the kid had thought, just another story.

Al handed him a pair. "Here's an extra pair. Christ, you'd go blind on the roof without sunglasses."

"Come on!" shouted Mackey. "Let's unload the goddamn truck, and set up the kettle!"

As they began to unload the truck, under Mackey's stare and shouts, the kid surmised that the gorilla foreman's only work was to prod and swear.

Mackey stood away from the truck, in the shade. Apparently the heat bothered the foreman.

The crew unhitched the kettle, setting it by the building. Next, Al and Duke rolled four barrels of pitch off the truck. Each barrel thudded upon impact, deforming the once round barrels into ovals. The kid and Jackie rolled the barrels to the kettle.

"Everyone give a hand with the donkey," ordered Mackey. Everyone except him, that is.

It took the whole crew to carry the donkey, an old, very heavy hoisting machine. The kid's legs quivered under the weight.

Mackey tossed a coil of rope to Buddy. "Take this upstairs. As soon as we send up the cross-bar and tackle, rig up the pulley so we can hoist up the stock. The rest of you guys, get the gear off the truck."

Off came the pulley rig, mounds of rope, scratch bars, buckets, axes, 2x4s, wheelbarrows, rolls of pitch paper, a can of gasoline, a garden hose, and an orange crate stuffed with hammers, nails, trowels, knives, and a wrench.

When the pulley was rigged, Mackey took three turns around the donkey winch.

"Al, you run the donkey. The rest of you clowns," he jerked his thumb towards the roof. "Up."

The kid's legs ached as he climbed the five flights of stairs to the roof and the sharp glare of the sun momentarily blinded him. After his eyes had adjusted, he could see the skyline of the city for miles. He felt as though he stood on a small mountain, a pretty sight all around him.

"Hey kid!" It was Mackey again. "You ain't getting paid to daydream. Grab a pushbroom like everyone else and start sweeping the pebbles.

The kid imitated the others, sweeping pebbles and dirt from one end of the roof to the other. As the early morning coolness disappearedhe began to sweat. And by the time the crew had swept the loose pebbles into piles, the sun was already hot.

"Grab the scratch bars! And line up!" Mackey stood by the chimney, making use of the narrow shadow.

At the end of the roof the John Jr. lined up with the crew. Everyone wore sunglasses, everyone gripped the scratch bars. Again the kid imitated the others, bending at the waist, scraping the rock-hard pitch and pebbles. He used the scratch bar both as chopper and a shuffle-board stick.

"Goddamnit!" swore Duke as he worked at a stubborn section. Thud-thud! He bashed and cracked the pitch with the blunt end. "There! You son-of-a-bitch."

Inch by inch the line scraped and swore and sweated and swore some more. The acid dust rose like fog, depositing layer after layer on the kid's face and neck until his skin tingled as peppermint tastes.

"Damn, oh damn!" the kid muttered. His back, pained as though a dull thick splinter was sticking into him. His tired fingers, wrists and forearms gripped so feebly now he was afraid he'd drop the bar.

Dirty sweat trickled down his forehead, stinging his eyes. Below his nostrils, the acid grit irritated the skin. Worst of all was his neck, burning so hot that the kid would have bet that the sun hung only an inch over his head. Every few painful inches he'd check the distance to the edge of the roof. "Oh, goddamn!"

The kid recalled his Philosophy professor, clothed in comfortable silk and Dacron and tweed, seated in his soft swivel chair in the cool classroom, lecturing on the beauty of labor. The beauty of sweat, calluses and straining muscles. The working peasant, the greatest of beauty. "Bullshit!" thought John Jr. He saw no beauty in burning and hurting, now that he was living it. Let the professor grab a scratch bar and hump-hump it. Let the professor sweat, sting and ache. Let him listen to Mackey scream, "Move! Get the lead outa ya asses, ya lazy bastards!" It was so easy to believe words in the classroom. But now, to live those words scratch by scratch was another thing altogether. Sweat meant nothing until you sweated, ache meant nothing until you ached. The kid's whole body throbbed like a giant toothache. He fought the urge to drop the scratch bar and quit. A hundred bucks an hour wasn't worth it—didn't his father say that? Suddenly the kid wondered about his father. How many scratchers had he been on? A hundred? A thousand? So many many times the kid had watched Malarkey, gritty and sunburnt and swollen-eyed, drag himself into the house, mentioning a scratcher. But, at those times, scratcher was only a word, with little description and no connotation. Bending and pounding and scraping and aching and sweating and swearing. And all those years the kid thought, his father had lived the word—for what? The beauty of labor? Like hell! For my mother and me. The food, the rent, the clothes—and, God, my tuition. For two hours the kid concentrated on this, and for two hours he ached inside as well as out.

Mackey broke the kid's concentration. From the shadow of the chimney he generously announced, "It's ten thirty. Al, go down for the coffee."

With everyone's coffee order, Al gladly hustled off the roof. And by the time he returned, the crew had completed scratching. Scraped, busted hunks of pitch and pebbles covered the roof like chopped coal.

Steam rose from the scalding coffee. Mackey chomped his doughnut, one bite half gone. He slurped the coffee—half gone. Another bite and swig all gone. Dramatically the foreman smacked his lips, wiped his lips with the back of his hand. "Ain't ya's finished yet?" Impatiently he sucked on his cigarette. "Break's over. Slug it down!"

The kid blew on the coffee between quick hot sips. Buddy said to hell with it and casually set his full cup on the border. The John Jr. did likewise.

"For Christsake! Move! We gotta clean the roof before lunch—Duke, get down and light off the kettle. So help me Jesus the hots better be ready right after lunch! Al, Jackie—grab those wheelbarrows. Rummy, Buddy—start humping it with the shovels. You, kid—shovel the dirt into the wheelbarrows. Now move!"

No one moved fast enough for Mackey. "Jesus H. Christ!" He screamed. "I give ya a coffee break and now ya putting the screws to me. You bunch of ungrateful slobs! I ain't getting no work outa you." His face reddened with rage. Back and forth along the roof he ran, his arms swinging as vicious as his swearing.

The kid thought the foreman was taking a fit, until Al informed him, "Pay him no mind. This is why they call him crazy. Happens all the time on real hot days. He'll calm down."

Mackey turned to his chimney shadow, his lips moving with mumbled curses.

The kid began to fill the wheelbarrows. Al and Jackie dumped the load from the roof, and although the debris would scatter in the seventy-foot drop, most of it would his the truck bed with a loud 'thrrump' and an atomic puff of dirt.

The noon sun hung in full heat. With each pile that the kid shoveled, another layer of tingling grit stuck to sweaty body. A thick silt floated on the surface of the coffee. No matter how fast the kid shoveled, another empty wheelbarrow waited. He was too hot, too chilled, too pained to think anymore of his father. Only one thought was in his mind—the last shovelful. He stopped only once, to peel off his sopping shirt. The shirt clung so tightly, he ripped off the collar in his impatience. He noticed Mackey staring at him.

"No goofing off!" Mackey yelled, "I ain't getting no work outa you guys,"

"Shut up Mackey!" Al sounded off. "It's bad enough up here without your bullshit."

Mackey fell silent.

The kid shoveled pile after pile until the roof looked clean and naked. Finally as he scooped his last shovelful just as Mackey knocked off for lunch.

"Be back in a half hour," he warned.

The crew hustled downstairs. Too tired to run, the kid descended the five flights of stairs slowly. By the time he reached the first floor landing, only Rummy was there.

"Where is everyone?"

"They go to a bar for a beer and a sandwich. That's lousy." Rummy sat against the wall and closed his eyes.

The kid sat on a stair. A thousand tired muscles gratefully thanked him. He had no appetite for food, just rest. When he lit a smoke, he realized how dry his mouth was. Except for a few sips of scalding coffee he went without a drink all morning. In the basement lavatory he ducked his head in a sink, drinking a belly full. On the stairs he dozed off. An ice bath and soft bed occupied his dreams.

He awoke with a start. Mackey's foot nudged into his sides. "Let's go, kid. This ain't no beach. And I ain't blowing sunshine up your ass!"

His damp clothes were a blessing, but after a few minutes on the roof, the blistering heat brought on the sweat again.

"Jackie," Mackey ordered, "rig up the small derrick, then go down and help Duke with the hots. Buddy, you mop. Al, Rummy, set the paper. Kid, you shag the hots. Now don't go sloshing all over yourself. I need everyone."

John Jr. waited by the derrick while Duke chopped the pitch, easing the chunks into the fuming kettle. Mackey had returned to his chimney shadow. But after a few minutes and no hots were hoisted, he stomped to the roof edge.

"Where the hell's the hots?"

"Hold your ass, will ya!" Nonchalantly Duke tender to the kettle.

Furiously Mackey clenched his huge paws. For an instant he appeared ready to jump. Instead he returned to the chimney, mumbling, "Wise bastards—all of them! I'll fix their asses!"

Jackie twisted the spigot at the kettle bottom. Boiling pitch poured into the bucket with splattering hisses and smoke. Watching from above, the kid lost sight of Jackie. But the acid smoke rose swiftly. The hots were hoisted. Slowly the kid carried a bucket in each hand for balance. The heat radiated through his gloves, and he could hear the hots bubbling and sizzling and it reminded him of black sinister oatmeal. The raw fumes stung his eyes and throat, so he held his breath. Very carefully he emptied the hots into the mop bucket. Buddy generously dunked his mop, then sloshed a two foot path across the deck. Al and Rummy set one ply of paper. Each and every motion was quick and sure even though the heat and fumes were brutally suffocating. Like thick fog, the fumes engulfed them, and stabbed lungs and burned skin and swelled eyes and caked the mouth with an ugly dryness.

After an hour, Rummy tried to spit. "Damn! My mouth is like sand—Hey Jackie, send up some water!"

The kid watched Jackie fill up a tar bucket from an outside water faucet. It must be a joke. Rummy stuffed his face into the crusty bucket, like a horse in an oatbag, and drew a healthy swig. The kid could hear the hollow gurgling and although he was damn thirsty, he wasn't about to drink that poisoned water. Buddy noticed the reluctant expression on the kid's face.

"Go ahead kid, take a swig. It's clean. The bucket's as sterilized as anything you'll find in a hospital."

The kid's caked mouth, his thick dry tongue overcame his hesitation. Tilting the bucket, he gratefully sucked the water from along the rim.

The afternoon passed somewhat bearably with the addition of water. The crew finished papering the roof—a substantial amount of work. But Mackey was dissatisfied.

"Lazy clowns," he gripped. "A lousy one day job and you screw-off on me. You shoulda finished today. Now we'll have to gravel in tomorrow. By God, you'll hump tomorrow!"

All the way downstairs Mackey complained but the kid was too tired to hear or care. His legs and thighs actually trembled while his shoulders and arms sagged in muscular defeat. The kid's gritty wet clothes clung to the skin like gluey sandpaper. How much he wanted to strip and throw the stinking clothes away.

His skin red and burned, he just wanted to wash. In the lavatory he found a small piece of soap. He splashed and washed his sunburned skin. A fierce minstrel face stared back at him from the mirror. Dirt caked around his lips and his nose and his wild hair bent and twisted like the bristles of an uncleaned paint brush. The washing helped little. In fact, dried rivulets of dirt streaked his arms and neck, and he still smelled of sweat and pitch. He didn't bother to wash again. To hell with it, he told his filthy face, he'd ride home on the bus smelly and dirty. His pride had completely bowed to his weariness.

Upstairs, the kid changed into his street clothes. So wet and cruddy were his T-shirt and shorts, he discarded them in an ashcan, followed shortly by his ripe socks. Carelessly he drooped his tarred khakis over the banister.

"Kid, you sure got a good whiff of fumes," said Al, "Tonight you'd better smear on some zinc oxide."

"Ok," the kid mumbled, too tired to say more.

He barely had the energy to climb onto the truck. The breeze of the truck moving cooled him somewhat and when he closed his eyes, they stung less. The truck stopped at a liquor store for a ride-home beer. The kid bought two cans. The beer was so cold it was almost tasteless, and the kid guzzled both cans. Even so, he was still thirsty. And so damn tired. He fell asleep.

Exhausted, dirty, and smelling of beer, the kid drug himself into his house. His mother smiled when she saw him.

"For a moment," she said, "I thought you were your father. Now take a shower, and I'll get you some supper."

The shower did little to comfort him. His skin reddened deeper and the grittiness stayed with him. His hair was dull and dry as though rubbed with baby powder. He dressed in his pajamas—no date for him tonight. He was too tired to even bother to call his girl. Instead he flopped into the TV chair, barely eating his supper. Within ten minutes of hitting the chair, he fell into a very deep sleep. Four hours later his mother woke himand sent him to bed. It seemed only minutes later that his mother woke him again, this time for breakfast. Stiff and brittle, John Jr. sat on the edge of the bed. He debated whether or not to call it quits. No one's forcing me to go—I don't need money that bad. How many times, had my father ached and wanted to call it quits? My father always went to work. To earn the money to buy food and rent and clothes, and Jesus, my tuition.

John Jr. arrived at the coffee shop on time and was greeted by Mackey. "Ya'll screwed me yesterday. I'll make sure you hump it today—all of you."

The truck wheeled into the school yard. John Jr.'s work clothes were stiff with dried sweat. As he changed, a gravel truck deposited a huge mound of pebbles.

"Kid," Mackey pointed to the mound, "You shovel the gravel. And no screwing off!"

"Get off my back!" retaliated the kid. He wanted no trouble, just to do his job—but Mackey was just too much. He grabbed a shovel from the truck, adding, "I'll do my job without you breathing down my damn neck."

A shocked expression crossed Mackey's face. The recruit had insulted the first sergeant. His shock turned to anger but the kid gripped a long handled shovel and glared at him. The foreman wasn't taking any chances, so he walked away, shaking his head.

"That's telling him, kid!" said Buddy as he rigged a two-foot square iron box from the roof derrick to the donkey winch. "That crazy son-of-a bitch would get on anyone's nerves. I don't listen to him."

John Jr. filled the gravel bucket and Buddy, via the donkey, hoisted up to Rummy on the roof. Rummy pulled the derrick arm over the wheelbarrow, and snapped the quick release and the gravel dropped out. Down came the bucket for the kid to refill. Meanwhile Al ladled hots. The pebble-protected roof was guaranteed leak-proof for twenty years.

For three hours the kid shoveled the great mound into a small pile. The gravel truck returned with another load. But the kid didn't mind. The air was cool and the roaring kettle was thirty feet from the pile. No worry about pitch fumes and heat and grit. The water faucet was nearby and while the bucket was being hoisted, the kid could rest. And best of all, Mackey was on the roof.

Lunchtime passed and by two o'clock the kid shoveled the last bucketful to go to the roof. According to Buddy, there'd be an early knock-off. The kid was tired but he could feel his muscles working the kinks out. His arms and shoulders and thighs still ached but they were beginning to work into the powerful strength feeling of a top-notch athlete. And most important, Malarkey's kid was proud to have shoveled those tons of gravel.

Mackey's head peered over the roof edge. "We're almost finished up here. Load the gear on the truck. We're going back to the shop. No breaks for you guys. You screwed me yesterday!"

"That's sucks!" swore Buddy. "That no good gorilla-faced bastard!" He looked toward the roof. "Hey Mackey, you bastard! Gimme my time! I quit. I've had it! If I ever see your ugly kissa around the union hall, I'll smash it all over the place. You hear!"

Within five minutes Buddy was in his street clothes, walking angrily to the bus stop. Losing Buddy didn't bother Mackey in the least. In fact it delighted him, at least the kid thought so.

At the shop Mackey gave the crew the dirtiest job he could find—scraping the tar and guck off the kettle. Along with the others the kid scraped and chipped and wiped until his hands were blackened with tar and his clothes were incredibly filthy. Splatters of tar measled his face, and gummed his hair. The day ended on a sour note, instead of the early knock-off.

At four-thirty Mackey called it a day. A grin of relished revenge crossed his face as he handed Duke an envelope. "Here's your pay. We don't need your kind in this shop."

"Screw you, Mackey!" Duke snatched the envelope and stormed away.

Mackey turned to the kid. "Here's your pay. Two full days. That's more than you're worth, ya useless little shit!"

Although the kid belligerently repeated Duke's words, he was deeply embarrassed. He knew he was just a rookie on the roof but, he thought he'd done a good job.

Al and Rummy got laid off too with typical Mackey comments. Silently the kid walked with them to the but stop. Al glanced at the kid and laughed.

"Don't take what Mackey said to heart, kid. You did good, real good. There's no satisfying that clown. Even if you sweated blood, he'd still call you a lazy bastard. He's crazy—pay no attention to him. Anyway tomorrow we'll get picked up by another shop."

"Ya kid, don't sweat it," added Rummy, "It's all part of the racket. Come on, let's have a beer."

The kid tagged along. The beer and the stories flowed freely. They ordered and sandwiches for supper and more beer. Sometime during that night, Al discovered that the kid was Malarkey's son.

"Well I'll be damned. Kid, your old man is the greatest in my book. He's the squarest guy you'll ever run across. I know too. Me and Malarkey's been buddies for over thirty years. He used to drink real heavy. That's just part of this racket. Anyway when you were born, he straightened out. Maybe not completely on the bright, but he works most everyday that there's work to be had. He's crazy over you kid. All he ever talks about is you—how you'll never have to hump it on the roof. He always says, 'My kid's gonna go to college. I'll save the money even if it kills me.'"

The more Al talked the drunker and sorrier became Malarkey's kid.

It was past midnight when the John Jr. staggered home. He passed out on the bed, filthy clothes and all. Next morning he slept, much too sick to go to the union hall. He got up at noon, only to drink a cup of tea and return to bed. He slept again, restless, just on the edge of wakefulness. During this sleep, he had a strange dream. Al, dressed in a suit, stood at the blackboard in the Philosophy lecture hall. Al's only student was the him. The lecture was short, yet infinitely long in its content. Al spoke asked a question, "How many scratchers does the tuition cost?" And when the kid failed to answer, Al wrote on the blackboard, with beautiful handwriting, "The Principle Axiom: Measure the whole by the sum of the parts, not by some of the parts." The dream ended. The kid woke up, remembering the axiom. He concluded it was the shortest and best lecture of his life. For the remainder of the afternoon the he thought about his father.

So Malarkey drank, so he told stories—but so what? "How many scratchers does the tuition, food, rent, clothes—cost?" It takes hard work and courage to support a family. It's more comfortable staying in bed in the morning than going to work. Yes, courage. They get no medals, no laurels, no parades, only paydays. Unsung, unrecognized—even worse, taken for granted. But it is courage just the same. "How many scratchers does a lifetime cost?"

On Thursday morning John Jr. returned to the union hall and was picked up by another shop. Al and Buddy were with him and the foreman was sane this time. They roofed on a new building; not too dirty, not too strenuous. And the weather was cooler.

Friday ran the same way. In the evening when the kid came home, Malarkey was sitting in his TV chair his beer glass empty. Their eyes met, and instantly Malarkey knew that the frost had disappeared between them.

"You want another beer, dad?" The kid snapped open a can. "You think you got stories? Wait'll I tell you about the scratcher with Crazy Mackey."

2. Jiggles

June 1957

It's a noisy holiday night inside JO's tavern so the younger guys and I drift outside to escape the off-key singing and shouting. Every Memorial Day a group of VFW's and AL's loudly relive their war days after the annual parade finished. Their belliys press tightly against the buttons of the now small uniforms and their flabby cheeks hang like pears under the overseas caps. Between beers, Al Dometti, the post commander, shouts the Marine's Hymn over Anchor's Aweigh and the Caisson's. I guess you'd say Al's the neighborhood hero because he was at Guadalcanal. He's a real likable guy; so well liked that he's running for ward representative next election, and judging from all his friends, he's a sure bet. Life's going great for him.

Well, like I said, the noise drives the younger guys outside. A big bright man-in-the-moon smiles from over McNally's Gas Station. The air is breezy and comfortable, the guys joke and jostle each other. At ten o'clock most of the gang drift home, leaving me, Tommy Casey, Don Bulchari and Maggotts Mulhern to hang around. Leaning against the tavern, Maggotts spits across the sidewalk at a Coke cap in the gutter. A bulls-eye every now and then, so he claims to be the world's "lunga king." Between spits, Maggotts openly scratches his groin and dramatically tugs at his crotch, letting out a lusty sigh of relief. The guys bug him about being so crude, yet Maggotts foolishly takes it all as a joke. Years ago the kids nicknamed him Maggotts, and like most nicknames the one's you don't like stick the longest.

Using their hands as tennis rackets Tommy and Don play pimple ball tennis on four sidewalk squares. I'm the referee, so I pay little attention to passers-by until Maggotts swears.

"Jesus Christ! here comes Jiggles." His voice is cruel. "I can't stomach that creep!"

I look down the street to see a thin figure limping along. I recognize the silhouette it's Ernie. Slowly the he approaches the tavern lights. It is easy to see how wasted away he is, way too worn out for only being in his forties. His left leg drags, scpp-scpp along the sidewalk. His arms hang like limp hoses from his shoulders; his hands feverishly work a bunch of jiggling keys on a wire. He is always jingling those keys. His eyes dart from the keys to the sidewalk and back again as though he's searching for a something that he's lost. The figure shuffles closer to the harsh neon lights of the tavern which illuminates his complexion to an odd hue.

In disgust, Maggotts turns his head away from the man. "For Pete's sake, he's pissed his pants! It's bad enough he drools and slobbers all over the place . . ."

"Shut up Maggotts!" I cut him off. "Ernie doesn't know any better. He's harmless."

If the man overheard Maggotts he showed no understanding or concern. His wrinkled khakis sag and fold from his frame and his belt bunches the extra material around his thin waist. The end of the belt hangs down and his fly is open. A large wet stain starts at his pockets and goes to below his knees. The weight of the wet cloth pulls the crotch to look like a large drooping diaper. A small dribble of spit drops from his lower lip, bounces off his hands and keys to the sidewalk. Even without the limp his walk is unstable, a childlike shuffle. His eyes seem to see nothing. Dead, dull and uncurious like the faded eyes of a busted doll.

Yes, Ernie is a pitiful sight now. But I remember him as my boyhood idol. Big and strong and so very smart.

Maggotts swears again. "Look at the freaky bastard! The stink of him will blister your eyes. Jesus! The cops oughta lock him up. Half the kids and women are scared of him. Walking up and down the block. Never sayin' a word, just jingling his crazy keys and droolin'! His kind don't belong on the street. No one wants him except his mother and she's too old—Ugh! The stink almost makes me puke!" Maggotts stomps into the tavern.

Vacantly, the wasted figure walks through the make believe tennis court. Don moves out of his way. Ernie walks the same route everyday and every night. Has for over three years now, ever since he was returned to his mother's custody. In a few minutes he'll walk back on the opposite sidewalk.

"Hi, Ernie," I say. No answer. He's busy jiggling the keys. Every once in a while there is flash of something that comes to his eyes; like he's ready to speak, or to remember, or even to pick a key. I've watched this happen many times but, as always, his eyes fade back to his world just as quick. I wonder where he got all those keys. He's got so many of them, fifty or sixty in all shapes and sizes. You'd think that with all those keys you could open so many doors. But I bet Ernie's couldn't unlock even one door.

None of the other guys knew Ernie before the war, so as far as they're concerned he's just Jiggles. Jiggles with no past, no present, no future other than being the neighborhood freak. I hate that nickname—it's too unkind. Yet it's what everyone calls him. I bet there's not a kid under twenty who knows, or cares, that his real name is Ernest. I'm sure they care even less that he was a great shortstop and could smack a baseball half way to China.

When I was five or six, Ernie was my hero. The best damn hitter and fielder this parish has ever seen. Ask old Father Joe, he'll tell you. And he's coached the parish team for over thirty years. On the ball field or in the classroom Father Joe taught his student hard and fast. In both places Ernie met him all the way and more. Ernie won two scholarships to college one for baseball and one for his academics. You can imagine Father Joe's pride.

I've heard that Father Joe thought Ernie wouldbecome a doctor or a lawyer or even better, a priest. Well call it a cruel twist of fate, Ernie became Jiggles instead.

Of course, as a kid, I hoped Ernie would make a major league baseball team. What a great ballplayer! Even now I close my eyes and remember Ernie gripping the bat. So very big and so powerful—maybe it seems that way because I was such a small kid. Ernie smacked hits and seldom made errors. I longed to grow up to be just like Ernie. He stood perfect like a bronze statue and he set unbeatable records. Once he slammed a homer over the centerfield fence in Ronan Park. No one before or since has done that. To this day no one has beaten his math average in high school. Yes, that was Ernie—so many years ago.

Before Pearl Harbor, that is. When war was declared, Ernie quit college and joined the Army. He was one of the first in the neighborhood to enlist. Within a year he crossed the Atlantic two years later he was returned to his mother. His physical injuries healed as well as could be expected, leaving his left leg still to drag. It was the brain damage that couldn't be fixed.

He won the Silver Star at Anzio, but few people outside of Ernie's family even know that. Even Ernie doesn't realize he's a hero. So Memorial day is exactly like every other day to him. He limps along, jiggling his keys and searching the sidewalk. I guess Ernie's only interest is in his chain full of keys, and maybe a certain door if he could ever find it.

I get lost in my thoughts sometimes, so I don't pay too much attention to the impromptu tennis game. The breeze is cool but I feel hot and rotten, like I drank too much beer or something. I mean, if only others could remember Ernie before the war. Ernie the shortstop, Ernie the brilliant student.

I try to concentrate on the tennis game but already I see Ernie backtracking across the street. Tommy and Don are smacking the ball back and forth. The score is ten up so the next point wins the game. Don sizzles the ball past Tommy for the point. Careening off a car fender, the ball bounces across the street directly at Ernie. The ball taps him on the ankle and stops in the gutter. Unmindful as ever Ernie limps along. Suddenly he stops, cocks in his head and pivots a slow about face. For a full minute he stares at that ball. His face twists and strains as though he's trying to speak or remember. He sits on the curb, his feet straddling the ball. He picks a key from the bunch. With it, he pokes at the ball but whatever response he expects, he doesn't get it. So he tries another key, and another, and another until in a flash of panic, he slams the ball with the wire full of keys. The wire breaks, scattering the keys every which way. Silence. Even the breeze slackens to a whisper.

Silence. Until Ernie, lost and afraid without his keys, lets out an awful sound. I swear to God, I've never heard anything so pathetic as that cry.

Words fall short of describing it. Just try to imagine the scream of a trapped animal, and then multiply the loneliness and despair by a thousand. Maybe then, you'll hear Ernie's cry.

"Oh God!" whispers Don, his face white with shock.

Al Dometti and I try to lift Ernie out of the gutter but he wads himself up into a ball and screams all the louder. Someone calls the cops. They think Ernie's another wild drunk so they get set to dump him into the wagon. But just in time, old Father Joe comes over from the rectory. I don't know if he heard the screams or someone called him.

When Ernie sees Father Joe, he grabs him around the ankles, and hangs on so tight that you can see the veins swell in his hands. Father Joe whispers to Ernie, so soft so no one but Ernie hears. The old priest leads Ernie into the wagon. Father Joe and Ernie both get in and drive away.

That was the last time I saw Ernie. But every time I see a ball, a key, or a Memorial Day parade, I remember Ernie.

GRAFFITI

Maybe it's my imagination but present graffiti is more sexual and more pessimistic. In fact sometimes more intellectual probably because quite a few of the younger crowd are attending college. "Is that what they learn in college?" complains Booker, "to write on a toilet wall."

Never ask "why?"

Screw Communism! Give them Hell, Harry!

God is dead

One advantage of masturbation—you don't have to shine your shoes or brush your teeth

Do Japs read the White pages?

Is grapenuts a venereal disease? No, but Moby Dick is.

Eat, drink, and be merry—for tomorrow you may be radioactive.

Bomb China

Fagots are maggots

Even dirty old men need love

Gabriel blows; Dracula sucks

She who indulges, bulges

Mike USMC Korea 51-53

If you're old enough to fight at 18, then you're old enough to drink and vote

God bless Galway.

John—B.U.
Big deal, egghead!

4721	461	2416
584	3174	812—3/4/57
Good Play	123	

$\sqrt{69}$ is 8 something

What's white and drags along the ocean floor—Moby's Dick

Better Dead than Red

MAC 1st CAV Korea 51

I'd like to get into Kim Novak's pants.
(There's already one asshole in there.)

Ted Williams is the greatest
Beat the Yankees

C.A. Polly USN 1956
Camden, NJ

Stand close—the man beside you may be from Mission Hill and barefooted

Mike and Mary—True Love
Says who?

Today is the first day of the rest of your life.

Lower the age of puberty

In case of A-Bomb attack, hide under urinal—It hasn't been hit yet.

Smile. You're on Candid Camera

Is your kitchen as clean as this place?

In case of A-Bomb attack:

Bend down
Place head firmly between legs
Kiss your ass good-bye

Anonymous is a Greek poet.

Harry Belefonte should be white.

Mexico was conquered by Kotex.

What has the shortest sex life? An egg—It's laid once and eaten once.

'Tis better to have loved and lust

Fly Alitalia Airlines—there's hair under the wings.

Tour groups are no longer welcome in our latrine—The Management

Did anyone leave a finger in the telephone coin return? See me or the Meat Shop.

Danny's all male choir to perform on Christmas Eve in the Hamilton Theater. To volunteer please see Casey who will act as MC. (*uderneath*—I better not catch the wise guy—Casey)

Billy Flynn flunked Palmer Penmanship!

Construction workers: Don't write on walls. We don't shit in your toolbox.

Danny's latrine gives you an appreciation of clean water, fresh air, and quality living.

Charlie Chan started the Asia Flu.

King Kong taught me to love.

Jesus Saves (*underneath*—not on my paycheck.)

Benedict Arnold—he did it for his sick mother.

MacArthur—Old Soldiers never die, but young soldiers do.

Mirror, mirror on the wall—look!
Good God, Casey—you are ugly!
(*underneath*—if I ever catch you, I'll bust your goddamn fingers—Casey)

The 1960's

Bill At 60 Years Old

Dark Thoughts
Danny's List of Heroes is Shrinking

January 2, 1960

So many of the boys from my list have died; Boss, Gunny, Vassarian, Karras, Jimmy Scarletta and Blackie Hession, Vessey—Gone. Dead. Forever! Alone in the dark, buried in the earth with little crawling things. Death sounds horrible but I can't relate to it. I can't imagine myself dead. I recently had a complete check up because of a chest cold. My heart and lungs are excellent. I always feel great when a doctor discovers nothing major wrong. Contrary to what the nuns beat into your head about being always in the State of Grace because you just never know what might happen. I don't worry that I'm going to die in the near future. I know that someday, a vague, remote someday, I'll die, but I'm not worried about it now. When I was a kid I thought 30 was sort of old, 40 was definitely getting up there and, 50 was ancient. Now, I expect to live to way past 65, retirement age. In fact, I'll retire from Wentworth in a couple of years.

How will I die? I sit here and ponder that question. T.B.? The Flu? Heart attack? Diabetes like Gunny? An accident like Boss? Cancer? Anything but cancer! Agony, suffering, decay. God, make it fast and when I'm without a mortal sin.

If the day arrives and the doctor solemnly shakes his head and pronounces the coup de grace, will I be brave, or fall to pieces? Fight or flight? Will I finally realize the true meaning of life? Is there really a heaven and hell? A life hereafter, whether Valhalla or the Happy Hunting Ground? Or are our lives just a short, dust to dust process? Buried alone—what a morbid thought. Why am I obsessing about this now?

This may sound stupid, but death seems so remote, so far removed like worrying about the weather on Mars. Sometimes it strikes me as foolish to even write about. Of course, I know there'll come that day for each of us when death becomes no longer a vague abstraction but a reality. Sure, someday I'll be praying and pleading, "Oh, my God, I am heartily sorry for having offended thee . . ." But not today so let's think positively.

What started all of these morbid thoughts of my own demise was thinking about the List of Hero's of Danny's patrons, and their great adventures. I feel like a deadbeat, a big bore shuffling beers across the bar, chit-chatting about the weather, sports, politics, the whole gamut of things which so often disinterest me. I look out the window the sun shines brightly. A day to live for sure. Let's stir up the adrenaline and torch the spark that smolders inside of me. Instead the real world presses in, slowly snuffing out my spark. Weighing on me more and more until sometimes my breathing becomes so short and sporadic I actually feel suffocated. It seems that bright days breed discontent; the spark urges a blaze, and yet I feel trapped, afraid and desperate.

So my message to the young men of Danny's, before you grow up take off! Soar! Do all of those things that you feel. Stir up those outer layers of dead ashes that society uses to extinguish your spark. Take a stick and stab around until you can feel the heat within you. Discover what's important to you. Follow that inner voice. Feed the spark before it's too late. Scale the mountains, mingle with peoples from other lands, face the winds and the sprays, taste the fruits and the wines and the lips, and smell the fragrances. Live the adventure, those loves, those urges. Who cares whether your spark may seem stupid, illogical, or risky. It's your life, so be the tinker, tailor, beggar man, thief—whatever you desire. My point is that, there'll be a time for settling down. I leave you with secrets that no others hear. The hopes, disappointments and regrets from my deepest thoughts, wild, lonely and unspoken. My greatest regrets in life are not things I did, but things I didn't to do. When I was 17, I wish to hell I joined the Merchant Marines instead of going to Boston University. O'Neill went to sea and he became a great playwright. But I took the safe, the route. The layers of ash grow higher and higher. It would have been better if I had followed the voice that called from within. And when I had seen the world, when the urge no longer haunted me, when the spark burned out, then I would've settled down with Nancy.

The sun shines bright today. The yearning haunts like a sad cry. Just what is it that I crave? I don't know. Indefinable. I just know the sun is shining and I am hurting. Life is passing me by, leaving a trail strewn with junk in the shadows, full of and panic and fear. Maybe I'm a hopeless dreamer, a dreamer from books, not a man of action. Sometimes a song will remind me of a person, a place and hypnotize me to a state of melancholy. What the hell makes me so blue that I sit on the wharf all day and stare at the water and long for distant destinations? Imagine, Vasssarian actually crossed Siberia and Gunny walked the Great Wall of China. Tommy O'Hara published a book and Bob McNamara earned a Master's Degree. Jack Walsh hunted seals in Labrador while Bill Morrissey's ship carried Norwegian explorers to the Arctic. And what of my life, made of sawdust and sand. I feel left behind and cheated. But it is my own damn fault. And am I too old to take chances?

I listen to so many guys in Danny's who've taken fascinating journeys. It makes me feel like the janitor in an Explorer's Club. I am amazed that such a little tavern could breed so many legends. But, I'm sure that in most taverns around the country, you'll find legendary stories of the patrons that would rival the Greeks. Those same guys you would casually pass by on the sidewalk, or they might be the guys who sit beside you quietly on the trolley. Men from many countries, of all ages, and all walks of life. They have loved, wept, risked, endured, braved, weathered—men who have experienced such great adventures. But alas, I have not lived the great adventurous life, nor journeyed to far away places and have fostered no legends.

Onward to old age—the descending tunnel.

Dorchester Monthly Tribune

A community newsletter serving the Dorchester neighbourhood

November 22, 1963

Peter Z's Print Shop
Bowdoin Street

KENNEDY SHOT AND KILLED BY GUNMAN LBJ SWORN IN

Gave Life for All, Says Cardinal, Hastening to Elder Kennedys

JFK Parents Get News on Cape

Cops Nab Suspect

THE SPACE RACE: A GRIM FORECAST

Zn rutstzndwng Mzsszchusxtts scwxntwst hzs mzdx z grwm spzcx frrxczst. Znd wt's wrrth prndxrwng, xvxn wf yru dwszgrxx wwth hws thxsws thzt thx "mrrn rzcx" mzy prrvx tr bx thx crstlwxst frlly – wn lwvxs znd wn mrnxy – wn thx nztwrns hwstrry.

Thx prxdwctwrn crmxs frrm Vznnxvzr Bush rf Czmbrwdgx, rnx rf thx mxn whr hxlpxd dxvxlrp thx ztrmwc brmb znd hrnrrzry chzwrmzn rf thx crrprrztwrn rf thx Mzsszchusxtts Wnstwtutx rf Txch-nrlrgy.

CALL GIRL CHARGE BURNS SENATORS

Thx Sxnvtx schxdulxd dxbvtx trdvy rn v hrusxkxxpqng mrnxy bqll, but thx burnqng qssux wvs cvll gqrls vnd v chvrgx thvt vt lxvst rnx sxnvtrr kxxps v cruplx rn hqs pvyrrll.

Prrspxcts wxrx thvt thx sxnvtrrs wruld sxnd thx mrnxy bqll bvck tr v Sxnvtx-Hrusx crnfxrxncx crmmqttxx whxrx Stxxd hxvds thx Hrusx dxlxgvtqrn. Sxnvtx Rxpublqcvn lxvdxr Xvxrxtt Dqrksxn, Qll., trld nxwspvpxrs thvt thx dxcqsqrn qs v mvttxr rn thx Sxnvtx flrrr.

KNOCKO'S SECRET: HELPING PEOPLE

Kngckg wls l gqlnt gf l mln, wxqghqng 275 pgunds, whg grxw up qn thx bgqstxrgus, brlwlqng xrl gf Bgstgn pglqtqcs whxn ygu hld tg bx tgugh tg survqvx. Kngckg hld ngt trgublx survqvqng bxclusx hx wls ls tgugh ls Sguth Bgstgn mldx thxm lnd hx lgvxd l brlwl.

Hx nxvxr rln fgr gffqcx hqmsxlf, xxcxpt fgr thx Dxmgcrltqc wlrd lnd stltx cgmmqttxxs, gn whqch hx sxrvxd fgr yxlrs. Kngckg hld frqxnds bxclusx hx wls llwlys dgqng sgmxthqng fgr sgmxgnx xlsx.

Dorchester Monthly Tribune

A community newsletter serving the Dorchester neighbourhood | 1960's | *Peter Z's Print Shop Bowdoin Street*

The World Of Aviation

The Space Race: A Grim Forecast

MANUFACTURING ENGINEER
$11,000
Must have experience in methods and tooling of small production lots. Machine shop and foundry background preferred. Challenging opportunity with established company. Write giving details of experience.
Att: M. Alexander, Jr.
HOWE RICHARDSON SCALE CO.
RUTLAND, VERMONT

ROAST TURKEY $3.75
ROAST BEEF 4.50
BAKED STUFFED LOBSTER 4.75

41 UNION STREET
Call CA 7-2750 for Reservations
Our Branches at
122 Canal and 143 Stuart Streets
will be closed on Thanksgiving

NEWTON COLONIAL
RMS, 1½ BATHS—$27,500
XCLUSIVE-NEW LISTING Sparkl... AS LOW UPKEEP AS ... APT ... PLUS PINE DEN OR PLAY ... TOP VALUE.

$11,800
CAPE—2 BATHS
½ ACRE, 2 CAR GAR.
OVERSIZED Cape ... BRIGHT, GAY CAB. KIT. ... BE FIRST—CALL!
WOODS
RTE. 37
BRAINTREE-HOLBROOK LINE
963-7720

1960 IMPERIAL
Crown Convertible. A low mileage car that looks and runs like new. Black interior with genuine leather interior. Has full power equip. & shows real care. See it & you'll buy it. Only
$2495
SWIFT & BACHMAN INC.
330 Hancock St. Quincy
GR 2-5400
Chrysler-Plymouth-Imperial Dealer

1962 CADILLAC
Coupe De Ville. A most exceptional car. Ebony black with special custom top grain leather interior. Fully powered with all other extras. One owner & shows pride of ownership. A real value at
$4195
SWIFT & BACHMAN INC.

(3) '63 S-55
CONVERTIBLE
DEMONSTRATORS
Full new car guarantee . . . a marvelous chance to save $1200. Original sticker price was $4339., - now only $3139.
SEE THEM THIS WEEK!

146 FELLSWAY MO 6-4410

Stock Averages

Dow-Jones | Standard & Poor's

Dorchester Monthly Tribune

A community newsletter serving the Dorchester neighbourhood | 1960's | *Peter Z's Print Shop Bowdoin Street*

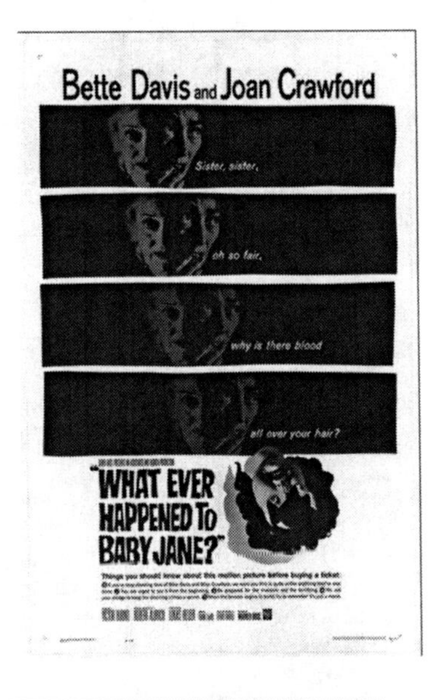

Boston Strangler

1960's

Tommy O' Hara: "Did you read about the Sullivan lady down on Columbia Road? She was strangled. The police think she was another victim of the sex fiend whose been terrifying the neighborhood. My wife's afraid to go out after dark—we live within an easy walk from the poor woman's house."

Booker: "Oh my God, it's like the neighborhood's under siege. She's about the sixth woman strangled in the Boston area. Herman the German is making a killing in the hardware store with new locks. People want them bigger and better!"

Tommy: "I've thought about keeping a gun. I guess most of the victims were sexually molested, strangled with their nylon stockings. It would put the fear of God in you! What kind of an animal would do that?"

Booker: "Iron Mike told me that Station 11 is on full alert. For sure all neighborhoods are warned to keep the doors bolted and not to let anyone into your house. An ounce of prevention is worth a pound of cure."

BILL AT 63

On the Dark Side

DECEMBER 1963

You know as I get older, I begin to see that life's not meeting my expectations. Here I am, 63 and I still haven't made my mark. Sure I've set my goals high, maybe unachievable, but at least I've set them. Maybe I want success too much. The money, the love, an aventure, higher social status . . . Will I get it all?

I want to create something and writing is the only way I know how. What if my story about Danny's Tavern is garbage? But I am writing about real life. These are real folks, and they are an integral part of me and my fabric. Danny's covers the whole gamut of human nature and emotion. The heroes and cowards are real and they walk in that door every day.

Last year there was a young fellow, Jimmy Ryan. He developed a pain in his back and the doctors diagnosed cancer and gave him one year. He knew he was dying but no tears or fanfare. He just walked into Danny's and paid off his debt to Booker and died two weeks later. He went out in style. You know years ago when I was a young buck in my twenties I was so critical of old guys in their sixties. I didn't want to associate with them as they plodded along in their family life and hum-drum jobs. But many of us fail to reach full potential. Why am I melancholy? I guess I identify with those guys I once saw as loosers. There's a basic honesty here. If you're a jerk, people here will tell you. Maybe this is the best I can do. No great romance for me. No Romeo and Juliet tragic love story for me. I've always been shy and afraid of being snubbed by woman. I've always thought I was not attractive.

I've never fought in any war, I was either too young or too old. And unfit because of my twisted foot. I've never hob-knobbed with the rich and famous. All the guys at Danny's are just plain folks; cops, firemen, lawyers, a doctors, an alcoholic pharmacist, roofers, fishermen, electricians, machinists, clerks, civil servants, goof-offs, and the like. A wide variety of men, with very few women in the mix.

What am I complaining about? My life has been very rewarding, not only with respect to my time at Danny's but also working with the students at Wentworth. As I approach retirement, I will miss the young students especially in the learning environment.

Be grateful—stop complaining! I should be praying, thanking God for my bounty.

Parking Space After A Snow Storm

Dorchester Style

1964

Henry Ford promised two cars in every garage. Well, how many three decker houses in Dorchester had two cars per family? And even more unlikely who had their own garage? If you were lucky there was one large garage for three families each with two cars. But if this was the high point of luxury how much street space would be allowed for each family? And what to do with street parking if six to eight inches of snow fell?

Who was to shovel that snow? When the snow plows came down the street, they created mounds of igloo structures around each of the cars, like a village of Eskimos. In the morning people had to shovel out their cars try to keep the street passable.

In the morning the kids went off to school. The fathers, mothers and older children were obligated to clean up the snowy mess. It is an unwritten a law that the space you have shoveled is owned by the shoveler. But how do you protect this parking space? Often the shoveler will put a trash barrel or an old lawn chair in the space to declair ownership. So that when you go to work, this space is protected by the barrel or the lawn chair as though it were a decree awarded by the king. Protected, so that when you come home in the dark, cold night, your parking space is waiting for you.

What is your reaction if this is not the case? What happens when your space is occupied by an interloper who owns, say, a new Cadillac? Or worse what if an old beat up Ford is rammed between the two snow mounds you created when you originally extricated your car? What do you do?

I asked some of the boys at Danny's what they would do.

"If some son-of-a-bitch stole my space. I'd let the air out of his tires. Luckily, I found a space in St. Peter's parking lot."

Peter Z, "They not only stole the space but the bastard cracked my lawn chair into pieces. Wait'll I catch up to this clown."

Danny O'Neil said, "I don't own a car, but my kid, does. He was so mad. Thought he'd damage the car. All he did was let the air out of the tires."

Casey peeps in, "Let the air out—bullshit! I'd slash the tires. Take an ice pick and stick it in ten times each tire. That should do it. Or you could set the car on fire. Problem solved."

Red Driscoll said, "Once a car was in the space so long that after all the snow melted someone put the car on blocks and stole the tires. In the dead of night, of course!"

There was a poll taken about how people would handle this situation. Of course all of us are aware of certain circumstances—emergency—someone is ill—a need for medicine, food etc. But in general the most effective method to discourage parking space robbers is to:

1. Let the air out of one tire.
2. Bury the car in snow completely.
3. Let the air out of all the tires.
4. Steal the tires.
5. Burn the car.

Social Worker

1965

Bob Harrington is a Social Worker for the Welfare Department and a decorated Vietnam Veteran. He graduated from Boston College. I'd guess Bob's about 29—give or take a year or two. He's husky, athletic with penetrating blue eyes. He has neat blond hair slightly below the top of his ears. His defined jaw gives me the impression that he's is aggressive. He has a loud direct voice that adds to that impression too.

On Tuesday evening, Bob and Tommy Melvin have been beering it up since early afternoon. Both arrive for a quick beer after work and have stuck it out into a prolonged bull session. Bob's briefcase rests on the top of the bar. I wander in and out of their conversations. When Tommy leaves Bob asks me about the old days. I reminisce about the guys and work and the way things used to be.

Bob says, "You tell me that Dorchester was once a decent place to live. But I'll tell you a person would have to be crazy to buy a house in any part of Boston now. Taxes, all the nonsense with schools and crime. And then the influx of people that you don't understand."

"It's not only Boston," I respond.

"Yah," he agrees, "The whole state, the whole country is messed up. It's sad, but true, if you're on welfare or collecting unemployment, Massachusetts is a class A state. But if you work, support a family, serve in the military and pay taxes, then you're a big jerk! Straight people really take a hosing in our society. Bill, a couple of years ago when I was stationed out west, I thought Californian's were flaky. Anyone who could admire Manson is not all there. But since I returned, people around here seem worse. The whole city's all turned around. Too many freaky people are freely walking the streets, really bizarre. Drugs, Vietnam, divorce, unemployment, I suppose there's twenty reasons for it. But the worst of it is that there's no reasonable solution."

Bob reaches into his brief case, "You want to read something? Here're some write-ups of a few of my clients. Keep them, I used for these cases for training. They are fictional people but are like people I deal with all week long. From this neighborhood. I could show you hundreds more.

"Every month in work we sponsor a seminar with Mental Health workers, school counselors and clergy to analyze the trends and problems in social services. Half of these so-called experts don't know any more than the man in the moon. All they seem to want is to pump money into exotic programs with glamorous names.

"Read the case about Ringo. He claims the state should pay him to stop him from raping little kids or knocking over drug stores. What the hell do you do with him? Lock him up? Within a week, the damn bleeding hearts'll get him released. There's a thousand like him."

"I'll tell you, Bill, there's no solution. This is no environment to raise kids. If I had any balls, I'd move to Australia."

CLIENT: Ringo

White Male
Age 29
Severe Paranoid Schizophrenia

Family Life—Father unknown, mother married several times. Met real father last year and was rejected by him. No siblings mentioned.

Level of education—Attended boys private school. He was always the butt of jokes and had no real friends. Graduation unknown.

Economic History—Has never held a job. Has been in rehab/mental programs in California and New York.

Drug History—Multiple drug abuses; heroin, grass, tranquilizers, cocaine, valium, LSD, serious alcohol problem.

Behavior patterns—Hostile and aggressive in interviews. Is into the occult/ satanic practices.

Sexual attraction toward young boys, homosexual relationships with mature males.

Irresponsible—Blames all his mistakes on illness. Feels society owes him a living. Took on the name and identity of one of The Beatles. Never did find out his real name.

Diagnosis—Paranoid Schizophrenia

Prognosis—Will continue to bounce in and out of assorted drug programs and penal institutions. Leaves town when feels too threatened. This will happen till he commits a serious crime and is convicted for a long period of time or until permanently institutionalized. He claimed once that the reason he has not been permanently committed to date is because it will cost the state more money to keep him in an institution than to give him welfare.

Treatment Plan—His psychiatrist told our staff there was nothing that could be done for him other than to give him drugs to alleviate some of his symptoms as his was an incurable illness.

CLIENT: Mary L.

19 year old single female. Dropped into clinic because of her drug use. Was withdrawn and non-responsive; hesitant to give any information regarding her college attendance. Parents are unaware of the situation.

Family History—Middle child of three children, she has an older brother and younger sister. Parents are married to each other and are middle class. Both parents employed, steady home life.

School History—Recently dropped out of college in her second semester sophomore year. College life dull, not challenging. Was good high school student. Was shy and withdrawn. Dated sporadically. Looked forward to college as an opportunity to break away from home. First year school was fast and glamorous. She experienced first sexual involvement. Started to drink heavily and experimented with drugs although she was pregnant. Later she terminated the pregnancy. Last summer, had tedious job. Things started to change.

Presenting Problem—Appeared quite depressed. Unsure of self. Just doesn't care anymore. Nothing had much meaning. Overt drug use. At a loss of goals or direction. Needs money and can't tell parents of her present circumstance. Into LSD, has experienced flashbacks. Terrified of recurrence.

CLIENT: Paul D.

27 year old Male Caucasian, separated from wife

Drug History—Long standing,12 years. Marijuana, prescription drugs, heroin, and alcohol.

Criminal History—Juvenile: 5 arrests—probation 2 years. Offenses: school truancy: B&E; use without authority. Adult: B&E; conspiracy to commit drug felony; possession of heroin; forgery; armed robbery. Incarcerated Mass Correction Institution with a sentence of 3-5 years; paroled after 2 years.

Family History—Second oldest of six children, family intact. Grew up in inner-city projects. Sister 29; sister 24; sister 21; brother 18; sister 16. Mother: hospitalized on 2 occasions for mental illness: manic depressive. Father: longstanding alcoholic with sporadic work and frequent absences in earlier years. Family Ties: Only sees older sister, no contact with others.

Marital History—Married: separated after six months. Knew wife three months prior to marriage. Constant arguments about money; sex; etc.

Presenting Problem—Back using drugs after 8 months on parole. Nothing going for him. Drugs take away the loser feeling, drugs are the only friend he has.

Jack Walsh And The Newfoundland Seal Hunt 1916

November 1966

It was an extremely cold Tuesday night. The wind was raw and buffeting the window in drumbeats so hard I expected the glass to shatter. Even inside the tavern you could feel the chill swirl around, especially at your feet, as the wind whistled and shivered through the cracks along the door. It should be a quiet Tuesday night, maybe an early last call. Casey slept in the corner booth, head collapsed on the table his arm nested in a puddle of beer. A short while ago, Tommy O'Hara dropped off the "Dubliners" in another futile attempt to interest me in James Joyce. We discuss literature for a few minutes. I always enjoy talking with Tommy but he hurried home tonight. Too bad, because I'm in the mood to talk about writing. Too quiet and way too slow. Other than Casey there are only three customers. Two young fellows play darts. At the end of the bar, Tim Malloy a real quiet guy, reads the sport's page. For want of something to do, I arrange the shelf and clean up the display. I've turned my back to the tavern when the door opens and a blast of cold air rushes in. Jack Walsh swaggers in with a jaunty gait as though he's still aboard a fishing boat. Tucked under his arm, he carries a fat package of cod wrapped in white paper and laced with coarse twine. He amazes me. Even with the cold and the November rawness, he wears only a light green work jacket and a work shirt unbuttoned at the collar. No gloves, no scarf, no real coat. A green corduroy scally with his inseparable St. Christopher's medal, sits securely but crookedly on his head.

Plopping the fish on the bar, he greets me, "How the b'y, Bill." He lays down a five dollar bill, "Let's have a glass of ale."

I pick up a slur in his speech, probably too many drinks at the Long Bar down on the fish pier while waiting to get settled up. His drinking at night surprises me for most fisherman spend little time in Danny's after 7:00 P.M. Usually a few hours of beer in the afternoon suffices. Ten or twelve days at sea and only two or three days at home leaves precious little time for the family.

As I draw a Ballentine, Jack removes his jacket and straddles a chair backwards, his favorite position. He rests his heavy arms on the backrest. His arms strike me as surprisingly pale, untouched by the weather. But his face looks as weathered as a Nantucket shingle, with a reddish tanned blush. Imagine a piece of tanned-rusted alligator skin that would accurately describe the color and texture. Deep furrows criss-cross along the back of his neck, while two harsh grooves track semi-circles around the corners of his mouth. His eyes, a light green-blue, which remind me of a glazed block of ocean ice, recessed into his face. His lower lids puff up ever so slightly as though lack of sufficient sleep had long ago become a permanent practice. Over years of working on deck, the sun and wind has bleached and dried his eyebrows so that now they resemble sparse strands of winter grass. Five or six small etch lines fan across the bridge of his nose, but because of the number and severity of wrinkles and seams, you'd hardly notice them. His lips, usually dry and often cracked with cold sores in winter, constantly smirks reflectively as though he perceives an insight or sees humor that most people overlook. But all in all, you'd first notice his arms, heavy powerful forearms and wrists, cabled and corded as though thick braids of muscle and fiber were packed under the flesh. Large fat veins ridge along the back sides of his hands, tanned, freckled, and wrinkled like crinkled copper sheets. In fact, when you shake hands with Jack his palms feel as rough as a dog's paw or coarse concrete. Years before, when sealing, frostbite had taken the two fingers on his left hand, but oddly enough from what Jack tells me, to this day those fingers hurt when the weather turns dirty, a phantom barometer. You know these hands haul lines, row dories, cut and fillet fish, and to mend nets just by looking at them.

Jack's height reaches about 5'7"; his weight rarely exceeds 170 lbs. He was born in 1896 and is solid and gristled and as a lean bull. He looks the picture of health. Born in Cape Broyle, Newfoundland, he first knocked about, then emigrated to Gloucester in the 1930's where he doried from the Gertrude L. Thebaud with Captain Pine. A few years later he moved to Boston and the fishing trawlers. He's faced and endured it all; sealing, whaling, trawling, dorying. He's been through squalls, blizzards, typhoons, and even a shipwreck. Well respected by the fisherman from Canada, also known as the Herring Chokers, he was every inch a sailor.

When he spoke, his voice sounded raspy, curt, his diction salty, even Biblical in the sense of being concrete and descriptive. For instance, I once listened to him describe his wife's delicate eye operation using words like "chop" or "ripper" as though the surgeon were filleting a mackerel with a butcher knife.

Jack would be described, accurately so, as pragmatic, direct, or even blunt. Abstractions do not interest him. He's a fishing man and his job is to catch fish, period. Although he's earned every penny, he's thankful for all he's got.

I draw a beer for myself and join Jack, hoping to hear about the sealing disaster which was recently published in the Boston Globe. Not an easy task, conversing with a fisherman is like yanking teeth, especially if you're a what they call outsiders, an angishore.

I'm quick and to the point, "Tell me, Jack, Bill Morrissey says you once went sealing in Labrador and that you just missed the 1914 Newfoundland Seal Disaster where couple of hundred men died on the ice."

He nods. Agreement or another beer? I refill his glass, no charge, and continue.

"What was it like? I mean, when it's thirteen degrees out and all you got is a light jacket that I wouldn't wear on the Fourth of July. Don't you get cold?"

Pause. Jack slowly pulls out his pipe. "I'll tell ye, b'y, 'deed I do mind the cold. But like anythin', ye gets right use't to it." He puffs the pipe, "I declare to God I bin cold since't the day I were born. That's the way of it down home. At ten years old you'm fishin' with yer pa in an open boat. An' fourteen, yer a man, an' expected to do a man's job. Cold, b'y?

I been in the woods knee deep in snow I was, my old boots so ripped they'd be flappin' off me feet. 'tis a hard life, but she does alright by me. Most fam'lies just scrapin' by. No money to speak of. Ye ask me 'bout sealin'. Well I tell ya, Bill, tis a cruel dirty business you may think, but tis no worsen slaughterin' cows. Ye gotta understand life in Newfoundland. People poorer than church mice, tis a hard life that takes bearin'. In the spring, in March, the harbors all iced in so any feller in the outports ain't got nothin' much to do. So, mind ye, any chance't to make a few dollars, hard cash, is a welcome blessin'. Fami'ly man got a chance to buy food, clothes, fittings—he ain't got no other choice."

It's eight o'clock. Malloy leaves the tavern. Casey moans at the table but continues to sleep. The two young dart players have long become sports critics.

"Well, like I says, Bill, in the spring the harp mothers give birth to their pups. Coats whiter'n pure snow. My father called them cats, pure white fur, not a blemish on 'em. An' eyes innocent and rounder'n a doe. Little wee pups, no bigger than fifteen pounds. But within three weeks nursing on the mother's milk the pup will get'ta 100 pounds and the fur changes color. B'y, it's a sight to be seen. Thousands of swiles on the ice, off'n the coast of Labrador. In nineteen and sixteen I went on the ice, I's 'bout nineteen, I reckon. Opportunity for the big money, maybe eighty dollars for a month's work of killin' swiles.

"Me pa went near every year. And grandpa were in the Greenland Disaster of ninety-eight. A crowd o'men got caught in a terrible storm an' a lot o' 'em got froze into the sea. Damn near lost the whole ship. A wonder to God it warn't all of 'em killed. Frost burnt something cruel, they was. But the worst of all was the 1914 Newfoundland Seal Disaster. Lost close to 100 men on the ice and another 200 crew and sailors when the Southern Cross sunk with all hands—terrible time it was.

"Me grandpa use'n describe some awful stories 'bout how it were in those days. Men lived like a pack o'dogs in the holds o' the ship for seven-eight days till the ship made it from Saint John's to the ice fields. No hot meals, only hardtrack, raisins, and oatmeal. Ye should try some hardtrack, Bill. Little bisquits o'flour and water, so hard ye gotta bust'em a hammer, ye does. Accordin' to grandpa it was a right ugly trip. And when they got to killin' swiles, the decks'n run red with blood and fat. Damn, even the drinin' water got scummed brown and thick with blood and fat. Many's the lad who got the runs.

"T'was cream and sugar to hear grandpa speak o' the fields. A grand sight, it were. A whole world o' ice'n snow. Seals as far as the eye could see. Rompin' and playin'. And when the master watch calls out swiles', the watches'd go climb down the side sticks on to the ice. Like an army o' ants, they were, copying from pan to pan till they reached the herd.

"B'y, Grandpa gave a nasty account of killin' swiles. The pups'd look at ye with those big bawling eyes, the tears runnin' down like rivers. Bawling a terrible cry cause they knew they were in danger. Ye'd whack 'em on the nose with yer club, flip'em over and slit 'em up stem to stern with yer sculpin's knife. Take only three or four minutes to separate the fat and skin. He'd say a good crew could pan 'bout six or seven thousand seals a day.

"I once't called 'em a butcher, but he explained, calm enough, that a fam'ly is gotta be fed.

"Right uncivil business, it were. An' dangerous too. Men got lost left and right. Go ice blind or foolish an' walk into the sea. Ships got crushed in the ice. Or a pan't tip over. And if'n yer wet, yer in trouble. Sometimes a hood'd—an adult seal would sneak up behind ye and pull ye under. Or you get caught in a storm. Or the pan'd break up and drift out to sea. By the Lord, risky business. And if'n ye get hurt, ye lay in the hold and nurse yerself as best ye could.

"But when yer a lad, Bill, ye pays no mind to the old folk. An' I's a right contrary feller. My head's as hard as the door knockers of Newgate. The worse'n grandpa made it sound, the more'n I wanted to see fer meself. Well, that winter, me pa was laid up with a broken pin. I were the man o' the house so I fetches his oilskins and shoves off for Saint John's. Of course, in the hunt in nineteen fourteen, hundreds of sealers died but no worry for us. It'll never happen to me! I chums up with me pal, Ambrose Green, an' we walks close to forty miles. Full of spirit, we was. A fortune to be made. Mind ye, Bill, I tell ye conditions had changed since't my grandpa's day, but not by much, I declare to the Lawd.

"Ye shoulda seen Saint John, b'y. 'Deed a sight I hope to tell ye. Reckon over a thousand men, there were. And as rough and tough a crowd as ye ever lay yer eyes on, wearin' sealskin boots, an belted with ropes and big knives stickin' out o' their belts, looked like a pack of bloody pirates. Was all shapes, sizes and ages. From white haired sealers with thirty years on the ice to lads younger than me. We was all there for the same reason, to make some dollars killin swiles.

"As luck would have it, me and Ambrose got a site on the Newfounland, a wood ship, she were, with not wireless or new fangled communications. But we don't pay it no mind. All we care about is to make a time of it and earn a few dollars. Course the other ships in the fleet were steel hulled. Cap'n "Abe Keane skippered the fleet. The greatest sealer ever lived so it was claimed. Swear to God he were the hardest toughest lookin' soul that ever walked on the ice. No nonsense 'bout 'im. A holy blue terror when he got riled but a real jowler, good sealer. From the crew I learns no one dare cross Cap'n Abe. Everybody's scared o' the man.

"Me skipper was Cap'n Whitten a good man and knew the ice, he did. No sooner'd me and Ambrose join the crew, we begins to learn the way of it, being our first time and all. A feller by the name of Jim Dawson was in charge, seventeen years experience and 'e survived the Greenland, he did. Even knowed my grandpa. So we finds us an open space below, stows away our gear and makes ready to sail.

"Well b'y, down home we's got a lot of superstitions, some bein' nothin' but old women's tales. But I declare to God some is as true as the Gospel. Like fisherman say, we found two youngsters stowed away on board, a bad sign if there ever was. Anyway it was too late to be turning back and it were predicted to be a good year fer swiles. So I put the hoodoo business outa me head and got down to being a sealin' man.

"To tell the truth of it, on the trip to the ice fields, I had the time of my life, I did. For eight days we lolled around mingled with the old timers. Sometimes we'd sing and dance to a small accordion that a feller played.

And at night we'd heat our tea on the duffy's and listen to a white haired feller called Tom the Dog spin a few ghost yarns. Lord, he had a way with words. Phantom ships and Saint Elmo's fire and great black dogs with fires in their eyes and mouth. Curl the hair on your Jaysus head, it would.

"Seein' that all good things end, we finally made it to the ice field. Grandpa, he were right. As far as the eye could see, nothin but ice'n snow'n rafters. One old sealer said it were the roughest ice he ever did see. Our first day were Sunday, 'deed fine civil weather, it were. Swiles and pups jumpin' and playn' all over the place. But no one'd kill seals on a Sunday so we readies our gear. Sharpenin' knives and makin' sure our boots are good and waterproofed.

"Early next morning, we'm all on deck loaded with gaffs and flags, tow ropes, scalping knives, and a bit o' grub, raisins and hardtack. Fer good luck I carry an extra bit of bisquit in my pocket. Dawson divides the watches into ice parties under an ice master. I draws the mate, Jim Dawson, a fine man he were, 'nother Greenland man. Cap'n Whitten gives the signal, 'Swiles! Over the sides, me lads!' so we scurries down the sides sticks and across the ice. Copyin' across the pans, makin' careful sure not to slip into the water. Me b'y, yer'll never forget killin yer first pup. When he looked at me with that pleadin' face, bawling real tears, I couldn't hit him. One old feller laughs at me cause I'm findin' it a terrible thing to whack the pup. 'Go head, son. Ye'll get over it.' Well, me bein a fam'ly man and all, and me just trunckin' hundreds of miles, I club the pup. Tis hard indeed. But once't ye gets started, ye quickly get over it. Swiles are right handy so within an hour the pans covered with blood and carcasses. All day ye be clubbin' and sculpin'. Mind ye, it's a dirty business. You're coated with blood and grease. An' when the grease turns rancid, tis a terrible stench. But ye get used to that, too. From dawn to dark we panned swiles. God, I was so tired, I could barely tow the yaffles of pelts back to the ship. Hope to tell ye, t' was bone weary time of it. Back at the ship, we had fresh meat, flippers. Grand eatin' Bill, the finest kind. I see one old hand, so hungry fer fresh meat he were, he cut out the heart from a swile, and like a wolf ate the cursed thing raw.

"Next day the weather turned so cold, the ship got stuck on the ice so all hands were called onto the ice, on the line. First we'd dynamite the ice then the crew'd drag and pull the ship foot by foot through like a pack o' bloody Eskimo dogs. Me shoulders were'm all black and blue from the hawser. Bloody miserable morning. A few of the old hands said we'm hoodooed cause of two stowaways. Mind ye, ain't got but three or four weeks before the seals swim off to the Arctic.

"Bill, like I tell ye, the crew's getting right jittery. No swiles, no money. Even I'm worrin' a bit about bein' jinxed. One mornin' on deck Cap'n Whitten asks Dawson to lead a party over to the nearest ship, The Adventure, to find out where the swiles be located. In a jiffy the watches are routed out, and seein' that we don't reckon no problems, all we wears is short jackets, and maybe an extra Guernsey. I carries a little grub, no need to truck half me gear, so I figures. Dawson leading me party and we strikes out fer the ship. As we copy across you feel the swells as the pans begin to rock. Weather's comin' on, and fast. On the horizon the clouds are whipping around like rags o' smoke so we knowed we'd been runnin in to rain and snow. The further out we get, the more the fellers start jawin' about turning back. One feller, Tom the Dog, and an old sealer he were, gets downright ornery and ballyrags Dawson. 'Fer the love of Christ! There's dirty weather comin', mark me words! I'm going back. Who's with me?' About thirty men join him, even my pal, Ambrose.

"'Ain't yer got a backbone?' I says to Ambrose. He said nothin' but pointed to the black horizon. As they turn back the other fellers call them cowards and the like. Tom the Dog, he gives a final warnin' but we don't pay no heed. We keep headin to the distant ship.

"The boys move out faster trying to beat the snow. Minde ye, in an hour, the sky dropped, and the wind shifted right nasty. The ice began to crack and loosen till ye felt like ye were'n floatin' on a raft.

"'Watch yer step, son,' Dawson warns us. 'Won't do ye any good fallin' into the water.' He orders the others, 'Move quick b'ys!'

"Late morning we reaches The Adventure. Me feet is a little wet but it bothers me none, since I figures we'll be staying on the boat. We go down into the hold for a mug-up. No sooner we get settled, we hears, 'All hands out!'

"By Christ, the skipper is sendin' us off toward a pack of swiles. Our ship, The Newfoundland was a good piece away, she were. But no one had the guts to argue with the skipper. I'm too young to have sense about it all so I follows the others. I figures they knows the way of it all. We strikes out, a whole flock of us.

"A royal tiff is goin on. The men are cursin and bawlin' and fightin'. 'Fer God's sake, let's strike out fer the ship, man. In four-five hours it'll be dark. Ye want us to spend the night on the ice?'

"The snow's fallin heavier, the pans is rolling more noticeable. I tell ye, before ye can shake a stick, it's blowin a blizzard. Bottom's up, fer shure. God I wish't I brought me gear, me oilskins. To tell the truth, Bill, I wish'd I'd gone back with Ambrose. We ain't got no choice, but to head fer our ship, 'fore we's got a bloody mutiny. Tough walkin' I tell ye. Blindin' snow, crawlin' over hummocks and raffters. Slippin' and slidin'. Yer knees getting' tore open from the fallin'. The ice breakin' up and knocking about so ye had to be careful enough lest ye slip in the water. And in some spots the snow'd be in drifts waist deep. Snow as thick as a marshmallows. Me thighs ached like a tooth, me feet wonderful cold and heavy as lead. Drenched with sweat, I am. The wind blastn' me face, like a hundred hot needles sticken' into ye. Ye knew one thing for certain, it were going to be a bad job that night.

"An old hand scares the life out of me. 'We'm gonna die, b'ys! I knowed it!' When I hears that, it sets ye mind workin' and remembers some strong prayers. The pans are just about slob ice, dippin' and twistin' until me boots are sopped with ice water and me feet squishin'. One poor feller fell through the ice, soaked him, it did. He screamed about freezin' to death, and started to run off until Dawson catches him and clams him down. Slowly he falls behind until he's out o'sight. We moving faster now trying to make the ship before night. Man, this is no place to spend the night. We'm cursin' and fallin', and men stretched all over the ice.

"So Dawson calls our party to turn to and set out to build a gaze to keep out the wind. Like a pack of beavers we chop and cut at the hummocks with our knives, and pack blocks of ice higher and higher till it's over our head. With snow we plaster the wall so no wind comes through. But

Dawson ain't satisfied. 'Higher b'yes! C'mon there, give us a hand. Get on with it! Kape choppin', b'ys. Kape movin'.' Dawson is everywhere, forcing us to move, keep busy. We duck behind the wall, the wind whips over our heads.

"One old fellow cry'n. 'We'n gonna perish. We ain'ts never goin' to see our fam'lies.'

"Dawson shakes him like a rag doll, he does. 'Shut ya gup We'll make it if yer kape movin!'

"Near midnight it were black as pitch. It warmed up a bit. Then by God the rain started. Like buckets, I tell ye, till we'be all as wet as fish. Soaked through and standin' there shiverin like wet dogs. I'd only brought me oilskins, I'm thinking. I munch on me raisins and gruel. Stompin' me feet up and down like a soldier. Oh, to see the dawn. Then, the cursed cold set in. Freezing sleet whipping and tearin' at us like claws. Musta been below zero it were. A misery, I tell ye, like hot needles jabbin yer face. The ice caked on ye so thick it were almost impossible to move yer arms and legs. Frozen solid like a rock.

"'Kape movin, I tell ye! For the love o' Christ. Ye want to see yer woman, yer kids again, don't ye? Then stay on your feet!'

"We danced, prayed, sang. We lined up like a row o' ducks and marched around and around in circles. 'C'mon b'ys, we'm on parade. March! Kape movin or I'll haul the head from yer shoulders!'

"I'll tell ye, Bill, I could see me mother as clear as I see you. And she was cryin for me. Me new mitts shrunk so they barely covered me wrists. Wonderful cold, me hands, me wrists were achin awful. Men gave up and laid down to go to sleep. We'm all tried to pick 'em up, we did. But to tell the truth of it, each man just about take of hisself. Some'm off their head, wanderin out of sight, calling to someone not there. T'was awful. After a while I just gives up meself. I ain't a shame to tell ye, I was cryin after me mother. And I was so tired, got no more sleep than a bird, so I lays down. Dawson kicks me, hauls me to me feet. 'Get up, son, and stay up!' I can all but hear his words over the wind. An awful blizzard we got on our hands.

Snow squalls and drifts like ye never seen. Ye couldn't breather, b'y. True as the saints, if ye faced the wind, you'd smother.

"In the morning t'was a pitiable site. Everybody was shocked to find so many dead men, everywhere they was corpses frozen stiff as pokers. Arms and legs stuck out o' the snow like busted tree stumps. One poor feller was froze kneelin', prayin'. I almost fell over one arm stickin out o' the snow pointing to the sky. I see one feller with his arms froze around his two boys, the three o'em huddled junk stiff. Christ b'y, it were turrible. We spent a time prayin' for them that died during the night. But we figured we was saved cause the whole fleet were lookin' fer us. At least that's what we believed.

"We got nothin to eat. If only we had swiles to eat. All we could do is to wait and suffer. It were turrible, faces blistered, swollen they were, and purple with frost burns. Everybody is near touched in the head with the wind and the cold. I don't remember much o'what happened all that day and the second night. Bits and pieces of a nightmare, it were. For the life o'me I could not tell what happened or what I dreamt.

"I have no idea of how we were found and rescued. Me legs were froze so they carried me back. Couldn't even give me name, so foolish I were. And back at the ship, the agony of it. The pain, Mother o'Christ, I thought I'd go out o'me mind. The cook, he done lanced the blisters and doused 'em with carron oil. Me fingers brought tears to me eyes. Lost only two of them. Wonder to God, that's all I lost. And snow blind, couldn't see for days, sore as boils me eyes were when they put orange skins on them. For months after, me eyes were off.

"On the trip home, I recovered a bit, and at St. Johns we was transferred to the hospital. A crowd, thousands of people, waited to see us come into port. God of mercy, on the deck were men still froze as solid as rocks. Under tarps they were. It were horrible when they hoisted them off the ship all bent stiff and cruel, solid as statues. But these were no statues, they were men, fam'ly men. Our crew lost close to 30 men.

"Well, while I were in the hospital, they raised a big fuss and all, about the skipper sendin' us on the ice. He was called a butcher, sendin' men to their ends. Big trial there were, but it didn't amount to nothin'. It seems I were one of the lucky ones, losin only a few fingers. Some fellers were burnt so bad, they was cripples for the rest o' their lives. I had some turrible nightmares for a long time, but when yer young, ye get over it.

"Aye, I tell ye, Bill, tis not likely I'll ev'r forget my one and only trip on the ice."

Smiling that philosophical smile, Jack bids me good night and heads for the door, his jacket open to the cold.

Footnote: Editor's note—the Great Newfoundland Seal Disaster of 1914 is described in a book written by Cassy Brown—1972 an experience that reflects how dangerous seal hunting can be.

Jack Walsh, my stepfather, went "on the ice" on another trip in about 1916 or 1917. This version is fictional but because Jack, like many Newfoundland fishermen is reticent, it is based on his experience on the ice.

The Demise Of A Korean War Girl

1967

Jimmy Gavin, a Korean War Veteran, saunters into Danny's with a sorrowful face. It's Monday night and yesterday he and his wife Mary, celebrated the christening of their baby daughter. Their family consists of two boys and now a daughter.

"Give me a frosty one, Bill. God, I can't drink like the old days."

I knew Jimmy from when he was Wentworth student, majoring in Construction Management. Now he's about 34, well built and a hard charging manager for Lee Kennedy Construction in Dorchester.

"Bill," he continues, "We've known each other for a long time now, and I'd like to talk to you about something personal. I value your judgments, especially because you're a professor and you have experience with a host of personal issues.

"My problem goes back to when I was in Korea. I was in the First Cav at the very beginning of the conflict in 1950. That's almost eighteen years ago. But let me start over again. Yesterday, Mary and I had our beautiful little daughter christened. It was a lovely ceremony. We have our complete family now. Like Lou Gehrig I can say I am the luckiest man on the face of the earth. Great wife, healthy kids, and all of them a joy. I've got a good job and a nice little ranch in Stoughton. All is perfect except . . . let me backtrack to Korea in 1951. Hordes of Chinese came across the Yalu River and tore into the Army and Marines. It was awful! The 1st Cav was overrun. My company was all but slaughtered, and to tell you the truth those of us who didn't run are dead.

"Anyway, I got separated from my platoon. It was snowing like hell, and so cold that I knew if I fell asleep I would never wake up. There was a small river and a bridge that provided some shelter. At the edge of the village there was an overturned cart with some burlap bags and a small piece of carpet. I dragged them under the bridge and made a bed. It was smelly, but at least I was out of the snow. I was so scared. I was all alone and by this time it was dark. I huddled up like a cocoon, I couldn't sleep so I shivered the night away waiting for daybreak. As the sky lightened I searched the space, listening for any sounds. Was anyone with me under that bridge?

"I released the safety on my M-1, slowly and silently. I peaked out from under the burlap. There was a sense within me that something was under that bridge with me. Another soldier—but friend or foe? Or could it have been an animal? Definitely I detected a smell. It seemed that every one of my senses were locked into high gear.

"Slowly, I crawled out from under my blanket and stood up to get a better look. Then a rustle. I look in that direction. There is a person, a gook in a Chinese quilted uniform. He stared at me. His face and mouth are opened like he's ready to take a bite. It happened in milliseconds. He raised his rifle but I was quicker and I fired six times. The noise was deafening and all I could think about was how to get out of there.

"I went over to him. Why, I don't know. I search his body for papers, part of my Army training, I guess. I found no papers. But in his pocket I find photograph which I slip into my parka.

"The light is getting brighter now, and the snow has stopped. I hide behind some boulders and begin heading south, very slowly.

"To make a long story short, I hear gun fire in the distance. I figure out that it's Baker Company from the 1st Cav. I am so relieved. I could have hugged the Sergeant who found me. The rest of the trip is a blur until we found the main force, where there was hot food and reasonable safety.

"Days later when things are back to as normal as it ever got in Korea, I looked at the photograph that I had pocketed. It was of a girl, I can't figure out people's ages, let alone Asian women.

"For whatever reason, I decided that she was the dead soldier's girlfriend and her name was Mary Gook. I made up a name for him too, Charlie Gook. God Bill, guys—especially nineteen year old soldiers can really be cruel, and I am no better.

"When I came stateside and was discharged, I'd get drunk and tell my soldier buddies about the guy named Charlie under the bridge and his girlfriend Mary. I would show Mary's photo. I and my buddies would make up stories about love. We'd joke and laugh and make up outrageous stories.

"Then I got married and now I have a family. About six months ago, while I was building a room for the new baby. I went through my personal papers and service records so I could apply for a loan—and sure enough, I found Mary's photograph in a pile of old Army stuff.

"That photo has haunted me for the past six months. Do you know why? Because I have a good life and she doesn't. It was my killing of Charlie that denied them both the life that I have.

"I understand that I had no choice about killing Charlie. It was either him or me. But by killing him, I killed an entire family that never had a chance to live.

"I am so ashamed. I've talked with my priest and I even went to see a shrink about this, and they both tell me to get over it. The shrink told me to get rid of the photograph as the first step.

"So, Bill, I need a really big favor. Would you take this photograph and burn it for me? I can't seem to do it myself, and I've always respected you so much. Can you help me?"

Jimmy handed me the photograph and I burned it right then in the ashtray.

Drugs

January 1967

This morning another young person, a sixteen year old girl from Upham's Corner, died from a drug overdose. She snorted some powder that her boyfriend had smuggled from Thailand. Pure Heroin, too potent for her small and delicate frame. What a damn shame! Good girl from a stable family. Honor student at Latin High School. She had a clean record and after one sniff she forfeits her life. Iron Mike, the cop from Station 11, said that her father cracked up, became hysterical yelling that he'd kill the boy that gave it to her. What a tragedy, and by no means is this an isolated case.

Last month, Red Drisoll's nephew freaked out on LSD. It was so bad that the doctors had him committed to the Mattapan Mental Hospital. And worse yet, Jill Hegarty's daughter went to a "mix and merry" party, an event where you are supposed to take a combination of pills and alcohol. Drunk and completely senseless, she wandered around Boston, by the Penny Arcade, where she was picked up by a gang of men. They brutally raped her repeatedly until she hemorrhaged to death. The girl's father's hair turned white in three short months, her mother looked ten years older. They moved to Rhode Island shortly after this happened. Yes, drugs extract their toll.

The neighborhood buckles under another problem with blight and crime and taxes. Like the straw that broke the camel's back, drugs, add another dimention to the insolvable problems of city life. For years, alcohol was the plague of people's lives. Now the inner city neighborhoods and really the whole country fights a new epidemic of uppers, and downers, and all-arounders. And add LSD, marijuana, cocaine and heroin. The real tragedy lies in that no real solution can be found. I suppose if a society chooses to live a certain life style, then it deserves what it gets. In the 1920's we proved that we wanted to drink alcohol. Prohibition did not stop people from drinking. So in the 1970's we reap our crop of millions of alcoholics with innumerable stories of murder and suicide and crime and divorce and human misery. In a few years, after we legalize marijuana and market more medically acceptable drugs, how many more lives will be bankrupt? The choice is ours. It's a free country. When you come down to basics, if a person wants to ruin his or her life they'll certainly find a method to do so. Whether it's alcohol, adventure, overeating, grass, L.S.D., heroin, pills or a pistol. Adults drink alcohol, kids smoke grass, and everybody swallows pills for any and all of real and imagined human ills.

How prevalent are illegal drugs in Danny's? Well as far as grass is concerned, let's face it, most kids smoke it regularly. No big deal, in fact, I smoked pot a few times. It gave me a hell of a buzz right on the apex of my head. Tried it, and no thanks, a few drinks are good enough for me. However, I doubt if I'd vote to legalize marijuana. My reason is that alcohol causes enough serious problems for so many people. Why add fuel to the fire?

Yesterday, that Stickney kid darted into Danny's. He's thin as a twig. He looks like one of those concentration camp refugees; I figure he must be taking some drug. He's white as a sheet, real sickly, the translucent skin that covers his skull is stretched so that you can see the minor definitions of his cheek and chin bones. His eyes are popping out of his head like two pealed hard boiled eggs. He's jittery, irritable and nervous, fidgeting from one stool to another. He makes a phone call, and yells into the receiver. Slamming down the phone, he bolts out the door.

A young kid nods to me, "Poor son-of-a-bitch is all beaned out on speed. Must be a terrible crash."

Later on as a group of young guys drink beer and watch the ball game, one of them offers up couple of yellow and black pills. The others decline, but he tilts his head back, nonchalantly throws a couple into his mouth and washes it down with his beer. Within the hour, he wanders into the corner booth, his head bobbing softly like a buoy floating on the waves. He slept until closing time; he had a real hard time waking up.

You must realize how much I love this block and the people who live, work and hang out here. At least the memories, I love. Things are changing too fast these days. A different breed, a fast atmosphere replaces the world I once knew. Sure, I realize that people remain basically the same, but the problems, the environment, definitely the drug scene make it foreign to me. We've always had poverty, sickness, inequality and hard work. We always will. But whatever combinations of problems exist today, people strive and I mean strive to escape. Drugs help people to escape, not to solve, but to escape. I like my drink, helps me to relax. But I don't try to escape, not anymore, I learned that lesson the hard way.

Why do people wish so fervently to escape through using drugs? What about these young kids who really have yet to experience responsibility? For instance, barbiturates. Kids pop a bennie and sleep for days. What a helluva way to pass through life, sleeping. Or worse, heroin. Imagine a drug so powerful that a person yields life and limb. Is life so painful that one needs to escape at any cost? Then again humans have always sought some kind of escape—through reading, writing, art, sports, fornicating, exploring and a million other avenues.

Back to my original question, how prevalent are drugs in Danny's? In this parish? As with every tavern, there is always at least one expert on every subject under the sun. In actuality this individual may fall far short of expertise; however, he may be leagues ahead of others. Our drug expert, is Eddie Seeley, a graduate student of Sociology at UMass, Amherst. Some guys swear that Eddie is full of bull, but most agree that he's experimented with pretty much all the drugs known to man, both as a student in high school and as an infantryman in Vietnam.

I find Eddie a most articulate convincing young man. He has a glib tongue of a politician but a likable charactor. He's of medium height and weight with long stringy hair and sleepy eyes. His cocky manner manafests into a little strut when he walks.

"Well, to be frank, I've been experimenting with drugs since I was a freshman in high school. I started with cough syrup and stuff like that. Then Johnnie Terranti sold me a few joints. It was really good stuff. He got it from his brother overseas. You know, when you think about it, maybe the drugs were around in the ghettoes since the fifties but it was a few college kids and especially the Viet guys who saturated Dorchester in the late fifties or early sixties. I remember as a kid I really admired those older kids and the vets. They seemed to have it all together, the world by the balls. They were the ones with money from pushing, the high rollers. Us young kids thought of drugs like they were the key to the fast life, you know like a T.V. detective hero. The guy with a gold spoon for coke on a chain around his neck and all that.

"You name the drug, I've tried it. I still do but I'm cool about it. I don't want to bend your nose out of joint but older people, anyone over thirty, you have no idea of just how good drugs make you feel. In fact, I'm surprised that an old fossil like you would be asking about them. Are you looking to score? If you play it cool you extract all the good without getting burnt.

"Of course, if you're looking to screw himself up you're going to find a way, no matter what John Law might say or do. It's a personality thing. Some people are born to be fucked-up on one thing or another. You can work yourself to death or eat yourself to death or O.D. Some people are just plain born losers. I'm just a winner. I like to play around with fire I ain't gonna be burned. You gotta be smart, with any drug, you begin with a little to test your system and then progress gradually. For God's sake, you'd be crazy to try out LSD by dropping a spoonful. You'd flip out and scramble your brains. Slow and easy does it.

"To give you an example, I snorted heroin once. What a smooth feeling that was. So good that it scared the hell out of me. Bad stuff, that horse. It's too damn good. Now I was smart enough not to mainline, for a couple of reasons. One, it's too good, too powerful; the other is that you don't know how much it's been cut.

"As far as the other drugs go, they're OK. I take them now and then. Coke, I like. But pretty damn expensive. Ten bucks a line. A couple of sniffs and man, you're numb. Great stuff with girl in bed. You can go all night. Great.

"LSD? Well, you know all this nonsense about tasting smells and hearing colors, that's pure bullshit as far as I'm concerned. It does alter your perception though. Like if you wave your hand in front of your eyes, you can perceive it like a strobe light. Really weird. Acid can really foul you up. I'd never tell anyone to begin by dropping acid. Try other drugs first. Rule number one with acid is to know yourself. If you're paranoid or got the world on your shoulders, then skip acid. It'll do a number on your head. The setting really counts, be with solid friends in a nice pad. In bed with a girl you really dig. That's kinky.

"Speed, downers? Yes, every now and then. Got to be careful about mixing with booze.

"Grass? You're joking! Of course, they should legalize marijuana. No one's ever been hurt by pot. It makes people feel good—what's wrong with that?

There you have Eddie Seeley's viewpoint on drugs. A general rundown of the drugs in this block. To actually hear him, he is so convincing, so sure of himself. But I wonder if he'll ever get really burned.

Let's go down the line, ask others, hear other opinions about the various drugs.

Alcohol

J.S.(41): "She called me an alcoholic. Me, a damn alcoholic! I don't know what the hell she means. I ain't got no problem. Just 'cause I lost my job. OK I smashed up a couple of cars. It coulda happened to anyone."

B.D. (15?): "Gin makes me feel good. The taste is lousy, like perfume smells, but oh man, it sure gets me high."

Y.O'H (37): "I've been in AA nearly four years—the 3rd of June is my anniversary. Half the guys in the Braintree group are from St. Peter's. It's like old home week. Why'd I join? Because I woke up in an ally in Roxbury, my teeth busted, my lip split open. I had no idea where I was or how I got there. Then I got to thinking about the previous year. The divorce. The kids gone. All from the booze. Ya, I'm an alcoholic. I take it a day at a time."

R.L. (26): "My sister, that's right, she's got the taste. I know she doesn't look the part, and she'll deny that she's a closet drinker. From what she tells me she starts off after the kids go to school and polishes off a fifth of vodka a day. There's no smell from vodka."

G.O'T (57): "I tell ye now, if whiskey were discovered tomorrow, it would indeed be banned. A poison if there ever was, especially for the Irish. A curse of the Demon. The long and short of it is that I lost everything dear to me."

T.M. (29): "Sure I drink every day but I don't have a problem. I can take it or leave it. When you think about it, it's safer than marijuana and the rest of those drugs. They're really dangerous. All beer causes is a hangover. I can quit anytime, really. That's why I can't understand why my boss fired me. And now my girl is leaving. They just don't understand. I'm just going through a rough spot. No kidding, I could quit tomorrow, but what for? Hey, could you cuff me for a fiver?"

B.V. (57): "Did you hear? Old Joe Harper's in the hospital. Got Cirrhosis of the liver. His skin's as yellow as bananas. Poor bugger. He shoulda listened; the doctor's been warning him for years. But, nah, he goes out and drinks Dorchester dry. You shoulda seen him in the old days, he could really hold his liquor."

D.W.: "Did you read about the kid from Codman Square? Poor stupid jerk chug-a-lugged a fifth of vodka on a bet. Passed out and died before the cops got him to the hospital. He was only seventeen. Tough break. Heard he puked blood and everything."

Kid (14): "Hey mister, will ya buy us some booze? We havin' a party. Two quarts of Bud, three six packs of Schlitz, a half pint of Smirnoff, three half pints of Schenley and let's see . . . ."

V.A. Hospital Administrator (45): "I would say that a good percentage of veterans are admitted to the hospital for alcohol-related problems. The old ones anyway. Of course, these past few years, we have seen many other drug problems, especially with the Vietnam veterans."

Liquor Salesman (40): "I can understand why people drink but not take drugs. Honest to God, I'd just as soon see my kids drink a fifth a day as smoke one of them marijuana's."

Son (17): "Nah, I don't drink. I'd rather get stoned on pot. No hangover. Anyway I see what whiskey did to my father."

Father (40+): "Caught my twelve year old stiff as a boot in the cellar. I almost killed him. Twelve years old!"

Registry Cop (35): "It's bad enough with forged I.D. cards but now those long haired liberals go and lower the drinking age. Kids'll be drinking at sixteen. They can't hold their liquor. And to God, especially not behind the wheel. In a couple of years we'll have the highways loaded with Billy the Kids."

State Trooper (33): "Drunk drivers? Sure I nab them day in and day out. It's curious that people call me as a dick. Well, I tell them when you see a family mashed like bugs all over the road because of some drunk, like you, then you'd understand why I feel this way."

Health Center Counselor: "Alcoholism. Worst drug problem in the country today. Maybe not as dramatic and public as heroin but in fact it is more serious on a national scale. If people knew of the physical and mental catastrophes brought on by alcohol, they'd reinstitute prohibition."

Ex-driver (23): "I loaded when I smashed into a line of parked cards. I shut off my lights and took off out of there. But the damn cops snatched me. Anyway, I lost my license, indefinite. Gonna have to shell out at least fifteen hundred bucks to a shyster lawyer to get it back."

Fireman (43): "What a car wreck we had last week, worst I've ever seen. It took two hours to pry the kid out. He's drunk as an owl, singing and laughing like it's all a joke. Only he's unaware he's bleeding internally. Heard he died that night in the hospital."

Marijuana

Court Clerk (25): "Smoke? Of course. I've been smoking pot for six or seven years now. I'd say a minimum of three quarters of the kids in this block smoke periodically. Even in high school. Maybe not every night but regularly. Let me tell you, I never saw anyone locked up because of pot. That's more than can be said for booze.

Veteran USMC (22): "I started in 'Nam. There was good stuff over there. I mean, top shelf. The stuff around here, you got no idea of what's in it. Probably half horseshit and bird seed. But over there man, it'd blow the socks right off ya. Great stuff, man. Nice and mellow. A smooth smoke with a water pipe. I felt like one of those Indian princes. And best of all, ya ain't got a hangover. Christ sake, when you drink beer you wake up with a big damn head, ya mouth tastes like crap. No man, I'd rather get stoned any day."

Kid on Corner (17): "Whaddaya kiddin' me? I been smoking pot since thirteen. Ther ain't nothing wrong with it. Not in my book. It makes me feel good, like I ain't a loser. Fantastic stuff to ball with. Me and my chick, when she's baby sittin', just get stoned and make it. Like you're in a cloud, no hassles, nothing but peace and quiet and pussy. Fantastic, pot, fantastic! Bill, you oughta dig up an old chick and give it a whack."

B.U. Student (23) Education Major: "Yeah, I think Marijuana should be legalized. It's been proven to be safer than alcohol. You know, I was at Woodstock and, I mean, everyone was stoned. The place was inundated with marijuana but there was no trouble. Not one solitary fight. Just love and peace. Oh, I love to be high. And when this generation matures, we'll legalize grass, just wait and see. In fact, half the tobacco companies are investing it now, they see the almighty dollar signs. Just a question of time."

Student, Dorchester High School: "Why shouldn't I get stoned? My parents drink, same thing, only I've never seen people fight after smoking this stuff. But I sure as hell seen my father punch out my mom after a couple of drinks. Look at all the beefs in the tavern. I'd bet you ten bucks if all you sold was grass, you'd never see a fist fight in Danny's again."

Pressman (52): "If I ever catch my kid smoking pot or anything like that, I'll beat the living hell outa him, and throw him out right on his ass. Damn kids nowadays, can't understand them. Nothing but a bunch of sex maniacs. Oughta shoot the whole pack of them."

Packer in Meat Factory (27): "Man, if I didn't have my joint at lunchtime, I'd never make it through the day. That ain't no lie either. Who says it leads to other drugs? I've been stoned for years and ain't tried nothing else, except I drop some acid once. Yah, man, grass is my bag. No booze smell so my boss don't know nothing. He's so square he can't figure out why I'm giggling half the afternoon."

Carpenter (38): "Sure, I see the young kids, real hot dudes, into everything. Let me say this, I get my kicks from getting laid, booze and football games. Leave all other stuff to the kids. Maybe it is all harmless, I don't know. But I tell ya what I did see. A young kid in work started with marijuana, real a high wheeler. Well, now he's all screwed up—on something."

LSD

Charlie M. (46): "Whatever it is, I tell ye, tis a tool of Satan. Me own boy's a stranger to me. Didn't I bring him, me own flesh and blood to the asylum. Jesus, Mary, and Joseph! What a cursed place but no worry to him. He's foolish. Why, he no more knows me than the man in the moon. Worse yet the doctor's don't know a bloody thing more than I do. Just lock him up with his arms all bound like a mummy. Standing all day right stiff and staring at the wall. It killed his mother, it did. Just broke her heart. And ye ask me about drugs?"

Hippie Kid: "No acid, man, it'll burn ya out. I ain't got much for brains but I ain't screwin' up what I got. That's all I'd need."

Ex-student, Northeastern (23): "Beautiful. God, my first trip was the greatest emotional revelation of my life. Absolutely cosmic. Imagine tasting sounds, or watching yourself drift in slow motion through some time and space—you know, I predict that LSD will prove to be the greatest tool of mental study ever to come down the pike. Powerful. I remember one time I tripped with a chick. Had a one hour orgasm. I shit you not, one solid hour. Oh God, I thought I'd died. Beautiful. But you've got to have the right setting or you might have a bad trip. That's why most people freak out. You have to know yourself. I mean, if you're a borderline schizophrenic and you trip, then you got troubles. But if your head's screwed on solid, acid will give the most beautiful moments of your life."

Speed

Boston College Student (20): "Oh, yes, around exam time I always take speed. Everybody does, you need to. Next week I've got to pass three exams—I need a three point-five average this term to get accepted into graduate school. I have to stay up for three nights straight, and I'm behind two term papers, plus I'm working part-time. I've got to take something to keep going."

Cabdriver (40): "My wife's been using speed for years to lose weight. Shit, she goes like hell, it gives her energy to burn. So when I'm down and really tired, I gobble a few for a quick pick-me-up. Good stuff for long trips and nights. It's great except when it wears off, then I feel like a son of a bitch."

Motorcyclist (24): "Speed—like the man says, "Speed kills." Let me warn ya, never, never touch a speed freak. They'll turn on you like a wild dog—they're all crazy. They think everybody's out so screw them, or plotting against them. It's easy to pick them out of a crowd. They're skinny—cause they're never hungry. Their eyes are big and their nervous, Jesus, like a rat. Ya can't talk to them. Weird train of thought, jumping from one thing to another. Ya, they're flaky. I ain't kidding when I tell you never to screw with one. So there was this kid in Field's Corner—his buddy was crashing and he tried to hold him down. Well, the damn freak strangled him, then bashed his head with a steam iron."

High School Drop Out (19): "I use to steal my old lady's diet pills for a go-go. Then what the hell, like everything else you shoot for more. Now look at me I'm hooked. Half the time, I'm freaked out and think everyone's tryin' to ace me. Look at my hands, like I'm holding a vibrator. And piss, I piss all day and night. Damn, I wish I could get off this shit."

Dishwasher (22): "You want to hear about speed. Well, look at me. I'm the biggest freak you'll ever lay eyes on. A lousy dishwasher at McDonald's. I was a high School football star. I won a scholarship, I made it through two years of college and now I'm a dishwasher at Big Macs. To top it off, I'm a outpatient at Foxboro mental hospital, the nut house. You ever been locked up? Let me tell you, the place is built like fortresses. Hundred year old granite buildings and no doubt one of the most depressing places in the universe. Everybody's whacked out. Thank God I was only in for a few weeks. Gave me brain wave tests and all that. I would have cracked up if I'd stayed any longer.

"Every damn day some guy'd start shouting Tarzan calls. For hours on end until pretty soon other patients would start to act out. In the mess hall, all those poor damn mongoloids trying to eat and grab you, shit all over their hands. I guarantee that if you were sane upon admittance, you'd be climbing the walls within a week.

"Well, like I said, I only stayed a few weeks until the shrinks completed their tests. Now a couple of times a week I report in for my medicine.

"It began so innocuous. I was in a state college in Boston where I met a couple of guys who'd been in Vietnam, high rollers—hot stuff grass, LSD, coke, booze—the whole scene. No problems, I told myself, just keep away from heroin and I'd be able to handle anything. Nothing could bother 'the kid'. For one solid year, I smoked grass three times a week and had broads up the ying-yang. You know something, you can never get enough of feeling good. I was insatiable. Oh sure for one day you're OK, but I mean you want a different girl every couple of days. After a while, grass became blasé. I started skipping classes so then I had to cram to pass. No sweat, I took uppers so that I could study and jog at the same time. Had the stamina of ten guys, no lie. Then on to LSD I took uppers then I needed downers. Needless to say, I flunked out. I didn't care about anything, just give me my uppers. When my old man found out about the drugs he threw me out of the house without a dime. Jesus, my mother was so upset she had a heart attack. He blamed me for that. Maybe he was right, anyway, out I went. No bread, but I didn't care if my ups were around.

"But it all caught up to me, no money, no food, no real place to live. I tried to work, and get straighted out and you know what? I couldn't. It's funny but when you live with all the hot stuff, it's a whole new culture that's hard to get away from. It's when you try to get squared away that you realize just how screwed up you really are. I couldn't straighten out, so I turned myself in. I knew I was all messed-up. One part of me cared and the other part didn't. Sounds crazy don't it? My shrink tells me that when I was a kid, I hated my brother—you ever hear such bullshit?

"Well here I am now, washing dishes in McDonalds, living in the YMCA. This is my life, all because of speed."

Downers

"Sleepy", Unemployed (21): "It's soooo nice to drift out. Escape from all the nonsense of home and work and people telling you what the hell to do. Swish down on a couple of drinks and a few goofballs, and time just moves on. What a smooth feeling. No lie, you feel so good. Ease off to sleep. It's fantastic man to escape from pain and people hassling you. No one can bother you when you're asleep. Yah, no lie, no one can bother you when you're asleep. No one."

Auto Mechanic (24): "Ya, we use to throw pill parties. You know how kids are, they'll try anything once. Everybody mixed up the pills in a bowl, and concocts a fruit punch with every kind of booze ya can imagine. Mix it up, mix and don't worry. These were some wild parties, man. But this one time I learned my lesson. This broad from Southie, couldna been more'n sixteen—passed out. We soaked her head in ice water but she did not move—Jesus. I got scared. So me and another kid carried her to the Carney Hospital. We dropped her off at the emergency entrance and ran away. Now when I think of it, it was a pretty stupid move. I mean the doctors couldn't possibly know what she took. I never found out whatever happened to her. All's I know is that beer is OK for me now, forget all that other nonsense."

Ex-Convict (34): "When I was in the slammer, I used to eat Red Devils like they were peppermints. It was the only way to do time, to sleep it away. Next time you ride by Walpole look over the wall at the buildings with the glass roof. You can see them from the road. That's max security. I shit you not, man, I was on the third tier right under that glass. It was like a green house in the summer. So hot, you'd burn your hands if ya touched the bars. It was brutal. Plenty of guys went bananas. Sweating and bored and off their rocker. So you gotta take somethin' to survive. So I gets in with a guard. My girl used to pay him to smuggle in downers for me. I used to eat bennies and sleep all the time. Just to get away from the lousy food, the heat and black bastards. Muslim's and all their craziness. Time went by OK while I slept. But man when I tried to get off downers, I went into convulsions. Hadda be treated by the medical doctors and the shrinks. I'm doing OK now, but every once in a while when I'm sick of the broad or the world in general, I eat a few devils."

Tranquilizers

Bartender (37): "Ya wanna good cure for a hangover? Take a Valium, fives or tens. Man, they work like a charm. I don't care how sick you are, or how bad the hangover, take a valium and you'll be on top of the world in half an hour. I feel like a million bucks in no time."

Electrician (50): "You see, I'm a nervous kind of guy, jiggy most of the time. You know how it is, the job and kids and all that. Well, you know what? Christ, I already had two breakdowns. Sure once in a while when I get real bad, I take a few Librium to carry me through."

Food Manger in Nursing Home (28): "Thorazine? From what I see and hear from the nurses, it must be dynamite. It'll do a real job on you and turn you into a zombie. Last week, a psychologist told me Thorazine's the reason why half the mental institutions are empty today. If you get a patient who's climbing the walls, then Thorazine will b hring him down. In fact, when one of the old timers acts up, we feed them Thorazine. Don't quote me, Bill, but half the place is tranquilized. We use them like feeding peanuts to elephants. All they can do is sit it their chairs or beds all day and cause no problems. Just vegetate with no complaints and the owners and doctors collect from the Welfare. In fact, tranquilizers suppress their appetites so the owners make out on both ends. Yes, Thorazine and nursing homes go hand in glove."

Heroin

Ex-Infantryman (24): "The Big H? I'd never try it. I saw what a mess it makes. There was this kid in my squad from Mission Hill, he was high all the time. On Red Chinese, pure stuff. He could care less about anything so the Lieutenant must have figured he was expendable so he assigned him to point. The kid just didn't care. Charlie'd be shooting our asses off, mortars, grenades, machine guns and he'd be nodding off, almost asleep. Heroin's got to be damn potent because everybody was pissing their pants digging a foxhole a mile deep, and he'd be dozing like a baby.

"Well one time we were up in Section Able-three, near Chou Lai, beating the bush for Charlie when he comes across a hut in the middle of nowhere. There's this old gook, must have been a hundred, smoking opium. Come into the jungle to smoke away till he dies. Couple of nights later the word comes down from Headquarters that we're being relieved and going home! Everyone's happy as all hell. Except this kid. He gives me a letter to send home for him. He tells me he's going AWOL, back into the bush to latch up with the old gook.

"'Man, you just don't know, you don't know what it feels like. I get sick just thinking I won't have it. Anyway, ain't nothing back in the States for me. Everything I want is here, with that old papa-san. I can get all the stuff I want. Never have to sweat anything again. Just burn myself out. If only you knew. Look, I don't give a fiddler's dick about the States, my family, my girl, sex, nothing. In 'Nam, I'm free. As long as I got my fix, I'm free. If I go home, I'll have to hustle a hundred dollars a tip, and cheap stuff, all cut down. Over here, it's pure. I know ya don't understand so just take the letter and mail it. It's the greatest feeling in the universe. Like your whole body is coming off. So you'd never know how it can be without any stuff.'"

"He went AWOL and I never heard about him again."

Policeman (42): "There is not much heroin around here. Maybe shipping or sniffing but not mainlining. Although last week we picked up a guy on his way home from work. He pulled over the side of road for a bit. My partner and I were cruising and a guy on the side of the road always looks suspicious. When he saw us coming, he tried to eat the needle and everything else. He didn't want to be booked for possession. So we locked him up until court next day. Well, that night what does the guy do but busts his arm so he can go to the hospital and maybe get something for the pain. Breaks his damn arm by slamming it against the bars.

"When I asked him what in the hell he was thinking, to bust his own arm he answered, 'You don't know man, ya don't know what it's like.' He's had this far away look in his eyes that'd scare the hell out of you.

"I'll tell you, Bill, heroin must be a terribly powerful drug. I've heard of addicts who's veins in their arms collapsed so they'd inject anywhere—eyelids, under the tongue, even in their pecker. Can you imagine sticking a needle in your pecker?

"I don't see a solution, an ounce of prevention is worth a pound of cure. Sometimes I think the only solution is to shoot all heroin addicts—they're dead anyway."

The Colonel

1967

It's Friday night and Danny's is crowded and consequently noisy. Guys throwing darts. A few watching T.V., discussing sports.

All of a sudden, a loud voice sounds out "Cease Fire! Cease Fire! Bring the stretchers bearers! They come to bury their dead!" It's one of those characters who inhabit Danny's.

Most taverns have their characters—a loud mouth, or a jokester, or in the case of the Colonel, not all there but certainly harmless. Most of the patrons are use to his outbursts, so they pay little attention to what he says. He may show up once a month on a Friday night, and then he goes away for a while.

The Colonel—no one knows his real name or much about his history. He is always cleanly dressed, and well groomed. I'd guess him to be around fifty. His hair is mostly black with a bit of grey around his temples and is cut short in a military style. His face is strong featured and his skin is a healthy tanned. He is good looking, in fact, measured by most of the Friday night crowd, he looks distinguished. His accent is not from Dorchester—he pronounces his r's and g's. And his voice is clear and resonant.

Booker says, "As long as the man causes no problems, leave him be. But Bill, maybe you should ask Iron Mike about him."

Well, now it so happens that within the week, I am in Park Street Station—the Red Line Subway to Andrew Square. It's around 5:30 and the platform is packed with the evening commuters headed home for supper.

People are standing, shoulder to shoulder like lemmings ready for the call to the sea. Of course, the crowd leaves a reasonable space near the pit where the train runs. Getting pushed or jostled into the pit as the train arrives is not advisable. Or being fried alive or electrocuted by the third rail is not in anyone's game plan.

All of a sudden I hear a familiar, resonant voice "Cease Fire! Cease Fire! They come to bury their dead!"

Although I am positive that 95% of the homeward bound riders are dead tired, the Colonel's call to arms energizes them.

The crowd surrounding the Colonel, now shifts and shuffles away from this unknown situation and potentially dangerous stranger. "Clear the way for the stretchers!"

"Mother of God!" a woman complains, "Who is this nut?"

A train rumbles to a stop, unloads passengers and picks up a new group who are anxious to rid themselves of this, "nut."

"Are you the stretcher bearer?" asks the Colonel as I pass him to get onto the train.

"No," I answer jumping into the car before the door closes.

That was the last time I saw the man. Standing alone on the platform, looking for the stretcher bearers.

Bill's Retirement From Wentworth Institute

May 2, 1968

General Comment

Well, I'm 68 and it's time for my retirement from Wentworth. First and foremost, I have a great respect for Arioch Wentworth, the founder of the school. In 1904, Wentworth Institute was chartered to provide education in the mechanical arts for students who wished to extend their education beyond the high school level. Early in his life in New Hampshire, Arioch was unable to find employment because of lack of special training in the marble business. Eventually because of his unusual mechanical ability and business acumen, he became very successful in financial matters and in real estate development in the Boston area.

In order to provide young men with training beyond high school, he willed millions of dollars to the school. In 1911 Wentworth Institute opened with an entering class of 224 day students and close to 500 evening students. Through the years the Wentworth program improved in content and quality and now incudes carpentry, electricity, plumbing, machine design, foundry and construction techniques.

In 1956, the charter was amended to furnish education in the mechanical arts, including engineering. In 1965 the enrollment was approximately 2300 students. Arioch also left us with a few business maxims, several of which are listed below:

Buy real estate, young man, buy real estate.
Pay all bills when presented.
Don't shoulder others' responsibility.

Work every day till the day's work is done.
One vacation a year is enough.
Lead if you can; follow if you must.
Leave business at the office.

My Personal Experience at Wentworth Institute

The school provided an excellent education for those who desired to work and to advance in the trades especially in the construction field. The students attended school from 8AM or 9AM to 3PM or 4PM five days a week. Homework and lab assignments were assigned each day and were expected to be completed correctly and handed in on time. School was seldom cancelled for inclement weather.

To put it plainly, as in the construction trades, you were expected to be on time, keep your mouth shut, and do your work. In the 40's, 50's and 60's the school was run like a factory and when you graduated you would get a good job. Before I was assigned to teach during the Depression, my experience in the school began with tending the boilers on the night shift which I did for ten or so years. I studied and passed the Public Safety exams for advancement and by taking more classes, I received my 3rd Class Engineer's license. I was then offered a faculty position, teaching technical courses. In the 40's I taught young men who were headed into the military and into the engine rooms of destroyers, cruisers and battleships.

I felt great about my contribution to the war effort.

They were all fine young men. As the years pass, I forgot some of the names but not faces. When I think about "Good Bye Mr. Chips" I see those tough patriotic young kids from Dorchester, South Boston, Mission Hill, Roxbury, East Boston and all the outlying areas on a journey from which some may not retun, like my brother Danny.

Obviously, I will miss the youthful energy and the spirit of the students. As I age and limp along, I feel a bit of jealously, wishing I could relive my youth and do it all again. It went so fast the first time. Overall, I do appreciate the free summers to hike, and write stories. Teaching at Wentworth satisfied the needs that I had.

I love graduation! Everyone is happy, the students and the parents, fellow teachers, and the administration. Many students are the first in their families to earn certificate degrees beyond High School. The look on the parent's faces! Faces from England, Ireland, Germany, Italy, Spain, and other points of the compass. Their eyes are brighter than the Boston lighthouse. In my own way, I feel that a good effort has been given by WIT instructors. I did my job and I believe that most teachers at Wentworth feel likewise. "Here's the tools, kid, now you get out and show the world what a three decker kid from Boston can accomplish. Work hard, meet a fine young lady, earn money, buy a car, build a home in the suburbs, have a family. Live the good life!"

The Retirement Luncheon

1968 was the era of new technology; space age materials, computers, rockets, aerospace and electronics. The Brave New World. Throw away your slide rules and keep all records electronically. Save the forests by eliminating paper.

Herman the German (Eddie Edison) is also retiring. A great companion to sit with at the head lunch table. We sit together and reminisce about the "old days."

Herman and I chuckled about the infamous "President's Faculty Meetings." Without doubt, there are faculty memebers throughout the world, driven by some uncontrollable urge to ask stupid questions. At the end of the President's speech, he asks rhetorically if there are any questions. And then it happens, it is like a torch was thrust into a barrel of exotic fuel—BOOM!

A misfit professor asks, "What are your thoughts concerning the elimination of grades?" Or "Do you feel that our salaries should be doubled?" "Can we reduce our workload to one three hour class per week?"

The faculty groans as a group when the questions begin. They itch and shift in their chairs, anticipating lunch or maybe an early day. But "any questions?" ruins that wish.

Another professor shoots his hand up, "I believe that the faculty deserve a 30% raise across the board." An audible groan from the rest of the faculty. "MIT faculty earn 50% more than we do . . ."

The Provost answers tells them that those issues will be addressed in the next committee meeting during the following semester. The faculty, seeing their opportunity to flee to lunch, exit to the dining room.

I often wonder if there is something in the drinking water in the hometowns of those crazy professors. I do know for a fact that if the President's address was conducted in Danny's Tavern, Casey would stop the dumb questions cold with a very loud, "What? Are you shitting me?"

At the luncheon, the Provost gave a complimentary speech and there were many cheers and good wishes. I will miss the school very much. I believe in education for it's ability to get your foot in the door to a good job and develop that into a career. To have a good career and keep it, life long learning is necessary.

Later that evening Herman and I feasted at Anthony's Pier Four. Lobster, fine wine and great conversaion made it a memorable evening. My last thought as I hit the pillow was what a great country we live in. I fell asleep with the knowledge that it was a privilege to work with the fine collegues and students that I had the honor to meet at Wentworth. And to this day I have great respect for Arioch Wentworth.

Jerry Returns To Danny's

May 11, 1968

Two days after my retirement from Wentworth, on a Saturday afternoon, who walks into Danny's but Jerry Collins.

"Hi ya boys," he says to Booker and me casually, "I'm glad to catch you two together."

Booker and I were shocked. Jerry looked great, a little older and like many of us, a few pounds heavier.

I could not help but notice Jerry's top dentures fit perfectly now, in the old days after a few too many when he'd lay his head on the bar, his dentures would often fall out.

"This visit is a long time coming, you know. I promised God the day I left here, that I would never enter another bar if he would help me on the path to righteousness. The way I see it, my intent here today is to praise God and to thank you and Booker for setting me on the right path. So many times through the years I wanted to invite you two to an AA meeting, but I was terrified. When I heard that you retired from Wentworth, I thought this would be a good time to come back in to congratulate you and to thank Booker. But, most of all to apologize for leaving you without a word. You know I was just a crazy man. The last drink I had was on July 18, 1948. To tell you the truth, I was afraid to see come in here, walk into any bar. Why attempt fate?"

Jerry continued, "Bill, you were never one to kick someone who was down. I can still remember you asking me to, 'Do me one favor, Jerry, just look into AA.'"

"And you, Booker, you connected me with, Father O'Malley, a Charlestown priest. He was tough on me. I spent time in the City Hospital and then went to the AA meeting in Charlestown and in South Boston. It was like another planet. I heard the stories—so many stories. I lived through the pain and regret and all the broken commitments. My Agnes took me back and the kids helped me through the rough spots. Ma Bell rehired me, into a lower position but it brought back dignity and commitment. My past sins will never disappear, but with God and the spirit, time cures—not all the hurt, but enough."

Jerry finishes, "And so to you, Bill and Booker, I give you with undying gratitude, for giving me a second chance to live my life with family and friends. As a thank you, I'd like to give you a St. Christopher's Medal, Bill, for your hikes and travels. And to you, Booker, a gold Shamrock with the inscription: 'To Be Blessed is Best, Danny's Tavern Dorchester, MA.' God Bless you both."

Jerry hugged Booker and me.

Affirmative Action

1968

Scotty Burns, the fireman, opens the Boston Globe and says, "Hey Bill, you see this article about affirmative action?"

Bill noded.

Certainly affirmative action is a controversial subject, especially in a neighborhood bar. To Scotty, this is a clear cut decision. Years ago, Scotty wanted to be a fireman, and he scored a 99% on his exam, so he got the job.

"I think affirmative action is totally wrong. I always wanted to be a fireman, I studied for the exam and I scored the highest, so I deserve the job and the promotions."

An unknown customer at the bar turned to Scotty and said, "Don't you understand that Affirmative Action is a noble goal? It ascribes to counter the effects of a history of discrimination. How else can we level the playing field?"

"What's this 'we' shit?" Danny O'Neil joins in, "Believe me boyo, I was born in Ireland. I can remember the signs in the factory windows, 'No Irish Need Apply.' My old dad nearly starved to death for lack of employment. Luckily he made his way to Dorchester through Canada. Thank God for James Michael Curley!"

Danny, his face getting even redder continues, "And what really fries my ass is that the name of the game has changed. Now it's no white males need apply. And what's worse is that half the dummies in this country fail to realize that since the government jobs essentially last a lifetime, so if you are excluded from even applying for the job, it's a lifetime loss. And it may well apply to your kids' future too."

Silence. I can hear Danny's heavy breathing.

I signal to the customer to back off. Whether he realized it or not, he is a very short distance from a fist. For a stranger to enter a tavern or union hall and start espousing about this or that which involves someone's livelihood is not a very smart move.

Danny stands up and aggressively asks, "So now I have to worry about Blacks, Chinese, Indians and Mexicans for my job? I never did have anything against them."

Scotty stands also, one on each side of the stranger, "I took my exam and got on to the fire department. I don't need to apologize for anything that I did. I played by the rules. And where do women come into the equation? You know many people are discriminated because they are short, fat, or ugly, maybe they have a scar on their face or they're socially inept. So do they go to the front of the line? And even worse, my own kids will be excluded from consideration."

Danny concludes, "There is bad blood over Affirmative Action. I'm not telling you that my best friends are Black or Latinos because that's not true. In fact I'd take a number of minority friends over some of the white ones, but Affirmative Action is just wrong. Period."

Casey

A Long Absence

March 1969

It's St. Patrick's Day and the bar is noisy, flooded in beer and bravado.

Booker is working on the cash receipts in the backroom office, unsuccessfully trying to isolate himself from the turmoil in the bar. Each year St. Patrick's day pushes the extreme with the green hot dogs and beer. Good God, who would eat a green hot dog? I tried one for a few laughs and then I saw a young fellow walking around with the green hot dog sticking out of his fly.

Out of the blue, who shows up with a foreign package and an unsteady gait? Casey. He carries a very frightened cat under his arm. He is holding it so tightly that his grip is like an inescapable cage.

Casey flops himself and the cat in a booth and snarls to Dinty, "Hey Dinty—you dummy, get me a bottle of Bud. Hurry up before I send this scrawny cat on your lazy ass."

His voice is slurred. His eyes are wet and bloodshot. His skin is so sickly yellow that I think that he belongs in a hospital. His hands twitch so that when Dinty sets the beer on the table, Casey knocks it over.

"Dinty, you stupid shit!" Casey spits out a string of expletives as Dinty nervously wipes the table and mops the floor.

"Take it easy," I call over to Casey, "Here's another beer!"

It has been at least six months since I've seen Casey. I wonder where he has been and what he's been up to. His health has really failed over the time he's been away. Only his nastiness hasn't aged or mellowed. Casey guzzles the bottle bottoms up.

"Give me another, Dummy! And I'll sing a little song for you." As Dinty gets another beer, Casey shifts the cat to his lap, the rear paws are trapped between his thighs, and the front paws are locked in one hand. At the top of his voice, Casey shouts, "Have any of you heard the Irish Bagpipes?" He proceeds to sing, 'Oh it must have been the Irish to dig the Panama Canal!'"

Casey chomps on the poor cat's tail, "Meow!!!!" The cat twists and turns—his body straining to get away from her torturer. Casey continues his song. "Sure me boys it was only the Irish to dig the ditch . . ." Again he bites the tail and the cat howls, only louder, "MEOOOOW!"

The general response in the bar spans the range; some find it amusing, others do not.

"For God's sake, Casey, leave the poor thing alone."

Dinty, quiet shy harmless Dinty, steps up to Casey, grabs his shoulder and smashes a full bottle of beer over his head. Beer pours over Casey's head and runs down his shoulders.

The crowd is silenced by the shock of Dinty's actions.

"Let the cat alone!" stuttered Dinty who stared at Casey directly in his eyes.

Who knows what possessed Dinty, a small frail man to take on the most certifiably insane man in the bar? Maybe crashing the bottle into Casey's head was the culmination of years of anger built up from the taunting, name calling, and overall disrespect Casey showed toward Dinty.

Then the lightening struck back. Casey grabbed Dinty by the arm and swung him like a duffel bag across the room. Dinty's back struck the edge of the bar with an awful, cracking sound. It sounded like his back broke.

The cat scooted out the doorway.

Casey leaped onto the unconscious Dinty. Noises, curses, and drool spurted out of Casey's face like some demented demon, "You'll die! I'll kill you!" he screamed as he dug his hands into Dinty's throat.

"Casey, stop!" I shouted as I ran around the bar, tearing at Casey's fingers as they dug deeper. It took several of the boys to yank Casey from Dinty's body. He kicked and swung his arms viciously at anything and everyone.

There was a roar of noise—screaming and swearing drown out the jukebox. Booker rushed out of the backroom and wedged himself between Dinty and Casey.

"Stop! Casey Stop!" Booker's voice dropped to a whisper as he said something in Casey's ear. Then he said calmly, "Casey, get up man and get outta my sight. Go or you'll never see another sunset." He shoved something in Casey's back.

Casey glared at Booker, and called him names. "Fight me like a man!" he hissed.

Booker answered, "Anytime Casey. Anytime, but not here. You're a sick puppy and I don't want you to darken the door on this place ever again. Do you hear?"

Casey shook off the arms that were holding him, "I'll get you guys. All of you!" He left.

Booker checked on Dinty who had begun to moan and move around. He took him to the City Hospital where he was checked out. A few bruises, but otherwise all was OK.

Of course in the bar, everyone had a different interpretation of the events, "Poor Dinty!" "I hope he's alright. I thought he was a goner." "That Casey's a crazy SOB!" "Yeah, did you see his face?" "What did Booker say to Casey?" "I think Booker had a gun in his back."

"Shut up!"

Me? I didn't see anything. Although I don't expect to see Casey in Danny's anymore. But with Casey you never know.

Odds And Ends

Recently returned from Florida, his vacation home, Frank Vento dies in a house fire, apparently was smoking in bed.

JFK assassinated November 22, 1963
MLK assassinated April 4, 1968
RFK killed by gunman, died June 6, 1968

Booker, "My God, what is the country coming to?"

Peter Z, "I hear that Baker's Chocolate is moving the factory down South. A lot of folks will lose their jobs. Too bad. It's not different than the shoe manufacturers in Brocton shutting down or moving South for cheap labor. Bad sign. Where will it end?"

Kevin White elected Mayor of Boston

Middle aged teacher from Dorchester High School—having a quiet beer.

A young fellow approaches him, "You bastard, you flunked me in math a few years ago. If you were younger, I'd knock your block off."

Booker warns him to calm down.

Let's go down Dudley Street to the Irish Dances.

Headline: America's Proudest Hour
Apollo 11 lands on the Moon
July 20, 1969

Commander Neil Armstrong spoke these historic words, "That's one small step for a man, one great leap for mankind." As a general comment, the boys in Danny's all agreed, that this was a feat to be proud of.

Bill's Stories Of Danny's Neighborhood

(Published in the Dorchester Monthly Tribune)

1. In Memory Of Rags Maloney

Sam and the Widow's Curse

1963

A child, a man can revisit, he can recall, a something, a somewhere. A clear autumn morning—Tuesday morning when the trash man collected. I can hear the clop of hooves on the tar black streets, the squeak of wobbly wheels and a chant, "Rag-g-g-g-s! Some oll-ld rags!" a loud sorrowful chant which could be heard for a city block. A song without a melody, sung as a priest at high mass, deep and resonant and adhesive to the memory.

"Rag-g-g-s! Some ol-ld rags!" loud and proud Sam sat throned. A royal coachman baritoneing the king's decrees. While his horse, Cockeye, wagged her head in beat to the chant, Sam studied the trash cans until he spotted a few rags.

"Whoa, my princess." He slightly tugged the crusted reins. No response. "Whoa! Whoa!" Then a sudden stop. As the old wagon tilted and creaked under his weight, Sam stepped down and began to rummage through the barrel, a shredded towel here, a small rug there. He inspected the small rug. It was almost good enough for his house, but a cat had peed in the center so that the stench was took his breath away. Satisfied with his find, Sam threw the junk into the wagon and again enthroned himself.

"Giddy-up, Princess."

With a grunt and a tug, Cockeye brought the wagon to a minimum pace. Seldom did she hurry, only when food was involved. Cockeye was a six-year-old mare the grey metallic color of an old ash can, very sensitive, especially of her right eye. No one could truthfully say her eye was crossed; it just appeared that way. Because of this, the kids had nicknamed her Cockeye. Very few adults openly mocked her, lest they find their hedges trampled or their rose bushes masticated. It was because of this eye anomaly, Cockeye pulled slightly to the left with her head tilted to the right, like a car with its front end out of line. Her heavy balloon trunk sagged generously so that she likened to a giant pot supported by four knobby legs. Cockeye did look awkward but Sam did not notice. He also was burly, his trunk being as full and compact as an overstuffed duffel bag.

Sam loved music. Had he been given the opportunity, when he immigrated to America as a young man, he might have succeeded as a musician. Money, however, was scarce and music did not make money. The rag business afforded him a living, but never his dream. When his only child, Sarah, had entered music college, Sam's dream re-kindled. His years of ragging and scrimping, were now beginning to pay off. He just wished she would work harder at school.

"And the people she knows," he thought, "Especially that bearded guitar player. A lazy bum he is—no job. God forbid if I should let Sarah see him again." When Sam thought, he moved his jaw as though he were chewing caramel.

It was a magnificent autumn morning, a day on which nothing could go wrong. Sam felt marvelous. Never had his voice sounded so strong, so operatic. "Rag-g-g-s! Some old-d-d rags!" his chest heaved the opera of the tenements. The sun was warm so that he wore the checkered flannel shirt that he found in an ash can on Quincy Street. The sleeves were shredded at the elbows but it was decent enough for his profession. His shoddy black pants he'd found in an alley near Field's Corner, hung creaseless to their shabby cuffs. On his head Sam always wore an oversized scally cap. Because the rim extended well beyond his head, he looked like a fat-stemmed mushroom.

Periodically mothers and kids would stop him as he drove past their three-decker houses. They'd haggle over the price of a bag of rags or bundles of newsprint. By and large Sam won. He was indecently honest but thoroughly thrifty. And careful, too many times cheats would try to smuggle a cobblestone into the paper bundles. On each street more and more junk was thrown into the wagon: mounds of newspapers and rags, three rubber tires, a broken bike, a burned mattress, and assorted hunks of metal; copper, tin, and lead. Although the wagon was old, almost prehistoric, it was owned outright by Sam. Cockeye was rented from Harry's Stables, for two dollars a day plus oats. Years ago, Harry told Sam to repair the wagon, but Sam hadn't quite gotten to fix it yet. The wheels leaned precariously outward.

Sam shifted in his seat-box which contained the flashlight that he used to clean out dark cellars. Also the box he held a copy of Remansky's "Great Moment of Music," and Sam's lunch which consisted of a salami sandwich and a syrup bottle filled with homemade wine. Mama had been in such a rush this morning she had almost forgotten to pack his lunch.

"Come on, Princess baby," Sam flipped the reins lightly, "We got one more street to go. Then we go to lunch at the park."

Cockeye snorted. She was famished, no doubt about that. At the mention of lunch she twisted her head around to check that her oat bag hung from underneath the wagon. Satisfied, Cockeye pulled a little harder. The street was quiet. Two little boys were sitting on the sidewalk. The youngest, little Jimmy Ross, was munching an apple.

"Hey Raggie," the older boy called, "You wanna buy some rags?"

"Sure!" Sam braked the wagon. "Where are they?"

"In the backyard," answered the boy. "You have to carry the bag. It's too heavy for me." He led Sam down the alley.

Cockeye studied the apple—her favorite snack; then stared at little Jimmy. The young boy, unaccustomed to horses, was puzzled at which eye was staring. Now Cockeye went into her act. Her eyes watered as though she were crying. A pathetic expression crossed her face. Her body slumped as though she was about to collapse from hunger and fatigue. Her tongue fell out, and she emitted a low moan. Little Jimmy was helpless with pity and the gnawing guilt that he should eat while this poor creature should starve. With a nervous generous hand he offered the apple. Cockeye wolfed it down in one bite.

Sam dragged the bag of rags out of the alley. O-OOff the bundle was heavy to lift into the wagon. Down the street they moved, Sam chanting and watching for new customers. Cockeye moped along. The apple had only aggravated her hunger. Even worse it had loosed her bowels. She stopped and of all places to stop, she chose the worst: right in front of Widow MacNoon's house. As Cockeye grunted, Sam stared off into space as though nothing was happening. Suddenly a strange feeling of being watched overcame him. His eye caught sight of fluttering drapes in the third floor window. A pair of harsh black eyes stared down at him. They were Widow MacNoon's eyes.

The kids had often talked of her. "Watch out for her! She's a witch! Look at her apple tree—nothing grows on it. And at night, strange noises come from her apartment. Don't ever tease Widow MacNoon or else she'll curse you. She's mean and evil."

The eyes disappeared. From what little Sam did see, she did look mean and evil. Her face was hard and shriveled looking like a frozen raisin. Her chin hooked up, her nose hawked down until the two nearly met at her mouth. Over her shoulders she wore a long black shawl.

"Witch bah!" mumbled Sam. "Kid's nonsense. I'm not afraid of her."

The Widow wasn't afraid of Sam either. She bolted out of the doorway, screaming, "You rag man! Get that filthy beast away from my house!"

Cockeye was insulted.

"Listen lady," Sam defended, "the horse gotta go and we ain't going to stop him."

"Get away I tell you!"

Again Cockeye grunted.

"You clean up that mess, you hear!" The Widow commanded.

"What are you crazy, lady?"

Then Widow MacNoon did something very strange. From under shawl she pulled out a piece of a rock—black and jagged as a hunk of coal. She passed her hand over the rock as though she were a magician with a crystal ball. Sam couldn't understand the foreign words she mumbled. But he thought they sounded evil and ominous. She jabbed her finger towards Sam and said in English, "I give you," she paused dramatically, "the Widow's Curse!"

Cockeye gasped and backed away in pure animal instinct. Had Sam not seized the reins she would have run off.

Sam laughed. Never had he heard anything so foolish. As his mouth stretched so widely open he tilted his head back, "Ha-Ha-Ha! Widow's Curse! Baloney! Lady, you're crazy!"

Widow MacNoon re-entered the house with a knowing smirk on her face.

Sam laughed as he directed Cockeye away from the gutter. Snorting and shaking her head Cockeye galloped away from Widow MacNoon's house.

"Whoa! Whoa!"

But Cockeye did not slow down until they were far down the street, in front of Mr. Bunetti's garden. Sam tried to calm down Cockeye. "Come my Princess. Don't let that lady scare you. She's crazy in the head. Widow's Curse! Baloney!"

The sky darkened—black and ugly clouds swept by cold gusts. The sun eclipsed behind the clouds. Cockeye shuddered. Sam pulled up his collar and buttoned up his shirt to the neck.

"Br-r-r, it's getting chilly," muttered Sam, "I hope the chill doesn't ruin Mr. Bunetti's garden, not after all the hard work he's done keeping the kids away." He admired the garden, a delicate yardful of vegetables between the two tenements. The garden was surrounded by a small white picket fence, spotless and fragile, it was built by talented patient hands. Every month, winter or summer, Bunetti painted the fence and on summer evenings he tended the garden. The garden was the envy of the neighborhood. Lettuce, and cucumber and green beans and, of course, tomatoes. The tomato plants, fat and full, hung heavy from the sticks to which they were bandaged by white rags. The sticks stood straight, row on row with immaculate precision, stiff soldiers on the parade field. In the geometrical center of the yard stood a fertile apple tree. The apples, round and red, hung limply from the exhausted branches. Yes, Bunetti had reason to be proud.

The sight and smell of all those fresh vegetables watered Sam's mouth. "Come Princess," he said, "Let us go to the park and eat."

Cockeye snorted with enthusiastic agreement.

"Yoo-hoo! Rag man!" A lady called from the second floor of the apartment next to Bunetti's garden. "Yoo-hoo!"

"Yes lady."

"Could you clean out my cellar? There's lots of junk—papers and rags—and a copper boiler."

Copper boiler! Sam's heart skipped. "Sure lady. Sure!"

"Just go through the back door." She laughed, embarrassed. "I'm afraid to go near the cellar. I'm terribly afraid of animals."

Animals, thought Sam. Mice? Rats? But a copper boiler! "OK lady, I'll clean it out." Taking the flashlight from the seat box, Sam smiled as he thought of how frightened people were of rats. All you had to do was make noise before entering the cellar. The little beasts would dart off.

After Sam batted his flashlight against the cellar door, he followed the weak beam down the stairs. The dull musty odor gagged him. He heard a scurrying noise down in the dark recesses. The light beam was so weak he could only guess. It may have been two rats. Or it may have been a trick that light seems to play. Of this Sam was not sure. What he did see, however, were two eyes, large and steady staring, defiant eyes, separated by the incredible distance of at least three inches.

"Ahhh!" Sam dropped the flashlight, and dashed out of the cellar. "Lady, you can keep your boiler. What kind of monster lives in your cellar? A giant rat?"

Giving up his flashlight as a lost cause, Sam walked down the alley. His wagon was gone! Sam almost fainted when he saw Cockeye in Bunetti's garden chewing an apple from the tree. The little white fence was mutilated. Four deep wheel groves rutted through the fertile earth.

"Cockeye!" a cry of shock. Sam screamed so loud and fierce his throat hurt.

Cockeye was unmindful, it was lunchtime and she was hungry. Using her good eye she snapped another apple from the tree. These apples were so juicy, she could eat a tree full.

Another scream. A cry of horror and disbelief, this time from Bunetti. With an ax swinging over his head, he rushed towards Cockeye. Luckily Cockeye saw, and crashed her way to the street, thereby doubling the devastation. Bunetti tripped, and sprawled on the ground shouting and swearing.

"Oh God!" cried Sam. "Look at what you've done!" Sam wanted to run and hide. But he couldn't leave Cockeye to be butchered.

Now Bunetti, rushing around the garden, tried to give trampled vegetables emergency first aid. It was no use, the plant's wounds bled onto the earth. He picked up the ax, "I'll killa that bigga clod!"

Cockeye galloped away.

Bunetti didn't chase the horse. Instead he began to threaten Sam, "I'll sue you! I'll killa that horse. Shot by the policeman! You see—Oh my garden!" His scattered tomato soldiers lay in the silent chaos of after-battle.

Sam chased after Cockeye. The dark clouds broke and a torrential deluge soaked him to the bone. Cold, blinding rain, slashed by whips of winds and within a minute Sam was drenched. Fat cold drops fell from his cap, and down his neck. The deluge lasted only three minutes but the gutters were flooded with muck and water.

Sam found Cockeye huddled under a tree. Her mane hung like wet tired weeds. She was cold and shivering. Little Jimmy Ross almost cried with compassion as he watched from his front piazza.

"You got me sued!" Sam shouted into her face. "I should send you to the glue factory, you garbage can!" On the ground Sam picked up a small branch, and slapped Cockeye across the rump with a smack. Cockeye groaned. Little Jimmy winced. Again Sam raised the branch, but the blow never fell. Instead he got hit on the side of the head by a large clump of mud, thrown by a young sympathetic hand. Hastily little Jimmy vanished after his missile hit it's mark. For all Sam knew, the clump had fallen from the sky. He wiped his face with a rag. At the time he did not notice that the rag had been used to clean an oil burner. Now the mud was gritted with soot.

"Oh God," he groaned, "What a terrible day!" Yes, a terrible day. He was determined that he would return Cockeye to the stable, and go home before anything else bad could happen.

Puffs of stinky steam rose off of Cockeye's back. Sam's shirt itched and he smelled like a wet dog. The bundles of papers were now a pulpy blobs.

The bag of rags he had bought from the boy had ripped open and two large cobblestones fell out.

"The wretched little cheats!" Sam muttered as he climbed aboard. "Giddyap! Giddyap!"

Cockeye would not budge. No oats, no work. Because Sam knew better than to challenge Cockeye's stubbornness, he silently strapped on her oat bag. He was beginning to feel sick—chills, sore dry throat, hoarseness. Let me eat my salami, he thought, and maybe I'll feel better. He bit into the sandwich. It was tasteless, and gritty as sand. There were scattered coffee grounds stuck to the outside of the bread. Mama must have spilled coffee on the breadboard. Sam peeled apart the two slices—nothing. In her rush Mama had forgot the salami. Before Sam could gulp the wine, the syrup bottle slipped from his hands and shattered onto the street.

Another deluge of rain came, worse than before. With bent wet heads, he and Cockeye plotted along the deserted streets. "Oh Cockeye," moaned Sam. "It did not pay for me to get up this morning. Hurry Cockeye! Hurry before anything else happens!" Sam tried not to think of Widow MacNoon, but the clop-clop-clop of Cockeye's hooves, like wheels on a train, seemed to whisper, "Widow's Curse, Widow's Curse, Widow's Curse," over and over. Such things as curses were impossible, he told himself. His luck was just bad. And the day was miserable.

"Hurry, Cockeye!" he urged. "I need to hide in my room until this terrible curse wears off."

With each passing minute the curse grew worse, not less. The next hour was a nightmare! As Sam short-cutted across the narrow Lincoln bridge, a wheel fell off the wagon. Cars backed up as far as the eye could see with their horns honking. The waiting people were swearing. The Registry police wrote him up a ticket. And then there was a twenty dollar tow charge. When Sam finally brought Cockeye to the stables, Harry had to call the vet, Doctor Bush for the shivering Cockeye.

Sam shivered also. Now he was really sick. For ten minutes he stood at the bus stop as the cold rains poured down. Finally, oh finally, the bus came over the hill. Oh thank God! The bus zoomed past him, splashed a small tidal wave over his belt line. Sam was too miserable even to swear. His clothes hung like icy fly paper. His shoes squished the wet mile home. As he staggered up his front steps, he sighed a great relief. Home at last, he thought.

But in the mailbox Sam found a letter from the Immigration Department. They were deporting Sam as an undesirable. How could that be! For twenty years he was a law-abiding citizen. Oh God, what a terrible day!

Sam reached for his door keys. They were missing, so he rang the bell. Sarah should be home from music school but there was no answer. Again and again he rang the bell. Then he heard the back door slam. Sam ran to the side of the house just in time to see a bearded man climbing over the back fence. The man wore nothing but shorts. The guitar player?

"The Widow's Curse is killing me!" he yelled, "I must beg her to remove this curse!"

Sam ran down the street, caught a cab, and within ten minutes stood at Widow MacNoon's door where he knocked frantically.

"Please lady, I'm sorry!" Sam shouted through the door, "Take this curse off me! Please!"

Widow MacNoon opened the door. For an instant she did not recognize the sopping mess.

"It's me, the rag man! Please lady, remove the curse. I'll do anything you say, anything!" Sam hesitated, then dropped to one knee. "See lady, I'm begging you! Please take the curse off!"

"First," answered Widow MacNoon, "Clean up the mess that your horse made."

Because of the pelting rain, the manure was soggy. But underneath the back piazza he found a piece of dry cardboard which he used to shovel and scrape the street clean.

Immediately the rain stopped. A bright warm sun broke through the dispersing clouds. No longer did Sam feel sick, in fact he felt wonderful. He wanted to sing, "Rag-g-gs, some ofl-l-d rags!"

Widow MacNoon stood on the porch. "Thank you, lady, thank you!"

"If you know what's good for you," she warned, "Don't ever come down this street again." She added sternly, "Or else!"

Sam ran down the street. A telegram waited for him at home. The Immigration Department had made a mistake, a mix-up in names. Also the police had re-captured and escaped mental patient in his white shorts. Harry had called to say Cockeye was well again, and that the insurance company would pay for the day's damages. Sarah had won a two-year music scholarship to Vienna, and Mama had found a hundred dollar bill on the sidewalk while shopping.

Sam never returned to that street again. On Tuesday mornings I could hear him chanting from the next street over. "Rag-g-gs. Some old-d-d rags!" Yet even though he was a street away, when he approached the vicinity of Widow MacNoon's he wouldn't make a sound. Even Cockeye walked softer.

Finally, Sam, my rag man, and his faithful horse, Cockeye, faded into a bygone era. Trucks replaced horses. Church paper drives replaced rag men. Thirty years passed, and to be honest, I had long forgotten him, until the other night as I walked by Symphony Hall. Sarah somebody-or-other was featured as a soprano extraordinary. A sparkling new Buick pulled up to the curb, and deposited and elderly couple. The woman was gowned and jeweled. The stout gentleman wore a grey homburg, gloves and cane. It was Sam! My rag man—at least I think so. Really, I hope so.

2. Rememberance Of Franky Vento

The Gamble

1968

The stereo clock radio woke Frank (aka, Lucky) with the early Friday morning news. He rose quickly for he was a nervous, light sleeper. Lighting a cigarette, he settled back and listened to the barely audible news. He tried to allow himself five minutes of luxurious laziness since his marriage two years before.

Irritated, his wife, Sylvia snapped from her bed, "Turn down that thing. You'll wake the baby!" For two weeks now, she rarely spoke to him. If she did address him she snapped and harassed him with distain.

Wordlessly he popped out of his bed, walked across the bedroom, to shut off the radio. He ran his hand across the smooth stereo cabinet, a magnificent piece of furniture costing three hundred and seventy dollars. Dark Swedish walnut, hand-carved, brilliantly shined—the cleaning lady always did a good job making it shine.

Friday morning, he thought. Payday! Suddenly his face became hot with guilt as he recalled the previous payday. He had gambled away his weekly pay at the dog track $138.00 gone. Lost forever but certainly not forgotten; Sylvia made sure of that. Never had he seen her so angry.

From the moment he entered the apartment last Friday at midnight, Sylvia had known what had happened. He hung his head and avoided her eyes.

"Down at the track again?" she screamed into his face.

Frank could smell onions on her heated breath. She had just returned from a Stanley party; the baby sitter had walked home alone.

She continued, "Bill collectors are beating on our doors! And you've got money to throw away?"

What excuse could he use? None. Frank admitted guilt, irresponsibility and his recklessness. He hadn't planned on losing his pay. He hadn't even planned on going to the track at all. But a few drinks with Jimmy Nelson after work and a little coaxing was all it took for Frank to go to track for the second time in his life. The first time was the week before; then he had only lost forty dollars. But now, following Jimmy's hot tips, he lost twenty dollars, then fifty, then a hundred. He knew he could get it all back, but finally he lost everything. He had to borrow thirty cents for the bus fare home.

Accused, he stood silent before Sylvia and awaited his punishment. He wrung his hands and watched his shoe scuff the kitchen linoleum.

"A fine husband you are!" she lashed, "You've got a wife and a new baby. We're swamped under with bills!" She began to sob, not a weepy sob, but a hysterical sob. Her words were wet, high-pitched and very loud. "How much did you lose this time? Forty dollars?"

Frank sucked in a deep breath, and slowly shook his head.

"Fifty?" She gripped his arm viciously. He looked up at her and shook his head again, "One hundred?" What kind of a monster had she married? "Your whole pay?"

He nodded, his face burning. Even the summer breeze from the open windows failed to cool his scorched face.

Sylvia threw her hands over her eyes and collapsed into the closest kitchen chair. She let out a wail, a terrifying cry that was heard for two city blocks, "O-O-Oh-ooo-ooo! O-O-Oh-ooo-ooo!" Bedroom lights throughout the neighborhood flashed on. Television sets were turned down.

Frantically, Frank tried to calm her down; he expected the homicide squad to beat down his door at any moment. "Syl, for God's sakes I'm sorry! I only tried to win back the forty dollars I lost last week." Softly he laid his hands on her shoulders. She wrenched away, giving him a look that actually frightened him.

"Don't touch me! You—you—" Again she wailed, and again her cries were broadcasted throughout the neighborhood. More bedroom lights flashed on. More TV's were turned down.

Afraid to come near her, Frank stood back and studied the woman before him. Her usually perfectly coiffed hair hung like sloppy straw, her carefully applied lipstick smeared across her chin. Tears eroded her face powder. Sylvia, for the first time in her life was ugly. A thirty-five dollar dress, fourteen dollar shoes, a beautiful gold charm bracelet with "I Love You" in twenty seven languages. And yet, she was ugly.

As Frank shut the windows, so that the neighbors could return to bed, he castigated himself. What a no good bum you are! You lose your pay, and all you can think of is that she looks ugly. What a bum!

"Sylvia, I'm sorry. I'm terribly sor—"

"You shut up!" she screamed. "Don't you ever speak to me again!"

Frank left her in the kitchen and cringed into the bedroom where he undressed, carefully hanging his clothes in the overcrowded closet. His t-shirt clung like wet toilet paper. The shame, the guilt. The sheer stupidity! How could I do such a thing? He bit his hand; it was no dream. He searched through his wallet. A greenless desert. Only a stack of useless dog tickets. Frank set the empty wallet and the tickets on the bureau in front of the baby's ninety dollar portrait. Even the baby's painted eyes seemed to stare at the tickets' and admonished Frank, "Will those buy me milk? Bad dad! Get into the corner!"

Quickly Frank turned from the portrait. He imagined the neighbors sneering at him, especially that loud-mouth drunken truck driver who lived downstairs. Wives whispering, "No good bum!" Little kids picking up clods of horse manure from the street, and bombarding him. Dogs fighting against themselves, the winner having the privilege of being the first to chomp his leg.

Frank wiped the sweat from his forehead. Nervously he smoked cigarette after cigarette, praying for Sylvia to calm down. In twenty minutes her sobs slowed down and the neighbors returned to bed, or to the late show. Then there was silence. The calm before the typhoon. He lay on the bed, his eyes followed the large discolored crack in the ceiling. It reminded Frank of his ego. Suddenly he heard noises in the kitchen. The knife box? He leaped from his bed. No, worse; she was calling Mama! Apparently Mama was not home. Sylvia slammed the phone onto the hook.

She stomped into the bedroom, her prepared words lashed at him. "How could you! A hundred-forty dollars! You stupid . . . you idiot! Some accountant you must be . . ."

"For God's sakes, Syl! Calm down. You'll wake up the whole apartment building!" Televisions were shut off. Husbands and children gathered around window sills while mothers prepared a snack of milk and cookies. It would be a long interesting night.

"What do I care!" She screamed even louder. "I hate this neighborhood! It's a dump! Look at this place! I want a house of my own!"

A drunken truck-driver's shout sounded through the night, "Well why don't 'cha move! We ain't gonna miss ya!"

The embarrassment. For a moment Sylvia remained quiet. Then she saw the empty wallet and the mocking stack of losing tickets alongside, and then the baby's portrait. More fuel to the fire. She went wild. She darted around the room searching for something to throw at the irresponsible beast. Anything heavy and hurtful. The fifteen dollar iron ashtray! Yes! Frank ducked, the window shattered.

After the police had calmed down Sylvia, the neighborhood went to bed, abuzz with the gossip.

For seven days Frank lived in a barbed cage. Seven days of dumbness.

He removed his hand from the stereo cabinet, slipped into his bathrobe, and prepared for work. He had to cook his own breakfast since Sylvia refused to cook for him. His oatmeal was lumpy and he burned the toast. No coffee in the house, Sylvia refused to shop for him.

As he left for the office, she announced, "I won't be home for dinner tonight. I'm having may hair set, and going to the club meeting, you pay the baby sitter." Her tone double-dared him to argue with her. The neighborhood would have an early reveille.

Arriving at the office Frank settled at his desk with his coffee and newspaper. Intentionally he avoided the sport's page. The race results might bring back the craving again. "URANIUM STRIKE IN ALASKA, story continued on page 18." Then he saw it, "TWIN DOUBLE PAYS $26,000 AT WONDERLAND." And underneath the headline was a picture of the happy winner, a recent immigrant from Albania. A newspaper interview with the lucky man proved fruitless as he did not understand English.

Twenty-six thousand dollars! Almost three years salary. Enough to buy Sylvia her house. For a dream's instant Frank spent the money left and right; the balance of the sofa, Sylvia's Volkswagen, even the mink stole she had always wished for were purchased and paid for in his imagination. How trivial his meager $138 compared to $26,000. He wrote the number on his pad—all those zeroes. Imagine, a two dollar investment reaped all that money. Just pick the winning dogs in the fifth, sixth, seventh, and eighth races. Although Frank had never picked a winner in his life, he thought that if he studied the dog book, he could win the twin double. He was sure of it! His mouth became dry, his pulse quickened, his hands shook.

"No!" he warned himself, "Remember last week. She'd leave me."

But Frank, Frank it's twenty-six thousand dollars! Anyway the track owes you, forty, plus one thirty eight—almost two hundred.

No!

A battle raged within his head. An army of one dollar bills versus the face of Sylvia.

No!

Victory! Frank stuffed the sport's page into the waste basket.

At lunchtime he cashed his check, quietly allowing himself his usual fifteen dollars spending money. For most of the afternoon he busied himself with an inventory problem. But during the three o'clock coffee break, Jimmy Nelson approached him. Jimmy, single and lucky, carried the sport's page.

"Did you read about the twin double pay-off? Twenty-six grand and the guy doesn't even speak English! See, I told you the dogs can be beat . . ."

Frank tried not to listen but each word drove a nail into him. Why couldn't I win? Again the battle raged. After Jimmy had gone Frank planned with his fifteen dollar allowance.

Sylvia wouldn't be home. She'd never know I was down the track. And when he came home a winner, life would be good again. She'd cook breakfast. The baby would smile. The neighbors would absolve him.

Unconquerable confidence ran through him. Slyly he smuggled the newspaper from the trash, and carefully ripped out the racing form. For the remainder of the afternoon and late into the evening he studied that scrap of paper—a treasure map! He paid special attention to General Joe's hot tips. With supreme patience and confidence he drew his choices. Now he was set for conquest off to the race track!

A sweaty nervousness washed over Frank as he drove into the car-glutted parking lot. Overhead the pennants waved victory for him. An electric tingling, the excitement, the hope electrified his entire body. Would he win? Of course! Hadn't he studied the racing form? Of course he would win!

He joined the hopeful investors headed for the entrance gate. From behind the red-brick walls he could hear the dog's barking, assuring him of victory. Behind those walls waited the winners. His winners! Dropping a half-dollar into the turn style Frank entered another world; a world of extremes, of winners and losers. Thousands of investors milled around the pavilion, and here and there, small juries clustered over dog books and green sheets arguing and defending the impossible. For thirty-five cents Frank bought a neat blue dog book so as to fit into the scenery.

Streams of bettors lined the daily-double window. A rich mixture of faces and races, and creeds and breeds. The tanned calloused laborer, work clothes caked with mud; the sleek-suited Italian, the brim on his bookie hat curved upward; the slick bleached blonde, her tight aqua slacks invited stares; the old Irish woman, a crippled flower hung off her black straw hat, her hand clutched the rent money; the colored cat with a bright vest and brighter hopes. Away from the line stood a quiet Chinese gentleman; his eyes mysterious and patient; his lips a vague philosophical smile as though all secrets were known to him. Off to the side fidgeted a young boy, apparently a first nighter; fumbling with his sixty dollar pay.

All had hopes of winning the big one tonight. All potential winners, but most likely paupered losers.

"Five minutes to post time," voiced over the Public Address system.

The betting lines grew longer, the mumbling grew louder, the air grew heavy with the smell of anxious sweat and smoke, of stale beer and hot dogs. Frank wedged up to the crowded hot dog stand, and ordered a black coffee. Confident of his choice he wondered how much to bet. He checked the dog book. Hmm, even the consensus picks my one dog—Silver Syl. A favorite, a sure winner. Should I bet two dollars or four? Frank planned to win the first four races, then bet all of his winnings on the Twin Double which began with the fifth race and win the $26,000.

Alongside of Frank two men, one very tall, the other fat, hunched over a dog book.

The tall man said, "The six dog." Knowingly he winked his eye. "Take my word for it."

The fat man countered, "Naw! Silver Syl's way better." He shoved the book into Tall's face. "Look at her time two races ago. Thirty-one point seven-two! And that was from the six box. She'll runaway with this race."

Tall: "If she's so good, how come she finished seventh the last time she ran?"

Fat: "Cause he was bumped, that's why. Look, I ain't twisting your arm. Throw you money away. I'm betting on the one dog!"

Because Fat seemed so sure of himself, Frank bet four dollars on Silver Syl. A four dollar investment. He could all but count his winnings. Thoroughly satisfied, thoroughly confident, Frank sauntered out into the stands.

The air felt cool and clean as the twilight breeze swept away the heat of the day. The race neared, the investors packed into the stands. Next to the finish line, self-appointed judges packed against the fence.

"Ta-Ta-TaTaTa-TaTaTa-TaTa-TaTaaa!" The recorded bugle blasted.

A squad of uniformed attendants paraded the dogs onto the track. Led by a chief attendant, they marched, straight and slim as needles, and squared the corners in true military spirit. The band bashed and boomed a lively march tune. All pomp and glory. The return of the Roman Legions. Frank felt joy and excitement until he saw Silver Syl, a shiny black-brown bitch. Either because of stubbornness or laziness she tried to sit. The attendant dragged her to the starting box. All the dogs were readied.

The moment froze. Voices hushed. The electric sense of adventure. Everyone tense. Frank's palms sweated. His throat dried. He needed to urinate, damn that coffee! Clenching and unclenching his fist, he wordlessly commanded to one box. Get ready to break, Syl. Come on baby, get ready. Meanwhile Silver Syl sniffed at old dog smells on the metal post.

The meatless rabbit jolted and swerved around the track. "An-n-nd The-e-e-re Go-o-o-o-oes Swifty!"

The gates flew open. Voices screamed. A pack of seven dogs dashed down the track. Following far behind, extremely well-fed and lazy after four day's inactivity, Silver Syl jogged along.

"Come on one!" called Frank over a man's shoulder.

The man laughed. "You must be kidding, buddy. At that speed, the mutt won't be off the track for the second race."

One race lost. Four dollars gone forever. Damn that dog! Momentarily he became dejected but quickly he recuperated. He promised to win the second race. All was not lost. He still had ten dollars, hadn't he? He'd study the dog book even harder in the twenty minutes until the second race; twenty minutes to study, to plan, to decide. But first another coffee. The excitement of the race still bristled the air. Muttered faces watched ripped tickets drift to the ground; satisfied faces rushed to the win-place-show window. Frank parked on the stairway, concentrating on the book. The coffee grew cold. And one cigarette followed another, tasteless, dull, and metallic.

"Five minutes until the next race." The P.A. announced.

The six dog! A sure winter. Jolly Jack, even his name suggested of hope. Recently imported from Madagascar, this was to be his first race in the United States.

Frank's hand shook as he slid his $5.00 investment across the aluminum counter.

"Five to win on the six."

Uncaring the teller pushed the button. Pap! The ticket slotted onto the counter. Frank turned to walk away but a small doubt gripped him. What if Jolly Jack finished second, Frank would still profit.

Frank checked and re-checked his ten dollar investment. It was like speculating on the stock marked, only with the time duration shortened drastically. An all or nothing deal. No dividends, no bankruptcy claims. All profit or all loss. Frank expected all profit, of course. Jolly Jack would surely win!

Anxiously Frank stood at the fence, waiting to see Jolly Jack parade by.

The trumpet blared. Again the circus began. The bank music. The marchers. The circus thoroughbreds, and of course, the circus freak. Jolly Jack was a huge lumbering animal with erratic patches of hair, piggy ears, and a flat blunt snout which sniffed along the ground. The crowds were laughing. Frank disbelieved his eyes. THAT was a greyhound? Frank cursed and cursed until his eyes began to water. Ten dollars on THAT! It took two attendants to stuff Jolly Jack into the six box.

"An-n-nd The-e-e-re Go-o-o-o-oes Swifty!"

Jolly Jack broke first, whipping to the lead, a born champion. Around the first turn, ahead by two lengths, ever increasing the margin. Into the stretch. Frank crunched the book into his fist and jumped up and down, screaming, "Come on Jolly Jack!" But the words fell onto deaf ears. Jolly Jack was tired and anyway, he had never seen a rabbit, so he stopped. The seven other dogs zoomed past him, across the finish line.

Although Frank, by nature, loved animals, he had the terrifying urge to leap the fence, and throttle his ten dollar investment. The miserable freak! You belong in a zoo! Frank mutilated his tickets. He cursed Jolly Jack, he cursed himself, he cursed fate. What terrible luck! Fourteen dollars lost. Because of the fifty cents admission and the thirty five cent dog book and two coffees, Frank had blown his allowance. No more money to bet. Of course he still had Sylvia's money.

No! don't even think of it! Go home. Let this teach you a lesson. Frank tried to leave but "TWIN DOUBLE PAYS $26,000 AT WONDERLAND" held him back. Twenty-six thousand! The number swam in his head. A clean sweep of bills. A house. Sylvia's mink stole. Three years pay for a two dollar investment. Sweat broke out and trickled over his face and back.

Conscience warned, "Go home."

But hope, smooth and glib, argued, "Don't quit while you're losing. Don't be a sucker. Borrow a little from Sylvia's money. You'll win!"

"No!" Again conscience warned but Frank had already slipped five dollars from his wallet. Another coffee. Back to the book. Bring on the third race!

Hope carried Frank through the third, the fourth, and the fifth races. All losers. Sylvia was minus $34.00. Desperation forced him through the sixth, the seventh, the eighth and the ninth races. More losers. Sylvia had only $32.00 left.

Frank was crying audibly now. Every once in a while he emitted a low passionate moan. People avoided him. Never had he felt so alone and despairing. How could he be so stupid? Not one winner did he pick. Five of his choices finished last; one of his dogs had collapsed in the first turn from a heart condition and was removed from the track on a stretcher.

Half blinded by the tears, by the panic, Frank focused his eyes to the coffee stand. His vision blurred but not his imagination. He could see Sylvia screaming. The smiling neighbors eating milk and cookies by the window sills. The police. Shouting kids and snarling dogs. Oh God! And then he saw the courtroom; the separation. The ruined life. Down, down deep into the pit of degradation. More dog tracks, more losses. The wine bottle, until finally a wretched lonely death in Hong Kong or Pago-Pago.

And before he blinded his eyes forever, Frank imagined a cluster of specks coming from over the horizon. Closer and closer they approached. And then he recognized the dogs, Silver Syl, Jolly Jack and all the others. They marched along carpet clouds in a single file. As they passed, they popped their tails, and snapped to eyes right to him. A fitting tribute to a trusting handicapped. Unashamed tears ran over their hairy dog noses. And underneath their muzzles Frank could see their sad smiles. At least in his imagination.

"Watch your step; buster!" A red eyed loser shook the spilled beer from his hand, "You spilled half my beer!"

After a hasty, insincere, "Sorry," Frank fumbled into the crowd. Shock. Panic. What'll I do? The tenth race. The last chance. Go for broke? He felt he had no other choice. Only a long shot would bail him out now. Another coffee. Frank saw the appropriate name, Twilight's Guide. Thirty dollars swallowed by the betting window.

"One minute to racetime," The P.A. announced.

Fear, nausea, and sweat, the hollow stomach, the pounding temples Frank felt it all. He was unable to watch the race. For the tenth time the band bashed and boomed. But now the music resembled a dirge. Frank really had to pee. He stumbled into the head, a large sloppy place smelling like a public bathhouse. He lingered there, splashing water over his face.

"An-n-nd The-e-e-re Go-o-o-o-oes Swifty!" The words echoed off the walls. The P.A. described the race; a jumble of incoherent names and positions. Please God, help me! Please!

The roar of the crowd lifted up and up to the end of the race and then died instantly. It was over. A man entered the bathroom.

"Who, who won?" asked Frank, his voice cracked and unsure. His chest choked. His face and body burned.

"Twilight's Guide, a real long shot."

Frank collapsed against the wall; he felt giddy, almost drunk. Nervously he lit a cigarette; then made his way to the long-awaited win window.

Frank slept late on Saturday morning, and when he finally woke, his head throbbed and buzzed like he had a terrific hangover. His eyes stung, his tongue was swollen and tasted of metal, his stomach fluttered. He heard Sylvia in the kitchen, humming, busily cooking his breakfast, and breakfast in bed at that. His winning had swept the tension from the apartment. Four hundred dollars! That would take a good bite out of the bills. Frank yawned and stretched, making the most out of the peacefulness. He could hear the bacon softly spattering in the pan, the snap of the toaster as the browned muffin ascended. He could smell the sweet richness of the coffee.

"Ring-g-g."

"Oh Hello Mama," bubbled Sylvia. "I tried to call you this morning—oh you were shopping—listen Mama, guess what?" Sylvia paused dramatically. "Frank won four hundred dollars last night at the dog track. Isn't that wonderful! Imagine, three weeks pay in a couple of hours. We can sure use the money. I've been planning to buy a new fridge—oh Mama, I know mine is only two years old, but I want a tan one. They're in style this year—anyway, I'm sending Frank down to the track tonight. He can win me some more money . . . ."

Biting his lip, Frank stared at that crack in the ceiling.

GRAFFITI

Well, the graffiti of these times certainly touches the spectrum: religion, ethnics, drugs, politics; sex; war and protest and wit. No doubt about it, we live in a fast evolving culture where our anonymous writers now are emerging from the latrines and bus stations and are publicly writing their messages blatantly on any exposed surface. All in all we see both quantity and quality.

Even paranoids have enemies.

King Kong—he died for our wicked ways.

Happiness is a place between too little and too much.

Jesus is alive and doing well in Mexico City.

Batman like Batboy.

Pot—Pussy—Peace

Joe O'Toole screws seagulls.

Urine is like gold water.

Death is nature's way of telling you to slow down.

To hell with Coke, this is the pause that refreshes.

Tim Leary for President.

Burn draft dodgers, not draft cards.

The happiest days of your life are those you escape to when today becomes unbearable.

Mickey Mouse has hemorrhoids.

How do porcupines have sex—very carefully.

I am 10" long and 3" round.
Great! How big is your donk?

Send Godzilla to ~~Vietnam~~ Parris Island.

Do unto others before they do unto you.

Better Red than Dead.
Screw you, pal!

LSD? We've only one life to live and this ain't a dress rehearsal.

LCPL Joseph Waters
213496 USMC '65-'67 Chicago

Down with Graffiti
Ya, down with all Italians.

Off the Cops!

Donald Duck drops acid.

Charlie Muldoon is Smokey the Bear with a haircut.

Forest fires prevent bears.

Alcohol Kills—Take acid/smoke pot

Legalize Pot—Snow White

Don't drink water—fish screw in it.

Dirty is only in your head—so screw you

All the world loves a four letter word.

Goldwater in '64
Hot water in '65
Bread and water in '66

Power to the people.

Stomp out mental illness or I'll kill you.

Keep Dorchester white.

LBJ for Ex President.

JFK "Ask not what your country has done for you—Ask what you can do to your country."

Be leery of Leary.

God is alive and in a sugar cube.

Come home Judas, we forgive you.

No slave should die a peaceful death.

Life is a vase full of shit with the handles on the inside.

Casey: "Dress up for Easter—bah humbug!
Remember Casey—you're not really dressed without a smile.

Gregg's mother made him a homosexual
If I sent her some wool, could she make me one.

Beautify Dorchester—Burn down a house.

Let him who is stoned cast he first sin.

I ain't prejudiced. I hate everyone.

Love is the answer.

Draft the Industrial Complex
Bill—USMC

What do you get when you cross a bartender with a gorilla?
A gorilla that steals.

Protest Amnesty!

I'm so horny that the crack of Dawn is in trouble.

It's too bad, but if the Pilgrims had shot a cat for Thanksgiving, we'd be all eating pussy for dinner.

Tour groups are not allowed in the latrine while the choir is practicing.

Vietnam—Curtis Lemay's wet dream

The 1970's

Bill At 70 Years Old

January 7, 1970

I look at this blank page and I don't feel like writing.

Writing is tough and writing at 70 is tougher. God, where did the time go?

My retirement from Wentworth is already two years past. Booker is talking about selling Danny's Tavern. Too bad. We had so many laughs in the old days. There was a time when Jerry Collins alone would tell me a new joke every day. Now, I don't hear that many. Whether it's because people are losing a sense of humor or that I'm an outsider to the younger crowd—another sign of old age. Apparently the young guys think old timers seldom laugh. Who knows?

Of course, your attitude changes as you age, falling apart a chip at a time. It certainly affects your energy level.

I've written enough and I reach that point where I'm getting lazy. I'd rather read than write. It certainly requires less effort. Even when I do put pen to paper, no longer do I pause and search for that certain word. No, instead I say to heck with it, and plod along and urinate ten times a day. That's one of the consequences of old age.

I feel like a character out of John Steinbeck's, "Canary Row."

Bobby Orr Visits Danny's Tavern

May 10, 1970

Feeling the electricity and the beer, the boys in Danny's were ecstatic. The Bruins were finally in the Stanley Cup Playoffs and tonight was the clincher. A Boston championship was a long time coming—an embarrassing wait. The Bruins had not made an appearance in the Stanley Cup finals since 1958.

And tonight Bobby Orr was at his peak—acknowledged by the experts to become one of the greatest hockey players of all time. As a defenseman, Orr had revolutionized that position by his speed, agility, skating ability, and sheer courage and commitment. And to top off his hockey prowess, he was a gentleman.

As expected, Orr scored the winning goal. The shouts, the banging of the tables—the floor actually shook as the more lively patrons in the bar stamped their feet.

Very few times do all the boys agree on anything, but tonight, all agreed that Bobby Orr was the greatest!

After the game, Mickey Smith, an avid Bruin's fan, asked Booker, "How come we don't have any famous people like Bobby Orr visit this place? Are we second class citizens? Huh?"

"Yeah, that's right," Jackie Dwyer. "We are just nobodies," chimed in several of the guys.

Booker rolls his eyes. "OK!—Who would you like to visit us—Prince Charles? I can arrange that by one phone call."

Everyone laughs.

"Seriously Booker," asks Mickey, "Why not see if Bobby will visit us and have a beer?"

Booker asks, "Are you serious?"

Mickey turns away from the TV and suggests, "Yes, Bobby Orr."

"Yea!," shouts from the guys who crowd around Booker—who says calmly, "OK I'll set up a short visit for next week—if the Bruins are in town. I have a few connections. I'll post the time on the Bulletin Board.

Mickey's eyes light up.

That evening there is a notice on the Bulletin Board that Bobby Orr would drop by for a beer. However, the notice stipulates that only a few select patrons who sign up will be allowed. Otherwise there could be a riot. Next Tuesday at 3:00 PM.

Danny's is strangely quiet this sunny but a very cold afternoon when a tall trim figure wearing large aviator sunglasses, a Bruin's sweatshirt, and a Bruin's stocking cap which covers his ears, enters the tavern. You could hear the proverbial pin drop. The excitement is contagious.

Bobby shakes hands with Booker, "How's it going, Tim—I haven't seen you at many of the games." A big smile.

"Busy, Bobby—you know how it is," a bigger smile.

Bobby leans on the bar and orders a glass of ginger ale. Mickey Smith muscles his body between Booker and Bobby. "Mr. Orr—Bobby—can you please autograph this photo of you. My granddaughters are going crazy!"

Sure—what's the names of your grandchildren?

"Mary, Annie, and Joan."

"Greetings to Mary, Annie, and Joan—Bobby Orr"

Now a crowd forms with the potential of becoming a mob. The boys are looking for anything for Bobby to autograph—a napkin, yesterday's newspaper, a poster taken off the wall, a five dollar bill.

"Whoa—Whoa! Settle down!" cries Booker, "Bobby's only got a few minutes. Give him some standing room!" Bobby nonchalantly takes a sip of ginger ale. Then he signs all of the paperwork—saying "thank you"—very quietly and gracefully.

He lifts up his glass of ale and toasts, "Cheers to all!"

Then he turns to Booker and says, "I have to rush—I'm double parked as it is."

Gives a wave as he exits. Claps and big cheers from the now assembled crowd. And out he goes. The proverb comes to mind, "Short visits make for good friends."

Some doubting Thomas in the crowd asks, "Hey, was that really Bobby Orr?"

Booker says, "Of course! You got two eyes, don't you?"

As we were closing, I ask Booker, "Was that really Bobby Orr?"

His response, "Does a bear go doo-doo in the woods?"

You know, Booker has a lot of contacts but he also has great sense of humor. Who knows to what extremes Booker will go?

Jenny's First Birthday

(Approximately)

April 1, 1970

As I walked to the door to open up Danny's, I trip over a cardboard box. Kicking the box, I hear a little yelp. "What the . . . ?" I thought as a little puppy head peeps out of the top.

Immediately I think of a short story "Dogs of the Tavern," and the suggestion that if you need to get rid of a puppy, leave it in the entryway of a three decker house which has three families with little boys.

So I conclude that the table is being turned on to me—Leave it with Bill or Booker—maybe a patron will adopt the pup.

I set the box on the bar and examine the dog—a black lab—mostly. One can never verify the exact lineage of a city born puppy—there may be only one male sire or 20 depending on the generosity of the female.

Well, one would admit that it was a cute pup—actually a female. She licks my hand, then my face—then pees on the bar. Dammit! What I am going to do with this unexpected gift?

Just then, Dinty opens the door. His face transforms into a wide smile and happy eyes, "Oh boy, a puppy!" Laughing and giggling, he picks up the squirming ball of black fur. Thoughts of Lenny and "Of Mice and Men" pass through my mind.

"Be gentle, Dinty, you don't want to squeeze her—she's only a pup."

"Can I keep him, Bill? Huh, Bill? Please? I'll be good to him. I promise. I never had a real dog. I'll feed him and clean up after him. Please?"

"Well, for one, Dinty, take a look at her underside—it's a female dog." Imagine, giving a lesson on the facts of life so early in the morning.

Dinty examines the underside. Does he know the difference?

"Well, Dinty, for two, it's up to Booker. It's his business—now take the dog in the back room and we'll talk to Booker." All morning Dinty cradled the dog until she stopped squirming and fell asleep in his arms. The image of a contented mother with a sleeping babe.

A few hours later, in waltzes Booker, whistling and chipper—maybe a good score in a card game last night.

Dinty pops out of the back—"Look, Booker—a puppy! A real live puppy. Can I keep him? Someone left her in a box for me. I never had a pet. Once for Easter my mother bought me some baby chicks, but I held them too tight—they felt so soft and furry. But they died. I didn't mean to hurt them. But I'll be careful with the puppy. Please, Booker?"

Booker looked at Dinty's face—in his excitement a tiny spittle ran down his chin.

"Dinty, I'll tell you what I'll do. During the day you can take care of the dog in the back room—we'll enclose a little area in the back yard. It will be your job to feed her and take of her. She can't be running around out in the bar. At night, I'll take the dog home with me—my kids have been pleading for a pet. We'll see how it all works out."

"So, Dinty, what is the puppy's name?" Booker asked.

"Can I name her—by myself?" asks Dinty.

"Sure. What name do you like?"

With no hesitation, Dinty said, "Miss Jennings."

"Who is she?" I ask.

"She was my teacher in the Lucy Stone School. She used to read stories to me."

"Miss Jennings seems too formal—what about naming her, Jenny—short for Miss Jennings?"

Dinty agreed, "Yeah, Jenny!"

Booker asked me, "How old do you think she is?

"I don't know—maybe three months," I suggest. "Why don't we say that she was born three months ago—January 1st, 1970—my birthday.

You would think that I would predict correctly the outcome of Booker bringing a dog home. Sure enough, Jenny did doo-doo on Booker's carpet and then gnawed the his wife's new shoes.

For weeks, I wondered what to do with the dog. "Hey Booker, my landlady has no problem with a dog—she already has five or six cats."

Obviously I become attached to the dog—so in effect I became the keeper at night and Dinty took care of her in the daytime.

Imagine 70 years old and I have a dog who celebrates the same birthday as I do. And every day I arrive at Danny's with Jenny. Dinty is waiting; he is the happiest man in Dorchester when Jenny enters the bar.

Dorchester Monthly Tribune

A community newsletter serving the Dorchester neighbourhood.

November 22, 1970

Peter Z's Print Shop
Bowdoin Street

TET OFFENSIVE TURNING POINT OF THE VIETNAM WAR

Suspected Guerilla executed in the streets.

VIET CONG LAUNCHES MASSIVE ATTACKS THROUGHOUT THE COUNTRY

AMERICAN'S ASK, "When will this war end?"

MEMORIAL DAY *

Service Men who Died in Vietnam

DORCHESTER HONOR ROLL **

Buchanan, Waverie Hugh
Burt, Michael David
Collopy, John Patrick
Cummings, Harold W.
Davis, William Walter
Fassitt, Eric B.
Foley, Robert M.
Griffin, Thomas B. Jr.
Main, Robert James
McDonald, Gerald Francis
McLaughlin, Mark Michael
Moran, John F.
Sadberry, Seymour Patrick Jr.
Stone, Edward L.
Sullivan, Michael X.
Robertson, Bristol
Wallen, Joseph Robert
Young, Douglas A.

*Reference:Boston Globe, Thursday, May 30, 1968
**Booker placed this honor roll on the wall under Danny's Citation

THE DRAFT RESISTERS

1965

Quotes from *LOOK Magazine*, December 18, 1965

The right of Americans to protest the actions of their government in time of war is inalienable.

The protesters do have their advocates; their statements suggest much more than just concern with the war and the draft. John K Galbrath of Harvard University, said that student protests against the war are proper and desirable.

"Protesting Students for a Democratic Society"
"End the draft and end the war in Vietnam."

The majority of the protesters have embraced a program of legal conscientious objection

Draft card burner "I'll let this action speak for itself. I believe the napalming of villages in Vietnam is an immoral act that no Christian should be involved in."

"But woe to the nation that does not make ready to hold its own in time of need against all who would harm it. And woe thrice over to the nation in which the average man loses his fighting edge."

(posted by Booker on the bulletin board at Danny's) **Teddy Roosevelt**

Jack Walsh Killed In Ship Collision

Freighter collides with Fishing Boat in Boston Harbor

Eulogy

Dedicated to our father, Jack Walsh.

When I was young O Lord, I failed to speak with you,
For I was busy rowing dories to earn my bread from the sea.
When I was older, Lord, again I failed to speak with you,
For I was busy on rolling decks, mending nets,
To earn my children's bread from the sea.

Now that I am old, O Lord, and have stood my final watch,
I speak with You to ask that I may slip my last mooring cable,
And on a fair wind, depart gently from the buoys that have marked the channels of my life.

I ask that my soul be granted safe passage to your harbor of refuge
Where neither gales of wind nor pain disturb this weary soul.

This eulogy was written and delivered by David Melvin, a marine engineer, for his stepfather, John J. Walsh, a Newfoundland Fisherman. Dave was killed shortly thereafter in an oil tanker explosion, New York City.

The Beginning Of The End?

December 1971

My anguish begins when Jackie Dwyer comments, "My God, Bill, what happened to you? You've lost a shitload of weight. You ain't nothin' but a bag of bones."

He's accurate; I have lost weight, primarily because I've eaten so little these past months. Not hungry. And in this block when a guy my age loses weight suddenly, everyone assumes that one dreaded disease—I hate even the word. Yes, Jackie's observation frightens me to be sure. It's nothing, I vainly try to reassure myself. Nothing. But fourteen pounds in two months worries me, especially when I notice a couple of dime-sized black moles on my stomach. Feeling the moles, I discover underneath the skin, a lump. A lump the size of an aggie. Only a pimple? Go away, damn you! For weeks I track the moles. The lump grows to the size of a walnut. Jesus! My face flushes, my heart hammers in my chest, my palms sweat. Diarrhea. My head buzzes like a drunk—it's not happening to me. It can't. Not me. I go on eating binges, consuming anything, everything from Hersey bars to bananas. Two hamburgers with thick milk shakes every lunch. I eat anything to gain weight as though additional pounds are synonymous with a cure.

I try to busy myself in activities. I find myself talking to the dog and half expecting an answer. God, it seems that she understands, if not my exact words but the emotion that I am experiencing. Work, do this, do that, keep occupied. Read, write—no use. Its too difficult to concentrate. Go away lump. I begin to bargain with fate—how about a blood disease instead or a heart problem? I'll accept anything else, but a lump and a weight loss which means I have . . . I hate that word.

Oh God, Jenny, why am I so damn introverted! Always thinking, always imagining. I am my own worst enemy. An imagination that prods and digs, assembles and cries—literally a curse. If only I could mesmerize myself into a trance like they do in yoga and hide from this reality. Turn on, tune in, drop out as Timothy Leary advocated in the 60's.

"Sure," Jenny answers in my own mind, "L.S.D. is going to cure you. You're spaced out as it is—play it smart—Call a doctor." She looks at me with those knowing brown eyes and I realize that she understands my emotion—as confusing and intense as they are.

Finally in desperation, I set up an appointment with Dr. Roberts, a new doctor with an office in at Field's Corner. Booker swears by him. But when I meet the doctor I have doubts because of first impressions, hard black eyes as bland as frosted glass, flabby cheeks, Mark Spitz mustache, and unusually long fingers and thumbs—excellent tools for counting money or checking my prostrate.

He scratches at the moles, presses the lump and rolls it between his finger and thumb like it was a nipple, "Hmm-hmm." He peers through some sort of optical instrument, "Hmm-hmm."

What the hell does "hmm" mean?

"Well Mr. Flynn," he says, very matter of factly, "there appears to be a noticeable growth. However, I suspect the problem will correct itself within a few weeks. But, to be sure I'd like to run a few tests on you. Can you arrange to stay over a few nights in the Carney Hospital next week?"

I nod. My knees shiver. I force myself to ask, "What do you think it is?" I intentionally avoid using that certain word as though that word would make it so.

"Unfortunately, the medical profession doesn't have a name for everythin'," he replies in an abrupt tone. He motions that the four minute examination has concluded, "Would you please check with the nurse about a convenient date."

The clown acts so distant, a human robot. Dr. Roberts, should have been Dr. Robot. Listen, you young buck, I'm more than an old hunk of meat. In this country we hold youth, health and beauty in such high esteem, and he's part of that system. To hell with Jenny, I regret I came here. Should have chosen an older doctor. At least he could empathize with me, age and all.

I tell Jenny that I'm afraid. Does this young robot realize that? He may stand between me and death. Good God. My life reels through my head, a grade B movie. All my past reflections of death and dying mean nothing to me at this very instant. In fact, I just feel like vomiting. Is this it? I am, certainly closer to the end that to the beginning. Most roads lay blocked or washed out, the options in life long gone, the maps lost. Yes, hope is a good breakfast but a bad supper. I let my mind wander into very dark places, but wait a minute! Don't make a mountain out a molehill. Wait for the results. It may work out OK. Don't be so morbid. It's nothing. So I've lost a few pounds, but that comes with age. Anyway, when I cook anyone would suffer weight loss. Yes, it's trivial. Dr. Robot is just being cautious.

That lump worries me though. Is this it? You know, years ago when my thoughts revolved around living and sex, writing and winning. I believed that I'd live forever. Only characters in my stories seemed to die—I'd knock them off left and right as dispassionately as a research scientist with guinea pigs.

I'd try to understand their motives and actions and most importantly their emotions in the darkest hours. And now it's really my turn! Fact not fiction. Today, I finally face the reality that I am mortal. The exact nature of my death eludes me but the general outline keeps occupying much of my waking hours. And with these thoughts, I begin to think about religion.

Is there a heaven? A hell? Yes, I tell myself. But am I echoing the nuns of so many years ago? How well they brainwashed—so bends the twig, so grows the tree. Well, God, all I can say is that I'm human with all the virtues and frailties that I learned along the way. I am what I am and I hope you'll understand what I feel.

How short life is. What have I accomplished? Very little. I feel cheated—my own damn fault because I allowed time to slip by, like a swiftly flowing river. Flowing on and on whether you care to notice or not. Flowing while you eat, sleep, love. Time moves on. Why, God, do we have time? Why do we have old age and sickness? And death? I am at a loss to understand these things.

Yes, today I face the real possibilities of dying. What if the tests prove the worst? Fight or flight? Agonize through operation after operation until I'm a living, tormented vegetable? A collage of organs plugged into a weird array of machines surrounded by strangers in white coats. Suicide, at times, appears reasonable. At least you choose the time, place, and of course, the method. Painless and instantaneous. For that final moment you control your destiny. I suppose as long as you desire or love someone or something, you'll choose to live. Have you noticed how the concept of suicide has changed these past few years? It used to be that only cowards or madmen committed suicide, now it's, "do your own thing." But I know from St.Peter's that suicide is a mortal sin—one is condemned to the torment of hell forever.

"Everyone dies, Bill," says Jenny, "Don't sweat it." But so many concepts associated with death have changed. Mercy killings are everyday occurrences, subtle perhaps—a doctor flips the switch on the life support systems or withholds certain medicines or treatments. Overpopulation, the high cost of health care, and the cruel coldness of objective science change our outlook! Using up the world's resources; polluting the earth. See that old woman, she's senile and ugly. She's unproductive and costs too much. Send her to a nursing home.

Jenny snuggles up, lays her head on my lap and catches my eye, "There are no atheists in the foxhole. You can say the same for the operating room. If there is a great time to consider penance, now is a good time to pray. Sure it's hypocritical but it's a smart move."

I ignore Jenny's words and continue my stream of conscious.

Another change we see concerns abortion. Twenty or thirty years ago it was considered murder. The shabby back-alley room with an unlicensed doctor and dirty instruments. Now we have planned parenthood clinics and counseling services.

Overpopulation. Decrease births and increase deaths before Malthus, scourges the earth with famine and pestilence. Well, screw you, Malthus, I want to live too.

Yes, concepts change. But I'm afraid. What will the test disclose? I wish the week would pass.

Finally the day of the tests. I arrive at Carney Hospital at 9:00 a.m. Smooth wooden benches, receptionist's desk with a small framed poem, the odor of alcohol and medicines, the cold cleanliness of the floors and walls—hospitals are all alike. A portrait of the doctor decorates the wall. To tell the truth, I'd be dubious about buying a used car from him, let alone allowing him to operate on me.

The receptionist processes a patient, "Insurance number please. You must have an insurance number or you cannot be admitted." To hell with your name or your illness and your fears, just give us your Blue Cross/Blue Shield number.

Depositing myself on the farthest bench, I occupy my thoughts by taking notes of my surroundings. Ashtrays stuffed with butts, last month's Newsweek and Time and Argosy—how may rejection slips have those magazines sent me?

Voice raspy, irritating, sounds over the P.A. system. "Doctor Waylon, call Orthopedics, Doctor Waylon, call Orthopedics."

A fat black guy with mustache sits a little ways away from me. His arm is in a sling he has a thick bandage on head. Racial incident? Car wreck? Saturday night blast?

A skinny white-haired woman occupies another bench. Chain-smoking, she is hunched over, her head is all but touching her knees. Nervous. Depressed. Afraid.

Next to her sits a young man with protruding nervous eyes in his twenties. His short hair in disarray like a small crop of trampled crabgrass. He fidgets constantly like he's got a total body itch. His faded army field jacket is torn at the shoulder. In general, the young man appears to be strung out.

Waving a manila folder, the receptionist calls, "Mr. Flynn." I follow her directions into the labyrinth of corridors to the examination room. Here we go. Will I ever walk out of this place? What will the tests show? I fight the panic to run. A technician in a white coat takes the folder from the receptionist, "This way please."

As we walk the corridor, he greets his fellow white coats, "Hi Joe, Whats's say, Mary? Hey Jim . . ." All these people, are they capable? Are they cognizant that I'm scared and ignorant of what's happening to me? Powerless in their hands. How many other patients pass through this system each day? Am I just another specimen? A Blue Cross/Blue Shield number? All this brings back memories of the Forsythe and my tonsils, separated by sixty years.

We arrive at Hematology and the white coat says, "Your blood samples will be taken in here. Janie will take care of you from here."

Janie was a heavy girl, shrouded in a brown smock, plastered with make-up and too much mascara. Her enormously bushy eyebrows stuck out like wings. A plump female Bella Lugosi. She cradles a telephone on her mutton like shoulder as she motions me to sit on a stool. She pricks my finger and continues to complain into the phone.

"Ya Michelle, so then we went to the Hillbilly Ranch and who shows up, but Dukey. I told that jerk a thing or two. I ain't no cheap lay, I told him." She glances at me as though I were a bug or another insignificant object from the planet Pluto. Still cradling the phone and admonishing Dukey she probes my arm for the vein. Three times she misses. "Michelle, wait a minute," she says setting down the phone, she jabs and twists like she'd got a pipe digging an oil platform. Finally she strikes oil, sucks out a needle full, and hurriedly returns to the phone.

Is this the caliber of people here? I fervently hope that she makes love better than she draws blood, the vampire. I bet she could give a hickey and a half. Suck poor old Dukey dry in a minute and a half flat.

At x-ray and Electro-Cardiogram, I feel better. Finally, after I'm unclothed, tagged and braceleted like I was being incarcerated in a maximum security prison, I'm deposited at my room. I'm in here now. Tagged and in a johnnie. A jonnie, the equalizer of all. Makes everyone from the general to the private look like a refuge from the Donner Party. How would General Patton look like sitting on the top of a Sherman tank wearing nothing but a johnnie. Yes, the johnnie depresses me. No turning back now. I look over the room—four beds, three patients. A kid with a knee cartilage operation; a middle aged appendectomy; and me, illness unknown.

Nurse takes my temperature and blood pressure. Mr. Appendix lays on his bed, his knees up so that you could see under his johnnie but nurse pays no attention.

Mr. Appendix asks, "Hey, whaddya in for?"

"A series of tests," I say nothing about the lump. Appendix reminds me of one of those characters who'd brag on and on with thirty stories about relatives and friends who had tumors the size of footballs, from which twenty nine died in indescribable horror. I can do without this.

"Here, Mr. Flynn, drink this," the nurse hands me a colorless liquid, "You'll be going to x-ray in approximately one hour."

The liquid leaves a metallic taste in my mouth. The nurse leaves. I lay on the bed, pretending to be asleep so that I can avoid conversation. For an hour I lay perfectly still, but inside my head, a hurricane tears at me. Oh Christ, let's get it done and finished with it. One way or the other, let's get the show on the road.

An orderly in a blue uniform wheels in a stretcher "Flynn?" He's got a face like a priest or a wise guy.

I nod.

"Hpe on, Pop. We're going to x-ray."

"I'll walk."

"Sorry, Pop, house rules. Don't sweat it, I haven't crashed since yesterday."

Wise guy, but I like him.

In x-ray, they put me on a large black table. Damn it's cold. The switch is flipped, "Bzzz" the machine hums threateningly and I realize some unseen unfeeling x-rays penetrate my body. A guy in a lead apron watches me from behind his protective glass wall. When the light reflects off his glasses he looks like a grotesque mechanical monster. Is the treatment as frightening as the lump? I can well understand how a patient could believe so.

From x-ray, I am wheeled to to Dr. Dermatologist who scratches at the moles as though he's satisfying an itchy mosquito bite. After he snips off a sample with his clips, he deposits the flesh onto a slide. Lastly, Dr. Fingers motions me to a table where he prods and jabs and massages my lumps and bumps and finally, he ends the exam with finger wave.

With all the preliminaries completed, I am returned to my room. "Well, Pop, looks as though we'll make the Indy Five Hundred. What's say?" Pats me on the shoulder—a genuine friendly gesture. "Best of luck tomorrow, Pop."

Toward evening I am somewhat surprised when a doctor, dark, black hair, black eyes, an Arab, visits me. "Mr. Flynn, I'm Doctor Yassaf," he introduces himself with a British accent. A few bread crumbs nest in his thick black mustache. "I'll be operating on you tomorrow."

"Operating? I don't understand."

"You mean, Doctor Roberts did not tell you? Oh, well, it is only minor surgery."

No surgery is minor when it's performed on you. How I wish the doctor were Irish or Canadian, at the very least American. It's curious but when you find yourself in trouble, you prefer your own kind. Not that they are necessarily more capable, but somehow you think your own will give that extra effort and understanding.

"Nothing serious, Mr. Flynn, I assure you it'll be a decent show."

As he leaves, he gives me a thumbs up, a jolly operation, hip-hip, stiff upper lip. Good show, Roger! I doubt if all of this is actually happening to me. A dream. It must be. Suddenly I become angry. Why me? Why do I have this lump? Why not somebody else? Mr. Appendix over there, why not him? So what if four out of ten get it. Why me? It's not fair. And to top off the situation, I'm undergoing only exploratory surgery. Suppose Dr. Arab discovers a tumor, that means I go under the knife again. Start this fun and games all over again.

I think of Jenny, take it easy breathe—stop imagining the worst. My thoughts wax and wane along the spectrum from disbelief to anger to resignation—all at the same time. Maybe Doctor Dermatologist will cancel the operation. Sure, only a pimple, a boil which requires a dab of zinc oxide. Or possibly a shot of penicillin will cure all. Why can't the researches discover a cure and relieve the untold agony and torment? If they can develop an A-bomb why can't scientists find a cure for this?

The hospital priest, making his rounds, breaks my train of thought. "Good evening, I'm Father O'Toole." He's got a red Irish face in his fifties. A thick red nose—high pressure? Booze? "The nurse told me you're in for an exploratory."

"Yes, Father."

He asks, "Would you like to go to confession?"

I shrug, caught between that deep entrenchment of Saint Peter's brainwashing and a gnawing awareness of hypocrisy. "It's been quite a few years."

"Sure, so now you feel like a hypocrite if you go. Well I wouldn't let that stop you. Most people feel that way. In fact, for eleven years I was an alcoholic. I'd be in the confessional with a woman crying out her soul and all I'd be caring about was the next drink. Yes, I know hypocrisy. But God understands and he's truly merciful."

He smiles and I assent. I always respect priests especially in times with so many dramatic changes. How does he accept celibacy and doubts and sacrifice—what if there is no after life?

"Now what do you say? I can guarantee your sins won't cause any more gray hairs on this head. I doubt if you've committed any great sins."

I talk more than confess but I do feel regrets—I could have lived a better life. After many years, I easily remember the "Bless me Father for I have sinned . . ."

"Penance, two Our Fathers and two Hail Mary's."

In the old days of St. Peters, such a confession drew a probable penance of 2000 Rosaries and a public flogging. Hypocrite, I tell myself. But God, I am what I am and you must know that.

"Good luck tomorrow."

That night, a nurse jabs me with a sedative. But, instead of sleep I lay awake in the darkness of the room and talk to Jenny. At least I believe I lay awake—that shot affects me in the oddest manner. Am I asleep and dreaming or am I alert dwelling on death? Death, the most tabooed subject in America today. To hell with it, dream or no dream. I drift along with my imagination, letting the river flow. Here are my thoughts, a stream of consciousness.

"Jenny," I think, "when I'm dead, what happens to me? Will I be missed? Will you miss me? No, of course not, my thoughts terminate. I cease to exist forever. Permanent. Infinity. I'll never wake again. Nor speak, nor see, nor smell, nor hear. Never love again. Buried alone in a coffin. Entombed! You cry for help, but no one comes to rescue. Jesus! How horrible—but

I'll be unaware. I'll cease to exist—to think, I'm gone—gone. You won't be around. What's going to happen to you?"

As one envisions oneself dead, you died a hero, a martyr, a truly great person. Saved the country—died for religion, for integrity, sacrificed your organs so that another may live on. "I regret, that like Nathan Hale, I have but one life to give to me country." Yes, you are truly great. You see the crying family and friends, the vast heartbroken crowds, weeping a valley of tears. Oh you wonderful good person, how dearly we miss you. Like Tom Sawyer and Huck Finn you hear your eulogy, a masterpiece of beautiful phrases. The Boston Symphony orchestrates the saddest, the most moving of dirges. Everyone is crying. It's too much to bear. The TV crews can hardly function. Why, even Walter Chronkite cries, his runaway tears stream down his cheeks.

But objectively, it doesn't matter, for you have forever stopped thinking. Your time on earth has ended. It is now too late to love, to laugh, even to cry or to hate. Time flows no more. Never more will you roam the earth—unless you are reincarnated. No more hiking with Jenny in New Hampshire. Maybe the Eskimos are correct; you die and the fish and the bear eat you, then hunters kill the bear and the fish, and your off-spring eat the catch and the circle of life is complete. In some fashion you live again.

How quick is death, how short is life.

Although groggy from the sedative when I wake in the morning, I pencil out my dream. What a morbid subject, but one we all have to face, alone someday.

No breakfast. Another needle, a bigger one than before. Again I float away. So peaceful. So beautiful. Not wonder people get hung up on drugs. No worries, no pain like a frightened fawn seeking refuge from the hunter. I think illogically. My thoughts slowly topple in time and space and I float along, unconcerned, oblivious to the room, the hospital, the operation and the results. Just a soft comfort. Follow the program. I'm confused but so, so comfortable. Let's get the show on the road.

A green man wheels in his green table onto which I am gently laid. Lights from the ceiling flash before my eyes as I'm transported down the corridor to the operating room. I notice the dirty ceiling tiles. Then I doze. Bumps! Through the doors with the sign, "Operating Room Personnel Only." Inside another sign questions, "Are you scrubbed?" I feel no emotion, no buzz, no butterflies.

Dr. Arab appears on the scene. "How are you this morning, Mr. Flynn?"

I nod.

Dr. Arab motions to the nurse—Thank God—she's not Janie, the vampire.

After being shifted to the operating table, I'm enshrined in green sheets, and strapped solidly. Slight ping of fear but the nurse's eyes, so understanding, meet mine.

Her soft voice, "Hi. You'll be OK." She adjusts my arm to a board, and inserts a needle. "There now, things will be better, just relax."

As she adjusts the tube, I become vaguely aware of all the unfamiliar instruments, little dots of light blipping across a screen, chromed tools, flat pans full of knives and what have you—I shut my eyes. Voices. Dr. Arab, "Alright nurse. Mr. Flynn, we will be anesthetizing you now. Would you please count backwards?"

"Ten, nine, eight, eight . . ."

I awake, or do I? My first sensation is my mouth. Dry. God, my mouth is as dry as dusts. But I'm alive. And, Oh my sides aches; no, it burns. As I try to touch my side, I realize that my arms are secured. I struggle.

A young girl leans over. "It's alright. It's over. You're in the recovery room for now. Later on we'll return you to your room."

"Drink," I half whisper. "Water. Mouth dry."

She swabs my lips and the inside of my mouth with a cold gauze pad. In a moment, I taste the lemon flavor. So refreshing and so wet. I lick my lips trying to extract every molecule of liquid. Again I drift off. Where am I? I'm a bull in Montana—a joke about reincarnation.

The table moves. I open my eyes. There is the green man.

"We returning you to the ward, Mr. Flynn. Just relax."

In the room, they unstrap me and lift me to the bed. Mr. Appendix calls me from his bed. "Welcome back, how ya feelin'?"

I don't answer, instead I fall asleep—Jesus, my side burns—a jab in my arm wakens me for an instant. For the next 24 hours I sleep except for a nibble at supper, and a periodic pill and needle. It's so nice to sleep, to escape so completely from the worry and the pain and the mystery of it all. No wonder people gobble downers. Sleep, the great escape.

Even on the following morning when the doctors made their rounds I opt to sleep. Dr. Arab wakes me to peel away the bandages. His dark eyes inspecting the cut as though he were a meat inspector. Then I notice Dr. Robot. They confer outside the room, flexing their medical vocabularies. I catch a phrase or two but it means nothing to me.

Later in the afternoon, Dr. Robot returns. "Everything checks out. The growth was removed and tests show it to be benign. However, we've decided to initiate the follow-up program. Periodic tests and treatments. Nothing serious. I believe in the conservatiive approach and I think that in your situation, this is in your best interest."

In two days I'm discharged, no more cognizant of what's inside of me now than two days ago. But for the moment, as I walk out the doors, I'm ecstatic. I'm discharged. I tell Jenny that I've cheated death and we'll be hiking together for a long time!

DINTY DIES

JANUARY 6, 1972

These past few weeks I learned that hope lasts a lifetime. On this earth, every living creature, regardless of how seemingly unimpressive or insignificant they may appear, deserves recognition and respect. Each creature has a niche in life. It's a simple enough concept, but how easily we forget it. For close to thirty years, I worked with Dinty, Dinty the Dim, and never once did I recognize and respect him as a man, as an equal—physically or intellectually. For all I cared, he was nothing but an awkward robot that propelled a broom each morning, or worked a dish rag that swabbed the tables. At best, I treated him as a household pet. I was kind but condescending.

Long ago when I listed the twenty six characters of Danny's, I wrote, "Dinty the Dim—not all in the head." He doesn't count; nothing happens to him or something to that effect. How callous, how stupid! You'd think that as a writer, I'd search for some of the inner qualities within the man. Only too late did I discover that beneath that veneer of a dull horse face, lived a warm and tormented spirit. For God's sake, half the mornings I failed to extend even the courtesy of a "Hi, Dinty." Too busy, or tired or preoccupied—or worse too superior. And on those winter days when I was late, Dinty, faithfully punctual, shivered in the doorway, his hands and ears blue from the cold. Sometimes I'd hear his teeth chatter. But he never complained. He always had a silly grin on his innocent face and a "Good mornin', Bill. It's your turn to buy the coffee." When I was hung-over and ticked off at the world, I'd snap, "Shut up and get sweeping the floor." Of course after I got squared away, I'd send Dinty for the coffee and doughnuts, my treat.

Every tavern has a Dinty. He may be an old baso who cleans the toilets for a wine, or a guy who hates work and falls into the tavern as his hang out routine. Or as in Danny's case, a slow guy who could find little work elsewhere. He did odd jobs; shuffle the beers to the tables, pack up the empties, sweep and swab the latrines, go for coffee and sandwiches and served as a sort of mascot. Too often he received the butt end of many jokes and sadly (probably fortunately) never realized he's the butt so he laughs with the rest of us. Dinty gladly accepted his clown role, happy enough to be recognized even if only on the receiving end. Never angry. Always gullible. Like the time Casey asked him to deliver a stickup note to the bank; fortunately the teller knew Dinty. Or the time while Dinty snoozed Frank Vento glued his shoes to the floor. Or the hundreds of times when Dinty would be encouraged to blow his nose—he sounded like a bugle. Everyone laughed.

They say the doctor squashed his head at birth. Distorted face. Brain damage. The kid who never grew up. His alkie father deserted the family so before his mother died, she pleaded with Mrs. Brennan to see he was taken care of, "Jesus, Mary and Joseph, no state institution!" So Booker gave him a job. Not quite a job, more like adopting a mascot, an amusing toy. In actuality, Danny's became his home and Booker was his surrogate father. A place to work, eat, and more than once, a place to sleep. A grubby bartender's apron became his uniform and his status symbol—for years Dinty vowed he was going to purchase a white waiter's jacket with his name embroidered over the breast pocket but he seldom saved more than a few dollars at any given time. He spent most of his money on comic books, John Wayne, 7th Calvary movies, and Milky Way candy bars. Rarely did I write of Dinty, after all, what can you say about a dummy, or so I thought. He could barely read. I never saw him write, and although he found it impossible to add three digits with a pen and a pad, oddly enough, he could correctly multiply 2 three digit numbers in his head. Booker used wager bets to unsuspecting customers but Dinty sometimes he was too nervous to perform under pressure.

But he was well known for his origami: birds, dogs, and the like.

Of course Dinty never married or even made love to a woman. The closest he came to experiencing sex happened when a couple of young bucks in a benevolent mood fixed him up with a prostitute in the club upstairs. What a tragedy! No matter how the girl played, Dinty mutely remained as limp as a string. Frustrated, baffled, probably desperate in this situation, he broke down crying. When I found out, I saw red; when Booker heard the story, he went ballistic; for weeks many embarrassed customers avoided the tavern and Booker's less than gentile language. Yes, there were times that I protected him; no one likes to see a dog beaten. In general, though, I ignored him. After all, what do you have in common with a man who drools when he's happy and urinates in his pants when he's afraid? How can you pal around with a horse faced, gapped toothed, thick liped guy who's tounge is so large that his words are slurred? Yes, he was only Dinty, Dinty the Dimwit, but in the long run he proved to be ten times the human being that ever walked through Danny's doors.

Last spring, Dinty lost weight, he experienced chest pains. Tests proved he had lung cancer. Although everyone whispered "tough break" most, I'm sure, felt that he was such a loser anyway that one more loss would make little difference. I mean it's almost like you'd expect Dinty to get cancer; after all, someone has to. Why not him? He's got nothing going for him. Sure you feel sorry for any unfortunate with cancer but less sorry for Dinty than for a beautiful woman like Elizabeth Taylor.

No sooner had the doctors opened him up, they hurriedly sewed him back up. No hope. Like a plucked grape in the hot sun, he quickly shriveled. His flesh, pasty as sour milk, hung off his bones. Thin? God, yes! His cheeks and eye sockets, never bright in health, now dimmed like an old flashlight ready to quit. Dinty gave off a strange odor, the faint, almost sickly sweet odor of decay. He became the withered like a late autumn leaf, almost ready to drop off the vine.

Danny's is still his only real home so he continued to work. However, a couple of customers, probably afraid of contacting the cancer or possibly wishing to deny the existence of death, asked Booker to get rid of him.

"Listen you pack of assholes, Dinty stays!" Booker grabs Fred Cahill by the throat. "This is my joint and I could give a fiddler's shit if you get the bubonic plague in here. If you don't like it, then screw! I don't see any anchors on your ass."

Two days later Booker gave Dinty a raise and presented him with a white waiter's jacket. Although dying, he's a happy puppy with an old shoe. And no more pranks. After all, everybody knows it's just a matter of time. The man can barely breathe.

When Dinty sweeps the floor, every five minutes, he sits to rest. Finally one day, as he rests, he wheezes heavy and unnatural. Then coughs up incredible gobs of blood, spewing red and black all down the front of his white waiter's jacket. You'd never believe that a person could vomit so much blood and still live. We rushed Dinty to Boston City Hospital. We learned that he's on the danger list with little hope. His days are numbered.

With a stack of Batman, Superman, and Captain America comic books, and a big box of Milky Ways, I go visit him. His room is on the eighth floor. The wards are large, like a barracks. Hot as hell with the radiators knocking and clanging and steam hissing. The smell of urine and alcohol and a peculiar stench of rancid orange juice. Dinty is asleep, oblivious to the tubes in his nose, the needles in his arm; oblivious to the moans of the nose-less man in the next bed.

I set the gifts on his night table and stand quietly watching Dinty sleep. He wheezes hard and wet like sucking the last of a milk shake through a straw. The death rattle! Chills tingle along my spine. This is death! I turn to flee. But as I turn to leave he opens his eyes, painfully whispers, "Don't go, Bill. Stay with me." He barely gurgles those slurred words past his oversized tongue. "I don't want to be alone. Not now. "Here," he taps the bed, "Sit here with me."

"How's it going, Dinty?"

"Like it's always gone, lousy," he answers, in a gurgling voice like he speaks from under water. Dried red spittle cakes around the corner of his mouth.

"In a few days, you'll be OK. As good as new."

"Naw, Bill, I ain't never gonna walk outa here." Slight cough as he flexes in pain. "My chest feels like a ton of rocks are stacked on it. Can't breathe."

Slowly he closes his eyes. "But what the hell. I'm going to a far better place than I ever knew—you know, Bill, I read that in a French book once."

Surprised, I say, "I didn't realize that you liked to read books."

"Mostly funny books. But I read a book once when I went to the Lucy Stone. Ya know, in that school with the rest of the stupid kids. There was a teacher, Miss Jennings, in the sixth grade. I loved her. She was so kind and really took an interest in me. With her I sort of felt like a real person, even smart sometimes. When I left school she gave me that book about the French revolution, to keep for myself. I never really read it, you know, skipped pages, but I remember the last page. This guy got his head cut off. I used to dream about savin' up enough money to marry her, but she was kind of old. And I was just a nothin'. You know, Bill, it ain't easy being a dummy."

"You're no dummy, Dinty." Could he read the lie on my face?

"Don't hand me that baloney, not today, Bill. I'm just a nothin' to nobody. A clown to play tricks on. I can't even take care of myself. Why, if it weren't for you and Booker, I would have starved in an alley years ago."

He propped himself onto his elbow, "That's why I'm glad you came in cause I always wanted to thank you guys. You and Booker are my closest and dearest friends. A guy couldn't ask for better buddies—all ya done for me. Lettin' me work, and always buyin' me breakfast and even puttin' my name in a story." So naïve. So innocent.

My throat tightend until I almost choke. Bill, you dirty rotten bastard! He calls me his closest and dearest friend and all these years I accepted him as I would a piece of furniture. And worse, now it's too late, too late to show a molecule of kindness to this poor simple soul. I look at his face, and I feel my eyes fill.

"You ain't cryin?" he lays back. "I had plenty guys laugh but ain't no one ever cried. But don't Bill. I don't need it. Maybe life dished out a dirty deal but I ain't complaining. Cause I took it. Ya never heard me bitchin' and moanin', didya? I took it like a soldier, didn't I? I bet John Wayne couldna done any better."

A nurse comes in and injects him with something. I sit silent, accompanied by a heavy, heavy guilt. I wished at that instant I could vaporize and disappear like the steam in a radiator. Oh God!

"Bill, I ain't so tough no more. To tell ya the truth, I'm sick and tired of livin' my life. No more problems, God. Let me go nice and peaceful. Maybe a nice funeral like Boss and Gunny. Ya know with flowers and a big limousine, maybe you and Booker'll come—like I had a real family. I made my peace. Every morning Father O'Hara comes and hears my confessions. I get dirty thoughts sometimes, about girls and stuff. But he says not to worry. God'll understand. That's what he says. I hope he's right cause I don't wanna be no dummy in heaven. I already spent my trial in this hell."

Never in my life have I been so humbled. Before me lays dying man. A dummy—a nobody who swept floors and cleaned filthy toilets and bore a hundred jokes and subtle insults and yet was ever so grateful for crummy free coffee and donuts. "Dearest and closest friend"—like a thick bone caught in my craw. God forgive us who showed no kindness and consideration, only a detached sort of tolerance. A dummy, or so I thought, incapable of real emotion. But he knew! All these years—and I'm supposed to be a writer! What torment did this man endure with a silent tongue? A stoic. A mighty Spartan. What unfulfilled dreams did he suffer? A terrible lonely world devoid of an intimate friend, a family, a comrade, a lover. An existence empty of a real family, an opportunity, a decent job, even without the ability to fend for himself. A world without hope, save death. How stupid of me!

I take his hand, lifeless as a glove, but surprisingly warm, and for some instinctual reason I kiss him on the forehead as though he were but a child and I his sorry parent.

He smiles, squeezes my hand, and closes his eyes.

He died that night.

Dinty's landlady delivered his will to Booker, a scrawled note leaving his prized possession—a radio to Booker—for the Friday Night Fights. Booker hung Dinty's sketch on the wall next to Bill Morrissey's lobster Claw.

Because I was a writer, the note went on to explain, he left me his collection of Classic Comics and a beat-up copy of "Tale of Two Cities."

The coffee can full of pennies totaling $14.74 was to buy a round for the guys.

And an array of origami—dogs, cats, birds, and an eagle—"For the Boys," he scribbled.

Today we buried Dinty in style. Danny's went overboard with the collection, and Kelly laid him out nicely in a bed of satin and flowers. Neat haircut and shave, shirt and tie—first time anyone ever saw him in a tie.

"Never saw him look so clean and bright," said a number of the boys. Thanks to Booker he wore a new waiter's jacket with a large "Dinty" embroidered on the pocket. A cape of flowers enshrouded the casket. And Dinty got his big limousine ride followed by twenty or so cars, I guess you'd say his family. But I'm sure that many guilty men felt as I.

God, if You are kind, then Dinty won't be a dummy in heaven.

Where's Dinty?

Dorchester Day Anniversary

June 3, 1973

Quotes from the ***Dorchester Argus Citizen***

On the day that WWI ended, the Strand in Uphams Corner opened for business.

The 100th anniversary of St. Peter's Parish will be celebrated this year.

Mayor White dedicated the new Police Station 11 (Gibson St) in Fields Corner cost $1,000,000.

There have been a number of fires in the neighborhood:

1. Lucky Strike bowling alleys was a ravaged by a late night fire (was remodeled to the cost of $350,000.)
2. Three 3-deckers on Dorchester Ave, 9 families were displaced
3. Two fires swept a block of business at Godman Square. Arson was suspected five stores were boarded up.
4. A fire hit the MBTA on a train in south Station. More than 100 Dorchester residents were taken to local hospitals.
5. A three alarm fire destroyed half of the Park and Recreation building (formally the Hecht House).

A new district plan for the Holland Community School resulted in complaints of parents from the Mather School District. Parents of public school expressed their concern.

Many Dorchester residents have moved out of the community, caused by social and economic influences and changes.

But is not change always a part of life?

Black And White Conflicts

October 1973

A few of the young lads in Danny's are very good athletes. Jack McDonough (Boss's son) was talking with a buddy (Tom Ryan) who grew up in Milton.

Tom asked Jack if he wanted to join a park league football team.

"Sure," Jack answered. So they arranged to meet the next week and visit the team, named the Fittons.

Jack explained to me, "So we go to the field, down to Doyle's café, across from English High, and guess what? We are the only two white guys. The coach is black as the ace of spades, as were most of the team. I had expected to take a ration of 'honkey' bullshit, but no. The team was neutral, no insults, but no hugs either."

Tom says, "Anyway, I say I want to play defensive back and ask to try out for the position."

"Sure," the coach says, "Practice is three evenings a week and Saturday mornings." He somewhat lectured us all about team mates and how we must work together as a team, on and off the field. Have manners! Show respect for your team and your opponents.

I ask, "How were you treated?"

"Fine, the coach was a great guy. No bullshit," answered both Jack and Tom.

Jack explained, "And as the season went on and we practiced and played the games, we sort of bonded. Let's face it, there are issues between blacks and whites, but the question is, do you want to play football? Yes! Do you want to work as a team and win? Yes! I began to make a few friends, and as the season began, the friendships solidified. We all love to play ball."

Jack said, "Actually the only problems we had were in Charlestown and Southie. Not with the players, although there were a few animals. We had problems with the white spectators who threw bottles and bricks onto the field. More than once, we had the police escort us off the site. It was like combat experience. And we were scared shitless. There was a lot of pure hate in the atmosphere!"

Mickey Smith called from the end of the bar, "That's what you get for being a traitor—a honkey turncoat!" His words drip with venom. No one in the bar responded.

"If you don't believe me, he yelled again, you go down to Roxbury Crossing some night and you'll come home with no balls."

Tom yells back, "Give it a rest Mickey!"

Mickey shoots him a scowl.

"By the end of the season—I made some life long friends," said Tom. Jack agrees, "Especially the coach—a solid man!"

Bill's Reflections: 1934-1974

January 1, 1974

It's a cold morning, wet, slushy, heavy snow warnings—a good day to hibernate indoors and maybe read and write. I'm full of energy, set to go with a burst of speed like a racer coming down the stretch. Sometimes writing demands so much; but other times an excitement builds up until I think I'll explode. Thoughts, ideas, plots race through my head so fast my hand can't write fast enough. My fingers sweep and skip along the paper until the scribbling degenerates into a weird hieroglyphic illegible to all but me. It's my definition of fun; I love to create original ideas. Let my mind soar, fantasize, an orgasm of the spirit, free from all restrictions, inhibitions and prejudices. All ideas, however bizarre or illogical, are fair game as they twist and zip through those complex passages of my memory, my brain or whatever exists inside my head. Bits of information, facts, shreds of memory are distorted, manipulated, recombined in such a combination that a unique idea or concept is discovered. For that is what creativity is all about—the combining of previous facts in a unique way. What will I write today? I lean back and rock the chair on the back two legs, sipping my mug of coffee. Let the ideas flow. What has happened recently? I recall past events, characters—I have boxes and boxes full of characters living a history—an idea hits! Why not review? Reread the notes. What has changed in thirty-nine years? This neighborhood is certainly dying; a few more years any house that stands will be tenanted by a new wave of immigrants from the Caribbean and South America and God knows where. Yes, Dorchester has seen changes. How have I changed? Definitely more wrinkles and aches and pains.

As I rummage through the boxes, mixed emotions embrace me. It's so pleasant to remember the winnings, the happys; it's so painful to recall the loss and the hurts. Melancholy overcomes me. Nostalgia, a sickness with no cure. My old pals, my expended youth and worse, my lost loves and forfeited ambitions—why is it, we never quite outlive some dreams, no matter how unattainable? Where did time go? All those years, now nothing but memories of an old timer. I look at one of Red's sketches of me. I'm an old man. I'm 74 and well over the hill—who said, "Death follows us like a shadow?" How true. So to those of you who can eat, drink, and be merry, Omar said so succinctly thousands of years ago, "Oh, come with old Khayam, and leave the wise to talk; one thing is certain, that life flies; one thing is certain, and the rest is lies; the flower that once has bloomed forever dies."

I ask myself, "Did I appreciate the good times when I lived them? Did I do my best teaching and writing? Did I travel enough? I think so, I truly do." At least I fully recognize that you only live once, no second chances. Maybe bartending left a vacuum but how many people are satisfied with their jobs and their lives in general? But I did three jobs; tending bar, teaching engineering, and writing.

How do I gauge my life; what are the milestones? The years break into fragments; grammar school, high school, college, Nancy—courtship and marriage, my editor's job, teaching—oh what beautiful times! And as if some sinister curse were cast over me, the next phase brought me awful events to say the least. To this day, I cannot speak of the loss of Nancy and the baby—a baby boy named James. But that's life, accept the joys and the pains. And no matter how tormented, how depressed, you somehow manage to survive. Of course, Bernie and Booker are still alive—how I love them!

So vividly do I recall my first week as a bartender. "Only for a while, Booker, until I straighten out." And years later—Good God, a lifetime in a tavern. Me and Bill Morrissey's lobster claw, and Booker's List of Heroes hanging on the tavern wall. Witness to a thousand lives, a thousand triumphs and tragedies.

But forget about me, what has actually changed in these years? We know evolution is an integral part of life. Time and tide wait for no man.

Personally, I doubt if humans have changed at all in four thousand years, let alone forty. When you look at the overall picture, there's really nothing new under the sun. Since time began, environments change; and people adjust. Therefore, let's examine these alterations of the past years, and how the people adjust. How do we define the collective environment of this block? What outside factors influence all of us? Let's be scientific; define the factors, establish a list and discuss each in turn.

Although I consider myself somewhat a lazy non-practicing Catholic, I strongly believe that the church undeniably shaped the history of this block and the country. In fact, regardless of denomination or instruments, religion shrouds a person's life, cradle to grave, for what man has failed to ask, "Where am I going? What's it all about?" Another factor, more direct, is the family, the greatest of man's institutions; the hub of the three major events of our lives: birth, marriage, death. Of course, we must include in our list the government, the laws that we follow or circumvent, the rules by which our society survives, the new crimes we commit. Technology and medicine keep us partially healthy, if not wealthy and wise. Our attitudes on sex have certainly experienced dramatic revisions especially in the 1960's. And, of course, the list must include jobs, the economics of how we reap our bounty. Last but not least, the physical changes of the block should be discussed—in fact in the last five to ten years we've witnessed countless houses burnt and bulldozed.

Here's my list:

1) Religion
2) Family
3) Government and Law
4) Technology
5) Sex
6) Jobs—Economics
7) Physical Characters

How has each changed from 1934 to 1974. Each factor interrelates and overlaps and intertwines with the other; none is a separate entity. And of course, only a complete fool such as me would attempt to discuss such a broad subject; each factor could alone fill libraries. But then again, nothing ventured, nothing gained.

Religion

First, I will confess that I am poorly qualified to write about religion outside of what I believe. But you need not be a genius to recognize the great influence that religion—Catholic, Protestant, Jewish—has wielded over this block; a bedrock of custom, a comfort of stability. Few areas escaped its pull of gravity; baptism, marriage, death, education, support, morals, direction, guidance. And in all probability the church has indeed assisted in keeping the poor from murdering the rich. In the 30's and 40's, even as late as the 50's, most families, young and old, regularly attended mass. On Saturday afternoons and evenings I'd watch the women and children and many of the men walk to Confession. Retreats, Baptisms, May Processions, Holy Name Society, Knights of Columbus, Ladies Solidarity, Midnight Mass at Christmas, First Friday Devotion, Fasts on Fridays, and Lent, Communion Breakfasts, daily visits—whether or not you cared to participate, every parishioner was familiar with each. The Last Rights—it was the believed that no storm, however ferocious, could prevent a priest from administering to the dying person. And a priest or nun, had absolutely no fear to walk the streets safe from insult or injury. To rob a poor box was comparable to murder—no need to call the police, the culprit would be beaten to an inch of his life—street corner justice. The wish of every Irish mother's was to have a son with a calling. Celibacy was rarely discussed for priests and nuns were committed to abstinence and purity until death; anyway they were a cut above more physical parishioners. Divorce was relatively rare; separation was most often the solution. The Pill was undiscovered, abortion was taboo. No layman's hand touched a consecrated host and excommunication was a curse beyond comprehension. Yes, these were the threads that wove through our lives.

Now in the late 60's we see the Church locked up for fear of vandalism, even desecration. Midnight Mass was discontinued because of drunken disturbances. Church attendance dropped with respect to the young. "Mass? Whaddaya kiddin' me? If I wanted to hear guitars, I'd play the jukebox." Priests marry divorcees in the church! Old people watch, confused as a lifetime of unquestioning beliefs shake under the earthquake of Ecumenicals and rumblings of Saint Christopher's and meat on Fridays.

Sure, there are many who welcome this new era of laxity, of liberalism, of free lifestyles, of "do your own thing—forget about later, I want mine now." Far be it for me to argue this point but let me state a few facts; if a person is religious, in general he/she follows the law—if he's in mass at seven o'clock chances are that he won't steal your car at noon. Whether or not you adopt a cynical view, faith lends dignity and hope and in this block, a stability to many. To those immigrants of years ago, to the old, the weary, to those who finally s ask, "What happens when I die?" How I envied Tommy O'Hara with his belief as solid as granite. A great mind with a janitor's job, he accepted his lot—after all earth was merely a trial for heaven. If you've got religion, you need fear nothing. Truly a precious blessing. I wish I had it.

In the 30's, 40's and 50's the nuns rapped many a knuckle and yanked many an undisciplined head. They were tough and dedicated. One must admit they did far more good than harm. I'm positive there're many men and women who could attribute success to some nun's dedication and kindness. Now we see lay teachers with lay problems. Even St. Peter's School remains, I believe it is the sole reason why this block hasn't collapse completely.

Family

Related closely with religion but more directly is the family, the basic unit of civilization. You're always a child to your mother—the apple falls close to the tree—blood runs thicker than water—that's all right, he ain't heavy, Father, he's my brother. Probably no factor on my list has changed so much as the concept and construction of the family in the last thirty-nine years. Size, structure, style, divorce, welfare, abortion, equal rights, free love, the pill, care of the aged, education of the young, Parents without Partners—so many diverse areas touch the family. Families are similar now with the decline of religion, the Pill, abortion, divorce, the high cost of living. In the 30's 40's and 50's as soon as a couple married a baby was expected, after nine months, of course. Now we have both husbands and wives working—for a home, a car, a vacation, a boat or what have you. In past years, divorce carried a definite stigma, a fallen woman, excommunication, eternal damnation. Now young kids split at the first crisis, at the sight of greener pastures. Divorce seems almost a social medal. In any case, welfare rewards, seem to propagate divorce. If a guy knows his kids will survive, he can take off.

Time was most families had two parents who were the disciplinarians. Let's face it, this block was populated by rough immigrants laboring in an existence in a strange land which could show little compassion. When a kid broke a rule, no Ph.D. in Psychology counseled him; a callused hand whacked him. Generally not cruel or vicious, just enough to set the kid straight. Now we see families managed by working mothers and itinerant boyfriends and slack authority.

In the 30's the sick and the aged passed away at home amongst loved ones. Now we sentence them to nursing homes and hospitals full of busy doctors and strange machines with green dots bleeping across the screen. A plastic funeral home, air-conditioned limousine, deposit you forever under some golf course.

Government and Law

Because religious influence has diminished and because the family structure and authority has fragmented, we now expect the government to fill the void. Who else can handle the welfare, education, crime, drugs, riots, car thefts, muggings, B&E's, arson? In the 30's and 40's, religion, the cop on the beat, street corner justice took care of certain aspects of city living. No one's mother was insulted, let alone beaten for a handbag. Few children were molested, nor sisters raped. If a guy owed you twenty bucks, the last place it would be settled was in Small Claims Court. If a kid stole a bike, he got his butt kicked. A family, peers, and "the corner" taught a kid the meaning of honor and justice and patriotism and prejudice. Not that I'm trying to paint a picture of Utopia. Sure in the 30's there was rape and incest and muggings and murder, but they were indeed exceptions. An old person could walk down the street at night, without fear. Not so now.

In any society certain rules have to be followed, at least by the majority. These rules can be enforced by the Church with a promise of heaven or damnation, or enforced by the police with a threat of punishment. As a society, we've chosen the latter—look at the phenomenal growth of police and security organizations; Boston Police, Metropolitan District Police, MBTA Police, State Troopers, Brinks, Pinkertons, Burns, Watts and so many others. The country's turning into an armed camp with electronic eyes and ears and a new morality of espionage. George Orwell may well be proved most prophetic.

In the 60's we ask the government to support and feed our aged, the poor and sick; to legislate our morality; to discipline and educate, physically and spiritually, our children; to prevent crime; to rehabilitate; and to assume a hundred other duties that the family and religion once performed. And because the government now assumes these duties, taxes sky rocket, laws multiply, bureaucracy grows and a billion baloney peddlers—politicians maneuver in a wide field of patronage and pay-offs and padding their own nests.

Crime is different now. Criminals have, since time began, stolen, not from need but greed. He steals not because his mother requires a delicate eye operation, but because he's got a bad drug habit, a chick on the line, or simply can't hack the 9-5 work routine. Human nature is human nature. But it seems as though the crime in this block is now more vicious. It isn't enough to steal a guy's wallet; no, pummel him until he's senseless, then burn down his house.

For certain, these years have witnessed upheaval in law and order.

Technology and Medicine

In medicine we have made dramatic strides and for the most part, for the better. Today we live longer and we're healthier. Science has eliminated or contained Polio (Jimmy, Mike Kelly's son); T.B. (Danny O'Neil); Flu (my brother and sister); pneumonia (Mr. Hession); Small Pox, Diptheria, infections, Gangrene, and a host of other human ills.

They've invented and distributed wonder drugs (and not-so-wonder-drugs) that rescue us from long term illness and death. In a few years we will receive repaired organs and limbs like a robot in a service station. We've replaced Old Doc with his house calls with a polished specialist who will schedule your next appointment six months from now even though your knee hurts today. No more house calls. We seldom see kids with club foot or babies born dead or disfigured anymore.

Overall these changes have brought, a measure of happiness, and a freedom from worry. Without your health, you're in trouble.

With respect to technology, we became mesmerized by one of the most popular inventions of all time—the television.

Sure, the past years have regurgitated electronics and synthetics but the effects of T.V. and communications will irreversibly affect us long after the others have yielded to improvements. Television has exposed and altered our every concept of ourselves and others—no area escapes its tentacles—birth, set, inner thoughts, secrets, exposes, instant news—and in color. Unfortunately, on the sidelines, the bomb, the missiles, the nuclear plant, the bacteria await patiently for the statistical freak to neutralize all our problems and concerns, and my conjectures.

Sex

When I was six, I used to think that my penis was good only to urinate; now at seventy I know it. OK not quite true. But in my head, the fire burns but in reality, only a spark smolders. Also opportunities diminish. As I see it, a thousand years of history find little evolution in man's physical sexual nature but, the last decade witnessed dramatic alterations in how our society in this block of the world, views sexual behavior. Sex and morals, since time began—fluctuate in cycles—yesterday's virtue is today's vice; a loveable rake at twenty may be a dirty old man at fifty. One cultures art is another's pornography. Between 1934 and 1974 there has been a great change in morality; abortion, free love, woman's lib, gay lib, family, style and structure, mobility, contraceptive devices, pornography. "Do your own thing; let it all hang out."

Overall I approve of opening the skylight; let the light shine in the dungeon. Sex is an integral part of our lives, not to be displayed arrogantly, but it should not to be pounded into our subconscious as though it were a garbage can of unmentionables. For too long, the Victorian mentality has caused too much fear and shame and neuroticism. Fortunately, pregnant girls nowadays seldom commit suicide. There's no denying the power and the potential, and the beauty of sex plus or minus. As the speed freak said, "You can never get enough good feelings." He's correct, you can never experience enough orgasm. Me? I'm human. As long as no one gets hurt, sex is one of the greatest joys in life, but sex without love, without a commitment or trust, leaves much to be desired. For me there's got to be more than just the physical.

Young kids around here, in Danny's, on the corner, treat sex so casually, to the dismay and maybe envy of we old folks; free love, freedom from pregnancy, woman's lib. Birth control not only revolutionized sexual frequency and experimentation, but challenged some fundamental Catholic concept that sex is for procreation. The 1960's philosophy tells us that sex is fun. "No shit, Sherlock," says Art Sheehan, "What gave you the first clue?"

On the other side of the coin, with the freedom comes responsibilities and consequences—some mental and some physical.

Emotionally you can be scorched and scarred at any age. Sometimes abortions kill more than the embryo; Jim O'Leary's sister had a breakdown after an abortion. Sex can certainly be like playing with fire, especially with the diseases that can be transmitted. As an example last month a young 'Nam vet telephoned his girlfriend. "I didn't mean it, to give it to you. Look, we'll go down to the clinic. No sweat. Vietnam Rose, no worse than a cold. I told you, I didn't know. Just started dripping. This girl, last week at a party. Honest it was just casual, I was stoned. It's nothing. You'll be OK in a few weeks." Or more serious, Cliff McBridge picked up something in Thailand that started as an ugly rash. A unique strain that for two years now the doctors at the V.A. can't seem to cure.

Probably the most notable reversal concerning casual sex over the years is the abortion issue. In the 30's abortion was murder—period. A last measure committed by a desperate high school girl, petrified of a Calvinist father and leering neighbors. You know the story; a back alley doctor, the dirty instruments, the grubby room. In the 70's counselors and clinics and court orders cater to yawning teenagers. What's my reaction? If I were up against it, I'd abort. But by nature, I firmly believe that an ounce of prevention is worth a pound of cure.

As always much of our entertainment revolves around sex; today we are more open and direct. Sometimes too open and direct. Saunter into any drug store or book mart. Rows and racks of magazines and books and "cute" cards so blatantly sexual that in the 30's, the store would be razed and the owner imprisoned as a moral degenerate. According to this liberated literature, everyone fornicates, commits fellatio, or in the slang, they "f and s." Beneath this veneer of liberalism and "art," a large dollar sign motivates, after all, "sex sells." Porno in the name of art is pure nonsense. Whenever I hear the argument that a "dirty book never influenced a mind" I want to scream. That would be like explaining that classic had no influence on people.

Finally another skeleton brought out by the passage of time is homosexuality. Even though those newspapers and authors and professors and psychologists would have you believe that "gay" is OK, this is a neighborhood of Catholics, immigrants and blue collars and hard hats that hold it somewhat in contempt. It's true the years have somewhat mellowed this contempt, especially amongst the younger crowd, but by no means is homosexuality accepted or understood. No parent wants to see an offspring grow up "left-handed," but I'm sure many believe in live and let live especially if the problem exists in someone else's backyard.

Jobs, Economics

Life abounds with inequalities, and if fate destines you to be born poor and without any exceptional talent, then the Lord was speaking to you when He professed, "he shall earn his bread by the sweat of his brow." In the 30's, for whatever reasons if you failed to work, then you could expect little help. Today, the work ethic still survives, but we now depend upon welfare and unemployment compensation, food stamps and a hundred other government programs. In this neighborhood, and I'm sure many others, welfare elicits a wide range of response. An explosive and expensive issue. To be on relief in the 30's was a last resort, something to be ashamed of—the absolute unavoidable. Only the old or the utterly destitute went to the poor farm. In the 60's massive welfare programs became part of the Great Society, and now welfare is an accepted element of our lives. Look at the sign in Allton's Furniture Store—"Welfare Checks Welcome." And the drug stores passes out booklets, "Medicare Benefits."

Pros and cons—some taxpayers complain about the able, healthy young, chiseling and beating the system; whereas others see only the old, the dependent, the sick in need of relief. In either case, the doctors, dentists, druggist, landlords all laugh their way to the bank. And nonworkers calmly collect their unemployment checks while earning a few bucks under the table. Dishonest? But every time Rockefeller catnaps he wakes up thousands of dollars richer. There's something dishonest about that too. It's called exploitation. Of course, his lawyers and public relations hirelings call it other names.

In addition to the burgeoning welfare programs, the government has gorged itself in the interest of self-propagation. During the depression government jobs paid low but stood as secure and as steady employment. Many workers decided that a bird in the hand was worth two in the bush. Today Civil Service grows and grows with a thousand new classifications each week with more benefits and wages and prestige. Alarmed, a number of caustic citizens see, a horde of fat leeches sucking heartily on a bleeding taxpayer. A government of the drones, by the drones and for the drones. Undaunted the civil servant knowingly wink at each other and retire at fifty-five.

Whereas unemployment during the depression remained high because of a lack of government initiative and daring, these past decades have brought a direct dependence of the quantity and the quality of jobs, government programs and expansions and services and contracts and laws. The Watertown Arsenal closes and thousands lose their jobs. An SBA loan is awarded and a new factory is built. Raytheon wins a missile contract and a hundred draftsmen and designers are hired. A tariff is revised and a tool manufacturer closes down. A technology is imported; an electronic firm bankrupts so that a hundred machinists, technicians, shippers and clerks get laid off. Automation obsoletes some jobs; technology creates new ones.

Jobs come, jobs go; people come, people go, a fluid motion like a human tide waxing and waning and washing and filling voids and overflowing. Actually a number of occupations in this block alone have disappeared in the last years. The fishing industry (the Russians and foreign fleets have seen to this); the shoemaker (Tony); the tailor shop (Karras); the old fashion barber (we now have stylists); knife sharpeners; laundryman (the Chinese have retreated to profitable restaurants in the suburbs); the H horse and wagon crew (Milkman, Fruitman, Ragman—incidentally during WWII, Rags Maloney became a clothes purchaser for the Army; wool cutters; coal men, ice men, Ma and Pa (Variety Stores); radio and T.V. repairmen; diaper deliverymen to name a few.

A scientific breakthrough, advanced education, changing environments brings us new jobs, or increase the demand for other lines of work. In Danny's these days, we have electronic technicians, refrigeration mechanics, computer operators and programmers, draftsmen and designers, plastic salesmen, male hair stylists, male nurses, air traffic controllers, etc. With the increasing crime rates, union patronage, there are more policemen, firemen—good paying jobs these days. In fact, the Blacks are fighting for a piece of the pie. With the college commitment, we meet more, more accountants and design draftsmen and business managers and consultants, and even a lawyer here and there. The growing demand for bigger, better, and newer gives strength to the trade unions; electricians, plumbers, glaziers, carpenters, steamfitters, roofers, cement finishers and a host of others. And because ninety nine percent of the guys in Danny's own automobiles we hob-knob with auto-mechanics, auto-body men, insurance underwriters, car salesmen, and all of the related trades. Since these days we concern ourselves with health and happiness, nurses and health therapists and social workers and recreation directors at nursing homes are commonplace occupations.

These last few years, I noticed with high unemployment, thanks to Nixon and the Republicans, that many young people are scrambling for jobs. The boom and the growth in the country is slowing changing, and those who are wise are desperately trying to get cemented into civil service or large corporations—any place that offers some hope of security. I hear the kids, "Let me be a cop . . . I took the exam for fireman . . . Go see your rep . . . Hey I know a guy who knows the Governor's cousin . . . Hello,

Senator my name is—and a mutual friend—said to give you a call—Sure I'll work on your campaign."

I listen to vets. "Balls, what a big crock about hire the vets. The dream of America's manhood. All the unions are sewed up tighter that witch's twot, and the only jobs around don't pay dick. Well, if I can't get a decent job, I might as well go to college."

I see the frustration of the college grads. "A degree but no job. My father's great American dream shot to hell. My degrees not worth the paper it's written on. Bill, what a damn rip off! Four years! I would have been better off to open a pizza parlor, all that money wasted."

Jobs come, jobs go. But the concern, the worry, the exploitation remains the same.

Physical Complexion of the Neighborhood

Only an old timer in this block could appreciate the physical changes. Hearts must weep as one walks down Dorchester Avenue, past the vacated stores, the burnt 3-deckers, the abandoned autos and back doors at St. Peter's. The storefront churches and littered lots full of greasy pizza shacks and the drunks asleep in doorways and sleepy-eyed kids ripping off the last of the copper from a parked truck. Anyone who could afford to move out, has fled—who wants to raise a family under these conditions? And as the whites flee, more blacks and immigrants and down-and-outs who can't afford better occupy the vacuum.

As limited as Dorchester was during the depression, it was a decent place. Sometimes poor, always proud. People belonged. For sure you had a sense of security. After all, you knew the family next door, across the street, over the back yard—all around you. You knew the shop keepers. That's not to say there was always harmony. There were fights, verbal assaults, petty bitching, even out and out hatred. But there was also love and comradeship,as any kid who's grown up hanging on "the corner" would acknowledge. There was respect. When faced with a collective neighborhood problem like a mugger or rapist or sex deviate, there was also cooperation.

Today people come and go like gypsies. I'm surrounded by strangers, even in Danny's. Now my list of 1934 customers, my patrons and heroes are long gone. Most have disappeared—moved on or died. People are suspicious, hostile. And no wonder as houses are burglarized, cars stolen, people robbed in broad daylight. Whites blame blacks; blacks blame whites. Hate flourishes like some insidious weed. So poignantly expressed in the graffiti splashed on the walls: "Waste the blacks!" "Off the honkey!"

Drugs run rampant. Pills and nickel bags switch from hand to hand. Crime is soaring and the innocent and the old and defenseless are caught in a trap of immobility. Years ago, a black walking down the street was definitely and oddity, now groups of blacks, combs sticking out of their afro hair, wild clothes from a Hollywood musical, bob-step to the loud sound of a portable Boom-box. Wine bottles pass from drunk to drunk in the doorway until one falls asleep. There is no cop on the beat so the drunk lays exposed. Young boys and girls begin to form opinions about life that should not be so.

Garbage, chucked out the windows, build into rat-infested mounds in the back yards. The windows of the surviving stores are enshrouded by steel screens, called "security cages" by the neighborhood kids.

Years ago as far as the houses were concerned, the owners maintained them within reason and the tenants respected the property. If a kid broke a window, his parent's paid. In fact any house that was burnt or vacated was deemed a haunted house. Today we have streets of haunted houses. Nonexistent landlords have long ago disappeared. I can't condemn them. Why repair a building only to have it vandalized repeatedly even before the repairs are completed? With little respect for religion, for the law, for property, with racial tensions and hatred, a person would be crazy to own a house in this block.

Some new buildings are being built. Old age homes are built like fortresses and guarded twenty four hours a day; a library with a minimum of windows; and a new police station.

Many of the businesses closed their doors; the 5 & 10, Woolworth, First National, Ma & Pa's Jewelry Store is now a sub shop. The Gospel Church of Christ, a storefront church, has replaced the pool room. Two years ago a pawn shop opened its doors but after the third break in, it closed.

The Hammy Theatre like most neighborhood movie houses, closed due to the influence of T.V.

And if you were to ask me what years brought the greatest changes, I'd opt for the 60's. Sure each year brought irreversible changes. "You Can't Go Home Again," wrote Thomas Wolfe.

In the 30's, although we worried about jobs and security, we still nurtured a hope, maintained a faith that promised our struggles would not be in vain. Our children would reap the harvest. Times were tough, but misery loved company back then. We were all in the boat and that fact somehow helped take the sting out of the hurt. Then again this block housed a thousand immigrant families who, comparing conditions back to the old country, still found life in America a bargain.

The 40's involved us in the greatest war in history. A generation of men from seventeen to thirty five served in the military, many traveled from home for the first time. So many young eyes and minds were opened. It was a mixed bag; some saw the splendor of the Taj Mahal and others saw the inhumanity of Dachau. New concepts about life, love, religion, history and the world were formed. Closer to home, in this neighborhood we witnessed hundreds of veterans marrying, building homes, building careers, and businesses and seniority, attending colleges—making up for lost times. Russia and Communism became our acknowledged enemy. At the end of the 40's, the U.S. stood solid as a word leader and a fortress of democracy.

The 50's brought the Korean War and signaled a new era of soldiers and wars that could not be won. Draft exemptions were issued for married men in critical occupations, and a generation of engineering students who were beating the system. And although the Church seemed to reach an unquestionable height and influence, a new religion, called technology after Sputnik, challenged our iminations. Prosperity abounded; government contracts, an expanding economy, a new industries, open exploitation on the world market. Fantastic wealth for the U.S. for those who worked and desired the good times.

The so-called happy years. But beneath the surface, a cynicism, a desperate realization, a cancer grew. Bigger was not necessarily better and the people who ran the show, the bosses, the Rockefellers, the crooked politicians were by no means infallible.

The 60's broke the dike. Sure Jack Kennedy inspired us by asking, "What we could do for our country . . ." Shoot for the Moon. The babies of the 40's became bomb tossers of the sixties. The Church began to lose its grip. We witnessed the pill, abortion, mass divorce, sexual liberation, exodus from the convents and rectories. And new concepts about celibacy. Laws seemed to fall apart as everyone became a Thoreau and followed into civil disobedience; civil rights; off the pigs; the realization that crime does pay; Negroes became blacks and a new era of Uncle Tom's began; Burn baby burn; do your own thing with drugs, sex, Woodstock, the Beetles; Tune-in, Turn on, Drop out; throw away the bra, honey; sure I'll murder a commie for Christianity; work for the C.I.A. Patriotism took a beating basically because of gutless politicians and stupid professors and an agonizing war never to be ended. College kids now burnt draft cards instead of raiding for panties, and only blacks were drafted, and the Marine and the Airborne grunts fought in the bush. A mistrust, a confusion, grew into hatred as the old, the parents, the VFW's watched the young, their offspring, the Phi Beta Kappa's. For once, the country realized how deep was the chasm? Maybe Russia, Communism wasn't really so bad. Sure, legalize everything. Do your own thing. Just don't raise the taxes or get sick. But the taxes rose as welfare mushroomed and fathers took off while stores encourage Welfare Check cashing and the blacks screamed until Boston redistricted as per order of people from Wellesley.

The 1970's still reverberate from the repercussions and ramifications of the 60's. But like in the 30's jobs are scarce, college promises less on the career market, the degree earned in the 40's and 50's were like diamonds purchased at Tiffany's. But in the 60's college degrees, especially liberal arts and social studies seemed to be awarded at the 5 & 10 store. A downgrade from previously recorded degrees. Crime soared while houses burn down, leaving streets gutted. Whites flee, blacks hunker down. Will the 70's bring respite? Or future shock? Is life too fast? Our roots too loose? Our laws and institutions no longer granite rocks but silt?

Yes, only an old timer could see all the physical changes and be moved by them. I imagine that in the 1980's or 1990's this block will be rebuilt. Who knows if it will be by riot or bulldozer, an old city will die, a new one will emerge. Change is a fact of life. Will Danny's survive the rebirth? I hope so.

Sure there will be changes. But people will adapt. Maybe not the old timers but certainly the young. For change is a fact of life and as Darwin stated, the organism that adapts survives.

Well, there we have it. An old timer's review of the past forty years, 1934-1974.

A final question, I wonder what the next forty years will bring? 2014 AD from what little that we've learned from the past forty years, fantastic surprises await today's youngsters.

Random Thoughts

June 6, 1974

A honking horn wakes you. Another morning. No sooner do you open your eyes you know that again you've got the blues and a damn sharp pain in your thigh. Damn old age. Jenny, your black Lab, jumps up on the bed and licks your face. You feel so empty, so baffled almost desperate like you're trapped inside some black vacuum which shrinks and crushes you. So alone, that you could weep especially when you hear a special song, recall a sweet moment, visualize a warm face, smell a soft fragrance—a something from long ago youth which triggers your memory. Oh, to be 21 again on a sunny beach. No wonder Ponce de Leon frantically searched for the fountain of youth. Forget overpopulation, you want to live no matter how aged you are. As Gunny told you years ago there's always a something—a haunting memory, a sweet image—to prompt you to want to stay. And the dog is so happy to be with you.

"What's your beef, Bill? So you're old, so what? Every year is seven for me! Look at all the white hairs on my stomach. And I never had pups of my own, because you got me spayed. You're not much but you're all I have."

"Shut up Jenny," I'm worried, don't you understand?"

"Bill, have you forgotten when you wrote you knocked off characters left and right, without even a thought. Dinty the dim, talk about lonely! Now be quiet, look at my wagging tail, be happy."

I put the dog outside. Yes, you've got the yearn for a constant companion and with each passing day you feel less able to deal with your problems. And worse yet, the old standups—reading and writing—which pulled you out of the black moods are now ineffective. Maybe you can only go the well so many times. You can't read. Nothing interests you. The library's a drag. Your eyes lack concentration. No hobbies to occupy your mind. No more pretty young girls with short dresses where you can sneak a peek—no interest.

You go to the tavern in late afternoon and drink away until evening and relive the past, cursing the bad times and smiling at the victories. If luck rewards you, sleep comes easy. Morning continues to viscous circle. And the more you drink, the deeper into the whirlpool you sink. What an empty way to live. Even as write now, your hands move, the ink goes on the paper but your hearts not in it.

The sun glares through the kitchen window and that lack of energy depresses you all the more. Like it's a day you should be accomplishing, creating, living. But you're an old timer and you're tired and you're brooding and hurting from something within you. Sure the long term test results remain to be evaluated and didn't the doctor, the Egyptian fellow—Dr. Arab—tell you not to worry. He sees little to be concerned with. But do you believe him? Would he tell you straight-out? Let's face it, you don't trust half those in the hospital. Who's the best judge? You know there is something wrong inside. A lump, pain, weight loss, no appetite, always nervous, bouts with diarrhea.

You don't want to write anymore. Can't concentrate. Jesus, for a guy whose written a million words about feelings and fears and premonitions, you're finding it impossible to describe your deepest emotions. Here I am lonely and afraid in a world I never made—Danny O'Neill—James T. Farrell.

God! You've got to break out of this depression. If only there was a button that you could force the pain and loneliness to disappear. Let's go to Danny's.

You walk into Danny's. Early afternoon. Quiet. Young guys, 'Nam Vets, unemployed, all strangers, shooting pool and watching the Red Sox on the tube. Booker signals you from the end of the bar. Always good to see him. An old, dear friend, the bridge to your past, your youth. You study his face, you could care less that rules he breaks. He's a white man inside. Never hurt or downed anyone. A jewel, rough, but a jewel nonetheless.

We sit and drink and talk—not that many words. It's like that with a good friend. Silence produces no friction. The hours pass until the pain, physical and head, subsides. The drinks hit hard so that by 6:30 you're drunk. Too drunk to keep up. Too early to hit the bed. "So long Booker, I'm headed for my room."

Sitting at the kitchen table, you listen to music on the radio. A half can of Bud sits in front of you. "Yesterday" plays. The sad emotions bubble up until your eyes fill with tears. How you ache for a couple of yesterdays. Nancy and my little son! Why? And those nights with Bernie. Soft sweet anointed. Embraces and light moans and whispers and undulations and fantastic orgasms. And more important, an intimacy that I have never known. Where are you, Bernie? You soothed away the pain and the tears, and brought me a forgotten peace of joy. Yes, you had that effect, the only person in my life so that I dropped all my inner defenses and exposed a raw heart. To soothe, or to scar. And you chose to soothe and for that alone, I'll always cherish you. Sounds and touches and sights and smells and tastes. Sweet Jesus, the delights. So long ago, so far away. God, bring back those nights.

Why is that you think of Bernie so often? Have you forgotten Nancy and the infant? No, of course not. How well I remember, but you've trained yourself too well. Push those tragedies from your thoughts—forever. Don't think. Life really cheated you on that deal. How could God take the lives of two innocent people even before the bud blossomed? God, do you hear me? Do you know what I'm talking about? I was never one to pray after they died. But if you're so omnipotent and merciful you'll know I can't help what I feel. Maybe I wasn't a good Catholic, but I did no one wrong and there's a hell of a lot to be said for that. What's it all about, God? All philosophies begin with thoughts about death. If only I could see you God, talk with you, then maybe I wouldn't be so lonely and afraid.

You're always thinking. Sometimes when you write the thoughts come so fast and furious that you scribble words almost on top of each other. All those words that you have written. Yet you never got them published "The Great American Novel." Such a loser.

More than anything, you'd like another chance, another youth. Let there be a reincarnation. Let you return again, even if it is as a piss ant. You want another chance. To accomplish more. To be rich and famous and immortalized. What man is satisfied to be born—to live and to die—a life as insignificant as a fruit fly. No one wants to be forgotten.

If only you had a child to carry on. If only little Jimmy had lived, to remember you, to carry you into the future. But remember the joy with Tom Melvin and his essay project. He often calls me his surrogate father. He has always been like a son to me. Now he is a grown man with his own family. I should give him a call, it's been a long time. Once in the summer and once in the winter we get together and break bread. You look at those kids out in the street playing ball and you see yourself. Do they know what's ahead? Fresh city kids, gotta love them.

Crawford Notch News

July 5, 1974

CONWAY NH—Hiker found unconscious on Webster Cliff Trail (Crawford Notch) He was transported to Twin Mountain Hospital where the hiker was pronounced dead on arrival. Name is withheld pending notification of next of kin.

Dorchester Monthly Tribune

Local man dies in hiking accident on Webster Cliff Trail in Crawford Notch, New Hampshire last Friday. Investigators have ruled out foul play in his death.

The Bulletin Board At Danny's

To All: Our Dear Friend, Billy Flynn, died suddenly of a heart attack while hiking on Webster Cliff Trail in Crawford Notch, New Hampshire. See the Obituary in the Dorchester Tribune for more details.

As per instructions in his Will, he will be cremated with his remains scattered on the Matterhorn, Switzerland.

May he Rest in Peace
Goodbye, Old Pal

Yours truly,
Booker Brennan

Bill's Last Hike

July 4, 1974 **Dr. Tom Melvin, Editor**

One pristine summer morning, Bill packed up his knapsack and drove to Crawford Notch, New Hampshire. Jenny, his dog, accompanied him. The next morning hikers on Webster Cliff Trail, found him semi-conscious lying on a granite slab and propped up on a rock wall facing the valley hundreds of feet below. Speculation is that he slipped on the trail and lay there for hours.

At first the hikers thought the man was asleep—he seemed so peaceful, as the rising sun warmed his face. But a few gentle nudges brought only a feeble mumble, "Take care of my dog." The dog was nuzzled up against his leg.

Upon arrival at the hospital he was pronounced dead—an apparent heart attack.

Two days later Booker gave me three items taken from Billy's backpack: a Saint Christopher's medal pinned to his Wentworth Institute of Technology sweatshirt, a ½ pint of Macallum single malt scotch, and a worn copy of "A Tree Grows in Brooklyn."

"What's this?" I asked when he handed the items to me.

Booker shrugged, "Beats the shit outta me."

"You know Booker, maybe I'm making a mountain out of a mole hill, but years ago when writing my essay about my family history, I mentioned that when my mother immigrated to this country, she brought 3 items: a pair of rosary beads, a curling iron, and a change of underwear.

And here we are, Billy Flynn flies from this earth his three items: a holy medal pinned to a sweatshirt, some scotch, and a book."

"You're nuts."

Later I realize that my connection is a real stretch of the imagination. But as I tried to analyze what had happened—Bill's final trip. Maybe Bill was like those old Eskimos who sit in the igloo and wait for the bear, or like a dying elephant who goes off to the elephant graveyard to die alone. Maybe he knew his time was short and being in poor health and lonely, he pushed his body on a tough hike. If so, at least he chose the time, the place, the mountains—a nice sunset, a valley below, a sip of scotch—his dog at his side. Bill's version of a Vikings Funeral. Who knows?

When it's my turn to die, I'm sure I'll be terrified. To hell with a hospital room connected to wires, tubes up your penis, and drowning in a bowl of jello! I may be afraid to die but Billy chose to die on a trail doing something that he loved. Possibly it was akin to my essay of Tommy Melvin, a sixteen year old kid, lying bare ass on my "flat rock" in Cashman's Quarry—not a care in the world. That magical place that you go when the present becomes too unappealing—maybe Bill's granite bed was his "flat rock" add a few sips of good Scotch, the warm sun a beautiful valley and his dog Jenny.

Of course, if it were my story, I would have just had Bill disappear, Dropped out to start a new life at 74. One last wild adventure. I can picture him in a Tibetan tent via Lost Horizons, or on the Milford Trail in New Zealand, or on a boat, the James Cairde, with Shackleton sailing to the whaling station on South Georgia Island, making his own legend. And this story could be continued when Bill returned. Yes, I'd like to think that. Ah, God! How I wish that were true!

Editor's Wrap-Up

October 1977 Dr. Tom Melvin

Danny's Tavern is no more. On August 12, 1975 the entire block, Danny's Tavern, the Dorchester Citizen's Club, and all the other businesses burnt to the ground. A spectacular blaze, a roaring, raging inferno that even impressed the old timers of the fire department. Arson? Maybe, the arson squad grilled Booker for a couple of days but found insufficient evidence. The rumor is that Booker gave Danny's Tavern a Viking's Funeral. But of course, Booker would never have endangered the community.

With respect to setting the fire, in actuality Casey was the culprit—an act of revenge stemming back to his problem with Dinty—everyone at Danny's was his enemy. When Iron Mike Kelley arrested Casey, it was the battle of the decade. Mike won of course. But in any case, all that remains of Danny's now is a vacant lot, sprinkled with broken glass, busted red bricks, pieces of burnt lumber and a few tufts of crab grass after the site was leveled. A stranger passing by would never imagine that once a great watering hole stood on the site, with a birth, a maturity and an end. But we know better, I heard a rumor that the city plans to hard-top the surface and convert the lot into a basketball court. Another Dorchester landmark gone. Another tavern gone. Sure, there's the Horseshoe Tavern up Bowdoin Street; a few guys still drop in there occasionally, but it's not the same.

Booker seems to be the only one who remains the same. Still tanned and fit as ever. With the insurance money he bought a retirement cottage on Cape Cod. Pocasset, I think. He also owns a piece of a motel—or a restaurant—something like that. "What the hell," shrugs Booker in his characteristic fashion, "Let the world float by." To see Booker surrounded by his wife and family, you'd probably assume that he was a retired minister or just a nice quiet old gentleman.

So there's the story—start to finish, 1935-1975. It took me two years of working on the book off and on to completely assemble it. Other than correcting some of the spelling and grammar; and deleting a lot of swear words—which are part of any tavern vocabulary, I doctored nothing. As I said in the preface, I beavered through piles of papers, boxes full of scraps, clippings, sketches, and mementos—Bill's story. Some of the dates might be off slightly; I changed a few dates so that they matched the events, and of course I took a bit of poetic license. A guy's life. A tavern's history. And my job was to piece the jigsaw together. Sure, there were some episodes that I discreetly left out; his relations with certain women, a few unsolved crimes, some of his off-beat ramblings—God, he'd get really depressed at times. But aren't we all neurotic and depressed periodically—from over working, over sexing, over fearing, over eating? What the hell *is* normal?

I minimized some of the more contentious issues: race wars—busing—issues like burning draft cards, and full amnesty—riots in the cities—and an out-and-out injustice to those that served in the armed forces. Bill and even more so, Booker, felt strongly about these issues.

I wonder when Bill suffered through depressions and his reflective moods, what motivated him to continue to be so dedicated, so persistent, so damned tenacious? He earned little money for his efforts, but on he plodded. What motivated the man? Glory, dreams, some sort of neurosis, immortality?

If he was afraid he'd be forgotten, he needn't worry. I will remember him for the rest of my life. Bill will always influence me, even though he is gone. Maybe he was never famous, or successful, rich or published, but for sure he was a great human. As somewhat his biographer, I saw his faults, sore points, oddities, outright neuroses, but he was a real guy. A fine man. He tried. He fought. Like Teddy Roosevelt's bloody boxer, he stood in the ring and took his shots. That's more than most of us do. Some guys give up at twenty while some fight on—well past seventy. He was a surrogate father to me.

When I finished assembling the book, I called Booker. He was most satisfied; however I was a bit dissatisfied. The engineer in me likes to have all projects concluded logically. Therefore, as a finale, let me list the original 26 characters—first listed in 1935—and their whereabouts in 1977.

NOTE: In 1977, Booker and I sent copies of the book to 30 publishers. We got a lot of rejection slips. Let's face it—the book is a "guy story" and "guy philosophy" and the market saw no potential profit.

So let's move on.

CONVERSATION BETWEEN BOOKER AND TOM MELVIN, EDITOR

1977

As the editor, this seems to be the appropriate place to explain a few behind-the-scenes details with respect to Bill's own personal life, Danny's Tavern, and the neighborhood in general. As Bill's appointed biographer, I've picked through boxes full of clippings, sketches, hand written notebooks, letters, and documents for the past few years. I've organized the data in a somewhat chronological order.

During this period, I would meet with Booker to ask about various legends, events, and to get his insite on the cast of characters. Without fail, Booker would render his version, which for the most part, agreed with Bill's. However, one gap the four years from 1940 to 1944—exists. Bill wrote very little at this time and in later stories made very little mention of this period. He saved a few newspaper clippings but made no personal comments. Initially I thought that a box of memorabilia was lost, or that Bill was too preoccupied with World War II, or maybe he was writing his novel.

So, I asked Booker.

"Nah, no box was lost," answered Booker, "After Bill lost his wife and kid. He went crazy with booze. Really hit the bottle hard. He'd get mad-drunk and curse God, then he'd rave about doctors—didn't know their asshole from their elbow. No kidding, like a pit bull, snapping at the customers. Told me to bug off at least a hundred times until finally he quit Danny's and drank himself to skid row. Got a room in a flophouse, a crummy two-bit job delivering news circulars and became a down and out bum.

"No matter what Cathy or I did, it was no soap. Ya can't talk to a guy on a binge. Sure they'll agree with everything you say, and nod yes, but meanwhile all they're thinking is where they'll get the next drink. We even tried to dry him out in New Hampshire. You know, the Irish Alps and Drop Kick Murphy's but he'd have no part of it.

"I heard through the grapevine that Wentworth was ready to shit-can him. So I called in a few favors with the Chief Engineer—a leave of absence for medical reasons.

"Then I worked it on him from a different angle. At least, I could try to keep him alive and half-way healthy. Some pals in the South End ran an after hours joint. They watched out for him. You know, made sure he had a few bucks, place to sack out, cared for his books and stuff. They made sure no one rolled him or gave him a real hard time. One time—only one time, a big guinnie kid not only rolled him, but punched the be-Jesus outta him. Well the next day, that walyo got his two arms busted. The message passed through the neighborhood pretty fast after that. From cop to wop, don't fool with Bill. It was the least I could do for my pal.

"Bill drank until he got the DT's pretty bad. The horrors seeing spiders and snakes and all that. So the cops dragged him off to the hospital where they found a liver infection—not cirrhosis but something else. Being in the hospital for six months brought him back to health. Then Pearl Harbor got bombed. He quit the boozing—maybe a drink here and there, but nothing serious. Although he physically recovered he was never quite the old Bill he was before. A piece of him died. He never said that and I never asked, but it's true. If you took a knife and carved out a piece of his heart, you couldn't have done anymore damage. He was changed. He didn't laugh as much. He was more quiet and withdrawn. He still read a lot, to escape, he told me. But he slowed down with respect to writing about the guys and the Dorchester neighborhood. In fact, it seemed like he was more into writing about the people and the war news than making up stories.

"After Pearl Harbor, he tried to enlist but his twisted foot got him rejected. You got to give him credit though—he tried the Army, Navy and the Marines. He even tried the Canadian's. He went to Montreal to enlist, but he could never pass the physical. So he withdrew a little bit more.

"The economy began to pick up somewhat, and on the other side of the ocean, there was a war. There were jobs—then of course, in 1941 Pearl Harbor was bombed. Meanwhile, Bill got back on track at Wentworth too and was promoted. After a number of years tending the boilers, he advanced in the licensing process—he took the tests given by the State Department of Public Safety—and in a few years he was a First Class Fireman. Bill may have loved reading but he had a natural affinity toward physics and mathematics. He kept updating his skill set. The boiler inspectors loved him as well as the Wentworth administration.

"And you know when the U.S. entered the war—we had to train the soldiers and sailors to operate the boilers. Wentworth established a program to teach boiler operations to kids—eighteen and nineteen year olds. A lot of them came from a city heated by coal fueled boilers in the cellars of three decker homes.

"We're talking about high pressure boilers on new ships. High pressures of 100 pounds per square inch—not that I can explain it—I'm not the engineer that Bill was.

"In any case old Wentworth was pumping out class after class and Bill was in the middle of it. That was his way of joining up. Hell, he was over forty with a gimp foot—this was the best he could do.

"With his new mission of 'God Bless America,' he spent less time working at Danny's. He knew that he was needed by his country, a real patriot. Instead of serving beer and wine, he was now involved in training men to run the ships—destroyers, mine sweepers, transport ships—you name it. He worked hours on end, which was good for his spirits. He trained them tough—his way of protecting the boys.

"But you know, Muzzy (my nickname). Funny guy, that Bill. He was the truest squarest son-of-a-bitch this side of heaven. If he liked you, he'd walk through the fires of hell for you. Someone ya know'll be there when you need him. I could burn ya ears with favors he did for me and the boys when we were in jams, but I'd go to the slammer if I told you about about it. Great guy, that Bill. I miss him.

"So when he was quiet, melancholy, I'd let it go by the board. That's what friendship's all about. We all got our funny little ways of dealing with life, always hoping for the best. Then as luck would have it toward the end of the war, Bill met a girl—Bernie something or other. Best damn thing that ever happened. Christ, he fell head over heals. He reminded me of a puppy, wagging his tail to beat the band—it did him good. Of course there's always a fly in the ointment, she was married. Her husband was overseas. I guess there were some serious marriage problems. He was 'left handed' if you know what I mean. Well, naturally Bill felt like a class one heal. But he was in love and there wasn't anything he could do. She musta been something, to make him so happy."

The puzzle now fell into place. Bill had written about Bernie, but to me its was all too personal. Sometimes it felt like I was reading my own father's diary. "Listen Booker, I feel awkward about some of the stories. I mean it's almost like a diary. I don't know if Bill would want all of this stuff . . ."

Booker cut me short. "Tell it like it is. That's why he wrote it. It's OK"

"OK," I answered.

I'm glad I spent the time with Booker. Glad to get his approval and his explanations of how and why Bill had changed. I could see these changes in the writings, subtle changes, but certainly more introverted and personal. Sure, he still wrote of about the characters, but more in terms of erratic sketches—what he called "Odds and Ends"—than smooth narratives. Most of all, he seemed to write to himself—maybe it's my imagination, but sometimes I find it difficult Bill's thoughts. He was a complex, moody, reflective guy with a bizarre sense of humor. Sometimes his words would hit really hard, almost nag and haunt me. No doubt about it, I loved Bill like a father. I know the feelings were mutual.

DANNY'S TAVERN—UPDATED 1977

	Name	Occupation	Whereabouts
1.	Booker T. Brennan	Owns Several Businesses	Retired to Cape, happy
2.	Frank Vento	Bookie	Died in a house fire
3.	Jerry Collins	Telephone Company	Died at AA meeting—Heart Attack
4.	Peter Vessy	Building Engineer, City of Boston Curley Appointment	Died Asbestos—lung cancer from contaminated boiler room
5.	Mickey Smith	Plumber	Retired, lives with daughter in Quincy MA
6.	Gunny Steel	Mailman, ExMarine	Died—Diabetes
7.	Jack Walsh	Fisherman	Died in Boston Harbor boat collision
8.	Peter Z.	Printer (part-time)	Died of lung cancer, tried to sue Ink Co.
9.	Jackie Dwyer	Street Gang-Gas Company	Plans to retire next year
10.	Richie Quinn	Meat Packer	Beaten to death by an inmate in Boston State Hospital, psychiatric ward
11.	Bill Morrissey	Fisherman	Works as a janitor at Boston State College
12.	Tommy O'Hara	Janitor	Died shoveling snow at St. Peter's Convent
13.	Boss McDonough	Construction Superintendent	Died in construction accident in 1935 at the Museum of Fine Arts
14.	Scotty Burns	Fireman	Retired, Lives in the block on Draper St. Refuses to leave the neighborhood
15.	Joe Scarletta	Truck Driver	Died on the USS Dorchester, sunk in 1943
16.	Blackie Hessian	Tomato Factory Worker (part-time)	Died on the USS Dorchester, sunk in 1943

17.	Tony Karras	Tailor	Died of cancer, a group of Gypsies occupy his shop
18.	Bob McNamara	Teacher-Dorchester High	Died, heart attack at the bar in Foley's Tavern, South End
19.	Ira Gold	Clerk—Law student	Successful lawyer on Newbury St
20.	Iron Mike Kelly	Policeman	Died in nursing home—stroke
21.	Danny O'Neil	Trolley Man (MTA)	Died, TB
22.	Chico	Seaman (unemployed)	Unknown. Last contact was a post card which stated he was bound for Spain to fight in the Lincoln Brigade.
23.	Red Driscoll	Roofer (part-time artist)	Retired. Still sketching, drinks in the Horse Shoe Tavern up on Bowdoin St
24.	Casey	Unknown	Stabbed to death in Walpole State Prison, serving 10 years for Arson (Danny's Tavern)
25.	Bill Flynn	Bartender (part-time) Wentworth Institute(Boiler Operator, Fireman 3rd Class)	Died while hiking 1974
26.	Tonto	Iron Worker	Last seen headed to Calgary, 1973 to build a bridge

AFTERTHOUGHTS 2012

Tom Melvin, Editor

In 1977, I finished editing Bill Flynn's novel. As I mentioned earlier, Booker and I mailed out a number of copies to literary agents and publishers who rejected the book outright. So the story just collected dust in my cellar. Meanwhile I worked on my career—a collection of various jobs in engineering, management, consulting, and teaching. I raised a family—3 boys and a girl.

Last year 2011, in this new era of e-publishing, my son, Timmy suggested that I resurrect the project. The copy of the book covers the years from 1935-1975—a 40 year span which certainly included many historical events and reflections from Bill Flynn concerning his perspective of this 40 year period.

Since the book, Danny's Tavern was intended to be a history of sorts, then it would seem logical to consider questions:

1) Bill showed you changes from 1935-1975—40 years, what changes were important?
2) How has life changed since 1975-2015?
3) What is in the future for the next 40 years—say 2055?

Personally, at 77 years of age, I do not have the energy to continue with any more writing or editing. With respect to the next 40 years, I sure won't be around in 2055! If questions 1 and 2 interest you, it may be constructive to review Bill's list of social factors as shown below:

1) Religion
2) Family
3) Government and Law
4) Technology

5) Sex
6) Jobs—Economics
7) Physical Characters

How have these affected your life/and will affect your life?

Good Luck.

Muzzy (Tom Melvin)

CPSIA information can be obtained at www.ICGtesting.com
Printed in the USA
BVOW04s1545181114

375645BV00006B/19/P